Gearhead
at Large

Gearhead at Large

A Backroad Tour of Automotive History and the Old Car Hobby

STEVEN ROSSI
with WEST PETERSON

McFarland & Company, Inc., Publishers
Jefferson, North Carolina

ISBN (print) 978-1-4766-8117-7
ISBN (ebook) 978-1-4766-3981-9

LIBRARY OF CONGRESS AND BRITISH LIBRARY
CATALOGUING DATA ARE AVAILABLE

Library of Congress Control Number 2021028935

© 2021 Steven Rossi and West Peterson. All rights reserved

*No part of this book may be reproduced or transmitted in any form
or by any means, electronic or mechanical, including photocopying
or recording, or by any information storage and retrieval system,
without permission in writing from the publisher.*

On the cover: Along the backroads of automotive history
with Steven Rossi and his 1924 Model T Ford, from the pages
of *Antique Automobile* magazine (photograph by Michael Rossi)

Printed in the United States of America

*McFarland & Company, Inc., Publishers
Box 611, Jefferson, North Carolina 28640
www.mcfarlandpub.com*

Table of Contents

Introduction	1
Historically Speaking	**3**
Bless the Bicycle	3
The Making of the Motor City	6
The Ascent of an Industry	11
Detroit in Decline	15
Bankruptcy and Beyond	21
Desperate Times, Desperate Measures	25
How the West Won: The Gestation of a Global Automotive Industry	34
Challenging Conventional Wisdom	47
The Return of the Retractable	58
The Unrecognized Origin of the Sport Utility	65
Flights of Fancy	**72**
Dialing-In a Cast Iron Carburetor	72
The Long-Lost Language of Antique Automobile Lore	75
The Best Way to Embrace the Future … Is to Appreciate the Past	80
Pipedreams and Other Flights of Fancy	85
For All Seasons and Reasons	92
Shipping Shenanigans	105
On The Marque	**112**
The Halo Around the Hyphen	112
Initial Impression	123
Good Things Come in Threes	130
Happy 100th	137
The 10 Most Significant Automobiles That Influenced the American Automotive Industry	149
What the Heck Is a Hotchkiss?	156
Life's a Learning Experience	162
Yeah, but … It's Only a Model T	171

A Pullman for the People	179
Been Thinkin' About Lincoln	187

People and Personalities — 198
My 10 Favorite Car Quotes	198
Enzo Ferrari in Emotion and Feeling	206
From Office Machines to Automobiles, Part I	212
From Office Machines to Automobiles, Part II	219

Technicalities — 229
The Roll of the Radio	229
Requiem for the Running Board	236
A New Beginning	244
Three-Peat	251
Talking About Torque	257
Power Density: Lessons Learned from Automotive History	264
Third Time's the Charm!	270
Persistence Pays Off: The V-6 Saga	279

Here's to the Hobby — 289
The Antique Automobile Hobby: The 10 Best Things That Ever Happened	289
Our Greatest Asset	296
Old Habits Die Hard	298
An Alternative for the Armchair Enthusiast	303
At the Crossroads: In Between the Car Show and the Concours	305

On the Road Again — 310
Survival of the Fittest	310
The Automotive Influence on America's Garden of Eden	316
Shake, Rattle and Roll	328
From Here to Gone: Architecture's Influence on the Automobile	332
Cars on the Cusp	342

Index — 347

Introduction

I'm often asked, "Where does all this stuff come from?"— these wide-ranging essays that I have written for *Antique Automobile* over the years. That's somewhat difficult to answer because the fact is, they've routinely landed from … here, there and everywhere.

Sometimes, a theme will simply pop into my head, which I try to capture immediately on the keyboard. Other ideas ran when parked, then languished in the lot until I could eventually find my way back and dust off the cobwebs. Then there were those that idled over the long haul, which were actively tuned and tweaked as time accelerated ahead, while a few others were inspired by salt-of-the-earth car-guy conclaves at Calamari's, an untouched-original tavern in Deep River, Connecticut. Finally, there are all the unanswered mysteries of automotive history that I've long pondered, and figured it was finally high time to explore and solve.

Most important, for me, is that I've enjoyed the latitude of not having to write any of this material on assignment. I figured that as a typical longtime AACA member, if I found a subject or topic interesting, it might resonate with some, if not many, of you. I've also had the luxury to not only write about whatever I wanted during the past 10+ years, but to write these columns as long or as short as I thought they needed to be. So, from where I sit, it doesn't get any better than that.

Such editorial license is thankfully due to the good graces of *Antique Automobile* Editor West Peterson, and the confidently accommodating AACA leadership. What might surprise you even more is that Editor West, who also serves as *Antique Automobile*'s art director, never knows what's coming his way until it arrives in his inbox—usually a day or two before his deadline. Then, he's challenged to burn the midnight oil and unearth compelling, most often inspiring, images—many of which have been sourced from the renowned AACA Library & Research Center (via librarians Chris Ritter, Mike Reilly and Matthew Hocker)—to graphically complement my copy.

What you now hold in your hands is the result of a proven AACA partnership that's been forged during the past decade, despite how circuitous the journey along the road less traveled may have been to ultimately arrive between the two covers of *Antique Automobile* magazine. Perhaps it's just an old-school excursion that simply ends up where it's supposed to, as opposed to what is now a more exacting editorial science that drives other commercial alternatives. I don't know for certain, but I hope you agree. After all, these feature articles and Back to the Future columns appeared in what is a nonprofit club publication, and the ultimate proof, and value as you perceive it, is in the product.

If you're not a member of the Antique Automobile Club of America, I urge you to visit AACA.org and join the greatest old car community on the planet. If you're already affiliated with AACA, I look forward to continuing to cross paths with you throughout the pages of each and every issue of *Antique Automobile*, because in order for me to write, and for West Peterson to further design and edit, we need you to continue to … read! And we sincerely thank you for that.

Steven Rossi

Historically Speaking

Bless the Bicycle

November/December 2008

It's often assumed that the wagon was the precursor to the car. After all, the very term "horseless carriage" seems to imply the automobile's origins. But that's not necessarily the case. In fact, the bicycle probably contributed more to the eventual existence of the automobile than any other influence.

By the 1880s, the bicycle boom that had been sparked in Europe was being very much fueled in America by concerns such as Columbia in Hartford, Connecticut. In an effort to satisfy insatiable demand, bicycle builders brought forth social, psychological and technological progress that was truly universal, on the order of what the Model T would achieve 30 or 40 years later.

The road that Henry Ford followed—and so many others after him—was, in fact, literally paved by the bicycle.

Back-pedaling a bit, be aware that before the turn of the 20th century, personal mobility was essentially limited to the train, the horse or just walking. To quote Hiram Percy Maxim (the chief engineer of Columbia at the time) from his memoir, "The reason we did not build mechanical road vehicles before this, in my opinion, was because the bicycle had not yet come into numbers and had not directed men's minds to the possibility of independent, long-distance travel over the ordinary highway. We thought the railroad was good enough. The bicycle created a new demand that was beyond the ability of the railroad to supply. Then it came about that the bicycle could not satisfy the demand it created."

It was the bicycle that first unlocked "the feeling of independence, the freedom from timetables, from fixed and inflexible routes, from the proximity of other human beings than one's chosen companions; the ability to go where and when one wills, to linger and stop where the country is beautiful and the way pleasant, or to rush through unattractive surrounding…" according to the January 1909 issue of *Harper's Weekly*.

But the bicycle not only set the stage for a truly private means of transportation, unconstrained by the schedule of a locomotive or the direction and destination of the track. It also bred familiarity with and acceptance of accelerated motion, and provided a first up-close and personal experience with vehicle dynamics and speed.

Indian bicycle.

"If we look back at the early days of the trolley car and the bicycle, it will be fairly evident that the introduction of the automobile has been very free [by comparison] of unpleasant incidents." So said a representative from Locomobile in a 1902 issue of *Country Life in America*. As still holds true today, knowing how to ride a bicycle went a long way in preparing to operate an automobile.

The technological contribution of the bicycle was just as significant. There were sophisticated metallurgical techniques, the concept of standardized components, mass production, and the development of a supplier infrastructure ready and waiting for the arrival of the automobile as a result of the bicycle.

If that weren't enough, the process to produce tubular shapes that were light and strong, the existence of the flexible chain, vulcanization of rubber for the pneumatic tire and the clincher rim were all brought forth by the bicycle ... to the benefit of the automobile. Dunlop, Michelin, Pirelli and Seiberling were all building bicycle tires before venturing beyond.

Then there was the existing network of bike shops and service points. Pope Manufacturing, for example, which produced the Columbia, had 600 outlets by 1892. The theory of evolution shows that many of these migrated from two wheels to four as the automobile industry took off and accelerated.

The bicycle also contributed to a technical understanding of mechanics, which further supported the acceptance of the automobile. While farmers already had a good degree of mechanical experience in rural areas with a forge, an anvil and a chisel, it was the bicycle that lent itself to such learning in the more metropolitan locales. And what bicycle mechanics amassed was an expertise in quality components, superior sprockets, fine gear sets and precision bearings that would certainly serve them well in the fledgling auto industry that followed.

In an effort to champion the bicycle cause and its acceptance, clubs such as the League of American Wheelmen and the National Cycling Association began. They contributed everything from route/tour guides and mile/sign posts along the minimal road system of the time to influencing municipalities to accommodate such traffic in parks and other public spaces. Yet again, the ultimate beneficiary would be the automobile and the die was cast for automobile associations that would soon follow.

Then there were those founding fathers of the industry who were bicycle boys before they became automobile men. So, so many of them first explored the world of wheels on board two. The Duryea Brothers were bicycle mechanics before they started building automobiles. Colonel Albert Pope was a bicycle tycoon before he became an automotive industrialist. Among others, the Dodge Brothers, William Metzger, Edgar Apperson, John North Willys and Thomas B. Jeffery all enjoyed early exploits aboard bikes. A good number of the earliest manufacturing companies that went on to produce automobiles began by building bicycles, too: Pierce, Peugeot, Rambler, Winton, Peerless, Columbia, Opel, Pope, Thomas, to name a few.

The concept of the "auto show" was derived from the bicycle display. "It was the editor of *The Referee*, a leading bicycle publication, who suggested that automobiles need to be displayed at shows, and a Daimler was thus shown at the Sportsman's Exhibition in New York's Madison Square Garden in 1896," according to James J. Flink, in *America Adopts the Automobile, 1895–1910*. This country's first actual auto show was then held in February 1899 as an adjunct to a bicycle display at the Garden.

Even the earliest auto racing epics owe their existence to the then state of the art that had already been established by bicycle racing. Innovations such as the board track were first built for bicycles, and racers such as Barney Oldfield, Henry Ford and John Wilkinson shifted gears from two wheels to four.

Finally, one of the most significant contributions that came out of the transition from the bicycle to the automobile was the very existence of a road infrastructure in itself. It was the bicycle industry, primarily through the effort of Columbia's Colonel Pope, that spawned the Good Roads Movement in America. Grassroots efforts by bicycle clubs and associations led to what finally became a national movement to turn mud-filled quagmires into paths of, if not to, plenty, paving the way for the automobile that followed.

So never forget. Those of us who worship antique automobiles should always give a little thanks, and … bless the bicycle.

The Making of the Motor City

January/February 2011

Having done three tours of corporate duty in Detroit, I've long been interested in the evolution of the American automotive industry along Michigan's navigable link between Lake St. Clair and Lake Erie. In fact, the city is named for the river that separates it from Canada, as the word "Detroit" is French for strait. But even the advantage of direct water access that's often been part of the folklore surrounding its industry origins is an unfortunate falsehood when it comes to the making of the Motor City.

Many of the factors that made Motown the cradle of the car are described in George S. May's *A Most Unique Machine: The Michigan Origins of the American Automobile Industry*, published in 1975 by the William B. Eerdmans Publishing Company (ISBN 0–8028–7032–5). Consider yourself lucky if you can find a copy of this 408-page publication.

When the automobile was in its infancy, there were thousands of makes being assembled here, there and everywhere by an odd assortment of back-alley builders and tinkerers. The cast of characters included *Pioneers, Engineers and Scoundrels*, according to the book written by Beverly Rae Kimes (SAE International, 2004).

Various locales, therefore, either gained a bit of traction and recognition as an automotive mecca as result of some early entrepreneur's success, or fell by the four-wheeled wayside when a homegrown inventive mind instead created an impractical curiosity. And there were many of them.

Kokomo, Indiana, was well recognized by the accomplishment of Haynes-Apperson, which began building internal combustion-powered products in 1896, boasting that they offered "America's First Practical Car." Cleveland, Ohio, was home to the Winton Motor Carriage Company, which started assembly in 1897 and sold their first car in 1898. White steamers hailed from Cleveland as well, beginning in 1901. Neither city could ever lay claim to being the true center of the fledgling industry. They were a speck out of an initial scattershot of automotive assembly.

The first true automotive incubator was New England. The industrial revolution of the Northeast was sparked by European immigration and fueled by natural water-powered resources. The mills and factories of the time quickly demonstrated a capability to produce both quantity and quality, and an ethic toward principles of precision lent themselves well to the arrival of the automobile.

The Duryea brothers are credited with assembling the first commercially available automobile in series and establishing a dedicated business for the specific purpose of doing so. In 1893 they were testing their invention on the streets of Springfield, Massachusetts, and during 1896 they produced and sold 13 more examples. You're probably already aware that the AACA logo celebrates this motoring milestone!

Another significant driver of early acceptance and commercial viability of the automobile was Colonel Albert Pope of Hartford, Connecticut. The two-wheeled tycoon was America's leading bicycle manufacturer by 1896, and he quickly accelerated his empire toward the future of four wheels. He established the Columbia Automobile Company in 1897 and then invested in the Electric Vehicle Company, while offering an array of Pope-manufactured products as well.

As a result of Pope's leadership in the then-booming bicycle craze, his automotive involvement enjoyed the competitive advantage of established sales and service outlets, along with advanced manufacturing methods and metallurgical techniques. More than any other entity at the turn of the century and in the early 1900s, Pope's variety of interests and product offerings allowed his enterprise to become the precursor of the conglomerates that would ultimately shape and define the automobile business ahead. Vertically integrated and applying the same mechanized production ethic as his bicycle business (which was similar to what was also being done by surrounding firearms and clock concerns), Pope was also an innovative and effective advertiser, which was yet another attribute that would become a staple of the auto industry and a prime mover in the Good Roads Movement. In fact, Connecticut's Pope Manufacturing was "general" motors before there was a General Motors.

But the Northeast's advantage would be short-lived. The visionary Colonel Pope was pushed aside by a more formidable foe than those who were also trying to simply cast iron and forge steel. Boom turned to bust when Pope's short-sighted blue-blood financiers of the Electric Vehicle Company placed a priority on quick capital gain. Attempting to arbitrarily engineer a monopoly on electric taxicabs for major metropolitan territories instead of sincerely trying to satisfy the demands of the free marketplace and its growing acceptance of the gasoline alternative, they undermined Pope's early advantage and quietly drove themselves—and Pope—into insolvency. When they were done, the primary asset they had left to try and leverage was the Selden Patent.

Meanwhile, while the primary, New England interests were trying to manipulate quick returns, critical mass was starting to take hold in the Midwest. Compared to the then-mature and industrialized Northeast, free-thinking middle–American trailblazers were never constrained by convention or the establishment—because there was none.

They were therefore left to concentrate on effective and functional solutions, which would be proven in service instead of in a banker's boardroom. For example,

Early in the morning on June 4, 1896, Henry Ford would take ax in hand and smash open the brick wall of his rented garage on Detroit's Bagley Street. He had just started his first gas-powered car, and it was too big to fit through the door.

in their world of abundant freshwater lakes, the development of lightweight marine motors for boats and launches was an early influence. Charles King was credited with driving the first automobile on the streets of Detroit in 1896, and to do so, he experimented with an engine from the Sintz Gas Engine Company of Grand Rapids, Michigan. So an established engine industry in the area contributed to the cause, along with the local tribal knowledge.

The proximity to expansive bodies of water did, indeed, impact Detroit's ascent as the center of the American automotive universe, but not due to logistic reasons as is often assumed. There were certainly many other areas across the country that enjoyed similar geographic distinction.

Another myth surrounding the making of the Motor City is its abundant access to raw materials, like lumber and ore. While there's truth in the premise that such resources supported the development of the automobile industry in Michigan, again, there were many other areas throughout America with similar natural advantages.

The lumber and mining industries did play a critical role in the story. These were Michigan's mature industries at the time, and these businesses' principals were looking for new avenues in which to invest their capital. While staid and conservative New York financiers wouldn't even give someone like the self-taught Henry Ford a second thought, local lumber barons, mine operators and coal merchants would, and did. And they were in it for the long haul, as they had been out in the forests and down in the mines.

Long before Henry Ford's universal success, fellow Michigander Ransom E. Olds was both practical and rational when he created his curved-dash Olds, because he strived to create a product that would be attainable and sustainable. He had to, because the heady reputation and collateral of the P.F. Olds and Son family firm, and later the Olds Gasoline Engine Works, demanded so. The curved-dash Olds is considered America's first mass-produced car and thus established a beachhead in Michigan.

Likewise, the curved-dash Olds demonstrated that intuitive and inventive solutions were both byproducts of the Midwest mindset. As referenced earlier, "Michigan mechanics learned their trade the hard way, and were not bound by orthodox mechanical training," according to George May.

The contribution of available labor into the automotive equation can't be dismissed, either. But it wasn't skilled trades that turned the tide from the Northeast to the Midwest, it was the unorganized and unskilled that did. Anti-union sentiment and a large pool of workers from the farms and fields ensured that wages were relatively low in comparison to other developed areas in America—for the time being, at least.

William Crapo (Billy) Durant's ascent from carriage maker to kingpin also

Detroit's General Motors Building, now a National Historic Landmark, was built as GM's headquarters during the period when the company, under the leadership of Alfred P. Sloan, Jr., became the leading automobile manufacturer in the U.S.

contributed significantly to the making of the Motor City and its surrounds. After amassing a fortune from the Durant-Dort Carriage Company, Durant applied a similar business model but unbridled the horse ... and unleashed opportunity. After saving Buick from an uncertain fate in 1904, he assembled an assortment of other manufacturers such as Oldsmobile, Cadillac and Oakland.

Through both fiscal strength and production scale, General Motors steamrollered itself into the position of an American automotive industry bookend, beginning in 1908. The other, following the unveiling and ultimate acceptance of the Model T, was Ford. Following in the footsteps of Olds, Henry achieved similar success by concentrating on everyman with his Models N, R and S. But his brilliance was with his universal car, and by the time the Model T was hailed with a hero's welcome in the marketplace, it carried Detroit right along on its shoulders ... especially after the opening of the Highland Park plant in 1910 and the arrival of the moving assembly line in 1913.

By 1914, May concludes, there was no looking back. Detroit had demonstrated its dominance and American automobile manufacturing accelerated into overdrive. Like a "perfect storm," it was a confluence of forces and factors that allowed Detroit to prevail as America's Motor City. But that's only the beginning of the saga.

The Ascent of an Industry

March/April 2011

Various forces and factors allowed Detroit and the surrounding Michigan area to assume the leadership role in the automotive industry by 1914, despite the fact that New England was out in front as the American auto incubator at the turn of the century. Although the automobile was finishing just its second decade of development in this country at the time, it was already a proven product. Initial apprehension made way for enthusiastic acceptance, and the horse was literally being driven out to pasture … in tow, behind an automobile. Engineering advances such as the self-starter and the closed car body, not to mention growing adoption and refinement of mass production techniques, ever-increasing economies of scale and continually demonstrated quality improvements, were transforming the automobile from a curious rich man's novelty into an everyman's commodity. And Michigan was well prepared to demonstrate its dominance in its continued creation.

With Henry Ford's Highland Park plant now on stream, some 200,000 Model T's were being produced per year. In 1914, he also introduced his legendary $5-a-day pay plan, which more than doubled the average worker's wages while decreasing the number of hours of work. While many blue-collar workers had to fight for and demand an eight-hour day, Henry Ford required it in order to implement a three-shift system that made the rest of the industry envious when they saw productivity soar. Those on the assembly line were on their way to being able to afford the product they were producing. By 1924, annual Model T output increased tenfold to almost two million the world over.

Meanwhile, over at General Motors, early chaos over corporate control had eased its way with the arrival of Alfred P. Sloan. With an eye toward the science of disciplined management processes, he established coordinated and centralized policy guidance, while providing for decentralized GM operations, with Oldsmobile in Lansing, Buick in Flint and Oakland in Pontiac, among others.

Sloan assumed what was left of Billy Durant's truly provident, though often vague and reckless, vision and focused it into an effective organization. He is also credited with engineering the annual new-model changeover and inventing market segmentation by providing "a car for every purse and purpose" through a defined

Top and above: **Motor City postcards.**

brand matrix and pricing ladder. Between Ford and General Motors, the American automobile industry was now in overdrive.

Michigan also laid claim to the pinnacle of automotive prestige and profit. While there were many upmarket manufacturers across America vying for the wallets of the wealthy, the Detroit-based Packard Motor Car Company truly succeeded in both volume and longevity by capturing a full 50 percent of the luxury car market—until the unfortunate (for Packard) expansion of Sloan's segmentation strategy with the Cadillac and LaSalle combination, that is.

Others added to the ascent of the industry in the area as well. Early Detroit automotive pioneers like the Dodge brothers leveraged their well-demonstrated success and expertise (and fortune) as a supplier for Cadillac and then, more predominantly, Ford Motor Co., and offered their own durable and reliable alternative. Down in nearby Toledo, Ohio, John North Willys used his natural-born sales ability to catapult Overland into early contention … and added even more critical mass to the Michigan-area equation. Walter P. Chrysler made what was left of Maxwell into a force to be reckoned with, and ultimately brought Dodge, DeSoto and Plymouth into his Detroit dynasty.

The arrival of Ford's River Rouge complex was yet another automotive industry milestone, and at the time it was the world's largest integrated factory. The U.S. government helped fund its original existence in support of Eagle anti-submarine boat building.

Wars came and went, and the Wolverine State prospered still. With its well-established infrastructure, Michigan's automotive industry became a prime mover in American armament and munitions manufacturing. In addition to keeping their factories running, war work kept automakers' cash flowing during the peaks and valleys of car and truck production.

In between, the Great Depression served to sort out the industry and its abundance of entries. By then, everyone was trying to get into the act and numerous examples of "assembled" cars were being offered: those made up of available off-the-shelf components, their unique attributes amounting to little more than a distinctive radiator badge and a catchy advertising slogan. With more availability than buyers, the Wall Street crash separated the strong and established from the weak and inefficient. It even shook out a number of recognized grand marques that may have been held in high esteem but, in fact, enjoyed more prestige than profit. They're considered Classics by the Classic Car Club and remain quite desirable, even though the market at the time thought otherwise and essentially said so.

Immediately after the Second World War, automotive demand outstripped supply. Americans were truly enjoying the spoils of victory. Postwar prosperity fueled the growth of suburbia and a new baby-boom generation. A new car in every driveway only added to the American dream of a Cape Cod (house) in Levittown (the archetype of Anytown, USA), where Mom, Dad and an average 2.3 children resided … all watching shows on their first TV sets. Anything on wheels would sell, and this was the point where second tier offerings by all sorts of independents enjoyed a heyday.

Henry Kaiser set up shop in a no longer active bomber plant in Willow Run, Michigan, just outside of Ann Arbor and Ypsilanti. Hudson hung on in an attempt to elbow its way into the big time with such advanced technology as the step-down body style and Twin-H carburetion. Long-standing yet staid, Studebaker also flexed its muscles in South Bend, Indiana, and tried to distinguish itself through inspired styling. And if that weren't enough, radio/appliance entrepreneur Powel Crosley, Jr., looked to tune in as well with his own half-pint of automotive expression, also out of Indiana.

Even through a recession that followed, Michigan automakers remained at the ready to ride all of the ups and downs that the American economy afforded. They did so by protecting their turf through consolidation, while simultaneously proliferating their model lines into numerous specialty segments, taking the concept of "a car for every purse and purpose" to a new extreme. This ensured that any chinks in the armor that the independents might have identified (like Rambler's success in the compact car category) would immediately be met head-on with more mainstream models from General Motors, Ford and Chrysler. Light-duty trucks became a rather considerable concentration, as well.

The time-tested Big 3 soon gained complete control. By the 1950s and into the 1960s, GM, for example, enjoyed an astounding 48 percent share of the U.S. new car and light truck market. The Michigan–based automotive business went from an American industry to an American institution, so much so that many thought "what was good for the country was good for General Motors, and vice versa." The popular proclamation of automotive arrogance—"what's good for General Motors is good for America"—was in fact a legendary misquote. But other than that unfortunate embarrassment, what could go wrong?

Detroit in Decline

May/June 2011

Just like the *Rise and Fall of the Roman Empire*, it is a story of unparalled triumph, followed by unprecedented tragedy. By the 1950s and '60s, Detroit assumed utter dominance of the U.S. automotive universe. General Motors alone enjoyed an astounding 48 percent share of the new car market. But the world was a changing place. Postwar prosperity fueled a population explosion, and the baby boom that accelerated the American market expansion felt the reactionary effect of a whole host of far-reaching market forces and consequences, the likes of which had never been experienced before.

The decline of Detroit really began with the innocent arrival of a few imports along our shores. Certainly, automobiles from abroad were nothing new. Some upscale examples from Rolls-Royce, Daimler (Mercedes), Fiat and more, had even been assembled here, so the postwar wave of cars from the Continent was readily accepted, particularly in an effort to support European reconstruction and because America, of course, has always been the land of free trade (with open borders). Many of these models were obviously unsuited for the expansive American operating environment and its more diverse climate conditions, since they were specifically engineered for local use in their home markets. But as always, cash was king and while war-weary buyers may have been few and far between on the other side of the ocean, desirable dollars were in abundance here, and many European manufacturers soon adopted an attitude of "export or die." It would prove to be prophetic.

When used for their intended purpose, a lot of these European alternatives demonstrated that they were competent, surprisingly cost-efficient and fun to drive. Americans began to understand and accept both the advantages and limitations of cars like the Volkswagen and Renault Dauphine, and thus, a beachhead began to be established, particularly in the more progressive (and crowded) cities along the East Coast.

Detroit was watching and, giving credit where credit was due, quickly mounted an offensive to help stem the tide. Of course, they ensured that their offerings were better attuned to the needs and wants of most Americans, and left the imports with

Top and above: **Abandoned Packard automobile factory, Detroit.**

extremely limited opportunity in but a few, small niches. The inroads they made were slow, but steady. So what happened?

Fast forward to the late 1960s and '70s. There was now an ever-growing strain on the American infrastructure and environment, due to the coming of age of the baby boomers. They were now consumers, and those 2.3 children from each home in the

Inside the former Packard factory.

suburbs like Levittown spawned many, many more. With more feet on the street, the social impact ultimately extended itself to the environment. Mother Nature began to feel the pinch and it forced our authorities to start to consider the control of the automobile and its impact on the world. Air quality and fuel economy mandates were about to alter the American automotive landscape forever—not to mention an incredible gas crisis or two, along with a conscious commitment to improved vehicular safety.

Simultaneously, the Japanese economy was starting to gain some serious traction. Unlike the European industrial experience, instead of simply reconstructing, they were literally reinventing themselves. They, too, turned to the lucrative American market and its open borders, and set their sights on California, along with the rest of the West Coast. Japan's automotive industry could not sustain itself in its home market, which afforded extremely limited opportunity (in Tokyo, for example, you had to prove that you had a place to park a car before you could even buy one). Their drive to export was, instead, fast and furious.

The true onslaught on Detroit was about to be fought from an invasion that would stem from both the East Coast, by the Europeans, and the West Coast, via Japan. Our quest for clean air and improved fuel economy was the first decisive blow in that battle. American products at the time were big, heavy and had little consideration for fuel economy. Being from the land of wide open spaces, American cars were developed to merely suit their surroundings. Gas was cheap, and the car had become a commodity.

Over in Europe and Japan, though, quarters were cramped, gas was like gold because it was so heavily taxed, and automobile ownership was still considered a luxury. American manufacturers were at an immediate disadvantage when it came to ensuring critical compliance with developing U.S. environmental requirements.

Our products suffered because they were so severely compromised from their original design intent, while the imports enjoyed an advantage and had an easier time adapting. Challenges that Europe and Japan had long grappled with were now being seen for the first time in downtown Detroit. The American industry started to struggle because an inordinate amount of our engineering attention went into significant re-adaptation of our existing automobiles. Our competitors, by comparison, were simply tweaking theirs.

In the effort to appease the Environmental Protection Agency, every dollar and engineering hour that was spent on emissions compliance was one less that would be devoted to building a better product. American innovation stalled, and we started to offer some pretty lousy automobiles. The Japanese and Europeans, meanwhile, may have had an easier time meeting our EPA requirements but they were building some pretty shoddy products as well, that still weren't totally suited to American operating extremes. Just as you don't see a lot of 1970s Chevrolets running around these days, nor do you see an abundance of Toyota Corollas or Volkswagen Rabbits. It was just a bad time to be in the automobile business.

Then came the downsizing of the American automobile. Huge investments were laid down to start anew with a clean slate, to build cleaner and more efficient cars that would be engineered from the get-go to satisfy ever-increasing regulatory standards. America was forced to learn how to create and manufacture products and configurations that competitors had been producing for decades. It would be a painful learning curve. Unfortunately, while we were regrouping and directing our full focus on the longer term, the imports—driven by the compelling need to export—were working hard to better adapt their products to meet the needs and wants of Americans and set forth on a quest to conquer with continuous improvement through ambitious market research and accomplished quality.

If that weren't enough, yet another curve ball followed. The typical middle American motorist had a hard time physically fitting into Detroit's shrunken sedans and contracted coupes. Many took refuge and found a corporate average fuel economy (CAFE) compliance loophole in light trucks instead, which only forestalled the inevitable.

Foreign competition made further gains into the heart of the American passenger car category, and gobbled up even more market share—particularly on both coasts, and particularly the Japanese. Conversely, American manufacturers held on in the heartland in places from Pittsburgh to the Rocky Mountains. By now, there were too many manufacturers chasing too little market opportunity. Then, things got even more complicated.

Being a very mature business, the American industry was burdened by infra-

Top and above: The ill-fated 1981 Cadillac V8-6-4 engine.

structure expense that the off-shore competitors did not experience. That playing field between Pittsburgh and the Rockies wasn't even level. Labor costs to produce in America proved to be much higher than abroad. Imbalances on the order of $1,500 per car put U.S. manufacturers at an incredible disadvantage, though that's not necessarily an indictment against organized labor. It could be argued that competitive labor was somewhat exploited, as well.

The battleground went way beyond the boardroom and the factory floor, to as far as Main Street, USA. With the American automotive industry now in steady decline, Detroit manufacturers were soon over-saturated with legacy dealers all fighting for a smaller piece of the pie. The local Chevrolet dealer's primary competitor became the three or four other Chevy dealers across town. State franchise laws that favored the dealers only served to compound Detroit's concerns to do anything about it.

The overseas upstarts instead enjoyed the advantage of being able to carefully pick and choose their retail outlets and ensure a more right-sized representation model. Thus, their dealers prospered and the financial health of the import establishments allowed them to invest in the market even more.

The vicious cycle was accelerating into a death spiral. A final blow was a newfound emphasis by American manufacturers on optimizing manufacturing efficiencies in an attempt to reduce costs and maintain any margin they could. Unfortunately, the tactic sucked the creativity and individual identities out of the product portfolios, and "badge engineering" became the buzzword of everything that was wrong in Detroit.

General Motors wasn't selling "your father's Oldsmobile," it was your Grandfather's, and it looked just like Aunt Mildred's Buick. And under the hood it had a Chevy engine, if not an incredibly crude Diesel (though that's a story for another time). The 48 percent market share that GM so enjoyed during the 1960s was eroding rapidly, and by the 1980s it was in the 30s and heading south, further still.

Brand equity and distinction that was crafted during decades and decades of development was lost, and the result read like a Greek tragedy. The odyssey would conclude in an epilogue that would rewrite American automotive history.

Bankruptcy and Beyond

JULY/AUGUST 2011

The American auto industry evolved from its infancy at the turn of the 20th century to achieve utter dominance by the 1950s and 1960s. Previously unknown market forces and competitive challenges soon followed, however, and accelerated the Detroit automakers into a battle they were ill prepared to contest. Environmental issues, the import assault, dependence on foreign oil and its manipulated shortages, labor disadvantages and a less-than-healthy dealer partnership all contributed to the decline of Detroit in the 1970s and '80s. But the story doesn't end there.

General Motors' 48 percent market share after World War II proved to be a slippery slope during the decades that followed. More than just eroding, the American automakers' performance plummeted. As explained in the May/June issue, even after Detroit's long, hard learning curve to develop and build globally competitive offerings and reinvent themselves, the imports were still producing preferable products.

The Japanese, in particular, routinely executed a demonstrated discipline of continuous improvement. Even when a bona fide competitor came out of the Motor City, immediately Toyota, Nissan and Honda would up the ante and outmaneuver Michigan with something better and more consumer satisfying. The American industry would eventually prove that it could build cars and trucks as well as the Japanese, but it never demonstrated that it could build them better.

The ongoing effort of continually playing catch-up resulted in Detroit's final loss of leadership. Had they been able to leapfrog the competition they could have stood a chance. And that's all before the influx of the next competitive threat—the Koreans.

By the new millennium, GM market share was down in the 20s. Worse yet, Detroit's brands were now irrelevant to a large portion of the buying public. Think about it: today there is a vast multitude of car buyers in their 40s and 50s that grew up with, own and have operated nothing other than a Japanese car. And it's been a truly satisfying experience, so what incentive could they ever have to alter their brand allegiance now?

But there were early signs of where our industry was headed. Chrysler was the first to falter, being the smallest and the weakest back in 1979. The Lee

GM Headquarters in Detroit's Renaissance Center.

Iacocca–engineered taxpayer bailout may have propped them up, but it only forestalled the inevitable.

If you recall, Chrysler gained a new lease on life, courtesy of the U.S. government, and innocuous K-cars would stem the tide until some true market distinction could be created through inspired styling. Unfortunately though, the beauty was only skin deep. Underneath, quality concerns plagued them still.

So yet another market imbalance emerged between the domestics and the Japanese, that being warranty cost. In an effort to appease the customers that still remained, Detroit automakers were taking it in the shorts by self-funding exorbitant repairs and recall campaigns.

There were examples where American automakers were able to innovate, but their advances were quickly thwarted by the competition. The creation of the minivan is a good example. Chrysler literally invented the segment. Today though, Toyota and Honda have toppled Detroit's stature as the minivan leader by continuously improving their Sienna and Odyssey models to the point that they are now the standard bearers.

In an effort to stimulate the American new-car buying experience, Detroit also invented the profit margin–sapping rebate and incentive game. Initially, it was intended to entice customers as a way to address an occasional or isolated inventory issue. Unfortunately, it became a way of life.

The cash drain was turning into a cash burn. A shadow of their former selves, Detroit automakers were soon shedding as many assets as they could to lay claim on cash. The factory press releases at the time proclaimed that it was in the interest of getting back to basics and refocusing on the core business, but the public relations jargon could only thinly mask what was being written in the annual reports.

Simultaneously, there was also a rush on mergers and acquisitions with smaller, specialty concerns as a defensive maneuver, which consumed even more precious resources, such as continued attention to the most important business at hand: long-term survival. Since Detroit was never able to achieve true traction in the overseas marketplace with its domestic offerings, the logic was that they could at least buy a presence.

The continual quest for capital also drove American automakers into the banking business. Rebates and incentives morphed into easy credit and subsidized financing/leasing. There was more money to be made through Detroit's captive finance arms than there was in the manufacturing and marketing of cars. It was yet another band-aid to help prop up the ailing new-car market, but it least it achieved the objective of keeping the factories going.

The straw that broke the camel's back was the great recession, which we remain somewhat mired in to this day. Through all the incessant market manipulation via rounds and rounds of rebates, discount financing and the like, a huge body of buyers were already driving cars that they couldn't rightfully afford. Like flipping a light switch, the credit crunch immediately took a massive number of potential prospects out of the sales bank.

The market shrank from what had been an inflated sales pace of 16–17 million units per year to what is now a more natural 12 million-ish rate. Of course, the domestics bore most of the brunt. Even worse, the associated mortgage crisis hit home in Detroit as well, since finance arms such as GMAC (General Motors Acceptance Corporation) were in the home mortgage market, too. GM was forced to sell this former lucrative cash cow, which previously helped see it through thick and thin.

As you're obviously aware, General Motors and Chrysler ultimately filed for bankruptcy protection. Ford narrowly escaped by leveraging everything it owned, down to its Harold Wills–designed blue oval logo.

The good news (if you can call it good) is that the crisis allowed Detroit to quickly perform some much needed restructuring. Saab, Volvo, Jaguar, Land Rover, Aston Martin, *et al.,* were sold. Damaged goods such as the Pontiac, Saturn and Hummer brands were quickly shuttered. The previous demise of Oldsmobile and Plymouth paved the way for the process. Debt was also eliminated, and only in bankruptcy were the domestics finally able to perform a much needed trimming of their dealer ranks, since the filing provisions overrode state franchise restrictions.

GM became what's been casually referred to as "Government Motors." Even more ironic, a big piece of Chrysler was simply given to Fiat, in response to their offer to step in and run it. You may not be aware that Fiat was previously on the brink of bankruptcy itself. But the Italian government protected their homegrown car company by levying hefty duties and taxes on imports across the country's borders, a tactic primarily intended, of course, to push the Japanese out. A home court advantage was therefore created for Fiat. At the opposite end of the spectrum, America remains the land of free trade.

In the end, the history of the American automobile industry remains incredibly complex. It's more than just an iconic business case that reached a crescendo and crashed. Certainly there were missteps and unimaginable market forces along the way, not to mention many other harsh realities of an ever-changing global landscape.

The sting of bankruptcy is sharp in any age.

If anything, our domestic automotive heritage is really nothing more than a reflection of our American culture and identity. Free and open borders, the land of wide open spaces with enough perceived market capacity to share, a between-home-borders sales sense, a comfortable case of complacency due to our tremendous economic engine and a never-ending dance with debt are all ethics that were likewise instilled in our automotive industry. Truth be told, American cars and trucks are merely products of the society that created them.

The powers that be deemed that the American automobile industry was too important to fail, so it's still here. Certainly, the impact on the economy would have been catastrophic. Though it's never been publicly stated, I also believe that the need for a heavy-iron industry to support our national security, as need be, was yet another reason to sustain it.

So Detroit no longer needs to concern itself about being the world's biggest automobile business. Hopefully, it can now concentrate on rebuilding American consumer confidence by simply being the world's best automobile business.

Desperate Times, Desperate Measures

MARCH/APRIL 2012

Walking through the parking garage at Bradley International Airport (Hartford, Conn./Springfield, Mass.) in search of my trusty Trollhättan-built 1988 Saab 900, I stumbled across a Saab 9-2X. In fact a Subaru in disguise, this "lost cause of motoring" (as noted automotive historian and museum-founder Lord Montague of Beaulieu might have called it) was a reminder of what can happen when the grim reaper is on the doorstep and knocking at the factory gate.

In yet another last-ditch effort for Saab survival, this "Saabaru"—as it's often being called among the Swedish brand's most ardent loyalists—was the child of a shotgun wedding, perpetrated as a result of its General Motors parenthood. Unlike the more usual badge engineering exploits that try to squeeze supplemental manufacturing efficiency out of a given investment (while simultaneously trying to protect brand equity and distinction), the 9-2X and its Chevy TrailBlazer–based sibling, the 9-7X (also referred to as the "TrollBlazer"), were a quick and dirty lifeline to help buoy a sinking Swedish ship. Like an Italian cruise liner's attempt to salute off the isle of Giglio, the bright idea didn't work.

It reminded me, though, of a few other desperate measures that automakers took during their own desperate times.

Franklin Olympic

Franklin was a proud company that hailed from Syracuse, New York. Distinguished by its air-cooled engines since the company began in 1902, Franklin was ultimately backed into a corner by the inherent engineering conflict that air cooling creates.

By the 1930s, the ever-demanding mid-level luxury car segment—the market in which Franklin competed—was simultaneously demanding higher engine outputs and still more refinement. The air-cooled innovator worked hard to keep up, developing some ingenious ideas during the years to deal with its thermodynamic dilemma. However, increasing horsepower required increasing the amount of airflow, and as you well know from running your bathroom fan or hair dryer, moving air consumes power and makes noise. Franklin also contended with a bit of heat-induced upper-end valve clatter and piston slap, not the most becoming behavior for a high-end entry.

Franklin did extremely well at crafting a compromise, though. Ultimately the air-cooled advantage would come with diminishing returns, particularly in the prestige car category. Cruel winds were gusting toward Syracuse. In an attempt to ward off declining sales, Franklin restyled its model range to include faux radiators so its cars would be perceived as the equivalent of their water-cooled competitors. While certainly producing handsome offerings, the tactic failed to generate the cash reserves necessary for Franklin to develop its next entries for the 1930s; certainly the Depression didn't help, either.

In 1932, Herbert H. Franklin and company found an inexpensive and expedient solution. In incredibly short order, they sourced "almost-complete" cars from Reo in Lansing, Michigan, and had them shipped to Syracuse, sans engine, hood and grille. After installing the six-cylinder Airman engine and its ancillaries and a Franklin front end, the games began with a new Olympic model. Its sales stamina would soon be tested.

The idea was to achieve a lower price point and hopefully attract a larger audience. At the time, a typical Franklin Airman sold for about $2,400. The Olympic was priced at roughly $1,400. Unfortunately, the threshold for more-affordable mid-market cars was on the order of $1,000, which is also where the original Reo offering was priced. So, in essence, the air-cooled alternative was accompanied by a 40 percent premium.

Despite its ancestry, like all Syracuse products, the Olympic was a fine Franklin and about 1,500 were built. It just distinguished itself differently than long-time Franklin aficionados had grown accustomed. Actually, it was somewhat of an early factory hot-rod with a larger six-cylinder engine stuffed into a smaller body.

Franklin Olympic.

Such strategy was, and still is, a proven formula to arouse interest and tickle the market.

But on the downside, Franklin's fully-elliptic comfort-quality springs were no longer in evidence and the interior was downgraded from what had become the Syracuse standard. They had already given up on the laminated wood chassis frame in 1929. At least an air-cooled Franklin emblem was applied over the space where the water temperature gauge was normally found on the Reo! And let's not forget those four Franklin hub caps…

During mid-1933, the Olympic enjoyed a slight restyle, but it was all too little, too late. Franklin failed to finish the sales race, took its last gasp and succumbed in 1934.

Reo Flying Cloud-bodied Grahams

The three Graham Brothers (Joseph B., Robert C. and Ray A.) found their first fortune in granules of glass. In the early 1900s, they invested in an Indiana bottle plant and nurtured it through investment and innovation. Continual expansion was enjoyed as a result of organic growth and strategic acquisition, so much so that by 1916 merger talks ensued with the Owens Bottle Company of Toledo, Ohio. The end result would ultimately evolve into what became known as the glass gargantuan Libbey-Owens-Ford.

Meanwhile, having spent their childhood and adolescence on the family farm, the brothers Graham now had the wherewithal to pursue another passion, light duty trucks that would earn their keep and put the temperamental horse and wagon out to pasture. No surprise, they began with Model T conversions. Henry's universal car met with universal acclaim when it was turned into a truck, so successful that by 1920 the three siblings were building their own Graham Brothers trucks.

Also off the farm, Ford certainly recognized a good thing when he saw it, and was quite capable of satisfying commercial interests on his own. A more recent start-up, Dodge, however, realized that it could utilize the Grahams' services to augment its developing line of products. Graham began building trucks for Dodge, and Dodge alone, using Dodge engines and underpinnings, selling directly through Dodge dealers. The collaboration between the Dodge Brothers and the Graham Brothers looked like a match made in heaven. Unfortunately, the big gate up in the great beyond would swing shut after only a couple of years.

John Dodge unexpectedly passed through those pearly pillars and headed toward heaven in January of 1920. His brother, Horace, followed that December. The family heirs continued to run the company, but by 1925 Dodge was in the hands of an investment bank. The Grahams remained in management and continued as directors, but the firm exercised an option to take 51 percent of the Graham Brothers' interests, so the boys decided to bolt.

Reo Flying Cloud-bodied Graham.

The Graham Brothers Corporation was formed in 1927, and it took over the Paige-Detroit Motor Car Company that same year. It would serve as the foundation for the brothers' next automotive adventure.

Fast forward to 1935. Having survived the early years of the Depression, what was now Graham-Paige was selling a series of mid-market entries and getting nowhere fast, despite the inclusion of a crankshaft-driven supercharger. The innovative and attractive Blue Streak specials were redesigned because sales were sagging, and the dowdy styling that superseded them was a disaster. A step in the wrong direction, the 1935 models tanked and Graham found itself at a loss for tooling funds to create new models.

But a cloud with a silver lining was about to arrive over the Graham Brothers: the Reo Flying Cloud. Like Franklin, they relied on the Lansing firm to ride to the rescue. The arrangement was the outgrowth of previous merger talks between the two, along with Auburn, Hupp and Pierce-Arrow. They were all battling as independents, but they all wanted to retain their independence.

An agreement to share sheet metal was about all that came out of the effort. On top of the cost to produce the coachwork, Graham would pay Reo a royalty of $7.50 per Flying Cloud. The collaboration would continue through 1937, with Graham buying the rights for Reo bodies.

In 1938, Graham was able to find the funding (partially by selling old tooling to Nissan in Japan) and tried to re-energize those distinctive days of its Blue Streak styling leadership with a new Spirit of Motion series, a.k.a. the Sharknose. This time, the design went too far in the other direction and the abstract extreme of the Spirit of Motion sank on the street. It wasn't long before Graham would find itself swimmin' with the fishes and trying to stay afloat again.

Hupp Skylark and Graham Hollywood

Hupp was yet another enticing independent that struggled to go it alone, lived a tumultuous existence and ultimately found itself underfunded. Hupmobile was the brainchild of Robert C. Hupp, who spent his formative years in the automotive industry with Olds, Ford and Regal.

He believed that "light was right," and wanted to produce products that would appeal to the masses. Although the Hupp Motor Car Company began in 1908, continuing disagreement with fellow directors concerning the market direction for the firm left Robert C. on the outside looking in by 1911. Without Hupp, the board rapidly expanded new model offerings and tried to be all things to all people. By 1925, they were even offering an eight under the hood, which was a long way from Hupp's original intention.

Most likely looking over its shoulder at LaSalle, Hupmobile likewise took an interest in aesthetics and became an early advocate of advanced design. Amos Northup was brought in to add a sense of style in 1928, one year after the arrival of Cadillac's companion car.

Sales surged, but such success was short-lived. The Great Depression quickly derailed any distinction that Hupp may have derived. Sales for 1930 were roughly 22,000 units, compared to 1928's all-time high of 66,000. By 1932, more than 10,000 Hupps crossed the curb, demonstrating the volatility of the industry at the time. Hupp was now fading fast, and in a fight for its life. Production even took a brief hiatus by the end of 1935.

Meanwhile, upheaval unfolded in the board room, and a scramble ensued in search of cash. However, money was in short supply and Hupp teetered on the brink of bankruptcy. Almost every asset, including real estate, was sold off in an effort to stay alive.

In a last-ditch effort, all hope was pinned on a new model, but Hupp couldn't afford to tool up for one. So they cherry-picked the remains of another bankrupt business in an attempt to leverage someone else's investment.

Auburn Automobile was down and out, and its distinctive Cord 810/812 body tooling was now owned by Norman de Vaux, who previously dabbled with the ill-fated De Vaux car. He was brought in as Hupmobile's new general manager and convinced the directors to produce a Hupp from the jigs and dies that he just happened to have in his hip pocket. The coffin-nosed car was now specified for rear-wheel drive, so John Tjaarda was tapped to redesign the front end.

Although a few prototypes and show cars were sporadically built between 1938 and 1939, the Hupp Skylark really arrived in 1940. When it did, it was in fact produced by Graham-Paige. The opportunistic endeavor just wasn't as simple as it may have seemed.

As discussed earlier, Graham was still reeling after its unsuccessful attempt to reverse its fortunes through a bold but botched Spirit of Motion design execution.

Graham Hollywood.

Before actually aligning with Hupp, de Vaux had previously approached Graham-Paige with a similar sales pitch for the Cord tooling, but all the cash they could muster had already been spent on the Sharknose. After witnessing all the inconsistency of 1937–38 Hupp Skylark output, Joseph B. Graham then came calling on de Vaux. Remember, by now Hupp had sold almost everything of value, including its factories.

De Vaux and Graham came to a desperate decision to share the Cord tools, in exchange for the former receiving shares of Graham-Paige stock. Graham was at least in a position where it could, and would, build two versions: its own, christened Hollywood, and the Skylark for Hupp under a licensing agreement. Among other immediate issues, though, the limited-production Cord tooling did not adapt well to mass market manufacturing methods. The cars required a lot of individual massage and hand-holding through the production process, which took its toll in time and money.

The hope was that the cooperative effort would be a win-win for both. Unfortunately, it was just the opposite, and by 1941 the experiment was over. Combined, Graham assembled about 2,200 Hollywoods and Hupp Skylarks, while Cord built more than 2,800 810s and 812s for 1936–37. Down to its bare bones, Hupp fell prey to the receivers, who were circling overhead at the end of 1940, while Graham fortunately found work at the 11th hour in support of the war effort.

"Packard-bakers"

The Studebaker-Packard story has been well chronicled, so I won't go into too much detail here. Like the other underfunded enterprises already discussed, the South Bend, Indiana, automaker came into its own cash crisis during the mid–1950s. Ultimately, what began more than 100 years before as the Studebaker Bros. Mfg. Co., "Builders of Fine Livery Turnouts and Vehicles for the Million," was purchased by Packard in 1954.

As independents, both were struggling with overcapacity and underachieving sales, particularly after the postwar seller's market became saturated. It was somewhat ironic, though, that the new combined company would bear the name Studebaker-Packard. After all, Packard was the more prestigious player and was the business entity that actually made the acquisition, not the other way around. Studebaker certainly had more market presence and a bigger, more powerful dealer body. There would be more surprises to come.

After the deal was done, the die was already cast for the near term. Studebaker products would proceed with utmost independence. Actually, they weren't paying attention to Packard because they were too busy trying to emulate Mercedes-Benz. It turned out, though, that they couldn't pay for the German cars they were importing for U.S. distribution, either.

On the Packard side of the house, after learning that Studebaker financials weren't all that they were cracked up to be during the due diligence, the challenge of logically rationalizing the product portfolios and dealer networks proved to be insurmountable. Something had to give. It would be Packard.

So in 1957, reappointed Studebaker Presidents were delivered to Packard dealers. The initial impression was that such insurrection would be only an interim measure. Packard purists were horrified that the Clipper was now nothing more than a

Packard-baker.

President with fins on top of fender fins. Then, the Packard Hawk landed in 1958, also derived directly from its Studebaker sibling, but you really wouldn't have wanted to "Ask the Man Who Owns One" because he was incensed that the namesake had been neutered. Adding insult to irresponsibility, the famous Packard plant on East Grand Boulevard in downtown Detroit was simultaneously shuttered. The proving grounds up in Utica, Michigan, had already been closed. Instead, the majority of corporate focus was put on the likeable Studebaker Lark, among other last-ditch defenses.

The handwriting was on the wall. Chasing even further efficiencies, there would be no 1959 Packards. In April 1962, Studebaker-Packard became simply the Studebaker Corporation. By December 1963, the crowning conclusion in South Bend took place as production ceased with a small run of 1964 Studes. And last but not least, the final Studebakers were assembled in Canada in 1966. In the end, Packard-plagiarized Studebakers were yet another lost cause.

Most ironically, the 1958 Packard Hawk—or "Packard-baker" as it was often (and still is) critically called (as was/is the '57/58 sedan series)—was one of the rarest of the rare, with only 588 assembled.

The "Hash"

In a further example of wretched excess from the 1950s, there was an additional attempt to ward off the wolf at the door in yet another Detroit neighborhood. Like Studebaker and Packard, Nash and Hudson were struggling when postwar prosperity shifted from a seller's market to favor the buyer. Soon, there were too many car companies fighting for too few buyers, since so many already owned an automobile. And if that wasn't enough, the Big Three were now very much leveraging their economy of scale advantage. In search of any opportunity, the smaller independents were forced to look in nooks and crannies to find any gap in the marketplace that they could fill.

Nash was well aware that there was strength in numbers—so much so that CEO George Mason aspired to create a "Big 4" conglomerate to also include Hudson, Studebaker and Packard. But Packard's play for Studebaker meant that Nash and Hudson would end up as the wallflowers, left to dance all on their own.

So American Motors was formed in 1954, with Nash of Kenosha, Wisconsin, in control, and operating out of Nash-Kelvinator's offices in Detroit. By now, Hudson was losing more money than it had during the Depression and thus became the subservient partner.

A year later, production was consolidated at Nash plants in Kenosha and Milwaukee. There would be no more Detroit-built Hudsons, the car that made its name on the back of its sponsor, the well-known Detroit department store magnate. But even more alarming was the news that the product platforms would be consolidated as well.

The first to fall victim would be the Metropolitan. A newly-introduced Hudson

Nash-Hudson "Hash."

Metropolitan was nothing more than a '54 Nash Metro with an "H" grille emblem. Then, and so much more significantly, the 1955 series of Hudson Hornets and Wasps would lose their distinctive sting as re-badged Nash Ramblers. The buzz was instead about the svelte step-downs that made way for an insulting array of Nash-based bastards, exaggerated by their garish grilles, trim and lamps.

American Motors was now trying to keep two essentially competing dealer networks alive with what was actually a single common car line. The public wasn't fooled. Losses from 1954 through 1956 amounted to almost $40 million. They would bleed another $12 million in 1957.

Obviously something had to be done, and it was. The Nash-based Hudson—or "Hash," as it's commonly referred to—would be gone by 1958. So would the Nash. Though solid citizens back in the day, both accelerated toward irrelevance in the ever-changing landscape of an increasingly competitive automotive marketplace, and became the answers to questions no one was asking. And oh-so-coincidentally, one of Merriam-Webster's definitions for "hash" is "A jumble, hodgepodge, a confused muddle."

American Motors then put all of its eggs in the Rambler basket. It would be an uphill battle from there, because automotive history had already shown that desperate measures taken during desperate times merely forestalled the inevitable.

And it has a way of repeating itself. Witness, Saab…

How the West Won
The Gestation of a Global Automotive Industry
July/August 2017

"The world runs on individuals pursuing their self interests. The great achievements of civilization have not come from government bureaus. Einstein didn't construct his theory under order from a bureaucrat. Henry Ford didn't revolutionize the automobile industry that way."
—*Milton Friedman*

From discovery to maturity, as a country, America evolved through fairly conventional means. Scouts went forth in search of basic understanding and assessed potential pitfalls and danger. Then, explorers reached further into uncharted areas to learn more and substantiate possibilities. With a level of confidence confirmed, pilgrims began to plant seeds in a fledgling infrastructure to seek opportunity, which paved the way for settlers to arrive en masse and fulfill the dream. Interestingly enough, it turns out that the world's automotive industry evolved in very much the same way.

The Scouts—Germany

It's well established that Germany gets credit as the birthplace of the automobile. In the early 1860s, Nikolaus August Otto began experimenting with compressed charge, internal combustion engines. Using the Lenoir double-acting (like a steam engine) illuminating gas engine as a basis, Otto began his quest by adapting its principles to liquid fuel. In an attempt to improve efficiency, he discovered that progressive combustion was a more effective solution than the more intense, explosive (and thus, destructive) process which was more common at the time. To achieve such an end, Otto concluded that the carefully choreographed four-stroke cycle (intake, compression, power, exhaust) was the most effective means of combustion control.

A commercial enterprise, N.A. Otto & Cie, was soon established to produce his engine, with a focus on large, stationary applications. As the company developed,

Otto's manager, Gottlieb Daimler, began to have other aspirations and believed that there was a future in smaller, lighter alternatives as well. Otto disagreed, and his name was on the door.

So Daimler went his own way in 1880 and partnered with Wilhelm Maybach to pursue his vision of a high-speed lightweight engine—if you could call 600 to 700 rpm "high speed." Along the way, there were experiments in fuel metering that led to the creation of the surface carburetor and improved ignition, which resulted in the hot-tube concept that allowed for the transfer of heat (essentially a glow plug) directly into the combustion chamber.

Ever the innovators, Daimler and Maybach continued to experiment. In 1885, they applied their engine to a two-wheeled *reitwagen* (riding car). A year later, Daimler installed his engine in a four-wheeled phaeton carriage. Meanwhile, 60 miles away, Carl Benz created a three-wheeler in 1886 as well (unbeknownst to Daimler), which was the first purpose-built automotive application. Which is why it was called the Patent-Motorwagen. Thus, the automobile was born.

In addition to stationary applications, small, lightweight engines were then deployed in boats, trolleys and balloons. Previously, Benz & Companie Rheinische Gasmotoren-Fabrik (Benz & Cie) was established in 1883, while

Carl Benz's first automobile, the Patent-Motorwagen.

Gottlieb Daimler's first automobile.

Daimler Motoren Gesellschaft (DMG) was established in 1890 as another supply source.

Both Daimler and Maybach believed in the commercial future of the automobile. DMG's cautious financiers felt otherwise, and pushed the pair of engineering innovators to focus primarily on stationary engines. Likewise, Carl Benz was confident in the opportunity of commercializing the automobile, and worked hard to sell examples of the Patent Motorwagen. Benz, too, had to face the reality that industrial engines would pay the bulk of the bills at the outset, which impeded Germany's commercialization of the automobile. Long after the first Daimler and Benz foray to create a functional/saleable automobile in the mid–1880s, Horch and Opel joined the fray with their own alternatives in 1901 and 1902, respectively.

Being so efficient, disciplined and thorough, yet fiscally cautious, it's no surprise that the proverbial slogan "Vorsprung durch Technik" not only sums up German culture, but its contribution to early automotive history. That being, Progress through Technology…

The Explorers—France

While the Germans demonstrated a rather empirical approach to their automotive exploits, the French proved to be a bit more effervescent. With a lust for life, they took to the automobile with boundless enthusiasm.

A Parisian bicycle maker by the name of Emile Roger was producing Benz & Cie engines under license and quickly became a Motorwagen customer. He then gained the sole rights for its sale in France, in 1888, and sold 60 percent of the first 69 cars built. According to Daimler.com, "It was only after [Emile] Roger had made this innovation known in Paris and imported and sold several cars there—among them one sold to Panhard & Levassor as early as 1888—that we were able to start production, and from then on, we had a lot of work." By the end of the decade, Benz had supplied about a third of its total production volume of more than 2,300 units to France. As a result of his success, Roger ended up with Benz distribution rights for all other countries outside of Germany!

Meanwhile, Daimler and particularly Maybach weren't sitting still, either. Another French entrepreneur (of German descent), Emil Jellinek, became infatuated with the automobile and ventured back to the fatherland in search of opportunity. He was impressed by what he saw at Daimler Motoren Gesellschaft and signed on as DMG's agent in France during 1898. By now Daimler was also licensed to Peugeot and Panhard, so Jellinek had to think and act quickly if he was going to establish a meaningful competitive advantage for himself.

He did so by pushing Maybach for the continuous improvement of Daimler products, to the extent that he began insisting that they be built to his own specification. His intention was to go racing! He was of the opinion, "I don't want a car for today or tomorrow, it will be the car of the day after tomorrow." Before long, the configurations Jellinek ordered were so unique that they were no longer considered Daimlers ... thus the Mercedes was born, in France. It was named after Emil's oldest daughter.

French aristocracy was consumed by motorsport competition, which followed in the racing-tire tracks of the bicycle boom that preceded it. As such, there was also an established infrastructure of good roads to support it. It's no coincidence that the earliest exploits in motor racing utilized the routes of such provincial contests as Paris-Rouen, Paris-Bordeaux-Paris, Paris-Marseille, New York to Paris, et al.

The visibility of such spectacles, along with the allure of personal freedom and exhilaration of speed, soon accelerated the growth of a French automotive industry all its own. From early Bollee and Serpollet steamers in the late 1880s to popular De Dion trikes in the 1890s, France was primed for an explosion of automotive production. Wealthy, ebullient Parisians proved to be a most enthusiastic audience.

By 1903, France was responsible for roughly half of the entire world's automotive output. They built almost 20,000 that year ... compared to roughly 2,000 that came out of Germany per annum. Panhard and Peugeot would compete with an increasing number of others, including Darracq, Renault, Delahaye, Hotchkiss, Delage, Rochet-Schneider, Delaunay-Belleville, Richard-Brasier, Mors, Mathis and many more.

Industrious and energetic as France was, its industry was bound by production constraints. Catering to such upscale and exclusive clientele led the French to concentrate on primarily expensive and ostentatious offerings. Though well proven in competition, they were essentially hand-built labors of love that sold in small batches and limited quantity, in comparison with what would soon follow. While insatiable demand was clearly established, it would prove to be an unsustainable business model, with too many Old World manufacturers in search of too few affluent buyers.

James M. Laux summed up the French exploration of the early automotive industry best in his landmark 1976 work, *In First Gear—The French Automobile Industry to 1914*: "In the 1890s, the automobile industry began in France due to the efforts of some alert and venturesome businessmen-engineers who together supplied a mastery of the technology and the financial resources to put cars on the good roads and streets of their country. Then, with their flair for publicity they stimulated the demand already awakened by the bicycle craze." He continued, "Such leadership in the face of the wide-ranging industrial achievements of Imperial Germany and Victorian Britain at the beginning of the twentieth century demonstrates a dynamism in the French economy…."

This is why Paris and its suburbs, became the world's first motor city.

The Pilgrims—New England

By the turn of the century, the world was a smaller place. The excitement, if not enlightenment, of the French automotive scene would then emigrate to America. As in Paris, the audience was primarily the wealthy elite who populated the established, and prosperous, Northeast.

Vanderbilts, Astors and others began to flaunt the latest four-wheeled French fashion with expression and passion. To quote *The New York Times*' "What Is Doing in Society" column from July 1899: "The automobile fad grows daily … nothing that was ever introduced here has caught the popular fancy as the automobile." Newport, Rhode Islanders routinely took part in parades, obstacle events and more across their expansive Ocean Drive estate lawns in rich imported (predominantly French) automobiles that were festooned with lavish floral arrangements.

The sport of "automobiling" was considered "good form," according to *The Times*, and paved the way for early acceptance of the automobile in America. The first closed-course race in this country was held at Narragansett Park in 1896. America's first short-track race then took place in Branford, Connecticut, by 1900.

Charles and Frank Duryea began dabbling with the automobile in Springfield, Massachusetts, and demonstrated their first phaeton in 1893. In 1895, Duryea won America's first recognized competitive open-road automotive event, the *Chicago Times Herald* race. Plans were then put into place to build the Duryea in series production, and the Duryea Motor Wagon Co. was then founded. It was this country's first commercial enterprise that was specifically established to produce automobiles. By the end of 1896, the company had built 13 cars. In honor

Frank Duryea with his first production car.

of its pioneering significance, the image of the Duryea is embodied in AACA's logo.

As if the *Mayflower* had landed, more "pilgrims" soon followed, "to plant seeds in a fledgling infrastructure," in New England, coincidentally. Flush with profit after selling their photographic dry plate business to Eastman Kodak, the Stanley twins of Kingfield, Maine, began experimenting with the steam automobile in 1897. Two years later, they had produced and sold more than 200, according to G.N. Georgano's *Cars Early and Vintage, 1886–1930*.

Locomobile was established in 1899 and began production in Bridgeport, Connecticut, during 1900. Frank Duryea went on to partner with the J. Stevens Arms & Tool Co., in Chicopee Falls, Massachusetts, to create the Stevens-Duryea in 1901. The Corbin automobile appeared in 1904 and was an outgrowth of hardware industry interests in New Britain, Connecticut. Having built the French Berliet under license, the American Locomotive Co. thought it could do better and began making its own ALCO automobile in Providence, Rhode Island. Even the Rolls-Royce would ultimately be assembled in Springfield, Massachusetts.

But it was Colonel Albert Augustus Pope who primarily established New England as America's first automotive manufacturing metropolis. As a bicycle manufacturer extraordinaire, Pope leveraged his success as a two-wheeled tycoon and accelerated full speed ahead onto four wheels.

All the necessary infrastructure was very much in place. The colonel had the assembly expertise, engineering know-how, metallurgical intuition, machining precision and manufacturing might to fast-track his entrée into the industry. In addition, Pope's vast empire brought purchasing power, an extensive network of sales and service outlets, replacement part resources, marketing and promotion expertise, and financial wherewithal with it, too!

The Pope Manufacturing Co. began producing electric automobiles in 1897. By 1899, more than 500 had gone out the door and the Hartford, Connecticut–made electrics became the staple of a burgeoning New York taxi trade … so much so that somewhat unsavory financial interests were drawn to it. These were the days of trusts and monopolistic tendencies, and the Pope organization was soon distracted by speculative endeavors, even including a stab at Selden Patent ownership and enforcement.

After supplementing the range with a variety of gasoline-powered alternatives, a hierarchy of Columbia, Pope-Tribune, Pope-Waverley, Pope-Toledo, Pope-Hartford and Pope-Robinson models emerged. While conventional wisdom holds that Alfred P. Sloan and General Motors invented the concept of market segmentation with a car "for every purse and purpose" in 1924, in fact, New England's Colonel Albert Pope did, some two decades earlier.

By the time the American bicycle boom went bust, which followed the previous French experience, so did Pope's automotive enterprise. The distraction of get-rich-quick schemes from financial influencers and hangers-on further led to the company's derailment. Pope first filed for bankruptcy in 1907, and died two years later. Unfortunately, New England was fairly set in its ways by then, so there was little interest elsewhere in picking up on a scale where Pope left off. The northeast industrial base was quite mature, while established banking interests remained comfortable with the safe status quo, such as the stock market, as opposed to the risky nature of the then new-fangled automobile business.

One of Pope Manufacturing's greatest contributions was not just in the making of New England automotive history, but rather the recording of it. Pope hired Hiram

Percy Maxim to lead his Motor Vehicle Department, so Maxim had a front row seat in the creation of the Connecticut colossus. In his 1937 *Horseless Carriage Days*, he not only reminisced about his earliest days and experiments from 1893 to 1901, but shared the cultural insight and social significance that influenced the invention of the industry, in quite vivid and visceral terms. It's become an automotive reference standard-bearer and is a highly recommended read, since it's been republished and remains available.

As a result, New England is best remembered as the incubator of the American automobile industry. According to the March 2, 1916, edition of *The Automobile*, "the zenith of automobile manufacturing in New England was reached in 1909 and 1910."

The Settlers—Detroit

By this time, the industry was migrating west. There was a groundswell of interest from tinkerers, backyard mechanics and self-taught engineers. Unlike established New England, which was steeped in strict, technical tradition, those to the west, and particularly the Midwest, learned by doing. They were untrained and unafraid to step out and experiment, because they didn't know any better! Many were enthralled by the idea of machinery to relieve the drudgery of farm work and chores out on the open range, and thus the automobile proved to be a prime mover to pursue such a cause. There was no constraint of convention.

With all its unobstructed lakes and rivers, the Midwest developed a burgeoning marine engine industry early on. It would prove to be a significant resource for many of those who would establish automotive settlements of their own. Meanwhile, regional capitalists simultaneously found themselves in a quandary. Their lumber and mining interests, particularly in Michigan, had matured and they needed new opportunities to pursue. Unencumbered, free, western spirit provided these individual investors, instead of established banks, with the courage to turn caution to the wind ... which conservative New Englanders refused to do.

Having developed stellite and stainless steel alloys, metallurgist/industrialist Elwood Haynes hired Elmer and Edgar Apperson to construct a vehicle for him in late 1893. He thought that an automobile could be the most effective way for him to inspect his Indiana gas field holdings, so he ordered a Sintz Gas (marine) engine from Grand Rapids, Michigan, and had the Appersons install it in a carriage of his own design. Haynes-Apperson would follow Duryea as America's second automotive manufacturing enterprise.

Ransom Olds joined his father's Olds Gasoline Engine Works in Lansing, Michigan, which produced stationary and marine engines. He began experimenting with steam-powered automobiles in 1894, but shifted to gasoline by 1896. That same year, Charles Brady King drove his first self-propelled automobile down the streets of Detroit. It, too, was powered by a Sintz marine engine. Of course, Henry Ford first turned a wheel aboard his home-grown Quadricycle later that same year, and Cleveland, Ohio's Alexander Winton began experimenting with automobiles in 1896 as well.

With all the excitement from these early automotive exploits, liberal and lenient investment capital was not far behind. Olds found financial backing from the wealthy Michigan Land and Lumber Company's Samuel L. Smith. By 1899, the Olds Motor Works was formed and automobile construction began. It proved to be something of a false start.

Olds was keen on providing a small, affordable automobile for the then-relative masses. Smith, on the other hand—who controlled essentially the company's entire block of stock—preferred a large, upscale French-inspired alternative in keeping with the social circle in which he traveled. Such preference would prove to be an unfortunate frailty among many an American investor at the time. Even Pierce promoted its Motorette as "An American design based on the best French experience."

So the success of the Curved Dash Olds was shorter-lived than it should have been. It was introduced in 1901 and was, in fact, America's first mass-produced automobile. The public was buying it, but Samuel Smith, the actual owner of the Olds company, was not. The fact that the factory burned down didn't help. Just as in the earlier struggle between Otto and Daimler, Ransom Olds was soon (by 1904) out of the company that bore his name, leaving Smith and his family to focus the Olds effort on more pretentious offerings. Ransom Olds went off and returned with Reo.

Ford found funding from various local sources such as real estate magnates, shipping czars and railroad captains as he plied along. After two false starts, he was buoyed by coal merchant Alexander Malcomson, among others, and Ford Motor Company was established in 1903. It's well known that Ford studied Olds, including its/his mistakes. He, too, became a disciple of the idea of an automobile for everyman.

Meanwhile, the New England ethic for precision machining began to invade the uninitiated in the Midwest. Having mastered his craft in the halls

A Curved Dash Oldsmobile runs up a hill.

Fordham Mahoney with his 1907 Oldsmobile in Bar Harbor, Maine.

of Brown & Sharpe in Providence, Rhode Island, and Colt Firearms in Hartford, Connecticut, Vermont–born Henry Leland advanced American automotive manufacturing capability to previously unheard-of extremes. His Detroit–based Leland & Faulconer machine shops were dedicated to the art of perfection, and as if an epiphany, it set America apart with its own identity in what was now an automotive establishment.

Cadillac was recognized as the first automobile with interchangeable parts.

Dr. Neil in a Model T Ford.

England's Royal Automobile Club recognized Leland's ability to produce exacting, interchangeable parts by bestowing upon what was then his Cadillac Motor Car Company with its prestigious Dewar Trophy. Accuracy of production parts to one-thousandth of an inch was an incredible accomplishment. No more filing and grinding required to assemble each and every component. The stage was set for the perfect storm, and a confluence of unprecedented automotive forces followed.

Automatic machine tools were now coming of age, as everything from office equipment to sewing machines was being produced in quantity. The study of metallurgy went from black magic to an applied science. The population was migrating from rural areas to city centers, bringing an abundance of unskilled (thus, affordable) labor with it. Finances were flowing. Traditional New England mill–inspired assembly halls were being superseded by purpose-built manufacturing complexes. The importance of a carefully choreographed supply chain was realized. There were plentiful untapped natural resources that were just ready and waiting, and having already been blessed by the bicycle (like France and New England before it), a massive American marketplace was now ready to embrace the arrival of the automobile, in keeping with the expanse of its vast geographic footprint and populace.

The pump was primed for Henry Ford to follow in the footsteps of Ransom Olds and create a car for an even greater multitude of the masses. When the moving assembly line technique was applied to the Model T Ford magneto at the Highland Park factory, it was as if a genie had been let out of the bottle. There was no turning back. Others went on to rub the lamp as well, and the ability to mass produce resulted in a tidal wave of American automobile production … and consumption. Progressive, if not aggressive, sales and marketing offensives followed, such as financing.

Success would now be measured in millions, instead of Europe's couple-of-hundred-thousands. By 1915, American automobile output dwarfed the rest of the world's, and the die was cast. The Midwest would accelerate ahead with Detroit—now Motown—settling in as the global manufacturing leader.

The dream was achieved; the west won and a new world order was established. The rest, as they say, is history—antique automobile history.

Challenging Conventional Wisdom

September/October 2017

Like a lot of other pursuits that chronicle past events, acts and ideas, accepted automotive history is grounded in a bedrock of traditional beliefs. But when it comes to the actual narrative that accounts for the happenings that shaped our favorite hobby, there are also a fair number of faded memories, fallacies and old wives' tales that have clouded the chronology of four-wheeled folklore.

As the automobile evolved, delivering results and proven success was vital. Recording such achievements for posterity, on the other hand, was obviously not as essential. So rather than simply letting bygones be bygones, let's try to separate fact from fiction, and challenge some conventional antique automotive wisdom.

Henry Ford Introduced the Moving Assembly Line

Beyond the often-repeated "you can have it in any color you want so long as it's black" anecdote, perhaps the most common Ford fable is that old Henry introduced the moving assembly line. There's no need to address the Model T paint color parable because most AACA members have seen and touched both early and late examples of "the universal car," and therefore recognize that it did indeed arrive in a variety of tones. When it comes to what went on within the walls of Ford's expansive manufacturing enterprise, the lore of the assembly line is not quite as clear.

It's well known that the industrial revolution fueled a transition from handcrafting techniques to a factory system. Having begun in Great Britain in the mid–1700s, industrialization migrated throughout Europe and further accelerated during the century that followed. The concept of bulk material handling was followed by a linear and continuous assembly flow, particularly in the area of textiles, before the next mechanized component was conceived.

The development of machine tools such as lathes and milling machines then contributed to an ability to produce interchangeable parts. This led to an unprecedented expansion of sequential manufacturing and the organized assembly process.

Firearms, sewing machines, clocks, bicycles, office machines and more were soon being produced through this industrial method.

As the Curved-Dash Olds began to enjoy early acceptance, Ransom E. Olds was soon producing in series, with interchangeable parts. He employed what was called progressive assembly, and relied on stands with casters to move the Curved-Dash along through the process. At the time, station assembly was the norm, where components were brought to a specific manufacturing point for installation by a defined team of workers. Henry Ford took note, and would go on to expand and institutionalize the Olds methodology.

It's said that Ford Motor Company was also influenced by the Swift & Company slaughterhouse in Chicago, but—just to clarify—that wasn't an assembly line, rather a disassembly system! Ford's operatives (not actually Henry) recognized the efficiency in the dividing of labor into very specific tasks as part of a clearly defined and mechanized operation with minimal motion and human interface and reported back to the Flivver King. In addition, there was obvious advantage in the automation of conveyors and overhead carriers with hooks, as also seen in Chicago.

After a few false starts at the Piquette Plant in 1908, Ford tested the technique of the scientific method again during 1913, in Highland Park's magneto assembly area. Through time and motion analysis, six or seven minutes were shaved off the time required to manufacture a Model T magneto, from 15 to about eight or nine. After the success of that experiment, the process was deployed throughout the plant with a vengeance. Engine assembly went from almost ten hours to about four, while chassis production dropped from 12 to six … to three … and even less.

As production times were driven down—and thus, manufacturing cost as well—Model T production rates soared. Before long, Ford Motor Company was supplying America with more than half of all new cars sold. It was Charles E. Sorenson who concluded in his book *My Forty Years with Ford*, "Henry Ford is generally regarded as the father of mass production. He was not. He was the sponsor of it."

So Ford obviously didn't invent the moving assembly line. But he sure improved it!

General Motors Created the Idea of a Car for Every Purse and Purpose

According to the GM Heritage Center, "Alfred P. Sloan explained his famous market segment strategy of 'a car for every purse and purpose' in the 1924 Annual Report to shareholders. Sloan divided the U.S. vehicle market into segments by price range. Each of GM brand's products was to be focused on one segment, with Chevrolet at the low end of the market and Cadillac at the high end."

It's well known that as General Motors' president and chief executive officer, Sloan brought order and management method into the wake of corporate chaos that followed Billy Durant's departure. Along with other boardroom breakthroughs and reliance on rational, corporate discipline, GM's market segmentation theory proved to be a ladder of success that propelled General Motors to the industry forefront, allowing it to ultimately eclipse Ford Motor Company and its lone Model T commodity. However, it seems that Sloan's greatest contribution was his ability to clearly strategize, carefully verbalize, and then ultimately execute segmentation as a competitive tactic.

The idea of a car for every purse and purpose was, in fact, previously employed by Colonel Albert Augustus Pope, who began producing electric automobiles in 1897. He then supplemented the range with a variety of gasoline-powered alternatives as well, and before long, a hierarchy of models was established under the Pope umbrella.

With a single cylinder, the Pope-Tribune was the least expensive offering in the Colonel's portfolio. It was produced from 1904 to 1908 and was initially priced at $650 before it was quickly lowered to $500. The Pope-Waverley was also built between 1904 and 1908, and it was an electric that cost between $850 and $2,250.

Next up was the Pope-Hartford. It included two, four and six cylinder variants, was sold from 1904 to 1914, and was priced from $1,000 to $5,400. The Pope-Toledo was predominantly a four-cylinder model from 1904 to 1909, and spanned the $2,000 to $6,000 price points.

Finally, the range topped out with the short-lived Pope-Robinson. Also a four-cylinder, it was produced only in 1903 and 1904 and retailed from $4,500 to $6,000.

Pope introduced automobile market segments.

In Pope's day, which preceded Sloan's presidency by some 20 years, the rough and tumble automotive landscape was still in its infancy. Marketing tactics were simply employed to see what would stick, as opposed to formal scientific principle. Thus Colonel Albert's contribution has essentially been ignored.

Sloan, instead, leveraged the idea of segmentation, put a proper corporate process behind it and wrapped it up in a clever sound bite that was presented to GM shareholders. It turned into one of the industry's most celebrated citations.

And the rest, as they say, is history ... automotive history.

Ford Used Wood from Packing Crates for Floorboards

Since more than one person I know is convinced that this is true, let me use Henry Ford's own words from his 1926 book *Today and Tomorrow* (in collaboration with Samuel Crowther) to dispel this old adage:

> We are saving nearly 100 million feet of wood a year by the salvage of old lumber.... Why should a crate or packing box once used be considered only as so much waste to be smashed and burned? ... Why should there be so much waste to dispose of? Answering that question has taken us into the salvage of all the wood that comes into our plants in crates and boxes ... each crate and box must be opened carefully without breaking the wood. Crowbars are not permitted.... All scrap wood eventually gets back to the wood salvage department.... Heavy stuff—barring serious flaws—is saved for sawing, resawing and planing to box size ... nails are removed.... Much of the lighter stuff needs no further treatment, and is simply sent on to where the boxes are being constructed.... The box factory also supplies, over and above its quota of containers, any amount of specially shaped blocks and cleats for shipping and packing automobile parts such as radiators and generators; tiny wood forms used in the coil unit assembly.... It is truly remarkable how far afield the pursuit of waste will take one and equally surprising are the results, for by following out the by-products, one gets the original material sought for next to nothing.

It's well known that Henry Ford was extremely progressive—if not a crusader. When it came to advanced industrial theory, he dedicated himself and the Ford Motor Company to the vertical integration of his manufacturing process and simply abhorred waste. So it's quite true and should come as no surprise that scrap wood and lumber were routinely recycled as part of the Ford manufacturing process; but, as indicated, the material was used to create new crates and boxes (in 14 standard sizes, by the way), shipping blocks and cleats, along with other generic applications ... *not* floorboards.

Think about it. By 1922, Ford was building more than one million Model T's a year. Simultaneously, the company was moving further and further into the realm of a fully integrated self-sustaining internal supply chain. Where would all the packing crates come from to create so many floorboards?

The answer's simple. Wood came from Ford's half-million acres of timberland in Northern Michigan, along with the 120,000 acres the company owned in Kentucky ... *not* recycled packing crates.

Did Ford use recycled packing crates for floorboards?

The 1927 LaSalle Ushered in the Art of Automotive Styling

The legend of Harley Earl and the creation of GM's Art & Colour Section in 1927, along with its influence on the art of automotive styling, is the stuff of ... well, legend. Certainly, I'm not going to argue about GM's critical contribution to the discipline of styling and design, but be aware that the truth of Albert Sloan's tenets that follow from a letter to Fisher Body President William A. Fisher does not indicate that styling was a GM invention. "I think," he wrote, "that the future of General Motors will be measured by the attractiveness that we put in the bodies from the standpoint of luxury of appointment, the degree to which they please the eye, both in contour and in color scheme, also the degree to which we are able to make them different from competition."

When the Duryea Brothers began construction of their second automobile, they made a conscious effort to hide the unsightly mechanicals underneath. Likewise, many a horseless carriage competitor worked hard to avoid any distraction from what could appear to be buggy origins, including the extreme of faux hoods up front. When they arrived, running boards and splash aprons at least helped unify an automobile from stem to stern before they were outmoded by increased speed, lower ride heights and, most conspicuously, more integrated design themes.

Meanwhile, in the luxury car category, custom coachbuilders were busy satisfying the every whim of upscale patrons throughout the Classic era with designs and

When did automobile styling actually begin?

styling elements to suit their individual heart's content. Certainly all the recognized houses simultaneously provided tasteful guidance as a function of their established savoir-faire. So no matter how incongruous the request, it was the staff's responsibility to interpret the client's interest and translate it into rolling sculpture.

The mainstream marketplace, however, remained driven by a manufacturing movement of improved efficiency and the continued engineering ethic of technical accomplishment. Due to the depth and breadth of what was now a well-oiled General Motors, Sloan, Earl, Fisher and company were able to subdue such emphasis and instead inject a new-found focus on style— particularly since the now-accessible automobile was a well-proven and reliable commodity.

Thus, the engineering labs were rivaled by what was sometimes referred to as the new "beauty parlor"—the Art & Colour Section—which would lead to an unparalleled GM parade of progress. Meanwhile, Ford was still struggling to sell what was now an anachronism known as the Model T … in colors again by this time, at least.

So to set the record straight, it's probably best to consider that "the 1927 LaSalle ushered in the art of automotive styling" to the mass market, due to GM's far-reaching and incomparable influence.

The Depression Destroyed the Classic Car Category

This one's pretty popular in the antique auto arena, and the usual story goes something like this. The Fierce-Sparrow was an incredible Classic and on its way to immortality. Unfortunately, it got derailed by the Depression. Otherwise, it would have certainly soared to new heights and been a huge success, had it not been for the Wall Street crash…

By definition, the Classic era was "distinguished by fine design, high engineering standards and superior workmanship," according to the Classic Car Club of America (CCCA), and spanned the period from 1915 to 1948. It was the wealthiest of the wealthy who had the ability to buy in this category, and quite often the only limitation was a function of how wide they'd be willing to open their wallet. So many a car maker and certainly all of the coachbuilders vied for a piece of this lucrative market.

As the industry matured, more manufacturers than you might imagine looked to this upper echelon in search of elusive earnings. Before long, the supply and demand curve was out of whack. As resolute leaders like Cadillac and Packard (and their dealers) upped the ante with such enhancements as V-16 and V-12 engines, the lesser second-tier attempted to follow suit. Marmon, for example, introduced a 16-cylinder engine in 1931, while Franklin added a V-12 in 1932.

The problem was that many of these smaller concerns were already struggling as a result of an early 1920s recession. As automotive history has demonstrated so many times—and continues to demonstrate—there were too many manufacturers in search of too few highbrow buyers during the Classic era. Being cash starved already, ambitious investment in innovation when it could least be afforded led a good portion of the Classic car contingent down a dead end of desperation and despair, as finances dwindled, and it drained the lifeblood out of them.

The fact is, many companies from the Classic car era were already on shaky ground before Wall Street imploded. By the mid–1920s, Franklin was clearly encountering resistance with its unconventional air-cooled appearance and designer Frank de Causse was hired to help lure buyers with a more mainstream appeal … that included an ersatz radiator. Marmon soldiered on with its long-in-the-tooth Model 34 and unfortunately stagnated, which forced the company to reorganize in 1926.

Pierce-Arrow fought the fight with the introduction of a lower-priced Series 80 in late 1924. The idea was to broaden the base of buyers, though at almost $3,000 to

Was it the Depression that destroyed the super luxury cars of the 1930s?

more than $4,000 a copy, the 80 certainly wasn't in the realm of the mass market. By 1920, Harry C. Stutz was out of the company that bore his name, and reorganization followed in 1922. Frederick Moskovics was then hired in an attempt to re-energize all the Stutz allure in 1926, with the arrival of the Vertical-8 powered "Safety Stutz."

So it wasn't the rage of a "perfect storm" called the Depression that led to the demise of many a Classic car. It was simply a "field of dreams" that foundered and nailed the coffin shut.

Underfunded and overwhelmed, Marmon ran out of gas in 1933. To try and stay afloat, Franklin resorted to repowering a Reo model that it called Olympic, and then shut its doors in 1934. Stutz succumbed in 1935, and after trying its hand at travel trailers, Pierce petered out in 1938.

After the dust settled, the luxury market quietly corrected itself—with Cadillac and Packard essentially in charge—and discreetly moved on.

The Big 3 Conspired to Put the Independents Out of Business

I heard it again just the other night. This time it was one of those History or Velocity channel TV shows that was discussing the demise of Tucker, and put the blame squarely on the shoulders of the Big 3. Excuse me?

No doubt, we all have a soft spot for the American independents, particularly from the postwar period. They were the Davids that did their best to go toe-to-toe with Detroit's Goliaths. The fact is, they were buoyed by an unprecedented seller's marketplace, where demand overwhelmingly outstripped supply. It's well known that after World War II you could sell literally anything on four wheels, new or used, and very much at a premium, too. Some, like Davis, even tried to do it on three wheels!

Generally speaking, though, the independents captured little more than a sliver of the market as America reinvented itself in response to newfound postwar prosperity. Sure, inroads were made by these smaller and more nimble competitors as the gargantuan Big 3 attempted to retool, but once the empowered industry poured on the coal, GM, Ford and Chrysler—with their expansive and established dealer networks, massive material supply chain and vast financial wherewithal—captured a commanding 90 percent of the market. That means that Studebaker, Hudson, Packard, Nash, Rambler, Kaiser, et al. were scrambling for a mere 10 percent share among the bulk of them.

Yes, the independents not only got to peek, but got a good look through a small window of opportunity after the war, but they were soon looking to the far horizon as the automobile establishment accelerated ahead and wartime economies of scale went into overdrive. Thus—as it always does—the market spoke.

So much for conspiracy theories.

Rarity Drives Value and Desirability

The prevailing school of thought is that the more rare a car is, the more valuable and desirable it's going to be. Maybe, sometimes.

Human nature is such that when we look in the mirror, we all aspire to a certain order of individuality. Likewise when it comes to our clothes, where and how we live, and what's parked in our garage. Most people just don't consider themselves as an "ordinary Joe." We are driven to be different.

So it's no surprise that many collectors aspire to own an antique that's simply unique because no one else has one. Limited production cars, one-offs, coach-built classics and more are the stuff that dreams and obsessions are made of. The interest in owning something within the category of "one-of-one" can be motivated by the desire to simply stand apart, to avoid being swept up in the mainstream sea of '57 Chevys, '65 Mustangs and Model A Fords. There's certainly nothing wrong with that, but care must be taken if you're going to head down a road less traveled.

History is full of examples of underdeveloped and underfunded automobiles that failed to achieve success in the marketplace. Thousands and thousands of early nameplates were extinguished by natural selection, leaving but a few with fortitude that proved they could competitively sustain themselves. Many of the also-rans simply failed to function properly in the first place, and retiringly rolled down memory lane into peaceful oblivion.

If you're like me, and lust after the more offbeat and esoteric, it's easy to get blinded by curious enthusiasm. While we'd sincerely like to see all of them rescued and restored, the reality is that what proved to be a marginal product then is still going to be marginal now, if not more so … despite how much modern re-engineering we might attempt to take on. In the end, the final outcome will primarily be valued as a function of past prowess because that's where an accepted benchmark was established.

So choose wisely, with eyes open and full understanding, if you head off into the antique unknown, because history has a way of repeating itself. Sometimes, they're rare for a reason … so curiosity and collector value don't necessarily go hand in hand.

"Pontiac Launched Muscle-car Era with GTO"

So read the September 14, 2008, headline in the iconic automotive trade journal *Automotive News*. They went on to report, "Pontiac's engineers got the bright idea to do at the factory what the hot rod community had been doing for years: Simply stuff a big engine into a smaller and lighter car." Well … yes, and no.

Since its inception the automotive industry routinely produced performance

In the late 1920s, Packard began using the "muscle car" recipe by installing a modified version of its most powerful engine onto the shortest chassis available, and fitting it with a body that was lighter, narrower and shorter than anything else. While many companies played with the idea since the dawn of the automobile era, Packard may have been the first to produce muscle cars in series.

alternatives by simply manipulating specifications during assembly. As early as the electrically driven Lohner-Porsche from 1900, which was upgraded to four hub-mounted motors, as opposed to the original front-wheels-only configuration, shoving more hardware into less real (wheel) estate is a long-established automotive industry tradition.

Willys-Overland found itself with an inventory of upmarket six-cylinder sleeve-valve engines, an abundance of entry level Whippet bodies and an empty Garford truck assembly hall, so it created the performance Falcon-Knight brand, which was produced from 1927 to 1929. Packard took a similar tack in 1929–1930 when it created its Speedster by mating a souped-up Custom/Deluxe Eight engine into a smaller Standard Eight chassis and fitting it with a much lower, narrower, shorter and lighter body. Ford outmaneuvered Chevrolet's inline six in 1932 with the arrival of a V-8 engine, and Cadillac included its then-recently introduced overhead-valve V-8 in the small short-tailed Series 61 Cadillac body for 1950. Then there are some who believe that the muscle-car idea originated with the 1957 Rambler Rebel, among the fastest production cars built that year, if not *the* fastest.

Meanwhile, let's not forget that Shelby Automotive was offering its version of the Cobra with "a big engine into a smaller and lighter car"—the AC roadster—two years before the 1964 GTO package appeared. So for the sake of clarity, the *Automotive News* headline should have really read, "Pontiac Launched the 1960s Intermediate Sedan Muscle-car Era with GTO." Although the idea did not originate with the GTO, it can be argued that at least the term "muscle car" did.

Sorry to be the bearer of bad news here, but so it goes when it comes to myth busting. Hindsight is now in sharper focus and interpretive analysis is more exacting, which is why we can and should challenge conventional wisdom in the interest of historic, antique automobile accuracy.

The Return of the Retractable

NOVEMBER/DECEMBER 2017

If you take stock in the old adage that history repeats itself—particularly, automotive history—then there's no better example than the romance of the retractable hardtop. After all, what could be better than the best of both worlds? Hardtop integrity to contend with the worst of weather, combined with open air enjoyment when the sun shines … at the press of a button.

It's an idea almost as old as the industry itself. The earliest inspiration came in the form of a working model by Ben P. Ellerbeck in 1919. He later built a prototype on a Hudson roadster. Ellerbeck promoted the retractable as a "shiftable top" and exhibited a working example at the Automobile Body Builders meeting in New York in 1922. According to Walter Gosden (*Special Interest Autos*, April 1979), it was manually controlled by a "gear and spring mechanism," which was cranked by hand.

Ellerbeck went as far as filing for a patent, and continually improved and simplified his idea. In addition to the practical advantages, he believed that his solution would help manufacturers reduce the number of body variants that they were forced to produce. A fair amount of publicity was also gained both here at home and abroad, but Ellerbeck's invention never reached production.

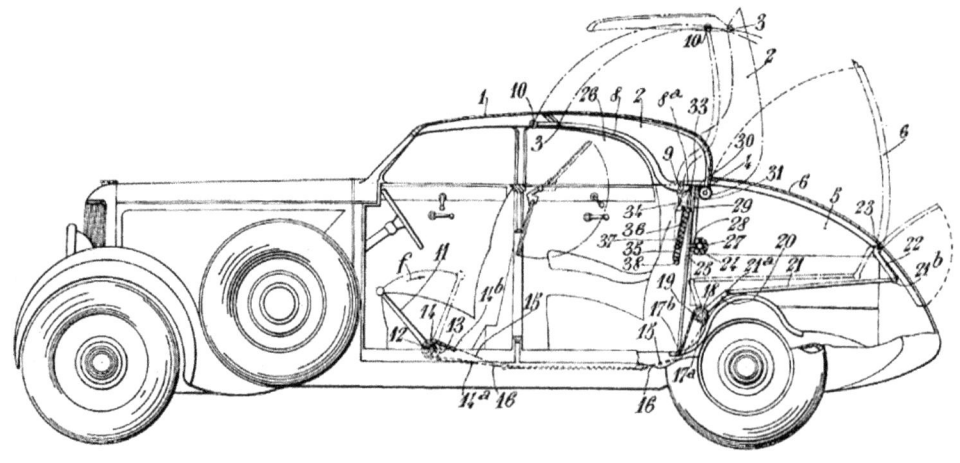

An early retractable design drawing.

Credit for the first successful retractable goes to Georges Paulin, who was a designer for Marcel Pourtout's coachbuilding concern, and Emile Darl'mat, Peugeot's Parisian distributor, who cooperated to create what was appropriately called the "Eclipse" roof. Leave it to the ever-innovative and fanciful French.

Top and above: **Peugeot 402 Eclipse top operation.**

The Eclipse appeared in 1934 on Peugeot's 402 model, and the top had to be manually unlatched from the windshield header. These initial examples also required the decklid to be opened first, by hand. Then, the top could be lowered. Carrosserie Pourtout went on to offer more versions of the Eclipse on the Peugeot 301, 401 and 601, along with the Lancia Belna, Hotchkiss and Panhard.

The retractable then made its way back to America. Chrysler's Thunderbolt concept car featured an electronically driven hideaway hardtop in 1941. It was designed by Alex Tremulis and Ralph Roberts, and five were built by LeBaron. The short-lived Brooks Stevens–designed Gaylord ultra-luxury sports car followed in 1955–56. Its retractable roof included a single electric motor with chain drive, and was backed up by a hand crank just in case. According to Richard M. Langworth, when GM Chairman Alfred P. Sloan witnessed a show car demonstration of Jim and Ed Gaylord's (heirs to a bobby pin fortune) top in action, he lit into the engineering entourage that surrounded him. "You bastards told me this couldn't be done. So how did these idiots do it?" (*Special Interest Autos*, February 1981).

Of course, the retractable hardtop poster child would instead be framed by Ford. The initiative originated with the Lincoln Continental Mark II concept. As development of the personal luxury car was underway, Dearborn designer Gilbert Spear convinced project leader William Clay Ford that such a distinction would set the flagship coupe apart. Some $2 million was earmarked to support the project in 1953, and a fully functional prototype was constructed. Unfortunately, it was soon realized that the Lincoln's limited sales potential would never offset the full investment required to put a retractable Lincoln into production, but the advanced engineering effort would not go to waste.

Chrysler Thunderbolt.

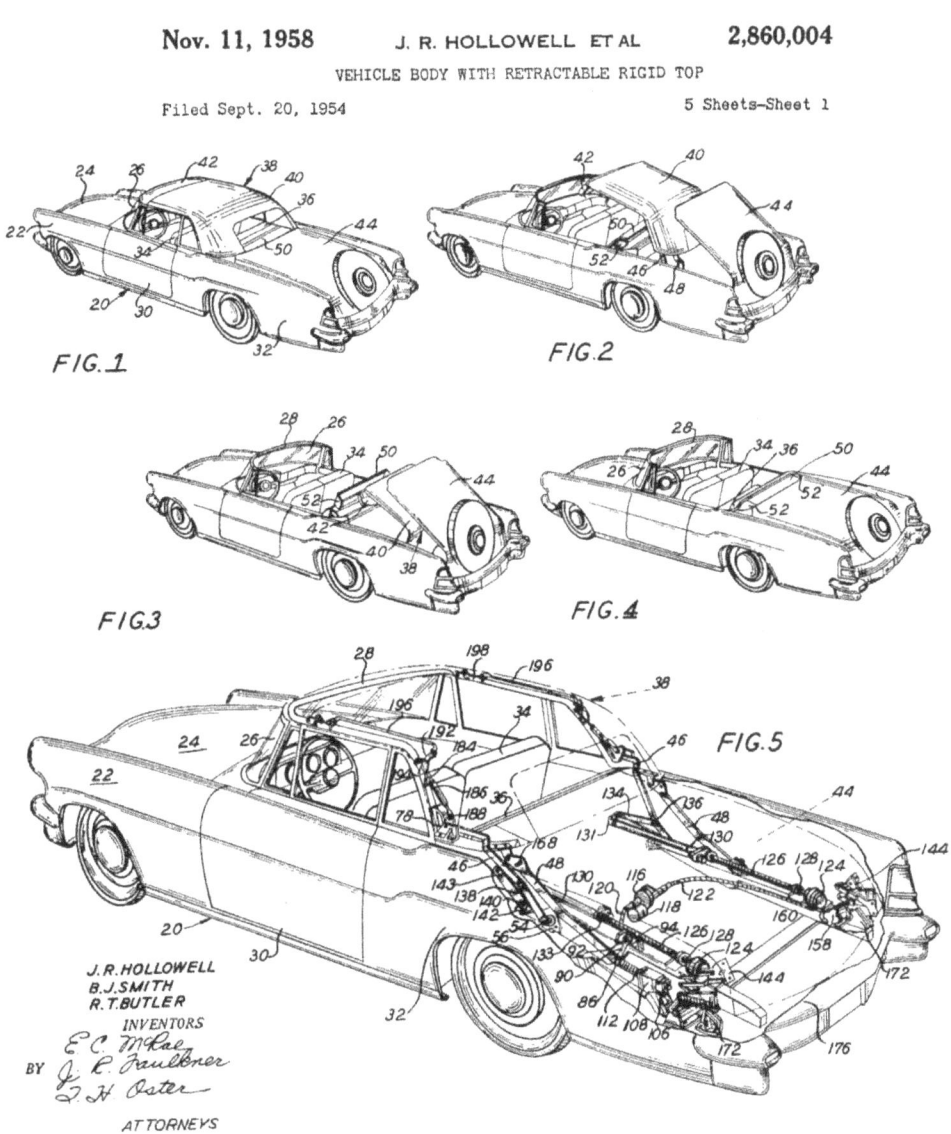

The patent drawings for Ford's retractable hardtop clearly show its Continental Mark II roots. Ford was issued a variety of patents related to the Skyliner program, including a header lock that was later used on some other fully automatic convertibles from Ford.

As the Mark II was making its way to market in 1955 as a 1956 model under the new Continental Division of Ford Motor Company, the retractable engineering project was transferred to the Ford Division. Obviously, it was assumed that the mass market channel would deliver better sales results that would justify the engineering expense, but it's also well known that Henry Ford II was no fan of the Continental, which may have also contributed to the migration of the mechanized hardtop over to the blue oval brand. The Ford retractable would ultimately make its way to the marketplace in what was then an already established 1957 to 1959 carline as the Fairlane 500 Skyliner, and finally the Galaxie Skyliner.

The design brief called for fully automatic electronic control. This immediately created a critical complication, because the full-length hardtop was longer than the decklid under which it was intended to be stowed. The solution was a separate "flipper" panel assembly on the leading edge of the roof that articulated down and tucked under when the waltz began and the top was dropped. Then, there was an abundance of automatic latching and unlatching that whirred its way along the process, as the hardtop lowered.

The result was a mechanism that required seven separate reversible electric motors and circuit breakers, along with ten relays and limit switches ... plus automatic screw jacks, locks, gear drives, flex cables and 600-plus feet of wire to manipulate all the mechanical magic. Certainly, it was a long way from the simple single-motor Gaylord concoction that set off Sloan.

After all the intricacies of the retractable mechanism were fully flushed out, turning it into a marketable production reality only produced additional engineering angst, because the structural architecture was already established for the then-current Ford line. Now, the roof height had to be lowered to allow the retractable top to fit under the rear decklid, which was reversed to open in the opposite direction from the norm. The rear seatback was altered to a more upright arrangement and the fuel tank relocated. The rear quarter panels took on a three-inch stretch, and the frame rails were realigned and brought closer together out back to carry what would turn into a 400-pound weight gain over a comparable convertible.

In the end, overall styling suffered and luggage-carrying capacity was confined to a mere small box beneath the rear deck. The redesigned full-size Ford line for 1960—which was softer and more "jet" inspired, and identified by its "long, sophisticated line that flows through the Ford"—led to the demise of the retractable hardtop. Fewer than 50,000 of the 1957–59 Fords were sold. It's doubtful that the Division ever recouped its investment, though it did redeploy a good portion of retractable technology on the soft-top Thunderbird and Lincoln Continental convertibles that followed during the 1960s, which also relied on rear-hinged decks.

The hidden-hardtop convertible was then stowed out of sight, and out of mind, for decades, until Mercedes-Benz dropped its disappearing concept "Vario" hardtop at the 1994 Paris Auto Show. Just as the Ford Skyliner did when it debuted at the New York Auto Show back in 1956, the SLK prototype met with critical acclaim.

Compared to the Ford, however, which was forced to rely on an already established design direction and adapted it accordingly, the Mercedes was a clean sheet of paper approach, and was purposely styled as a car with a folding hardtop. So while the aesthetics of the Ford Skyliner suffered proportionally, the SLK proved to be an exquisite execution when it went into production. It was named North American Car of the Year in 1997.

After that, the folding hardtop floodgates opened and retractables were offered

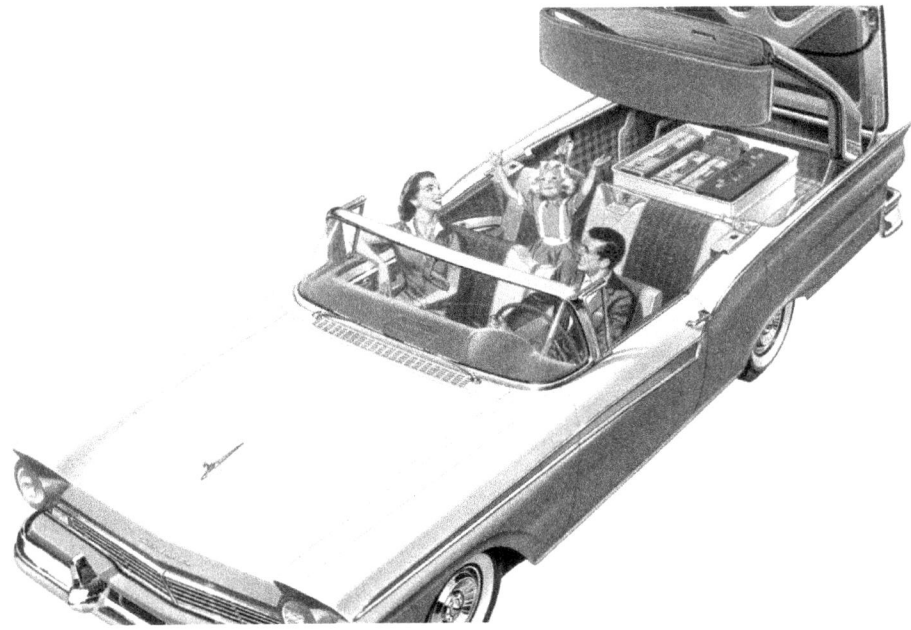

Here's How Ford's New Convertible Hardtop Works:

TOP DISAPPEARS INTO REAR DECK

The Skyliner's automatic top-operating system is operated by seven specially designed electric motors. Each of these high-efficiency motors is sealed and permanently lubricated. All are protected by circuit breakers. The top operates in the following sequence: First, after the control knob on the instrument panel is pulled out to lower the top, the rear deck lid unlocks and rises to the "up" position (1). Next, the top unlocks from the body and windshield header and begins to move upward and back (2). As the top moves, its forward section folds down and back to enable top to fit into trunk. The top continues its backward movement and eases into the trunk compartment (3), where it comes to rest snugly on cushioning pads. Rear deck lid then closes and locks itself tight. Entire sequence is reversed for converting back to a hardtop again. The transformation from convertible to hardtop or vice versa, takes less than a minute.

Top and above: **Ford Skyliner retractable.**

by everyone from BMW to Volvo. Most recently, I had the good fortune to spend some quality time behind the wheel of yet another alternative, the new Mazda MX-5 Miata RF. The "RF" portion of that mouthful of model designation stands for Retractable Fastback. The fact is, the power hardtop in this example turns the Miata into what many would consider a Targa, that being Porsche's registered trademark terminology to describe a removable center roof section.

Modern Mercedes SL retractable.

A true measure of the Mazda's muster is the fact that there's no sacrifice in trunk space or accessibility, despite the demand to stow the center hardtop section and rear window. It's the fastback structure itself that opens and serves as an articulating decklid for roof and window storage beneath it. The transformation from cozy coupe to delectable droptop is a 13-second mechanical ballet of churn and turn that would even amaze Harry Houdini, just as the Peugeot Eclipse "Decapotable" might have done back in the day.

So when it comes to automotive history, it's clear that the more things change, the more they stay the same. The retractable hardtop is yet another example of our antique heritage that's been reincarnated by going back to the future.

The Unrecognized Origin of the Sport Utility

MARCH/APRIL 2018

They're essentially everywhere, and since the passenger car now only represents some 40 percent of the new car marketplace, light trucks have proven to be the shining stars of today's automotive universe. The top-selling vehicles have routinely been pickup trucks, though the sport utility vehicle has been coming on strong. In fact, the market leaders for Buick (Encore), Cadillac (XT5), Lincoln (MKX), Mitsubishi (Outlander) and more are now all SUVs. Now let's take a look at the origin of this recent industry phenomenon.

There are those who contend that the Range Rover started the fad for a proper upscale utility offering. It was introduced in 1970 by British Leyland, as an offshoot of the original Rover Company's Land Rover. Intended to be more of a "road rover," as the prototype was called, it was more refined than the other English off-roaders that preceded it. The Range Rover featured unibody construction, coil-spring suspension (instead of leaf springs) and disc brakes. Although it was introduced with basic vinyl upholstery, an abundance of plastic trim and plebian powertrains, it quickly catapulted into a four-wheeled status symbol equipped with Connolly hides, V-8 engines and innovative drivetrain technologies.

It was marketed as an "all work … and all play" alternative and promoted as an all-in-one "Luxury car, Performance car, Estate car and Cross-country car." When it was launched, the Institute of British Carriage and Automobile Manufacturers immediately recognized it with a Gold Medal for "Best Utility Coachwork." The gentrified Range Rover was soon accelerating ahead as a premium SUV posterchild.

Meanwhile, there are others who believe that the Jeep Wagoneer created the Sport Utility category decades before the term SUV was even invented and while the Range Rover was nothing more than an empirical pipe dream.

In 1966, Kaiser Jeep took its utilitarian Wagoneer (which was introduced for 1963) and embellished it with such niceties as a pushbutton radio, tilt wheel, air conditioning, power steering, power brakes, power tailgate window, deep-pile carpet, a four-barrel carburetor, mag-style wheels and more. It was billed as a "Super Wagoneer." At the time, Jeep advertised it as "the most unusual luxury wagon ever built" to "go where other luxury cars can't." Production ran through 1969, with almost 4,000 being built, for what Kaiser sales literature referred to as an "epoch" in "excellence."

As a flagship, the Super Wagoneer clearly gets credit for setting the stage for some of the modern SUVs' most recognized liabilities: a premium price point and less than stellar fuel economy. It retailed for $5,943, the equivalent of a 1966 Cadillac or Lincoln, and gas mileage was a dismal 13 mpg.

Then along came American Motors, which upped the ante. They took control of Jeep in 1970 and immediately began to add refinement by mitigating noise, vibration and harshness. A larger, AMC-sourced engine and a full-time four-wheel drive system was just the beginning. By the late 1970s, a "Limited" edition was launched. Jeep referred to it as "The ultimate in 4-wheel drive." It included "real leather seats, extra thick carpeting for a quieter ride, woodgrain trim inserts both inside and out, an AM/FM radio with a choice of CB or stereo tape deck" and was "built for those who demand nothing but the best." In 1984, the opulent all-wheeler was rechristened Jeep "Grand Wagoneer." Suspension upgrades, trim improvements and specification enhancements would become an ongoing ethic of continuous improvement until the final, "Final Edition" rolled off the line in 1991.

Way before any of that, there was the original Willys-Overland Jeep station wagon. At the end of the Second World War, the military's rough-and-ready front-line friend was "civilianized" and supplemented by such models as an all-steel station wagon. Produced from 1946 to 1965 and designed by Brooks Stevens, it was an intentional attempt to stretch the Jeep brand into a broader market segment. Willys called it "a double-duty deluxe all-steel car with swanky good looks for pleasure … with ample cargo space for business." It was the amalgamation of functional styling, everyday convenience and rugged utility, so much so that the kaiserwillys.com website deems it "Arguably, the first sport utility vehicle in the world to gain mass appeal.…"

There was even an attempt to extend its allure with a "Maverick" upgrade (sorry, 1970s Ford fans) option. It was intended to be a more luxurious version with two-tone paint and matching interior appointments, stainless steel window trim and a standard AM radio. But it was only available in two-wheel drive with a four-cylinder engine, so one would be hard pressed to consider it much of a premium package.

So … was the Jeep station wagon the actual incubator of the sport utility idea? I don't think so. I'm of the opinion that the unrecognized origin of the sport utility vehicle dates back even earlier, with the infamous invention known as the woodie wagon, sometimes referred to as a "shooting break!" ("Break," as in breaking horses, for those of you who argue the correct spelling is "brake.")

Technical specifications aside (before everyone writes in and says that woodies didn't come with four-wheel drive, there were aftermarket conversions and, by the way, there are plenty of 2WD SUVs in places like Texas and Florida), it's the unique combination of purpose and promotion that leads me to conclude that the wooden wagon was in fact, the precursor to the SUV movement. I came to this realization while perusing numerous woodie advertisements and sales brochures, in the interest of understanding how manufacturers went to market with this oh-so-special cornerstone of station wagon history.

It's well known that the woodie was derived from the utilitarian depot hack. Among other duties, as a means to shuttle passengers from the train depot or hustle guests up to the upscale hotel, the first wooden-bodied wagons served as basic jitneys or taxi cabs. They could haul a healthy load of luggage in addition to passengers. These "carryalls" or "suburbans," as they were often called, were long on utility and short on just about everything else, since their intention was primarily commercial, but they got the job done.

As the automotive industry matured, production supply was pressured to keep pace with ever-accelerating demand, which led to the science of steel stampings for enclosed body structures. A faster and much more cost-effective alternative, the stamped steel body also offered more integrity and longevity than heavy squeaky-creaky wood-framed car bodies. Of course, wood wagon construction required more than its fair share of maintenance, which was expensive and labor intensive.

It's said that Buick produced the last woodie in 1953, having been previously distracted by the demands of war, like every other manufacturer, which is why the golden era of the woodie wagon stood its ground like a pair of bookends, from just prior through to the immediate post–World War II time frame.

But sentimental sightseers along the road less traveled would learn that the switch to steel came at the expense of the warmth and old-world charm of the wooden workhorse. Antique and classic boat aficionados still long for magnificent mahogany-planked barrel-back

1942 Buick estate wagon.

construction (instead of more modern materials), for just the same reason (***Editor's note:*** They also cut through the water much more smoothly). That was enough, along with a small market that was being sustained by independent coachbuilders for special customers and unique applications, to leave a meager window-crack of opportunity open for the woodie wagon.

So the woodie evolved into more of a luxury conveyance, which was only fitting because it was largely hand-built, and quite obviously from the very best of then-available materials. It was relatively expensive, too, in keeping with its niche appeal. That's when manufacturers got the bright idea to pursue the previously mentioned "unique combination of purpose and promotion."

Here's what Packard had to say about its 1941 timber-trimmed vehicle of versatility: "The smartest, most comfortable station wagon…. In every inch of its handsome sweep, this is a car that will pay generous dividends…. From any angle, its stunning good looks belong wherever smart people gather…. This beautifully finished Packard rides like a luxurious passenger car…. Yet it is abundantly roomy for eight…. Ask the man who owns one." Obviously, those are attributes that would be hard to claim just 10 years before, for something like the then state-of-the-art, more mundane Model A Ford station wagon.

Even more pronounced was the arresting imagery that accompanied the market positioning of the woodie wagon in period sales materials. Plymouth parked one beside a main-line suburban train depot. Mercury stationed its entry within a secluded fishing camp. Woodies were further depicted in town, out in the country, at the riding stable, in queue at the dog show, by sports stadiums, at the golf club, near the shooting range, outside of estate gates, beside the circus tent and more. All of these settings were essentially at the carefully choreographed intersection of sport and utility.

And if the ad copy and creative images weren't enough, there were the poignant headlines to ensure that the underlying marketing message made its way across the crossroads. Taglines such as "Perfect Playmate" (Plymouth), "More of Everything" (Mercury), "The Grandest Way to Go Places" (Pontiac), "A Family Affair" (Ford), "Glamour Girl … and Chore Boy, Too" (Dodge) all contributed to the woodie's prospects as "The All-Purpose Car That Has Everything," in 1940 Oldsmobile-speak.

Fast forward to more recent times, and it's obvious that today's SUV has assumed an equivalent existence, delivering the same value proposition, as the woodie waged. Chevrolet says that its current Equinox offers "Everything you need, to do everything you want" while Toyota claims that the Highlander is ready to "explore every possibility." Top-shelf accoutrements, grace, pace and space have allowed the modern sport utility to pick up not only where the woodie left off, but the Jeep station wagon, Grand Wagoneer and Range Rover that followed.

Along the way, Di-Noc vinyl cladding was specified on many a station wagon in symbolic salute to the long-lost woodie tradition. Simulated wood-graining would become a staple within the automotive industry, which stumbled onto the realization

The New Ford Station Wagon

The new Ford Station Wagon has been designed to meet the needs of large estates, country clubs and families having summer homes in the country or by the seashore. It is particularly well suited to such use because it combines the sturdiness of a light truck with the flexibility and comfort of a passenger car.

Seating accommodations are provided for eight people, including the driver. Baggage is carried on the large tail-gate. The seats in the rear compartment, though securely anchored when in use, can be removed quickly and easily when the car is used for hauling.

In appearance, the new Ford Station Wagon reflects its sturdy construction. The body has uprights of hard maple, with ply-wood sides finished in natural grain. The sill is unusually rugged. Fenders are full-crown, heavy and capable. Seats are wide, deeply-cushioned and finished in blue-gray artificial Spanish leather. Doors are wide, carefully fitted and substantial, with full-nickeled handles in conservative scroll design. The side curtains, which can be put up easily and quickly in bad weather, are made in tan-gray to harmonize with the body finish.

The new Ford Station Wagon brings you the same alert performance, ease of control, safety, speed, power, reliability and economy that are characteristic of all the new Ford cars. Its easy-riding comfort is particularly appreciated on rough roads.

FORD MOTOR COMPANY
Detroit, Michigan

1929 Ford station wagon.

that there was a fair amount of disposable income to be had from buyers who tended toward an active lifestyle, just as Eddie Bauer and L.L. Bean learned. Ford went as far as calling their 1966 Country Squire the "Son of a Classic," and their current Flex model includes a series of four horizontal striations along its flanks. *Car Design News* referred to them as a "styling reference" from "a previous era."

1940 Oldsmobile station wagon.

To get an idea how the sport utility segment has proliferated, here's a quick snapshot of what's now an unimaginable mix of offerings within current brand portfolios. From today's eight mainstream American, five German, nine Japanese, two Korean, two English, two Italian and one Swedish source, some 92 different SUV models are readily available in U.S. showrooms! Even niche players like Alfa Romeo have gotten into the act with its Stelvio, as has Bentley, which now offers its beguiling Bentayga, billed as "the world's fastest SUV" … and then there's "the Maserati of SUVs," the Italian automaker's new Levante.

In an irony of automotive history, like a colony of termites, the woodie wagon spawned what is now an SUV infestation (pun intended). So much so that a car-platform–based subspecies known as the Crossover Utility Vehicle (CUV) has since evolved, as well, which is further devouring the traditional breed of passenger cars. Is there any stopping them? The buying public continues to vote with its wallet, and routinely says *no!* Low gas prices further fuel the tinder.

With the clarity of unsuspecting foresight, perhaps Plymouth ad writers summed up the impending arrival of the SUV best, back in 1940: "No longer need you sacrifice smartness for room—this big car is the last word in graceful beauty. Gone is the necessity to give up comfort for the sake of utility." A year later, Pontiac proved even more clairvoyant in its woodie advertising: "It's the perfect travel companion wherever you find fun—in camp, at the beach, or just rolling the open road.

And it's by far the most convenient car for daily shopping and the inevitable school runs."

While it may have been a consequence of marketing happenstance, the unrecognized origin of the sport utility vehicle stems from the workaday woodie wagon. Inspired and cultivated messaging, which was combined with the artistic interpretation of an adventurous, if not aspirational, lifestyle, clearly continues in current SUV advertising and promotion.

A remnant of gracious acknowledgment of this woodie heritage remains with us, at the premium hotel that ensures that there's a well-outfitted, if not well-oiled, Cadillac Escalade or Lincoln Navigator at the ready, and waiting on a moment's notice to coddle its most prestigious clients. When it comes to automotive history, the more things change…

Flights of Fancy

Dialing-In a Cast Iron Carburetor

March/April 2010

With the wind howlin' and snow flying today, I wasn't *about* to head out in an old car. But as the Nor'Easter raced up the East Coast, that didn't mean I still wasn't up to my elbows in the science of stoichiometry—the chemistry of managing air flow and fuel quantity proportions.

So there I was out in the three-seasons room, trying to dial-in a big black throttle body that was sand cast in Vermont, rather than a delicate die-cast from the likes of Stromberg or Holley, if not Weber or S.U. At least I could continue my antique auto avocation in the dead of winter! Well, sort of…

Coaxing this carburetor out of its year-long hibernation required that I first drain the tank and clean the filter. Sound familiar? In this case, though, it was a tray of spent ash lingering in the belly of the beast (the equivalent of debris in the float bowl), and an obstructed lower air grate (think of a mouse nest in the air cleaner housing) that could easily keep it from running. That done, I was soon reminded that cold-blooded and temperamental fuel metering devices are not limited only to those that hang off intake manifolds.

To get this baby fired up, you must begin, appropriately enough, by applying the choke. This requires opening the primary air control and setting the air combustor to prescribed levels, adjusting the cold start enrichment circuit.

Then, it's on to some careful priming. To do so, an accelerator pump or priming cup makes way for some dry kindling or a leftover section or two of the Sunday *New York Times*. You want to exercise caution here because the owner's manual teases you into believing: "Burning wood is often said to be more of an art, than a science." If the old car out in the garage were to backfire at this point, it could singe your eyebrows. In this case, a backdraft could burn the house down!

Lighting it becomes the equivalent of cranking … and cranking … for as long as the battery (I mean, match) holds out. Once it finally gets going, the throttle will very much need to be feathered. Trying to open it up too soon will only stall the proceedings, but a good supply of high-octane fuel—like some dry, seasoned oak—will usually help the process accelerate well. Long story short, if you want this engine to really

Stromberg carburetor ad from *Motor Age*, December 9, 1920.

rev up and cook by, say, 6 p.m., ignition timing is critical. Plan to hit the starter (light the first match) by early afternoon.

Under these circumstances, I'd need to fire up my antique car the night before to make it in time for the Sunday-morning club tour. And this type of carburetor behaves like so, so many others, with a tendency to cough, spit and sputter until fully warmed up.

Coming off idle, you'll want to monitor the mixture as you normally would. Instead of reading a spark plug, the calibration in this case is considered via a probe port and thermometer. It can be used as "valuable guide to tell you when to open or close the damper to increase or decrease air supply, and whether or not to add more fuel." If you're still freezing after hours of tweaking and tinkering, you might want to go back to the basics and think about re-jetting. Or go back into that portion of the house with the luxury of thermostat control. Because the self-starter, electronic ignition and fuel injection really have come a long way ... i.e., the modern heating system.

For better breathing, the stove's front wood door or side access port can be opened to reduce the throttle restriction. Under extreme circumstances, the equivalent of a low restriction (K&N) filter effect can be had by cracking open a nearby window. With more air, though, remember you'll also need to go rich ... and load on the fuel. Economy will suffer, of course, and the increased consumption will mean more trips to the gas station (out to the woodpile), in the worst of the storm, no doubt.

From a volatility point of view, any sort of starter fluid (gasoline, oil, naphtha) is definitely not recommended. Sorry, American National Standards Institute (ANSI) sanctioning also says no nitrous, either. And you should never try to supercharge your cast iron carburetor with external fans or other air flow enhancements. Your wife, or significant other, won't appreciate the soot and cinders all over the family room.

Of course, you'll very much know when the time is right to lean this thing out when the whole housing starts to glow cherry red. The good news here is that at least you won't have to synchronize two or three of them to get the full effect.

As always, if the combustion process isn't efficient enough, the available energy just won't transfer into power, or in this case, heat. Instead, it will leave the engine and flow right out the exhaust pipe. In other words, right up the chimney.

So dialing-in a carburetor, any carburetor—be it an exquisite, aluminum four-barrel or a nasty, old, four-legged wood stove—requires experience, understanding, care, finesse, and patience. Maybe as spring gets ready to arrive, I'll be able to adapt some of the experiences I've enjoyed (?) with Vermont Castings, scale them down as appropriate, and put them to good use out in the garage.

Unless, that is, I freeze to death in the interim...

The Long-Lost Language of Antique Automotive Lore

September/Oct. 2012

As the most widely used means of communication throughout the world, the English language and its logic are certainly well understood. And even though the origin and derivation of our vocabulary is usually clear, language is still always evolving, with new terms, definitions and interpretations arriving at an incessant pace, and thus riding roughshod over earlier terminology and meanings.

Such is the case when it comes to the special dialect that's spoken within the old car community. It's a vernacular that even today's most educated and experienced master mechanic cannot quite comprehend. For example, to everyone else, the term **polarizing** most likely refers to a sunglass lens treatment, or else to somebody's objectionable personality. But to old-car guys, the word immediately defines the procedure to match the polarity of a generator to the voltage regulator through a surge of current to the generator, since a generator can deliver current to either a positive- or negative-ground system.

So before all the new definitions and silly slang kick our unique expression of antique automotive lore to the curb and force it to be forgotten, here are some more examples of what's becoming our long-lost language.

Packing is what people do when they're getting ready to go on a trip. In our world, it pertains to the rope seal that you'd routinely string around a water pump shaft in an *attempt* to create a seal. In fact, it's still available at home repair and hardware stores as a quick fix for leaky plumbing faucets.

So when it comes time to **repack the bearings**, that doesn't mean changing them from one suitcase to another. It's the dirty, old task of reloading them with grease after cleaning.

It's commonly considered that **arcing** is the electrical breakdown that allows current to flow through normally non-conductive surroundings, such as air. But some of us remember that it's also how we used to grind new brake linings after they were riveted or bonded to the brake shoes, to ensure an accurate fit within the brake drums.

An incredibly energetic individual who's also most likely a mover and shaker is often called a ***dynamo***. But it's really a generator that converts mechanical rotation into direct electrical current by way of magnets, coils and a rotating electrical switch called a commutator.

And it's not just some scaredy-cat that quivers in the corner on fright night that's a ***trembler***. It was also a small vibrating spring set that was set in motion by a magnetic influence to make and break an ignition circuit. While a ***vibrator*** was yet another solution that resulted in a succession of sparks—usually weak ones.

Filing ignition points has nothing to do with the Word folder you plan on using to store the bullet call-outs with which you intend to launch your next PowerPoint presentation. Of course, it's a time-honored technique to clean burned, pitted or oxidized breaker points in an ignition distributor.

A rude individual who elbows his way into a conversation is an ***interrupter***. But way back in the day, that was yet another name for breaker points.

Those who aspire to a life of uninterrupted leisure might consider ***dwell angle*** as an unfortunate demonstration of how long an unwanted visitor hung around, and what posture he or she may have assumed. Certainly, we're not about to take that lying down, because we know that it's the duration in degrees of distributor rotation that ignition points remain closed to energize the ignition coil.

Despite the myriad of Dyson Ball ads that appear all over the infomercial channels, ***vacuum wipers*** are not the latest patent on the company's clever carpet cleaners and floor sweepers. They came along during the 1920s, and relied upon the differential between engine manifold pressure and atmospheric pressure to drive a motor that would operate the windshield wiper blades.

Some might think that ***trimming an antenna*** is what happens when you take a pair of side cutters to an old radio aerial and snip off a couple of inches to ensure that it clears the garage door. But for those of us who have been screwing around with old cars forever, it is, of course, the screw adjustment within the radio for a variable capacitor to calibrate the capacitance of the antenna cable, to achieve the best reception.

In today's world of reality TV and notorious crime lords, most might think that a ***kingpin*** is simply the top banana. If not, perhaps a game show host, or at least the front pin in the alley down at the local *bowl-a-rama*. In fact, it was the primary pivot in a steering assembly between the stub axle and the outboard end of the front axle beam ... back when there were beam axles.

A nut with one conical end that secures a wheel to a threaded stud has long been known as a ***lug nut***. It's derived from a Scandinavian word that describes a projection that's used as a support. But be aware: it's become somewhat of a double entendre these days, because the same term is now commonly used for bolts, too, that screw directly into the wheel hub.

It's well known that a ***driveshaft*** transmits mechanical power from the transmission to the rear differential. In fact, though, it's a misnomer because it's actually a driven shaft.

The Long-Lost Language of Antique Automotive Lore

Checking the kingpin? (AACA Library archives).

The word *freewheeling* immediately conjures up the image of a happy-go-lucky individual who is not bound by social norms or convention. When it comes to antique automobiles, though, it pertains to an over-running clutch that disengages the rotation of the crankshaft (the *actual* driveshaft) from what we instead call the driveshaft (the driven shaft), to ensure that the wheels can't drive the engine while the car is still rolling at speed in gear.

A *fierce clutch* isn't necessarily heavy, or brutally hard to actuate. It's how they used to describe a clutch that grabs.

Charlie Chaplin may have been a master of the *slapstick* form of physical comedy, but drag racers recognize that it's a special performance shifter used on automatic transmissions, to allow gears to be engaged quickly in succession.

According to a period owner's manual, "an *emergency brake* is operated mechanically to insure braking ability in the event of a hydraulic system failure." Who in the world would ever admit to that and actually put it in writing in today's disclaimer-happy land of legal liability? That's why they're now referred to as parking brakes!

Of course, the English have to do it their way, so a *flyoff handle* is not necessarily an emotional overreaction. Instead of pressing the button to release the handbrake, you keep it pressed while you're setting it in a British sportscar. To put it down, you simply yank the flyoff handle handbrake back … so you can fly right off into the sunset.

A *cut-out* had nothing to do with skipping school en masse. It was/is a valve in the exhaust system between the engine and the muffler that relieves back pressure on demand to improve performance, particularly while climbing hills. They also justified its existence as a "warning device" to let those on the other side know that a car was coming. What a simpler time it was, back then.

After coming down to the wire, it might be easy to think that a ***clincher*** was the deciding game that won the series or championship. Actually, it's an early wheel design where the tire bead interlocks with a corresponding flange on the rim.

A ***stovebolt*** is more than just a slotted fastener that's used to assemble wood burning stoves that are fabricated out of sheet metal. Obviously, it's a six-cylinder Chevrolet engine that was introduced in 1929.

Computer-savvy car enthusiasts know that a ***firewall*** is a software security provision that controls online network traffic, and they're also aware that it separates the engine bay from the passenger compartment in an automobile.

It's certainly been clear for some time what a ***four-door*** car is. But the term was actually first employed back in the brass era to signify the arrival of front doors … or, the fore-doors.

Although a good portion of the general public may be aware that the ***Model A*** was a Ford from the late 1920s, many readers of this magazine recognize that before that, it was the first production Ford from 1903.

Venomous snakes aside, long before Carroll Shelby's well-known sports car, a ***Cobra*** was a lesser-known copper-brazed Crosley engine.

Literally everyone knows that ***Hershey*** is a delicious chocolate lover's paradise. But what's even more delectable is the fact we recognize it as the home of AACA headquarters, the AACA Library & Research Center and the AACA Museum, and our annual antique automobile pilgrimage to mecca.

De-coking isn't a drug rehabilitation program, nor is it a process to wean oneself off of a sugar-laden soft drink addiction. It was a common service procedure to clean carbon deposits from cylinder head combustion chambers and piston crowns.

Scraping a bearing is not what happens when you let an engine run low on oil. It was a delicate craft to contour babbitt (a soft, cast metal that's used as a bearing surface) and remove high spots between a shaft and the shell that supports it.

Although you might want to kick off a drinking binge with an aperitif or two, there's no need to get carried away and consume such alcoholic appetizers from a ***priming cup***. That, instead, was used to supply a small quantity of fuel to each cylinder to enrich the mixture and aid the starting of early engines.

Tickling a carburetor isn't something you do to provide entertainment and make it laugh. It's a way of manually priming a carburetor by displacing the float by hand, to allow gasoline to fill the float bowl.

To relieve nighttime congestion, people often rely on a cool-mist humidifier or ***vaporizer***. Surprise: it was also an early term for a carburetor that heated fuel in an attempt to aid atomization.

Although it may be a losing poker hand, we know instead that a ***pair of deuces*** is a twin two-barrel carburetor set-up.

Some might think that a ***uni-syn*** is something that you hope to achieve within the confines of the Sunday church choir. Actually, it's special tool that's used to synchronize multiple sidedraft and downdraft carburetors.

A ***dashpot*** isn't what you'd use to prepare food on your instrument panel. It's a damper within a constant velocity carburetor, like an S.U., and a variable choke that functions through changes in intake air volume, while simultaneously controlling fuel flow via a needle that retracts in and out of the main jet.

No, ***belt dressing*** is not some sort of new-fangled fashion statement or the latest concoction that you pour over a salad. Obviously, it's a spray-on petroleum distillate conditioner that restores drive-belt pliability, flexibility and traction to prevent belt slippage and squealing.

Dum Dum is not necessarily just an idiot or a give-away lollipop, it's also an old-school strip caulk that was often used to seal windshields and body gaps.

"Ellbo" grease: illustration from September 1930 *Motor* magazine.

Wikipedia swears that ***sea foam*** is created by the agitation of dissolved organic matter within sea water, which traps air and forms bubbles. We, unfortunately, know all too well that it's a petroleum-based additive that was created in response to ever-deteriorating gasoline quality, to help liquefy gum and varnish deposits … in the never-ending quest for clean carburetors and fuel systems.

Finally, if you go wandering the lubricant aisle at the auto parts store in search of a tin of ***elbow grease***, don't bother … you won't find it. While the old-car guy's cordless drill is powered by elbow grease, semantics aside, nowadays it would just be a recyclable plastic tub of unobtainium, anyway.

The Best Way to Embrace the Future ... Is to Appreciate the Past

January/February 2014

You're probably well aware that I spend a fair amount of time in my garage, and it seems that my "man cave" has again contributed to my old-car consciousness—which is no surprise, considering that we're in the middle of the cold January–February extremes of winter here in Connecticut. This time the subject matter is the result of my good old (40-year-old) Marantz 2230 AM/FM receiver that finally bought the farm.

Though it's now somewhat of a serious audiophile collectible, after 10 years of service I really can't complain. I only paid $35 for it when it was nothing more than just another used stereo ... which is not unlike a lot of secondhand cars I've acquired during the years as well.

So I replaced it with a more up-to-date secondhand Onkyo TX-8511 found on Craigslist. While this new(er), 100-watt per channel amp delivers essentially the equivalent audio performance, it's just not the same. Soft, warm, incandescent lighting wrapped in "wood-grain vinyl veneer" has made way for a sleek, black cabinet with a cold, hard LED digital display.

But there's more of a difference than that. A product that hailed from Chatsworth, California, has now been superseded by something from Osaka, Japan. Just another sign of the times, of course, but that doesn't mean it has to please me.

I probably jumped the gun too soon in search of a quick fix for the snap, crackle, pop from the right speaker circuit, which got to the extreme of complete unintelligibility. But what I walked away from is not so easily replaced. Crisply locking in to a selected digital station is just not the same as gently dialing in on an analog frequency via "Gyro Touch" tuning control, with final validation provided by the full deflection of the signal strength meter.

What was an active level of audio engagement has now given way to the instant gratification of tuning right in. It's no different than the compliant compromise that my 1933 Pierce-Arrow (which sits right inside my garage) affords when it runs down the road, compared to the precise accuracy of my 2003 Ford Focus SVT (which is just behind the Pierce ... outside, on the other side of the insulated door).

Built in Buffalo, New York, like a brick $#!+ house, the Pierce provides bank-vault–like integrity with the opening and closing of each and every door. The commitment to coddle extends to the extreme of leaf spring shackles that are suspended in ball bearings. They didn't call it "America's Finest Car" for nothing.

Think about it ... how much angular rotation can there really be as those leaf springs deflect under normal operating conditions? It demonstrates, though, that people like Pierce strived to do as much as they could with the level of technology that was available at the time. But it was meant to make a meaningful, operational difference for the end user, as opposed to simply creating some implied marketing advantage.

According to Fafnir Bearing Co. of New Britain, Connecticut, who supplied them, "Ball Bearing Spring Shackles can't squeak, can't bind, they never need to be greased, they never need adjustment, they allow your springs to flex freely, your shock absorbers to work evenly and smoothly, always. And furthermore, they greatly improve the riding." It sure sounds like there was some real benefit provided for the Pierce-Arrow owner (which I can confirm) who was simply the passive recipient of such technological advantage.

By comparison, with its 45 cross-section tires and SVT-tuned suspension, the Ford Focus is anything but passive. You become immediately engaged the moment you let out the clutch and bang the throttle. Feedback is immediate and exact.

Going back to my Marantz vs. Onkyo comparison, does the digital accuracy of the new modern receiver work well? Obviously, yes. Does it deliver good performance? No doubt. Is it a cost-effective solution? Absolutely. But its operation is more appliance-like than intimate—just like a modern car compared to an antique automobile.

Certainly, there are features and attributes that contribute to an improved listening experience with the new TX-8511, though there are others that seem to offer marginal advantage, at best. For example, I've gotten along just fine without "3 station group presets, with 10 stations per group" because I only listen to one or two stations anyway. And I'm still not sure how "2-mode Automatic Precision Reception" really helps to tune FM stations. I never needed any help tuning a radio in the past.

Most significantly, the new component is just not as intuitive as it could be. I'm not only unaware of what some of the features are, I haven't a clue how to use them. By comparison, when it comes to old stereos, if not old cars, simple functionality seemed to always take precedence. Both seem to have a focus on human interface that is obviously instinctive.

So even though my Pierce also has four-wheel mechanically actuated drum brakes, they work just fine ... considering. I'm well aware of the actual level of their in-use performance, so I drive that car with a heightened sense of awareness to

HONORABLE HORACE WHITE OF NEW YORK
is the owner of the Pierce-Arrow in the photograph
. . . a car which has been in the constant service
of the former Governor and his family since 1917

The Convertible Sedan of Group B . . . $3650 at Buffalo

SURVIVAL VALUE • A PIERCE-ARROW FUNDAMENTAL

What community today is without its ten- or twelve- or fifteen-year-old Pierce-Arrows . . . still superbly patrician, still rendering distinguished service to the original owners? Therein lies the deepest-rooted, most foundational, of all Pierce-Arrow characteristics —a quality that has been called *survival value*.

Because an essential part of its beauty is in its character . . . a part that is unchanging . . . the Pierce-Arrow of yesterday, or of a decade ago, finds complement in the smartest of today's models. And thus a great Pierce-Arrow fundamental becomes also a fine safeguard for each Pierce-Arrow owner's investment.

Twenty-nine New Models . . . with *Free Wheeling* . . . from $2685 to $6400 at Buffalo. (Other Custom-built Models up to $10,000.)

Above and opposite: **Two 1931 Pierce-Arrow ads.**

always pay attention and plan ahead. The SVT Focus, on the other hand, is outfitted with four-wheel ventilated anti-lock disc brakes, and, with major help from sport radial tires, can stop you on a dime. As a result, I'm a bit more relaxed behind the wheel of the more modern and much, much safer Ford—so much so that I often find myself letting my guard down. As comes comfort, so, too, complacency.

The Best Way to Embrace the Future ... Is to Appreciate the Past

PIERCE-ARROW
AMERICA'S FINEST MOTOR CAR

Mr. Adolphus Busch III, of St. Louis, is the owner of the Pierce-Arrow coupe shown in the photograph. Although more than eight years old, the car is used regularly by Mr. Busch.

•

Moving up and down and across the land, with daily satisfaction to their owners, are the visible, active evidences of Pierce-Arrow survival value.

To be prized in a man-made mechanism, as in a man himself, is long and faithful service.

Into the newest of Pierce-Arrows, with all their patrician value-of-the-moment, is built the traditional quality which creates Pierce-Arrow survival value, a unique attribute in motordom.

Thus a two-fold return on a Pierce-Arrow investment. First, the certainty that nothing finer or more modern is to be had among motor cars.

Second, the equal certainty that engineering and manufacturing utilize every sound means to preserve for years to come the prestige which literally is Pierce-Arrow.

In modern yet dignified design, in luxury, in long and economical life, Pierce-Arrow is today as always, America's finest motor car.

•

Twenty-nine New Models—
ALL WITH FREE WHEELING
$2685 to $6400 at Buffalo.
Custom-built models up to $10,000.

One of the reasons I can really appreciate how well the Focus performs, though, is because I've spent so many years with antiques like that rolling Buffalo-built bank vault. So I can recognize the amazing improvement in relative terms because I have a unique antique automotive frame of reference.

On the flip-side, with today's advances in electronic engine controls that yield instantaneous, flat torque curves, did that '03 SVT really need a 6-speed transmission? The answer is no. By comparison, there's no question that the three-speed behind the '33 Pierce's straight-eight is a perfect match. Again, it's a question that I can easily answer as a result of years and years of shifting gears, among countless manual gearboxes.

So it pays to not forget about the past in favor of the future. The price of progress should not necessarily force us to accept change for the sake of change. Real improvements in performance, economy, safety, emissions and in-use operating experience that provide true value are the ones that will drive utmost market acceptance, not just new feature sets that are designed to create product differentiation and little else.

Antique automobiles are essentially an analog experience, while modern cars are digitally driven. That means that old cars inherently include compromise. Like the signal strength meter on my old Marantz tuner, "near about" or "close enough" is good enough to get the job done—which is fine by me, because I still enjoy the latitude of being able to dial in things like mechanical and/or vacuum ignition advance and tweaking idle air/fuel mixture circuits. Maybe I should have restored the Marantz…

Modern iron, on the other hand, is more of a yes or no, absolute equation. Knock sensors will listen in throughout the operating range, overriding what I could have ever achieved with a timing light or dwell meter, and O2 sensors in the exhaust will keep the air/fuel ratio spot-on at any throttle opening, thank you very much. No need to bother with a hand throttle and manual spark advance to get the best fuel economy and lowest emissions. I can certainly appreciate that advantage, as well.

Of course, my frame of reference here is already 10-plus years old. The 2014 models now put my 2003 Ford to shame.

So is a factory-tuned high-performance SVT Focus a better car technically than an 80-year-old Pierce? Of course! Is a modern Onkyo receiver a more effective solution than a tired old Marantz stereo? You bet it is. But one of the main reasons I know is because I've lived with what came before, which has given me a level of appreciation that's matured with the passage of time.

As I've personally witnessed the ever-accelerating art of automotive (and audio) engineering, I've learned through experience that the best way to embrace the future … is to appreciate the past.

Pipedreams and Other Flights of Fancy

JULY/AUGUST 2015

I generally do not write about myself so specifically, because I prefer to keep the personal stuff a bit closer to the vest, but a few folks have asked me to share some of my own antique auto exploits over the years. If you're a regular reader of this column you might remember that the first car I ever bought was a Renault Dauphine. It cost a whopping $70—which I didn't have, so I went in 50–50 with a friend who was also 16 at the time. Believe it or not, I found it on the back row of the used car lot at a nearby Renault dealer. Those were the days.

With it parked at the house on Long Island, New York, on a 50 × 100-foot lot (which included the footprint of the home itself, and a one-car garage) there obviously wasn't much room to drive it around when my parents were home. When they weren't, it was another story. Young, foolish and full of enthusiasm, who needed a driver's license or plates to sneak it around the block every now and again? Not that we're condoning such actions, but times were different then.

Careening up the driveway after school one afternoon (before my mother got home), I hit the bump at the bottom down by the street at speed, which caused the driver's seat-back to break, catapulting me into the rear of that skimpy sedan and leaving me desperately stomping in search of the brake pedal. Fortunately, I didn't hit the house, or take down the fence on the other side of the driveway.

But the die was cast and it seems as if the hunt has continually gone on ever since. After I received a newly-minted driver's license at age 17, a VW Beetle followed, but not for long. Because I soon theorized that with ever-escalating 1970s gas prices, a fuel-sipping Volkswagen could be sold for $500 and replaced with an ever-depreciating 1960s Alfa Romeo for the same price. Proven right by the weekly Trader paper, I then enjoyed the advantage of a twin-cam engine, two Weber DCOE carburetors, a 5-speed transmission and four-wheel disc brakes. In short order, what also came standard was my ability to change blown head gaskets and correct valve clearance concerns by removing and replacing calibrated shims. After all, the antique automobile lifestyle is a learning experience!

By this time, Triumph sports cars were very much in the mix. We bought a 1968 TR-250 in 1972 that's still in the family, along with TR-3 after TR-3. The going rate was roughly $150 per for those earlier four-cylinder roadsters, and it got to the point that we built a bit of a local reputation for being a Triumph family—so much so that people would call for us to come extricate derelict TR-3s off of their own 50' × 100' Long Island lots, free for the taking.

On the opposite end of the spectrum, a $600 1941 Ford V-8 sedan was followed by a 1930 Triumph Super Seven, which was then the oldest known British Triumph on U.S. soil, and probably still is. The Ford was used for everything from ski trips to Vermont (it came with a vintage set of tire chains in the trunk), to wedding processions down to Washington, D.C. Meanwhile, the Super Seven was driven out to the Bridgehampton, N.Y., racetrack at a breakneck speed of 35 mph for the Vintage Triumph Register (VTR) National Convention.

Early on, I recognized that a lot of the fun came with using the cars and participating in organized events, from meets and shows to autocrosses, TSD rallies and track days. Meanwhile, having driven the Alfa out to Detroit after moving to Michigan, I also recognized the value of a good heater, so then it was on to $600 Volvos after I replaced yet another Giulia head gasket.

Never one to look at the investment value of antique automobiles, I soon began to do what I still do to this day: buy antique and special interest automobiles that I wanted to learn about and experience, such as the Model T Ford speedster and a Datsun 240Z. Before long, I got darned good at buying high and selling low, something else that I still seem to do with great abandon!

Buicks came next. A nice '56 two-door proved to me that "When better automobiles are built, Buick will build them." But it was a low-mileage 1937 Special that gave me an appreciation for untouched original cars with patina. It was yet another antique automotive affliction that was forged early on, and continues to drive much of my ongoing interest.

Though that was just the beginning, it should help explain why I'm "still crazy after all these years." Things then took a turn toward the more esoteric and offbeat. My Saab saga began with exposure to a very early, Triumph-powered (coincidentally) 99. Next I acquired the first production version of the Vignale-bodied TR-3 powered Triumph Italia from a Studebaker Avanti aficionado out in the back woods of Connecticut. The steering wheel came off one afternoon while *Autoweek* magazine was doing a retrospective feature on it, because for some reason the previous owner removed the attachment nut. I don't know if I was more embarrassed or freaked out. So once again, being an experienced Renault Dauphine pilot, I desperately went stomping in search of the brake pedal. Go figure.

All along, my interest was also leaning more and more toward technically unique examples of automotive invention, and an air-cooled 1930 Franklin convertible coupe made its way into my garage, as did a Ford-powered V-4 Saab 96. No doubt, I have to be the only lunatic to ever do the Woodward Avenue Dream Cruise in a Franklin

Steven Rossi and sons David and Michael with Franklin convertible coupe.

with two kids lounging around out back in its expansive rumble seat. I was confident that at least it wouldn't boil over! To ensure there was always something turnkey at the ready, there was still a trusty Triumph TR-3A in my ever-changing inventory.

At some point, I expanded my horizons and was determined to experience automotive technology from each and every decade. That's when my interest in brass-era automobiles really accelerated. I looked at lots, and ended up with a 1912 Overland 59T touring. At the time it was built, Willys-Overland was America's second largest car producer because they built good products that worked, and worked well.

Then I delved into the Classic (with a capital "C") category and went in search of an affordable Pierce-Arrow. I was drawn to the Buffalo-built rolling bank vault by its marque club, the Pierce-Arrow Society. Why? Because it proved to be a very close-knit community of like-minded enthusiasts who weren't afraid to get their hands dirty, and they routinely drove the wheels off 'em— like the time I chased a Minnesota-bound 1917 Series 66 from Buffalo to Detroit. Via the club classifieds, after a circuitous route through a northwest Packard broker (it's a long story), a fairly fine 1933 836 club sedan came my way.

The technology bug bit again and I sold the Franklin in partial exchange for a 1922 Wills Sainte Claire roadster. It embodied almost all of the attributes that I had come to appreciate by this time. An offbeat orphan with an Hispano-Suiza–inspired dual-overhead cam V-8 engine configuration. The only thing it was lacking was the all-original patina with which I had also become so enamored. But it had a robust restoration by Bill Harrah's shops back in the 1960s, which has since held up incredibly well. It, too, came through the underground via its single-marque owners' group, the

Steven Rossi with 1933 Pierce-Arrow 836 club sedan.

Wills Sainte Claire Club from Marysville, Michigan. The previous owner obviously had the right religion since he specialized in bronze antique automobile sculptures.

One of the reasons I sold the Franklin was because I was going to buy another Syracuse-made air-cooled example from an even earlier and desirable decade, a 1904 cross-engine. Unfortunately, even after a hearty handshake with an agreed-upon price, the owner had a change of heart. *Damn* … I've remained Franklin-less ever since.

Meanwhile, with all the lessons learned from that earlier experience with the Alfa Romeo Giulia Super, I went after a few more examples of automotive expression that appeared to be at the bottom of their depreciation cycles. Having never owned a 12-cylinder car—and with high-end Auburns being totally out of reach—I shifted gears in search of a silky-smooth BMW 850i. It rewarded me with the most egregious speeding violation I've ever received. What memories…

Having owned only one piece of 1950s automotive Americana—that 1956 Buick Special, back in the day—I couldn't resist when the Hershey car corral yielded a baby 1950 Cadillac Series 61 coupe, complete with manual transmission, roll-up windows, rubber floor mat and radio delete. Another Model T, this time, a '24 coupe, followed me home because of its fully-enclosed body. We could use it all year long. In January, I'd just bring the basset hound along to avoid freezing to death, and a blanket helped, too.

Steven Rossi with Aston Martin.

Before that, I got back to British with a 1975 Aston-Martin V-8. My wife and I took one of our most memorable road trips in that Newport Pagnell–produced road locomotive from Detroit to New Orleans on two-lane roads, including the beautiful 444-mile Natchez Trace Parkway. As I explained to her before we left, "Either way, this is going to be an incredibly memorable experience, because one of two things is going to happen. We're either going to have a delightful drive down and return home unscathed, or the car is going to blow up out in the middle of nowhere in Mississippi and, with all due respect to the Queen, we'll be royally screwed." Fortunately, the trip took the turn to the former road less traveled.

With the New Orleans excursion behind us, the only two cars that Mrs. Rossi couldn't stomach then materialized. For some reason, she never warmed up to my low-mileage all-original 1970 Buick Electra 225 coupe from the Kruse Labor Day weekend auction in Fort Wayne, Indiana. Perhaps it was because it was a literal land yacht, but that paled in comparison to her opinion of the 1980 Lotus Eclat that landed after that, which she only rode in once, which was quite enough. Oh well…

So where do you go after chasing technically-interesting offbeat examples of wild and wacky original orphan antiques? Why, you buy a Citroën, of course, which is exactly what I did. It picked up from where a pair of Peugeot 505s left off. The 1987 CXA GTi now rests on its belly in my driveway—yes, I just simply enjoy it as a used car, and it's always at the ready to rise to the occasion, on any occasion. It's certainly been a most rewarding and trouble-free experience and led me to a conclusion that I'd reached so, so many times before along this personal path of antique automobile enlightenment: Why didn't I just do this sooner? Let me answer that: The lack of money probably had an awful lot to do with it.

A one-owner 1988 Saab 900 had also joined the stable by now, as did a low-mileage 1987 Alfa Romeo Milano; so, I guess, I could re-experience my misspent Giulia Super youth. Together with the Citroën, I realize that unbeknownst to me, I was mining yet another rarefied vein of antique automotive aspiration: the last iteration of pure automotive examples from manufacturers that have since been bought out or forced to merge and were then pushed into the realm of shared platforms and powertrains. I think there's a story line in there, somewhere ... stay tuned.

Trucks have always been a mainstay within the household because they very much earn their keep. Being a fan of the postwar Chevy advance design series, I owned a pair of three-window ½-tons—1950 and 1954—that served me well. I also had high hopes for a cute little mid–1960s International with a grain dump body that found its way from Kansas to Connecticut, but fate decided otherwise. I did, however, learn the true meaning of the term "farm truck." Let me translate: "a rusted hulk that hasn't got a snowball's chance in hell of ever satisfying safety and inspection standards, or possibly qualifying for a license plate." I'm always learning, and as always, at my own expense (and peril).

Most recently, a gently-worn 1926 Stutz AA victoria coupe found its way into one of my outbuildings. I'm the third owner and, yes, it's a technically interesting antique and loaded with a ton of untouched patina.

Then there are all the ones that got away, like the mid–60s 250 Ferrari coupe that I could have easily bought for next to nothing at the time, but didn't ... all the Lancias, Lamborghinis and Maseratis that I looked at, test drove and passed over when I was, yet again, young and foolish ... Jaguars left and right, and more Morgans than you could shake an ashwood stick at, not to mention Franklins, Packards and Pierce-Arrows, all in readily available abundance ... even a steam car or two.

Now that I'm older—but obviously not much wiser—there are even recent opportunities where I brushed off a Locomobile, a Marmon, a Peerless and an early Lincoln. Though, admittedly, as time marches on, the lack of financial wherewithal certainly has had a lot to do with that, too. For some reason, you just can't seem to find 'em for a couple of hundred bucks anymore. But the fact that I've never bought a new vehicle has at least allowed me to channel the funds that were/are available into antique cars instead. Life is full of choices, and in addition to never having had a new ride, my wife has never gotten to park in the garage, either.

Many of my best friends live by the same code of conduct. They're the ones who also know that you can stuff three—if not four—cars into a two-car garage, and then surround them with a smattering of interesting motorcycles and old outboard motors among all the nooks and crannies. They, too, have a very up-close-and-personal relationship with their antique insurance provider and state motor vehicle office, and also like me, they essentially own stock in Deland, Florida's, Deltran Corporation, the provider of 6- and 12-volt battery tenders.

Though of course it's true that you can't buy 'em all, you can sure try, or at least dream of trying. It seems that my soulmate is well aware that the day I stop doing that is the day that she'll be dropping me into the ground. So in the meantime, the search goes on. I'll be the guy surfing the Internet, thumbing through *Antique Automobile* magazine classifieds, staining my fingertips with heavy *Hemmings* ink, cruising car corrals—etc., and so on and so forth—because some things never change. As far as I'm concerned, they never should, once you've been consumed by pipe dreams and other antique automotive flights of fancy.

For All Seasons and Reasons

JANUARY/FEBRUARY 2017

In today's times of attached garages, heated seats and remote self-starters, it's hard to imagine that in the days of yesteryear it took what seemed like an ice age for the automobile to practically warm up and gain traction as an everyday appliance, instead of what was a seasonal plaything. During January and February across much of the country, automobiles were simply "put up" for the winter when they were in their infancy because there was simply no other choice. As the thermometer dropped, so too did their ability to operate. Conventional wisdom was, like an ornery old cuss, horseless carriage hibernation was simply a way of life.

But despite the cruel grasp of Jack Frost's cold clutches, the thought of a long winter's nap in the back of the barn was soon met with a groundswell of second thought. The automobile was rapidly gaining enthusiastic acceptance and an impassioned public would quickly force its acclimation to four seasons. Here's what helped make it an ever-ready all-year-round overachiever:

Improved Carburetor Control

As a fuel metering device, early carburetors were pretty ineffectual. Sure, even the simplest surface instrument allowed an engine to splutter into life, at least under fairly steady-state conditions, but to accommodate the upsurge in demand as the automobile industry began to mature, the thought of coaxing a car to cooperate throughout the seasons was a commercial barrier that needed to be beaten. The challenge was that when the weather changed, inlet air density deviated and the inertia that naturally impeded fuel evaporation wreaked havoc on combustion control. In the words of the 1918 edition of *Putnam's Automobile Handbook*, when temperatures dropped, "gasoline wouldn't gas."

The Carburetor Handbook from 1925 eloquently explains how the problem was solved: "…stranglers or air chokes which reduce the main air supply by means of a suitable shutter or similar device, the use of which increases the suction on the main fuel orifice or jet, far beyond the normal state of affairs … make up for the loss of fuel

Rayfield carburetor ad.

due to condensation on the cold walls of the passages in the engine, and to give the added power required to run an engine that is stiff as a result of being cold…" Thus, priming cups made way for the choke. And to avoid associated carburetor icing, induction heating systems and hot water jackets soon followed.

Battery Ignition

After coming to grips with the need to properly calibrate the relationship between air and fuel with weather extremes, the source of stable ignition would prove to be another hurdle. Crude horseless-carriage hot-tube ignition was almost immediately superseded by the magneto, but that solution was quickly overtaxed with the migration to multi-cylinder engines of increasing speed. In addition, it was getting increasingly difficult to hand crank engines fast enough to get the magneto to properly fire in the first place, since its output was speed sensitive. In the words of R.C. Fryer from his *Automotive Starting, Lighting and Ignition* handbook of 1918, when addressing cold starting and ignition trouble, "There are a number of vexatious things to make the novice and prospective driver peevish."

It got to the point that redundant systems were often employed, which began with a starting battery, and then switched to running on magneto. Ultimately, such compromises led to the breakthrough of breaker points and battery ignition.

In 1910, a single coil with points (which served as a switch) picked up from where the rotating coil within a fixed magnet, or vice versa, left off. Not only did the battery system provide consistent output across the engine's operating range, but it was cheaper to produce, easier to service and certainly more reliable.

As engines got bigger and compression ratios rose, the move from 6- to 12-volt systems followed to provide still more ignition output, particularly with the changing seasons. Simultaneously, battery technology was improving, with available cold cranking capability and reserve capacity amping up as well.

Antifreeze

Meanwhile, antifreeze appeared in various forms soon after the arrival of the automobile, and included such alternatives as tea kettles full of hot water, alcohol, glycerin/glycerol and calcium chloride, among other concoctions. Each had its own shortcoming including corrosion, evaporation, erosion of rubber hoses and the potential to impede coolant flow as a result of coagulation. Such side effects caused the editors of the *Cyclopedia of Automotive Engineering* to predict during 1912 that "the substitution of air cooling for water cooling will mark a great advance in automobile development." With all due respect to the waterless Franklin Motorcar Company, however, the answer to fend off freezing came instead with the commercialization of ethylene glycol in 1917. At that time, it was used as part of the manufacturing process to make dynamite!

By the mid–1920s, ethylene glycol found its way into automobiles. In addition to lowering the freezing point, the synthesis of this phenomenal fluid proved prophetic and paved the way for the future, because it simultaneously raised the boiling point on the eve of ever-escalating engine outputs—particularly after cooling systems were

Whiz antifreeze ad.

later sealed and pressures rose. In addition, it served as a carrier of lubricants for water pumps and also accommodated rust inhibitors.

The Self-Starter

Like a high-speed blender, the self-starter stirred all the elements discussed above together and harmonized cantankerous subsystems into an accomplished

An ad evokes the advantages of the self-starter, powered by a Philco battery.

orchestra within the engine bay to get things going—particularly when the mercury plummeted.

If you've ever tried to hand-crank an antique auto in the winter (and I certainly suggest that you do, to gain an appreciation of what the challenge was really like), you'll understand why. Of course, the self-starter also very much expanded the automobile's market opportunity and helped transform it from a mere curiosity into a commodity for the masses. The worry of winter was waning.

A Garage

Pioneers and early adopters who invested in the automobile were certainly conscious of protecting their prized possession from the elements. Lean-tos, makeshift sheds and spare space in the barn soon made way for dedicated structures to house automobiles. Thus the garage, which was derived from the French word for shelter—*garer*—was born. Such an enclosed environment also allowed owners to perform service, which there was plenty of, under cleaner and more controlled circumstances.

Many of the earliest automotive garages were city clubhouses for like-minded upscale owners, where they could share experience and enjoy a bit of camaraderie. As automobile ownership evolved into opportunity for everyman, private garages soon appeared locally, as suburbs began to sprawl, which was also a result of the automobile's acceptance.

It's interesting to note that while the early garage didn't have the sanitary challenge of a stable, most were still separated from dwellings and houses due to safety

Garages caught on quickly in the automotive age.

concerns, such as perceived fire risk from gasoline and acetylene, among other reasons. It didn't take long for entrepreneurial architects to become engaged with garage construction plans, mail order kits and more, following fast in the wake of ever-growing automobile affection.

Enclosed Car Bodies

Now that the automobile had the technical capability to operate throughout the year and was always ready and rarin' to go—snug as a bug in its own four-walled cocoon—it was the innovation of the enclosed body that truly allowed the automobile to firmly and finally conquer the elements. While closed bodies were produced since the dawn of the automotive age, they were only available to the rarified few with the means to afford their exorbitant expense. Built from old world, carriage trade experience meant that they were heavy and ornate, which was coincidentally why they always found their way onto the big powerful chassis of the day.

It was the arrival of the affordable enclosed car that put the automobile industry into overdrive. That advance is attributed to the 1922 Essex coach. By 1925, the entry level Hudson Motor Company model was offering its enclosed car for the same price as its associated open touring alternative, or less. It wasn't the specific price point

Enclosed car bodies offered protection in all weather.

that moved the needle, but the fact that the premium for enclosed Essex comfort and weather protection was now nil. Even Henry Ford took notice.

Like the self-starter, the affordable enclosed car was a boon to automotive promotion that enticed previously uncommitted people who hadn't even thought about the feasibility of owning an automobile yet, such as the generally untapped female audience.

Here's an interesting statistic that demonstrates how the market was not only influenced but ultimately disrupted in 10 years. In 1919, the ratio of open to closed cars was nine to one. By 1929, it was exactly the opposite.

Heaters and Defrosters

To add to the enjoyment and functionality of the cozy enclosed car, heaters and defrosters soon defied Mother Nature even more. Lap robes, hot bricks, electric aids and rudimentary coal- and gas-fueled portable heaters made way for purpose-built solutions that preferably relied on an existing onboard heat source. Exhaust gas heaters showed early promise, but had limitations because they were difficult to regulate and their output was speed dependent.

Enter the hot water heater. With hot engine coolant flowing through an auxiliary radiator (*i.e.,* heater core), it proved easy to blow air across it, liberate heat and channel it back into the cabin. The hot water car heater proved even more effective with better water pump precision and the improved reliability of engine thermostats, which not only accelerated engine warm-up, but ensured a steady operating temperature.

Prior to thermostatic control, intrepid owners struggled with such alternatives as blankets, hot water bottles and radiator shutters/covers, which were marketed

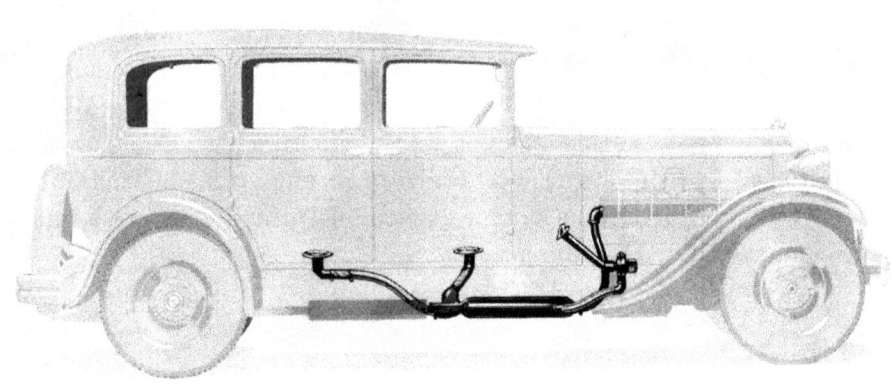

Early heater.

as winter fronts, to try and keep engine temperatures stable. Some even resorted to removing the fan belt during wintertime.

Installed as somewhat homespun add-ons during the 1920s and '30s, the specification of the car heater really warmed up in the 1940s and '50s as a defined line item on the option list. By the 1960s it was standard equipment, with windshield defrosting being federally mandated in 1968.

The defroster was created by funneling hot air up to the windshield. Rear defoggers began to appear when auxiliary airflow systems were similarly deployed to channel air through an opening in the parcel shelf. They were soon obsolete after the ascension of what is now the state-of-the-art electrically-heated rear window grid.

The art of cabin heating went on to further stimulate the science of air-flow management and ventilation control within the passenger compartment.

Windshield Wiping and Washing

Precipitation met its match with the invention of the windshield wiper. The earliest examples were manually actuated from inside the vehicle. Mary Anderson cleared the way with her invention in 1903, when she patented a "window cleaning device" for electric vehicles. The Tri-Continental Corporation (Trico) began commercial wiper production in 1917. The basic design of a pivoting arm with a blade attached remains with us to this day.

As windshield-wiper applications increased and the performance of the automobile was ramping up, the window cleaning device was soon powered by a vacuum motor to keep pace. Unfortunately, its speed was manifold-pressure/throttle-opening dependent (*i.e.,* upon acceleration, the wipers would effectively stop wiping).

A few alternative drive mechanisms were explored, such as hydraulic control on the Lincoln Continental and cable actuation via the transmission on the Citroen 2CV. In the end, the efficiency of electric control became the generic standard, and for good reason. It allowed for the later adaptation of intermittent and speed-sensitive controls.

The windshield washer first appeared in the aftermarket during the 1930s. *Popular Mechanics* magazine attributed it to the Richland Auto Parts Company of Mansfield, Ohio, and it was developed specifically "to keep the windshield clear of sleet and snow in winter." It relied on denatured alcohol during the winter, while plain water could be substituted for summer.

Tire Chains and Snow Tires

Of course, all of the above improvements were useless if the automobile was stuck in a snow drift or marooned at the bottom of an icy embankment. Traction aids

For All Seasons and Reasons

Windshield wiping—here done manually via an aftermarket accessory.

were part and parcel with the very arrival of the automobile, and were often required to simply plow through the abysmal road conditions of the day, let alone in winter extremes. As good roads began to proliferate, lessons learned in mud and muck slid over to snow and slush.

So it was quite common to tie ropes and straps around wheels and tires to increase traction at the turn of the century, and such provisions were staples on tours and in competitive events of the time, such as the Glidden Tours. In fact, the winning

Tire chains.

New York-to-Paris Thomas Flyer racer was identified years later—in severely dilapidated condition—by the divots left behind by such traction aids in its wheel rims.

The idea of the tire chain arrived with its patent in 1904, which was developed in New York as a "grip-tread for pneumatic tires." Temporary tire chains are still with us, and are routinely seen in locales like California and Colorado, where they're required to proceed through certain mountain passes during ski season. Of course, if you live in a place like Alaska, you're already familiar with such folks as Glacier Chain Supply in Anchorage.

It figures that the Finnish Nokian company lays claim to the invention of the snow tire, which first appeared in truck applications during 1934. Car fitment began in 1936 and provided an aggressive tread design with a "tooth-like grip," according to Nokian.

Snow tires were somewhat superseded by the arrival of all-season tires, which soon proved to be a bit of a compromise by not really performing in any exemplary way in either summer or winter. Winter tires have, therefore, been making a comeback, particularly now that the science of rubber formulation is such that compounds can be specifically tuned for cold weather extremes. They remain pliable as the temperature drops, while simultaneously resisting wear.

Studded winter tires date back to the 1960s, as speeds went up and road-clearing capability improved.

Multi-Grade Oil

While no surprise, here's another telling observation from *Putnam's*: "…while oil does not freeze, it does get very viscid and like molasses, flows stiff at low temperatures." As a result, early car makers had no choice but to provide oil recommendations that varied by season, with lighter viscosities specified for lower temperatures. While such guidance may have helped keep the machine in motion throughout the year, it certainly wasn't the most convenient or cost-effective solution.

As a classic case of necessity being the mother of invention, the development of multi-grade motor oil followed. Oil naturally has a higher viscosity (resistance to flow) when cold and lower viscosity when hot, which is the opposite of the engine's lubrication demands. During the 1950s, special polymers known as viscosity index improvers began to be added to oils to create multi-grade capability. Through the wizardry of chemical engineering, engine oil could now behave with lighter viscosity when cold to help starting, while simultaneously performing at full grade specification when hot.

Winter Fuel Formulations

More recently, gasoline began to be blended as a function of season to control the evaporation rate of volatile organic compounds. Winter fuel includes butane because it's cheap and abundant, and still remains volatile at low temperatures, which helps cold starting. In the summer, its light ends would quickly boil off and create harmful emissions.

As a side note, the ability of drugstore-supplied ether to serve as a potent starting fluid was realized early on. The only challenge was to convince the corner druggist that it was really needed for a cold cantankerous car … instead of for the exhausted, irate owner who was so fed up with cranking that he was prepared to end it all.

* * * *

Those are the reasons why we can now enjoy the automobile throughout the seasons. These days, it might be easy to take the automobile's cold weather capability for granted since it's evolved into such an obedient servant, but it took a tremendous transfer of energy across various mediums (which is the definition of heat, by the way)—engineering and industry mediums, that is—for the car to ultimately acclimatize itself.

So as you sit in comfortable confines and read this during the frigid winter, unlike the plight of early automobilists you can rest assured that they don't make 'em like they used to.

Shipping Shenanigans

March/April 2017

The clock is running down on the online auction and there's not much left of your fingernails, either. *Tick, tick* ... place one more bid, pull the trigger ... and up it comes. The online notification that exclaims, "You've Won." Well, all right, it's a happy day, indeed! Now all you have to do is figure out how to get the damned thing home? Oops...

While I've certainly had many, *many* great experiences transporting antique cars and old motorcycles all across America through the years, there have been a few less-than-stellar performances that I thought I'd share with you. They're filed under the heading of lessons learned, which may be of benefit to you, as the spring trading season unfolds. Because the last incident included here just occurred, I was prompted to put pen to paper, or in fact, fingertips to keyboard.

Yes, after 40 years of collecting, I'm still learning lots of things. Such as, that even while the vast, *vast* majority of antique automobile enthusiasts are solid, stand-up citizens, the old car community can include a few pirates and other scoundrels. Even if they are acting inadvertently and without malice.

The Pierce from the Pacific Coast

When I decided to buy a CCCA classic car, I set my sights on a Pierce-Arrow—a 1933 in particular, because among other reasons, I liked the way the then-newly updated fender-mounted headlights were a bit more aesthetically integrated into the overall styling. In addition, I enjoyed the camaraderie within the Pierce-Arrow club, where many members were not afraid to drive the daylights out of what's been referred to as "America's Finest Car," and also had no qualms about getting their hands dirty. Sign me up!

After months of searching, I stumbled across a '33 836 club sedan in Napa, California, in the classifieds of the Pierce-Arrow Society's publication. When I called, however, it was already gone. The day the deceased owner's wife mailed the ad in to the longer-lead-time club newsletter, she simultaneously put it in the more immediate local "Trader" paper. So you can guess what happened.

A load of new 1941 Buicks at the factory in Flint, ready to be transported in security and style (courtesy Buick Heritage Alliance).

Later that year, I was on a business trip out on the Pacific Coast and stopped to visit a well-known vintage car broker. Much to my surprise, there was the same 1933 club sedan that previously appeared in the Pierce publication. So a deal was done!

While I was preparing to make arrangements with one of the nationally recognized antique car haulers, the broker offered an alternative. He had an established relationship with a local shipper who moved all of his cars. In addition to saving some money, the enticement was that this trucker hauled cars one at a time in an enclosed trailer with white-glove attention, so the transport would be direct and right to the point, without any stops or detours along the way. I liked the idea that there would be no unloading and reloading en route, so I took his advice.

At the appointed hour, around dinner time, the Pierce arrived in Michigan, where I was living at the time. The car was unloaded, money changed hands, and I went back into the house to finish my meal. Before dark, I rolled the car into the garage.

The next morning I fired it up, backed her out and just sat there admiring all of its Buffalo-built brilliance. Then something caught my eye that just didn't seem right. The Pierce appeared to be listing to port, so I crawled under to find … a broken front leaf spring!

Obviously, that's what happens when you tie a car down with a chain around the spring instead of securely strapping to an axle or using wheel bonnets. So I called the broker concerning his reputable shipping partner and the answer I got? "That's absolutely impossible!"

After going back and forth over the phone in what turned into heated frustration, I finally learned the cold, hard truth. The shipper was, in fact, an old friend of the broker's who was down on his luck, and a well-intentioned Mr. Dealer was simply trying to help him out by having him move cars. So he asked me to "give the guy a break, since I gave you a good price on the car." Which I unfortunately did, to the tune of $500, in the form of a cold, hard broken leaf spring.

Early Morning Antics with a Bimota Motorcycle

A classified ad from a dealer in the Midwest drew my attention. Being a longtime Italian motorcycle lunatic, I'd always had the thought of owning a Bimota, the two-wheeled equivalent of a Ferrari, on my short list. Having followed the depreciation cycle on these things, it had finally flattened to the point where I was able to take the plunge. When I came across a former celebrity-owned example with essentially no miles, I made my move. The arrangement included transport to my door, because the dealer was already heading my way with an enclosed trailer to deliver a car to another client. So yet again, there were good savings to be had.

A few days later, the phone rings at 5:30 a.m. There's a truck and trailer in front of my house "running ahead of schedule" and ready to deliver. So we unload the bike in the black of the night and the crew-cab dually and tri-axle box trailer head off into the sunrise and I back to bed. I'm not about to fire up this raucous crotch-rocket at 0 dark hundred and romp around the sleepy suburban neighborhood on it.

Like a kid at Christmas, I run down at a more reasonable time in the morning and jump aboard my beautiful new Bimota. Much to my surprise, it will only idle, and won't develop any power whatsoever, so I can't actually ride the thing.

There was a more critical concern than just the dead fuel pump. Now that it was daylight, I discovered that the VIN on the title didn't match the one on the bike! Coincidentally "running ahead of schedule" at 5:30 a.m.?

So to this day, the Bimota carries the Michigan license plate that it had when I got it, because there were no inspections required when I was in the Detroit area. When I moved to Connecticut, however, VIN verification was required for any vehicle that enters from out of state, and I've been petrified to let the motor vehicle department know that there's a numeric inconsistency! Even though it was supposedly an honest mistake…. I was told that the celebrity owner had two identical motorcycles, and the paperwork got confused.

International Intrigue from the Heart of Kansas

It was the acquisition of a cute little light-duty International dump truck that taught me the true meaning of farmer's ingenuity, along with the definition of "farm truck."

With a decent amount of property to maintain here in eastern Connecticut, I concluded that things like fall clean-ups would be a lot easier if there was more than just one workhorse around here besides me. I became intrigued with the idea of finding an antique that could do double duty, simultaneously earning its keep by being worked. So the search began, but I soon realized that the majority of farm trucks were out in the farmlands, particularly the ones that hadn't rusted to dust.

Lo and behold, I came across a 1965 International D-series ½-ton with a 10-foot factory grain box. I'm in! Now, how do I get it home? Well, the farmer from whom I bought it also had a "connection" who was routinely running back and forth across I-80 delivering everything from cars and trucks to tractors and farm implements. The price was right, and it's not as if this thing was pristine anyway. So I engaged his guy.

When the International arrived, it was unfortunately in far-from-advertised condition. After a fuel-tank leak burned a hole in my driveway, I called the seller who just didn't understand my concern. His response? "Park it beside the barn and let it leak … you'll soon learn how much fuel to put in to get it to do whatever job you want" … and "You never asked if the windows rolled up and down or if the lights worked, and even though they don't, it's not my fault. That's why we call 'em farm trucks!"

He was also rather nonchalant about the manner in which it was transported. In fact, to make a long story short, since it didn't actually fit on his friend's beaver-tail trailer, this device-ful duo came up with the idea of extending the trailer deck with planks, and the International rode all the way from Kansas to Connecticut while hanging off of the back of a derelict trailer's derriere! No doubt, the neighbors thought that the Beverly Hillbillies had come to visit.

I ended up trading it to a local hard-core International collector, who never saw anything like it here in this part of the world because of the notorious New England tin worm. In exchange, I received a Dodge work van, which I planned to use as a combination motorcycle hauler and camper, because yet again, this incident was fueled by the idea that antiques can earn their keep.

An Aermacchi Adventure

Aermacchi was an Italian motorcycle maker that grew out of the remains of Aeronautica Macchi, which was forced to cease airplane construction after World War II. Having had a couple over the years, I was intrigued when one of the earliest-known examples popped up at a vintage motorcycle dealer, also in the Midwest. It remained in inventory for a while because nobody out there really knew what it was, I guess. So when I got around to finally making a lowball offer, I became its next owner. *Surprise!*

Since it was so small and light, I thought I'd try an online shipping auction alternative, figuring anyone could move it. Up went the transport auction and I began reviewing bids and scrutinizing each carrier's user profile. The source I selected didn't actually offer the lowest price, but was certainly competitive, plus his profile included a photo of a nice new Ford F-350 crew cab towing an equally crisp and clean color-matched trailer. Since he obviously had so much pride in his rig, I gave him the go-ahead.

A week or so later, the driver shows up at my house ... at 11:00 p.m. Instead of the flawless Ford, he's driving a ragged Ryder rental box truck. *Hmmm* ... wonder where the pretty profile picture came from. When he rolled up the rear door of the truck, I was horrified. In addition to the bike, there was a camping tent erected back there, along with a barbecue grill and lawn chair! The tie-down hooks for the bike straps were nails driven into the hardwood floor deck—and the ramp to roll the Aermacchi down to the ground on? How about a crusty old 2" × 10"!

From South Carolina to Connecticut, the Long Way

This last and most recent incident gets parked under the heading, "If it sounds too good to be true, then it is"—and I should have known better. Yet again, it was the lure of some sweet savings that swayed my judgment.

Having lusted for a pre–Fiat Lancia for a long, *long* while, I determined that if I was ever going to satisfy such craving I should probably do it soon. So that's what I did, since I'm not getting any younger. I had the good fortune to hook up with a very sincere seller who had a wonderful car, so when he recommended a shipping broker with which he had great experience, I figured what could go wrong, since it was just coming up the I-95 corridor?

The highly rated broker (99.8 percent positive, according to him) proved most congenial. The service he provided was to coordinate everything, and the value he added was in his relationships with known, proven carriers who would reliably get the job done at a fraction of the cost of the big boys. This was a new business model for me, but the broker's fee was reasonable, as was the independent carrier's.

Everything was proceeding along with utmost expediency and going according to plan, when the call came at 8:00 p.m. Tuesday evening. "We're in New Jersey now, and should be at your house in Connecticut between noon and 1:00 p.m. tomorrow." So I took a half day off from work and anxiously awaited the arrival of my little Lancia. At 5 p.m. or so, with no car hauler in sight, I started making phone calls. With no answers or return calls, I then resorted to email. The first electronic response I got back from the broker's office was, "Has the car been picked up in South Carolina yet?" What? The broker doesn't even know if the car's been picked up in South Carolina? Uh-oh, this didn't sound good.

A little later, the next email arrived. "You'll have your car by 8 p.m. tonight. The driver will call you 30 minutes before he arrives." Around 9:30 p.m. or so, and still Lancia-less, I called the broker again. This time he actually answered. Then the fun started, and true colors shone.

The conversation began with "You should be thankful I even answered the phone while I'm in the middle of dinner" and went downhill from there. I reminded the broker that I hadn't had dinner yet either, since I'd been on constant lookout for the Lancia since noon. He went on to say, "I have no responsibility for the trucker, he's an independent and I'm sorry you're mad." I told him I wasn't mad, just really disappointed, primarily in myself for doing such a stupid thing in the first place.

Thursday arrived and after Wednesday's half-day, I then took a full day off and waited some more, because I was told that the car would now absolutely, positively arrive no later than 6 p.m. Meanwhile, I learned that the Lancia was the last car loaded, hanging off the back of a gargantuan open transporter (from the seller who sent me a photo) and that it was going to be the last car delivered from the load. Which means that it went on and off the transporter some 10 times or so, in two days. Was the reward of a low price worth such high risk?

At 4:20 p.m. the dispatcher from the transport company called, reconfirming that the car would positively arrive by 6:00. Well, the Lancia finally landed on Thursday evening at 8 p.m. ... with the ignition on and red instrument panel light blazing bright, and choke fully actuated. So I said to myself, "I sure hope she starts, and the breaker points aren't fried ... or spark plugs fouled."

A long way from the original Wednesday 12–1 p.m. projection, it was a day-and-a-half late on an 880-mile jaunt, and I was certainly not a dollar short settling with the driver. At least wasn't 5:30 a.m. again. Wait a minute ... it *is* dark, I'd better check the serial number! Wonder what happens when these guys go cross-country? A week late, plus or minus either way, perhaps? I got the feeling that I'd just lived through a scene from *The Gang That Couldn't Shoot Straight*.

Fortunately, the car fired up just fine and otherwise arrived unscathed, and is just wonderful. The only casualty was my blood pressure, a few more gray hairs and a nice fresh raw gouge in the rear valence beneath the bumper, which wasn't there on the auction listing.

Having sat around so long twiddling my thumbs in wait, while my Lancia was obviously wandering around the pothole-strewn New York City metro area (judging by the other beat-and-battered leaky dealer auction derelicts on board the transporter that accompanied it), I could have just as quickly flown down to South Carolina and driven it home. Then, my new-found Fulvia would have been spared from all the oil, antifreeze and who knows what other excrement that dripped all over it in transport. Not to mention that fresh divot taken out of the lower valence. No doubt the memory would have been better had I done so. Instead, I got a great idea … and wrote this column during the time away from my full-time (real) job.

After that, do you think that the broker ever made contact to determine when the car arrived, if it did so intact, and if everything worked out all right in the end? Of course not, which makes you (and me) wonder. With that level of attention to detail and customer service follow-up, where did his "99.8% positive" feedback actually come from?

Albert Einstein supposedly said that the definition of insanity is "doing the same thing over and over again and expecting a different result." Having had so much positive, personal experience over the years with such recognized carriers as Reliable, InterCity, Horseless Carriage, Passport Transport and more, you have to wonder why I'd ever deviate and set myself up for such shipping shenanigans as those described above. Well, me too!

Obviously, I must just be insane. Don't you be—because I've already proven that there's yet another age-old adage that can make you as smart as Einstein when it comes time to ship your antique automobile. That being, "You get what you pay for!"

Happy shipping…

ON THE MARQUE

The Halo Around the Hyphen

MARCH/APRIL AND MAY/JUNE 2009

Throughout the course of automotive history, the hyphen has always signified something special in a car or truck's name. Quite often it served as the bridge between individuals, commercial entities, geographic areas or other interests. But it was always more than just pure punctuation. The strength and sophistication of the hyphen was not for humble cars, and still isn't.

It's no surprise that the hyphen immediately appeared when the industry was in its infancy. Partnerships and cooperative ventures were not only the norm, but a necessity. The knowledge base was nil, and the pioneers who prevailed were a unique combination of inventors, engineers, entrepreneurs and investors.

The Edwardian era is therefore best remembered by cars that were marketed with hyphens, and the French were particularly fond of them. In 1883, Count Albert de Dion was already in partnership with Georges Bouton when *DeDion-Bouton* emerged as a result. DeDion is perhaps best remembered as the leading engine supplier of the day, with roughly 140 firms relying upon them.

Clément-Bayard was the amalgam of early bicycle and pneumatic tire magnate Adolphe Clément and the 16th-century hero Chevalier Bayard, who saved the town where Clément had a factory. While many early manufacturers relied on chain-drive, many Clément-Bayards derived their motive force via shaft-drive.

Lorraine-Dietrich began as a manufacturer of DeDietrich railway rolling stock, and added the Cross of Lorraine to its radiator to highlight its French origin after acquiring the rights to produce Amédée Bollée's flat twins. The *Sizaire-Naudin* was a small, light French product from Maurice Sizaire and Louis Naudin. When the two later split, Sizaire went on to produce the much grander *Sizaire-Berwick* with F.W. Berwick, who had been the British agent for Sizaire-Naudin.

Just after the turn of the century, French locomotive and marine boiler maker *Delaunay-Belleville* appeared at the Paris Auto Show with a series of grand, four-cylinder T-head-powered models that were considered by many to be the best cars in the world. Julien Belleville had been building boilers since the 1850s, and Louis Delaunay joined Belleville's firm and married the boss's daughter.

Parisian builder *Panhard et Levassor* existed in one form or another from 1889 to 1965, before then being taken over by Citroën. Although René Panhard and Émile Levassor's quality cars were primarily marketed as Panhards, the name Panhard-Levassor apparently appeared as well.

Rochet-Schneider began in 1894, and later simply capitalized on the existing Benz and Panhard state-of-the-art, but built them better. They therefore created a reputation for conventional cars that were strong and fast. Edouard Rochet was a bicycle manufacturer. Theophile Schneider was a French industrialist, involved in armaments.

Georges Richard also began by building his own version of a Benz. But by 1902, after Brasier arrived via Mors, they were soon turning out the impressive *Richard-Brasier*. They went on to win the Gordon Bennett Cup in 1904 and 1905. *Rolland-Pilain* was a unique, upscale French alliance between François Rolland and Émile Pilain.

Yet another mouthful, Ernest Chenard and Henri Walcker's *Chenard-Walcker*, spanned from 1901 to 1946. They went on to partner with the delectable Delahaye in 1927, and were ultimately absorbed by Peugeot. The *Lion-Peugeot* was an upstart, breakaway endeavor by Robert Peugeot in 1906, named around the parent company logo that dated back to the mid–1800s. The Lion-Peugeot only lasted until 1913, when he then returned to the fold and reunited with the Peugeot family.

As the 20th century was getting ready to accelerate, so too was the fledgling automotive industry. With it came more hyphenated auto names from the world over. Many would go on to be recognized as some of the best in the business.

Elwood P. Haynes, Elmer Apperson and Edgar Apperson put their heads together in the very late 1890s to create the *Haynes-Apperson* in Kokomo, Indiana. Haynes dealt in various businesses including steel and oil, while the Appersons ran a machine shop. Together they created some short-lived, two and four-cylinder cars that were not only well built, but rather unusual with wheel steering on the left side as early as 1903. By 1905, these cars from Kokomo, which were known for their touring capability, were being sold as Haynes when the Apperson brothers went on to produce under their own name.

Italy's illustrious *Isotta-Fraschini* was created when Cesare Isotta and Vincenzo Fraschini began offering Renault knock-offs in 1900. Soon, in 1903, they were instead following Mercedes' practice and also got very involved in racing. They're best remembered for their dashing, luxury limousines, and were very much accepted by American aristocracy and ultimately the Hollywood elite. By 1936, however, Isotta-Fraschini was relegated to merely producing trucks, and the company ceased to exist in 1949.

Stevens-Duryea began in 1901 in Chicopee Falls, Massachusetts, and was the result of the J. Stevens Arms & Tool Company aligning itself with the Hampden Automobile & Launch Company. Hampden was organized by J. Frank Duryea, of pioneering Duryea Motor Wagon fame, after the falling-out with his brother Charles E. The Stevens-Duryea was sturdy and sedate, with a penchant for high quality at a high price.

1929 Isotta-Fraschini 8 Convertible Coupe with body by LeBaron.

Colonel Albert A. Pope appears to have also been high on the hyphen. Having made a fortune in the bicycle business, he set his sights on automobiles in the late 1800s, specifically electrics. His chief engineer, Hiram Percy Maxim, was a strong proponent of gasoline. Ultimately following market forces, Pope allowed gasoline to charge ahead of his Columbia and the *Pope-Hartford* emerged from the Pope Manufacturing Company plant in Hartford, Connecticut, from 1904 to 1914. While single- and two-cylinder models soon made way for fours and sixes, they very much focused on the mighty 50- and 60-horspower category.

Stevens-Duryea Model X.

Pope, however, is also remembered for preceding Albert Sloan with the premise of consolidation and a car for every purse and purpose. The *Pope-Toledo* was even more exotic than the Pope-Hartford, and was advertised as "The All Ball Bearing—All Alloyed Steel Car." Pope built it in Toledo, Ohio, from 1904 to 1909.

The more economical *Pope-Tribune* was the smallest and lightest Pope offering, and was made in Hagerstown, Maryland, between 1904 and 1908. The *Pope-Robinson* never found its niche, probably because after Pope acquired the Robinson Motor Vehicle Company in 1903, John T. Robinson died in 1904. Later that year, Pope-Robinson's Hyde Park, Massachusetts, assets were purchased by Buick for its Selden Patent license.

Of course, it's no surprise that an electric would appear in the Pope hyphen hierarchy as well, based on the Colonel's background. The Waverley Electric already had an association with Pope because it had a connection to his bicycle trust in Indianapolis. When Pope assumed responsibility, it became the *Pope-Waverley*.

Although Henry Royce, a manufacturer of electric cranes, had also been producing two-cylinder cars in Manchester, England, since 1904, it wasn't until 1906 that *Rolls-Royce* was established. It was the association with Charles Stewart Rolls, a pioneer motorist who was selling the Panhard in London at the time, that led to the halo around the Rolls-Royce hyphen. Rolls required quality. Royce delivered. Immortality soon arrived with the creation of the Silver Ghost. To this day, Rolls-Royce is considered by many "The Best Car in the World."

The George N. Pierce Company began by building birdcages and other household items, and then bicycles, in Buffalo, New York. In 1901, the Pierce Motorette motored out of the experimental shop and into the Pierce bicycle dealer's sales catalog, and was powered by a single-cylinder DeDion engine (as mentioned above). In 1903, a two-cylinder model was produced, which gained the name Arrow in 1904. Pierce then produced the Great Arrow, a four-cylinder car, in 1904 as well. The Great Arrow achieved such acclaim that by 1909 the company and its cars were now renamed *Pierce-Arrow*. Pierce-Arrow was, and to many still is, recognized as "America's Finest Car." It lasted until 1938.

While its origins are Spanish and go back to 1904, another marque became more famous after it began being manufactured in France in 1911. The name *Hispano-Suiza* was, in fact, derived from the combination of Spain and Switzerland. Elegantly engineered by Marc Birkigt, a Swiss engineer, the Hispano-Suiza was expensive, large and prestigious. In total, 6,000 were produced in Barcelona and some 2,600 in Paris. The Hispano-Suiza relied on then-exotic aircraft engine design principles and became a favorite of King Alfonso XIII—so much so that there was a model named after him.

John W. Stoddard began by building farm implements in Dayton. He and his brother Charles, however, were less passionate about plows than they were mesmerized by the automobile. With the help of H. Edwards, an English engineer, they turned their attention to a car that was "As Good as It Looks." The *Stoddard-Dayton* was produced from 1904 to 1913, and is well remembered for its superlative performance potential, particularly around the Indianapolis Motor Speedway.

"The Best in Motorcars" was the slogan of the shaft-drive Palmer-Singer, produced by a company formed by barrel maker Henry U. Palmer and sewing machine scion Charles A. Singer. They previously joined to sell Simplex, Matheson and Isotta-Fraschini automobiles on Broadway in New York. So it's no surprise that the bulk of their 1908–1914 production was in the upmarket 40, 50 and 60 hp category.

Although *E-M-F* was certainly a bit more middle-of-the-road than most of the others mentioned here, the car remains well remembered by the two hyphens that separated its founding fathers: Barney Everitt, William Metzger and Walter Flanders. All three were well-versed in the infant industry by the time they got together in 1908. Everitt enjoyed success as a body builder, Metzger had previously been associated with Henry Leland at Cadillac in sales, and Flanders cut his teeth in production with Henry Ford. They produced cars in Detroit through 1912, when the company was taken over by the wagon-building Studebaker brothers, Thus, another automotive brand was born, though sans hyphen.

Also in 1908, Frederick Osgood Paige, an early automobilist who made good with the Reliance truck (which had been taken over by General Motors), was put at the helm of the *Paige-Detroit* company. It was actually established by Harry M. Jewett, in Detroit, of course. The first Paige-Detroit was a three-cylinder, two-stroke that proved to be a disaster. By 1911, Jewett took control of the company, eased Paige aside, and launched a line of conventional, four-cylinder cars. Interestingly, they continued to be marketed under the name Paige. Only the "Detroit" designation was dropped.

Graham-Paige was created for the mid-upper market when the three truck-making Graham brothers (Robert, Joseph and Ray) bought out Paige-Detroit in 1927. But the Graham-Paige name was employed on 1928 and 1929 models only. By 1930, the name Graham appeared by itself. Production continued through 1941.

Willys-Overland was the brainchild of John North Willys, who was obviously also hyphen happy. The company existed in Toledo in one form or another from 1908 to 1963. Willys, a super salesman, took over Overland, which had originally been in Indiana, after he never received his order for the company's entire 1906 output of 47 cars, plus 500 more for 1907. In 1909, he moved production into the former Pope-Toledo plant and by 1912 was second in production behind Henry Ford. The cars, however, were marketed as Overlands. But when the rights to the Knight engine were assumed in 1914, those models so powered were named *Willys-Knight*.

Willys was also associated with the *Falcon-Knight*, which was produced from 1927 to 1929 to bridge the gap between the Whippet and the Willys-Knight. Essentially an early factory hot-rod, it used the big six-cylinder Knight engine in a small Whippet body, and was produced in Elyria, Ohio.

Stearns-Knight was yet another upscale automobile, produced from 1912 to 1929. Frank Ballou Stearns grew up rather privileged as a result of the success of his father's stone quarry. So it's no surprise that when the F.B. Stearns Company began

Willys-Knight.

production in Cleveland at the turn of the century, it catered to clients of wealth. Stearns were easily recognized by their white-line radiators, the perimeter of their shells being outlined in white. Having actually acquired the first American license to the seemingly refined Knight sleeve-valve engine in 1911, all Stearns products from 1912 were sold as Stearns-Knights. They were also the only company authorized to use the full image of a knight in their logo, all other Knight-hyphenated cars being limited to just the bust. They were powerful and impressive, and were produced in four, six and eight-cylinder varieties. Kalamazoo, Michigan's, *Handley-Knight*, from Handley Motors, was also Knight powered.

Although the coachbuilt *Crane-Simplex* was short-lived, it was certainly another grand hyphen marque that was the result of Henry M. Crane and Simplex coming together. At the time, the cost of a chassis alone was on the order of $10,000 and power was derived from a 564 cid six-cylinder.

E.R. Thomas' *Thomas-Detroit* became the *Chalmers-Detroit* after National Cash Register Vice President Hugh Chalmers bought a sizable interest in the company.

Some other lesser-known marques followed the fad to hype the hyphen, though they never lasted long enough to achieve the upscale status so rightfully earned by the likes of Pierce-Arrow and Rolls-Royce. *Abbott-Detroit* was established by the Abbott Motor Car Company in Detroit and relied on Continental four- and six-cylinder engines and a *Herschell-Spillman* eight. Herbert and Eugene Adams, along with Fay Oliver Farwell, produced the *Adams-Farwell* in Dubuque, Iowa, from 1904 to 1913. It was truly unique with its three- and five-cylinder rotary engines. The *Frayer-Miller* of Ohio was air-cooled, and built and raced by Lee Frayer and William Miller. They also

Crane-Simplex (West Peterson photo).

had an early association with a very young Eddie Rickenbacher (who later spelled his name Rickenbacker), who was also from Columbus.

The *Pan-American* was produced in Decatur, Illinois, from 1917 to 1922 and obviously aspired to span the continent. Meanwhile, a world away, the name *Russo-Baltique* defined that marque's Russian origins. Perhaps Michigan's *Dearborn-Detroit* just wasn't sure where its roots originated.

But the rugged *Scania-Vabis* bowed from Sodertalje, Sweden. Scania is a geographic region to the South in Sweden. Translated, Vabis stands for "Wagon Factory Company in Sodertalje." *Austro-Daimler* was the Austrian producer of Daimler products, when the German manufacturer established a factory near Vienna. Likewise, there was an *Austro-FIAT*. Also Austrian, the well-engineered *Steyr-Puch* was a product of *Steyr-Daimler-Puch*. The Steyr-Werke produced rifles in Steyr, Austria. We're all familiar with Daimler. Johann Puch was an early bicycle builder.

Coventry, England's, *Siddeley-Deasy* contributed most to automotive history when it merged with *Armstrong-Whitworth* and created the *Armstrong Siddeley*, eschewing the hyphen.

William B. and George B. Pratt's *Pratt-Elkhart* was built in Elkhart, Indiana, from 1909 to 1911. They continued production through 1915 but dropped the Elkhart designation in 1911. Then came the *Crow-Elkhart*, produced by Martin E. Crow from 1911 to 1923 in Elkhart.

Top: **1933 Austro-Daimler.** *Above:* **1953 Armstrong Siddeley.**

Up north, *Gray-Dort* was more successful than most, though it was never a premium product. The Gray-Dort was essentially an American Dort that was assembled by Wm. Gray-Sons-Campbell Ltd., from 1915 to 1925 in Chatham, Ontario. The *McLaughlin-Buick* was made in Oshawa, Ontario, after an agreement was reached between Billy Durant and the McLaughlin Carriage Company. It was considered "Canada's Standard Car."

W.A. Pungs and his son-in-law, E.B. Finch, collaborated in Detroit, Michigan to create the impressive Pungs-Finch between 1904 and 1910. It's best remembered by its "Limited" model's shaft drive and its overhead-camshaft four-cylinder engine with hemispherical combustion chambers.

Piano-maker and early Ford dealer Gustav Heine offered his short-lived *Heine-Velox* from San Francisco between 1906 and 1909. Heine-Velox then had another brief spurt in 1921, and its last gasp was in the custom-built, luxury category and included a V12.

James Scripps-Booth, of the newspaper publishing family fame, produced his own line of distinctive *Scripps-Booth* automobiles from 1912 to 1922. His first model was the V8-powered *Bi-Autogo*, which was a cross between a car and a motorcycle. He then produced a cyclecar, but soon moved on to luxury cars, some with Mercedes-styled V-shaped radiators. The firm was ultimately acquired by Chevrolet and very quickly lost its unique character.

Mercedes-Benz was rather late to assume the hyphen habit. It's a long story. Carl Benz designed and built the first functional motorcar (a three-wheeler), powered by an internal combustion engine in 1885. Gottlieb Daimler created the first motorcycle powered by an internal combustion engine in 1885, as well, but soon ventured into the four-wheeled world, too. By the turn of the century, Daimler's French agent, Emil Jellinek, began to achieve success with a Daimler racer he called "Mercedes," after his daughter. Jellinek began selling Daimlers to his wealthy friends and continually pushed the Works for greater performance. He soon acquired the Daimler sales rights for all of France, Belgium, Austro-Hungary and America, and sold the cars as Mercedes. In 1902, Daimler re-badged all of its passenger cars Mercedes. Benz, meanwhile, was enjoying success on four wheels as well and ventured into motorsports with its Blitzen Benz.

Daimler and Benz officially joined forces in 1926, and the result was Mercedes-Benz. The rest, as they say, is history—an incredibly illustrious one at that, which continues to this day.

Even Lincoln leaned on the style of the little line when it presented its aerodynamic Lincoln-Zephyr in 1936.

Maxwell-Briscoe was formed in 1904 by Jonathan Maxwell and Benjamin Briscoe, but their product only carried the Maxwell name to market. Likewise, *Kaiser-Frazer* produced just Kaisers and Frazers between 1946 and 1953 in Willow Run, Michigan, and a hyphen wasn't even hung on the Kaiser Darrin.

But numerous sports car marques certainly did cash in the cachet of the petite, yet powerful, point of punctuation. In this segment, it was the British who really leveraged the little link more than anyone else.

No doubt, *Austin-Healey* was the most prominent. Slotting in nicely between the upmarket Jaguar and the more mainstream Triumph, the Austin-Healey was the result of Donald Healey's gaining access to four-cylinder Austin mechanicals. Birmingham, England's Austin dated back to 1906, while the Austin-powered Healey was unveiled in 1953. The arrival of a six-cylinder in 1957 turned the Austin-Healey into a very impressive big brute of a sports car, and it was soon joined by a smaller Sprite in 1958.

The Austin-Healey was preceded by Donald Healey's *Nash-Healey,* which ran from 1951 to 1954. It was intended for the American market, and was produced in partnership with Nash-Kelvinator. Both 235 and 252 cid inline sixes were offered.

The last hyphen Healey was the *Jensen-Healey.* This was when Healey connected with San Francisco auto dealer and importer Kjell Qvale. Both were looking for something to fill the void the Austin-Healey 3000 left. The Jensen-Healey was produced from 1972 to 1976 by England's Jensen Motors, Ltd., and featured a 2-liter Lotus-built engine.

Lea-Francis began life as bicycle manufacturers and moved on to motorcars in 1904, in Coventry, England. Soon thereafter, Richard Henry Lea and Graham Francis were building Singer cars under license. By the mid–1920s they heavily leaned toward their own sports models, and are remembered for their early supercharging efforts. Lea-Francis cars were often referred to as "Leafs."

Sunbeam began by making bicycles in Wolverhampton, England in 1887, and built its first prototype car in 1899. Talbot was derived from the *Clement-Talbot*, which is what the French Clément was called when it was imported into England from 1903 to 1938. The import endeavor was underwritten by the Earl of Shrewsbury and Talbot. When Sunbeam and Talbot got together in 1919, and assumed control of Darracq in 1920, the name *Talbot-Darracq* was then often used. From 1938 to 1954, the *Sunbeam-Talbot* was a luxury version of the British Hillman and Humber models. The *Talbot-Lago*, or *Lago-Talbot*, was born when Anthony "Tony" Lago assumed control of *Sunbeam-Talbot-Darracq* in 1935. Lago's creations are best remembered for their svelte style, and soldiered on through 1959 when Simca took ownership.

Frazer-Nash was another sporting special, created by Archibald Frazer-Nash. There was no relation to Kaiser-Frazer, nor Nash-Kelvinator. Produced from 1922 to 1960, the Frazer-Nash utilized Meadows, Anzani and BMW engines, and is noted for its chain-drive transmission. Frazer Nash appears to have been a bit lax, though, on the strict and consistent use of the hyphen.

William Lyons' Swallow Sidecar Company, and later Swallow Sidecar & Coachbuilding Company, produced various *Standard-Swallow* and *Austin-Swallow* models depending upon the powertrain source. The British car became known as the S.S. for short, but as a result of simmering hostilities across Europe, the name ultimately became Jaguar. Like Frazer-Nash, its products were promoted both with and without the hyphen.

Arnolt-Bristol was an Anglo-American affair. Stanley Harold "Wacky" Arnolt was an American importer, distributor and dealer in Chicago who commissioned Bertone of Italy to build custom-bodied M.G.s during the early 1950s. When chassis supply became difficult, he turned to Britain's Bristol and produced a series of potent Bertone-bodied sports cars from 1953 to 1964. Similarly, the *Gordon-Keeble* was a high-grade GT during the 1960s, from England's John Gordon and Jim Keeble.

After ending an unhappy relationship with Citroën in 1949, Charles Deutsch and René Bonnet created the French *Deutsch-Bonnet*. Produced from 1952 to 1962, they were raced extensively and were marketed in harmony with Panhard.

Finally, the *Dual-Ghia* was produced by Eugene Casaroll's Dual Motors in Detroit beginning in 1955. It was bodied by Ghia of Italy, relied on Chrysler powertrains and was a favorite among celebrities such as Frank Sinatra and Desi Arnaz.

So there's a little look at some of the more memorable co-joined cars that all enjoyed the prestige and persona of a hyphenated name. No doubt, there were more. They all distinguished themselves by the de rigueur of the delicate dash, and will forever be united by the bond that fused their founders and foundations together.

Initial Impression

May/June 2010

Recently I wrote a two-part column called the "The Halo Around the Hyphen," addressing the many historic marques that were distinguished by a hyphen in the name of the vehicle that went to market. The column received good response, so I started thinking about other forms of designations that were used to set automobiles apart back in the day. It turns out that a smaller, though also unique, subset relied on the company head or founder's initials to create a brand or marque.

What I find interesting about this elite group is that initials were often employed in response to specific restrictions or conflicts of interest that arose from the individual founder's previous automotive endeavors. Unfortunately, none of them ever seemed to achieve the status of their earlier exploits.

No doubt, the most identifiable initial automobile was REO. Ransom Eli Olds enjoyed his first success with the Olds Gasoline Engine Works, before the Olds Motor Vehicle Company was formed in 1897. Because he was such a proven performer in the Michigan business community, Olds really didn't need to invest personally in the new company to get it going. That luxury belonged to the wealthy Samuel Smith lumber family, among others, who bought into what they considered a safe bet, if not a sure thing. Olds would regret it later.

Their future was secured with the arrival of the Curved Dash in 1901, which went on to become an early automotive icon. It was the first car to be produced in serious quantity in America. But even with all the success the single cylinder Model R (as it was cataloged) Olds enjoyed, the Smiths had other intentions. To them, achievement was measured in luxury and opulence. Since they held the purse strings along with controlling interest in what was now the Olds Motor Works, Ransom had little choice. Disagreeing with their direction, he did what he had to and defiantly walked out in 1904.

A year later, the Reo Motor Car Company was formed. It was supposed to be called the R.E. Olds Motor Car Company, but the Olds Motor Works threatened legal action and contended that such a name would cause market confusion. Using his initials was, therefore, the safe alternative.

Reo produced automobiles through 1936, then concentrated on trucks in various

1913 REO (Ransom E. Olds).

forms and alliances through 1975. Through the course of its history, the name was interchangeably expressed in all capital letters as REO or with just the first letter capitalized.

Indianapolis, Indiana, was home to the Stutz Auto Parts Company, which manufactured a promising rear-axle-mounted transmission. It was designed by Dayton-born Harry Clayton Stutz in 1910 after he left the Marion Motor Car Company.

Being situated in the mecca of motorsport, it's no surprise that Harry C. parlayed his auto parts success from the pit lane to the fast track. A strong showing with a race car he created for the inaugural running of the Indianapolis 500 led to the formation of the Ideal Motor Car Company, which would produce "The Car That Made Good in a Day."

In 1913, the Stutz Auto Parts Company and the Ideal Motor Car Company merged, and the Stutz Motor Car Company was born. Its racy Bearcat actually began production in 1912 under Ideal, and could be delivered with a 60-horsepower four-cylinder or a 70-horsepower variety. The two-passenger speedster would go on to be synonymous with the name Stutz, but a variety of other alternatives were produced as well, including roadsters, coupes and touring cars.

In an attempt to broaden the brand's appeal, the H.C.S. designation was first applied to a 35-horsepower, lower-priced Stutz roadster in 1915. It didn't last long though, and neither did Harry. In an attempt to raise needed capital, the firm went public. In 1916 a Wall Street speculator bought controlling interest in the Stutz Motor Car Company, and by 1919 its founder was gone.

No stranger to competition, Harry C. Stutz quickly regrouped and launched H.C.S. as a stand-alone entity, along with the Stutz Fire Engine Company, back home again in Indianapolis. Production began in 1920, and like the Stutz, the H.C.S. was

1920 H.C.S. (Harry C. Stutz).

fairly expensive and sporty. This time, however, it was something of an assembled car. Engines were outsourced from various suppliers such as Weidely. The Bearcat mystique unfortunately never materialized in Stutz's second effort.

Stutz succeeded in manipulating his former tag line and referred to the H.C.S. as "The Car Born with a Reputation." But he significantly damaged that reputation when he created the H.C.S. Cab Manufacturing Company to succeed the H.C.S. Motor Car Company in 1924. Performance became measured by taxicab fares instead of lap times, and it didn't take long for the meter to run out. By 1927, Harry C. Stutz was out of business. He died three years later.

The scenario that unfolded at Olds was not uncommon in the early days of the auto industry, and management would often forget their roots, ignore the common man and instead target the well-heeled in the interest of maximizing revenue and perceived profit. The Lozier Motor Company, on the other hand (which began producing automobiles in 1905), did exactly the opposite. Lozier initially established itself as a pioneer in premium products, drawing its inspiration from the likes of Mercedes and Panhard. Well known for engineering innovation and manufacturing excellence, the Lozier was originally produced in Plattsburgh, New York. The company routinely demonstrated its competitive superiority in such arenas as the Vanderbilt Cup and the Indianapolis 500.

The cars were so well received that supply could not keep up with demand. The firm relocated to Detroit after being lured by a group of investors who were looking for an offering of their own to challenge Packard. That was in 1910, and by 1912 Henry Abram Lozier was forced out of his own company when stockholders initiated a survival tactic by which Packard itself would later be best remembered. They decided to create a more popularly priced junior series, so Lozier resigned. His former company may have been going down-market, but he wasn't.

In 1916 he responded with the HAL, which was produced in Cleveland in a factory that was leased from the F.B. Stearns Company. Lozier luxury picked up where it had previously left off. Powered exclusively by a V12 engine, the HAL Twelve was a premium, 40-horsepower car on a 135-inch wheelbase. Shortly thereafter, toward the end of 1916, Lozier left the company due to failing health, and by 1918, the HAL Motor Car Company filed for bankruptcy protection. This time, they were both down … and out.

Finley Robinson Porter is well recognized by the over-achieving 34-horsepower T-head Mercer engine he developed for the Trenton, New Jersey, company (which was partially owned by the Brooklyn Bridge–building Roebling family). After four short years with Mercer, an apparent disagreement over its future engineering direction caused Porter to leave Mercer County, where the company was located, and head to Port Jefferson, New York. He established his own automotive venture there on Long Island in 1914.

With his background in the "raceabout" genre, he quickly set out to construct three Knight-engined racers for that year's running of the Indianapolis 500. Unfortunately, they never hit the bricks due to engine issues, and Porter shifted gears in an effort to out-muscle Mercer. A four-cylinder 100-horsepower entry was quickly developed and made available on three chassis: 110-, 130-, and 140-inch wheelbases. The two shorter chassis would lend themselves to raceabouts and runabouts, while the longer version would allow for touring and limousine alternatives. They were simply badged F.R.P., and only a handful were built from 1914 to 1916, after which Porter's plant was taken over to support the war effort.

Production resumed in 1919 in Bridgeport, Connecticut, but by now the car was called Porter. The wheelbase was stretched to 142 inches, and that was the only offering. Sporting pretentions were set aside in favor of attracting coachbuilt clientele, although engine output was simultaneously increased to 125 horsepower to help motivate the massive machine. By 1922 the reality of financial hardship prevailed over the ambition of exquisite engineering, and production ceased.

The Hupp Motor Car Company was formed in 1908 by Robert Craig Hupp in Detroit. Well-versed in America's early automotive industry, Hupp put his previous experience at Oldsmobile, Ford and Regal to good use to pursue the light-duty low-cost segment with a creation of his own, the Hupmobile. He surrounded himself with an experienced team of engineers, salesmen, and manufacturing executives and soon enjoyed significant success with a series of 20-horsepower four-cylinder models with frog-eye head lamps that included a sliding-gear transmission instead of the typical planetary unit.

Unfortunately, his "experienced team" soon got the better of him, and by 1911 Hupp sold his stock and left the company after continually clashing with management and the board. They wanted to build the company conservatively, while he was attempting to expand into adjacent market spaces and envisioned a company along the lines of General Motors.

Remaining true to his belief that light cars were the right cars, he formed a new firm, the Hupp Corporation, for 1912 to produce the R.C.H. The October 14, 1911, issue of *The Automobile Journal* quoted Hupp as stating, "The Hupp Corporation was named for my brother, L.G. Hupp, who was in active charge at the outset."

A court order restricted Hupp in the way in which he could use his name to promote the new venture, and forbade any "attempting to trade illegally upon and benefit from the reputation and standing of the Hupp Motor Car Co." Hupp was even limited in the size of the typeface he could use for his own name in R.C.H. advertising. So he cleverly turned the tables by using his initials and proclaimed in marketing materials that the R.C.H. was "distinct from and having no connection whatsoever with the Hupp Motor Car Company."

Publicized as the first sub–$1,000 car to include self-starting, the R.C.H. was powered by a 22-horsepower four-cylinder engine and the body had "decidedly English lines," according to *The Automobile Journal*. It, too, proved to be an immediate success, and immediately overtaxed the fledgling company. Unable to keep up with the ever-increasing demand for working capital, Hupp was soon on the outside looking in, again.

Throughout its existence, both R.C.H. and R-C-H designations appear to have been utilized. By 1913 R.C.H was in receivership, and by 1915, to avoid bankruptcy, production was stopped and the company refocused on the production of replacement parts. Hupp himself passed away in 1917.

Jay-Eye-See was an automotive entity comprised of initials, but at the same time it was not, because it was really a phonetic spelling. According to Bev Kimes' and Henry Austin Clark's *Standard Catalog of American Cars 1805–1942*, "The designation Jay-Eye-See was initially used for a racing special produced by the J.I. Case (Jerome Increase Case) Threshing Machine Company in 1914." In addition to its farm implements, Case also produced quality cars in Racine, Wisconsin, from 1911 to 1927, after acquiring the local Pierce-Racine concern (no relation to the Buffalo-built Pierce-Arrow). The Jay-Eye-See name was further used in varying degrees from 1923 through 1927 on some of the six-cylinder J.I. Case cars.

The R-O was built in 1911 by Ralph Owen. Since Owen had previously sold his Owen Motor Car Company to Reo, this time it was Ransom E. Olds and company who got nasty and threatened to file suit over Ralph's initial intent. But only a handful of R-O automobiles were ever assembled, so Owen moved on. Ralph and his brother, Raymond, a Reo sales agent coincidentally, would be better remembered for their Owen Magnetic that followed.

Those of you who follow the always entertaining British sportscar scene may have logically assumed that H.R.G. was the brainchild of Henry Ronald Godfrey. In fact, it was … but it wasn't. While he was indeed associated with the founding of the firm in 1936, so were Major E.A. Halford and Guy Robins. Obviously, Godfrey enjoyed an initial advantage that his partners did not. Technically, though, H.R.G. is not initial-named. Production ended in 1956.

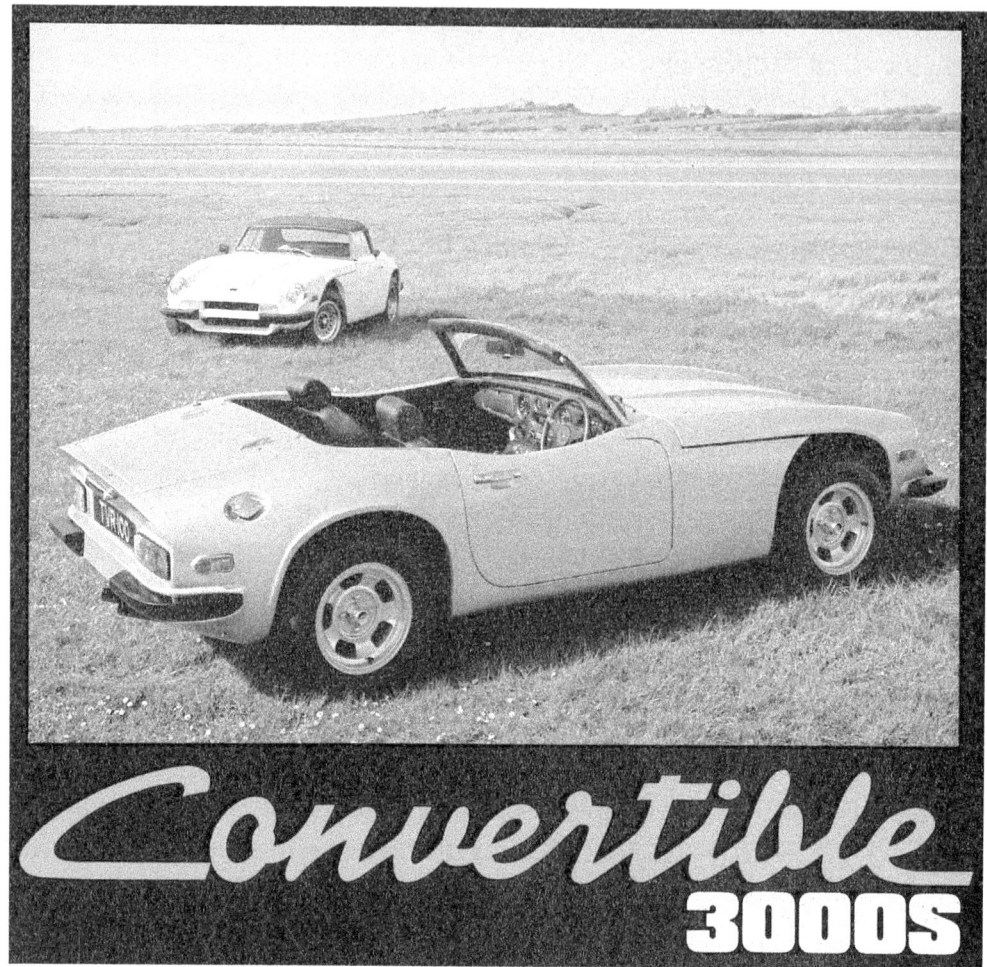

1978 TVR (Trevor Wilkinson).

An even more recognizable true English initial insignia is, and will hopefully remain, TVR. Trevor Wilkinson founded the English sports car company in 1946, and used those letters from his first name to brand it. The first TVR was built in 1947, but series production began with the Mk 1 (Grantura), which made a name for itself starting in 1957.

It included a fiberglass body over a tubular steel backbone chassis combination, which would become a TVR tradition. Numerous engine alternatives were employed during the years from such sources as Coventry Climax, BMC, Ford, Triumph and Rover, while their own AJP8 engine was produced as well.

In 2004, the Blackpool, England–based builder was purchased by questionable Russian interests. Most recently, production proved even more sporadic than it had historically been. In fact, TVR is now at a halt, while dedicated enthusiasts only hope that a British flag forever flies over the now Russian-owned uncertainty.

There were even more obscure examples of automobiles that attempted to immortalize their founder through a few illustrious initials. They spanned the alphabet from Amedee B. Cole's A.B.C. highwheeler that hailed from St. Louis to the W.F.S. built in 1911 and 1912 by W.F. Shetzline in Philadelphia.

Certainly, there were many more initial iterations in between. Within the supplier community, there are similar cases where a company founder relinquished or changed control of his initial enterprise and went on to identify his next venture with his initials. The classic case concerns the famous French bicycle racer, Albert Champion. After his success on two wheels, he emigrated to America seeking fortune. His competitive bicycle spirit soon accelerated to automobile racing, and Champion began assembling spark plugs based on established French principles. Initially a hobby to support friends and fellow competitors, his avocation quickly became his vocation with the help of a group of investors. The Champion Ignition Company was formed in 1908. A year later, after misfiring with his associates, he was on the street. But with backing from the Buick Motor Company, he then started the AC Spark Plug Company.

And J.A.P. engines from John Alfred Prestwich powered many a Morgan, along with numerous motorcycles and speedway bikes. But that's another story, for another time, because we wanted to leave you with just an "initial impression" and not lead you to initial exhaustion…

Good Things Come in Threes

NOVEMBER/DECEMBER 2010

Superstition says that bad things happen in threes. But I prefer to look at the glass as being half full, and try to recognize that it's good things that come in threes.

I was reminded of the ever-present pattern of this perceived natural influence while recently considering the wonderful heritage of the "three P's." For those who may be unaware, the three P's refers to the three grand marques of the early antique automotive era, particularly during the period before World War I, those being **Pierce-Arrow, Packard and Peerless**.

These three prestigious pioneers separated themselves among the elite through a consistent commitment to quality, performance, innovation, refinement, engineering and elegance. Certainly they were not alone, but as a group their reputations have withstood the test of time. The term three P's therefore remains well recognized within the antique automobile community, representing the epitome of automotive excellence from a time when a select few manufacturers could proudly assume a price-be-damned demeanor.

Packard was founded in 1899 and was certainly the most prolific. At the time, James Ward Packard was less than satisfied with his Winton. Offended by Packard's criticism, Alexander Winton challenged him to build a better automobile. So he did.

The company would go on to not only dwarf Winton, but very much outlast it. Surviving the Great Depression, Packard sought to improve its economies of scale by introducing lesser, medium-priced entries: the Light Eight of 1932, followed by the 120 in 1935.

In 1954, continuing the quest to compete via volume and its associated savings, Packard purchased Studebaker. But by 1959, the Packard name was pulled from the Studebaker-Packard portfolio. Soon thereafter, in 1966, Studebaker ceased production.

Pierce-Arrow is best remembered as "America's Finest Car." Produced in Buffalo, New York, from 1901, the company began with the production of household items and bicycles. Such experience ultimately turned into expertise and allowed Pierce to transition to automobiles.

Pierce never bowed to the commercial pressures that pushed Packard to create its "Junior" series, though they did introduce a slightly more affordable Series 80. Failing to respond to the market drove Pierce out of business in 1938. They did, however, go out in style, with the head of their infamous Archer emblem held high.

Peerless was a Cleveland, Ohio, concern that began by producing wringers and bicycles, and moved on to automobiles in 1900. Essentially, they built De Dion-Boutons under license, but Peerless quickly developed its own automobile. They promptly accelerated into racing and are well remembered by their Gordon Bennett "Green Dragon" entry.

Peerless built to exacting standards, and like Packard and Pierce, they were also heavily focused on trucks, perhaps too much so, as production shut down in 1931. They went on to quench their business thirst by brewing beer, beginning in 1936, under the now familiar Carling name.

The postwar domestic industry has long been identified by its Big 3: **Ford, Chrysler and General Motors.**

General Motors dates back to 1908 when William Crapo "Billy" Durant took Buick and began combining it with the likes of Oldsmobile, Cadillac, Elmore, Oakland, Reliance Motor Truck, Rapid Motor Vehicle and others.

All the acquisitions brought with them a good amount of debt, soon causing General Motors (GM) to be reorganized by its bankers and Durant to be forced out. But he would soon be back, bringing Chevrolet into the fold. General Motors ultimately became the General Motors Corporation and would go on to dominate the world's automotive industry. Through all the ups, downs and in-betweens, GM is still most commonly viewed as the combination of Chevrolet, Cadillac, Buick, Oldsmobile, Pontiac and GMC Truck.

Henry Ford founded Ford Motor Company in 1903, in a third attempt (coincidentally) to enter automobile production. His previous Detroit Automobile Company proved unsuccessful, while the remnants of the previous Henry Ford Company went on to become Cadillac—but without him.

Always the innovator, Ford remains best known for putting the world on wheels with the Model T, his "Universal Car." Add to that his Model A, the moving assembly line, $5-a-day pay, battling labor unions, building airplanes and tractors, the flathead V-8, his museum, a never-ending interest in science, materials and engineering, and much, much more.

Chrysler was the result of Walter P. Chrysler's success with Willys-Overland. After acquiring a controlling interest in Maxwell, he founded Chrysler Corporation in 1925. Innovative engineering at an affordable price would become a Chrysler hallmark.

Among the American independents, there was also a three-peat of unique entries that set themselves apart and almost went the distance: **Studebaker, Hudson and Nash.**

The Studebaker brothers began building wagons in South Bend, Indiana, in 1852. They ventured into electric automobiles in 1902 and followed that by producing their first gasoline-powered example in 1904. Studebaker established an early relationship with Garford and then took full control of E-M-F in 1910, which firmly established a foundation that would last for decades. They produced their last car in South Bend in December 1963, and automobile manufacturing finally ceased entirely in Ontario, Canada, in 1966.

The Hudson Motor Car Company was founded in 1909 and was initially funded by Joseph L. Hudson, a Detroit department store magnate. Best remembered by its trendsetting, step-down Hornet with its low center of gravity, Hudson went on to dominate the early NASCAR racing scene with its six-cylinder engine. In January 1954, Hudson was absorbed into Nash-Kelvinator to form American Motors.

Speaking of Nash-Kelvinator, Nash automobiles had been produced since 1916 in Kenosha, Wisconsin. Charles W. Nash, a former General Motors president, acquired the Thomas B. Jeffery Company, which was best known for its Rambler, to create his own corporate namesake that built cars "embodying honest worth."

The Japanese auto industry evolved over time into three primary players: **Toyota, Datsun and Honda**.

Toyota was an outgrowth of Sakichi Toyoda's Automatic Loom Company. They entered the automobile market in 1936, never looked back and are now recognized as a global powerhouse.

What many of us remember as Datsun, now called Nissan, comes from complex beginnings. Jidosha-Seizo Kabushiki-Kaisha (Automobile Manufacturing Co., Ltd.), Tobata Casting Company, the Kwaishinsh Co. and Jitsuyo Jidosha Co., Ltd., all had a hand in what became "Japan Industries" (Nippon Industries), an industrial conglomerate. The Nissan name was first used in the 1930s, while "DAT" dates back to 1914. No wonder the brand has had a bit of an identity crisis.

The Honda heritage, meanwhile, is much clearer because it was simply the outgrowth of the founder's passion and persistence. Soichiro Honda was a racing enthusiast who adapted small, surplus two-stroke engines to motorize bicycles immediately after World War II. By 1947 he was producing his own engine, and then moved on to complete motorcycles, and ultimately automobiles.

The German juggernaut of **Mercedes-Benz, BMW and Volkswagen** went on to define Deutschland's automotive expertise, expression and expansion.

The Mercedes-Benz name first appeared in 1926, after the merger of Daimler-Motoren-Gesellschaft and Benz & Cie, though in fact, Carl Benz is credited with the first patent for an automobile that was built way back in 1885. Coincidentally, Gottlieb Daimler harnessed internal combustion to what's now considered as the first motorcycle during the same year.

BMW, or Bavarian Motor Works (Bayerische Motoren Werke), dates to 1916. The company was rooted in aircraft engine production, but after the Armistice they moved into motorcycle manufacturing in 1923 due to the stipulations of the Versailles Treaty. Their first automobile appeared in 1928, and the rest, as they say, is history.

Volkswagen.

The Volkswagen heritage, or history of the "people's car," is best remembered by its original Beetle. Founded in 1937 by Germany's labor trade union, the Ferdinand Porsche–proposed alternative, among numerous others considered, best satisfied Adolf Hitler's state-sponsored "Volkswagen" initiative. Despite Germany's defeat in World War II, by 1946, 1,000 Beetles a month were being produced. Almost 22 million more would be made.

During the early part of the 20th century, the burgeoning French automotive ancestry sorted itself out among a triumvirate of principals, who still prevail to this day: **Citroën, Peugeot and Renault.**

Always unconventional, Citroën was founded in 1919 and quickly became France's number one seller. While most manufacturers carefully pursued a path of evolution, Andre Citroën—and even more, Michelin Tire, which acquired the brand in the 1930s—created an automotive revolution. And yes, the family name was derived from a pack of lemon peddlers.

Peugeot, very much a pioneer brand, began building automobiles in 1891. Prior to that, they were known for coffee mills and bicycles, and were contemporaries of Daimler, Panhard and Levassor during the dawn of the industry.

Louis Renault sold his first automobile in 1898, and was one of the first to recognize the goodwill and publicity value of racing. Today, Renault has taken over as the biggest car company in France, has enjoyed a successful alliance with Nissan and is still aggressively involved in motorsports.

Even when it comes to Italian exotics, there's truly a triumphant trio: **Ferrari, Maserati and Lamborghini**.

Enzo Ferrari was a recognized road racer who went on to run the Alfa Romeo factory team. In 1947, he produced his first Ferrari road car to essentially fund his Scuderia Ferrari ("Ferrari stable") racing team. The Ferrari name would go on to become synonymous with the term "Italian supercar."

The Maserati brothers were known as tuners for Isotta-Fraschini, and were dedicated to motors and motorsport. They built their first car in 1914, and, coincidentally, built their brand around the distinctive Trident logo that was derived from the Fountain of Neptune in Bologna, Italy.

The Lamborghini legend is somewhat similar to the story that propelled Packard. Ferruccio Lamborghini was an Italian industrialist who became dissatisfied with his Ferrari 250GT and decided to do something about it. He therefore accelerated the Italian exotic category into a more refined grand touring niche with his 12-cylinder autostrasse alternatives.

Even the more mainstream automakers from the land of linguini made their mark as a triad: **Fiat, Alfa Romeo and Lancia**.

Fiat, or Fabbrica Italiana Automobili Torino, was founded in 1899 and quickly established itself as a unique combination of functionality and emotion.

Alfa Romeo was established in 1910 and was an outgrowth of what had been Darracq's Italian enterprise. Nicola Romeo took control of Anonima Lombarda Fabbrica Automobili in 1915, and the Alfa Romeo emblem appeared soon thereafter in 1918.

Vincenzo Lancia was a test driver and racer with Fiat who set out on his own in 1906 to pursue his vision of research and advanced development. Lancia products have always set themselves apart through engineering innovation such as independent suspension, uni-body construction and inventive engines.

Three British sports cars have always defined the category as everyman's entry into the tweed cap community: **Triumph, MG, and Austin-Healey**.

The tried-and-true Triumph was an outgrowth of the famous English bicycle and motorcycle maker that entered those fields in 1885 and 1902, respectively. Automobile production began in 1921 and the company became best known for its torquey TR-series, from 1953 through 1981.

The MG was produced by Morris Garages, a dealer in Oxford, England, as a sporting alternative to the standard saloons (sedans) that were then being produced by Morris. MG began by simply re-bodying the modest Morris in 1924, and has been credited for building its first pure product in 1928. Its familiar badge has been defined as the "sacred octagon" and the brand is best known for its always spirited fun-to-drive quotient.

Austin-Healey was the result of Donald Healey's drive to produce a 100 mph sports car at an affordable price. The brutish Healey was powered by Austin mechanicals and would go on to set the stage for what would become a definitive British sports car. Production began in 1953.

The English elite set itself apart through its own trifecta of upper crust ambassadors: **Rolls-Royce, Bentley and Aston Martin**.

Rolls-Royce began in 1904 when Charles Rolls and Henry Royce pooled their respective marketing and engineering talents to create a car that would forever be recognized by its Spirit of Ecstasy emblem and Parthenon-styled grille shell. Cars graced by the "Flying Lady" continue to demonstrate that "the quality remains long after the price is forgotten."

The Bentley brand began in 1919 when Walter Owen (W.O.) Bentley, who was known for his rotary aircraft engines that powered the Sopwith Camel, came down from the clouds. Bentley quickly established itself by its sporting credentials, while simultaneously providing a rugged and reliable automobile. The company was sold in 1931 to Rolls-Royce.

Aston Martin was the brainchild of Lionel Martin and Robert Bamford. Martin was a regular hill-climb competitor at Aston Hill and produced his first car by combining a Coventry-Simplex engine with an Isotta-Fraschini chassis. Like Bentley, Aston Martin was underfunded throughout much of its history and often struggled to survive, but they, along with Rolls, continue to epitomize the finest of the upscale British automotive experience.

Meanwhile three legendary German automakers, who were not about to eat English dust, created their own upper echelon: **Mercedes-Benz, Maybach and Horch**.

Mercedes-Benz, as previously discussed, has historically covered the market from top to bottom with premium products. Its high-end entries have long been destined for kings and queens, celebrities and stars, and even the Pope.

Maybach was founded in 1909 by Wilhelm Maybach, who was also a Daimler director. The company began by building heavy-duty diesels and gasoline engines for Zeppelins and rail cars, and built its first automobile in 1919. It would go on to be recognized by its opulent limited-production automobiles, but is probably better remembered as an engine builder, since automobile production ceased with World War II. Daimler-Benz purchased the remains of the company in 1960, and recently reintroduced another elite Maybach automotive entry.

Horch was the shining star of the Auto-Union crown. August Horch was previously employed by Carl Benz and built his first car in 1901. By 1907, a six-cylinder engine was introduced and an eight-cylinder followed in series production by the 1920s. Horch set itself apart by introducing art into its advertising in an effort to communicate with the class of its clientele.

Even air-cooled enthusiasts recognize that only three amigos really tackled the thermodynamic dilemma of engine heat dissipation with demonstrated success: **Franklin, VW/Porsche and Chevrolet Corvair**.

Certainly there were many others, but Franklin was the first to enjoy broad acceptance of the air-cooled alternative. Herbert H. Franklin made a fortune in the principle of die casting and funneled it into the development of his own automobile.

1956 Ford Thunderbird.

Relying on the engineering expertise of John Wilkinson, a Cornell graduate, production began in Syracuse, New York, in 1902 and ran through 1934. It's been estimated that Franklin built some 150,000 air-cooled automobiles.

The VW/Porsche answer was a horizontally opposed, air-cooled configuration, and would go on to be the most popular and accepted solution. Millions have been built; even industrial and aircraft applications have been employed.

Chevrolet's air-cooled Corvair was a unique execution, particularly when compared to its other, more mundane Big 3 counterparts. Revolutionary instead of just evolutionary, the Corvair followed in the tire tracks already laid down by VW/Porsche, and utilized a horizontally opposed, six-cylinder engine. Production ran from 1960 to 1969; almost two million were manufactured.

Finally, there were also specific model runs that enjoyed a very special three-year span. The **1955–57 Chevrolet** has been recognized as a major milestone due to its debut of the legendary small-block V-8, also referred to as "The Hot One." These full-size Chevys have become just as much a part of America's social fabric as they have evolved into icons of automotive history.

Likewise, the **1955–57 Thunderbird** enjoyed its own celebrity status as a competitor to the Corvette. The first generation T-bird was positioned as a personal luxury car with an emphasis on comfort and convenience, and seriously outsold the Chevrolet.

A good portion of automotive history evolved around the triple progression. It's no coincidence that when it comes to antique automobiles, *three* is indeed the charm.

Happy 100th

November/December 2011

On November 3, 1911, the Chevrolet Motor Company was incorporated, following in the footsteps of the Little Motor Car Company, which was established just four days earlier on October 30, 1911. It was the seed of an idea that would ultimately blossom into an American institution, and it certainly wouldn't stay small for long.

Chevrolet's history began in the brain of William Crapo "Billy" Durant. Having lost control of General Motors the year before, Durant was on the hunt for a new opportunity. It arrived when the Flint (Michigan) Wagon Works ceased making carriages, due to declining sales as a result of the accelerating acceptance of the automobile.

Well known and established in the Flint business community, Billy bought the plant and its contents. He quickly moved to manufacture horseless carriages in the same space of the buggy that went by the wayside. Durant partnered with his former general manager at Buick, William H. Little, along with Charles M. Begole and William S. Ballenger. Timing being what it was, all eyes were on Henry Ford and his recently introduced Model T, so the Little Motor Car Company's commitment was in the lower-priced, competitive category.

Meanwhile, the Mason Motor Co. preceded both Little and Chevrolet, having been founded by a group of former Buick employees, who also had a connection to Durant, on July 31, 1911. The Mason mission would be to build engines to satisfy Durant's interests, the first being Little.

In the middle of this flurry of activity, Buick race driver Louis Chevrolet was experimenting with advanced car concepts in Detroit based on his former French experience (see sidebar). Durant liked what he saw, and capitalized Chevrolet's venture. More importantly, he liked what he heard: the sound of Chevrolet's name, along with the notoriety it gained after racing all across America.

In typical Durant style, Chevrolet exploded on the early automotive scene as a result of Billy's publicity machine. Although Louis assembled only a few prototypes, Durant was already doing a deal to procure land immediately across the street from Henry Ford's factory. A huge billboard was erected, announcing Chevrolet's imminent arrival, though Durant's birth announcement was a bit premature.

1912 Chevrolet.

Chevrolet spent the remainder of 1911 and 1912 not only experimenting, but perfecting both six- and four-cylinder designs. He was keen on producing a high-quality car that would command a high price, and focused his concentration on the six, a 299 cid twin-cam T-head built by Mason. Durant had other ideas, though, and launched the Little Four in April 1912.

With frustration rising and a dire need to generate positive cash flow, Durant hauled what there was of Chevrolet back to Flint. Durant may have been happy, but Chevrolet certainly wasn't. While Chevrolet and Ford would go on to become fierce and bitter rivals, they would never compete from opposite sides of the same street.

By 1913, Durant's new-found conglomerate of confusion began to settle down. Chevrolet series production was ready to commence in a former Imperial

1911–1914 Chevrolet logo.

Wheel factory that was owned by Buick, though it conveniently ended up in the Flint Wagon Works with Little and Mason.

Behind the privacy of the factory's four walls, there was still a little bit more Durant deception to follow. What was more than just a little of Little was quickly and quietly amalgamated into Chevrolet. The Little roadster became the Chevrolet Special Little Six. Louis's darling Type C, which would ultimately be called the Classic Six, remained part of the portfolio as a luxury offering—but not for long. Some of this Flint "coincidence" seems to have occurred while Chevrolet happened to be on holiday in France! Headstrong and hot tempered, Louis Chevrolet wasn't fooled, nor would he play the fool. After his return, he stormed out on September 17, 1913.

Durant's 1914 Chevrolet models were introduced in mid-1913, and forever cast the die for the bowtie brand, for this was the year in which the world-renowned Chevrolet trademark first appeared. The logo was supposedly the result of Durant's infatuation with a French wallpaper design he'd seen in a Paris hotel room, or else came from an unrelated newspaper ad that crossed his path while he was vacationing in Hot Springs, Virginia. Or…?

It's also the year that Chevrolet came into its own as a company with such popular H-series four-cylinder models as the Baby Grand tourer and Royal Mail roadster, which both sold for less than $1,000. The alluring model names alone secured their place in automotive infamy.

In 1915, Little production ended. Assembly alternatives now included the newly acquired Maxwell Motor Company plant in Tarrytown, New York. The meteoric rise of Chevrolet from the dusty debris of what was the Flint Wagon Works was a true Cinderella story that allowed Durant to regain control of General Motors. He was just getting started, though. Chevrolet would soon be incorporated into General Motors through an exchange of stock.

By 1916, Cinderella's carriage of choice may have been the $490 Chevrolet 490, designed to compete with the Model T tourer of the same price. The inclusion of a self-starter, automatic Connecticut ignition system instead of a magneto and a sliding-gear transmission ensured that it would enjoy a competitive edge, but the price wouldn't stay that low for long. Always the entrepreneur, Durant publicly positioned the car exactly where he wanted to in the marketplace … and then raised the cost to $550.

Louis Chevrolet, 1878–1941

Born Louis-Joseph Chevrolet on Christmas Day, 1878, this namesake of one of America's greatest brands proved to be a tragic figure in early automotive history. Son of a Swiss clock and watch maker, Chevrolet spent his formative years in France. Such early exposure to precision mechanical devices and their inner workings sparked his natural aptitude and led him, like so many others during the day, into the then-burgeoning bicycle craze.

While working in a French carriage and bicycle shop, his interest in gear sets and other mechanical elements fueled his fascination for racing and bicycle production. He created his own Frontenac two-wheeler, a name which would play a memorable role in his later life.

By 1900 he emigrated to Montreal, but quickly made his way to New York. His mechanical ability allowed him to find work at De Dion-Bouton in Brooklyn and then with Fiat in Manhattan. In addition to priding himself as an excellent mechanic, the burly and mustachioed Chevrolet was also recognized for his racing exploits. He routinely kept himself in fine physical condition, which was a virtual necessity to manhandle the big, brutish machines of the period.

After serving as a Fiat racing mechanic, he soon found himself behind the wheel. By 1905, he was turning lap times below those of Barney Oldfield at New York speed trial events in a 90 hp Fiat. He won his first race shortly thereafter, in Yonkers, N.Y. His reputation, and fate, were sealed.

Ormond Beach speed trials, Vanderbilt Cup races and land speed records would follow aboard entries fielded by Darracq and Matheson, in addition to Fiat. Louis and his brother, Arthur, were then hired by Buick in 1909, and that's when his career went into overdrive.

Buick not only led him to the Indianapolis Motor Speedway, it allowed him to establish a relationship with William C. "Billy" Durant. At the time, Durant was about to lose control of General Motors, while Chevrolet was dabbling in engine experiments that were being funded by Durant.

In an effort to immediately regroup, Durant purchased the plant and property of the Flint Wagon Works and organized the Little Motor Car Company (William H. Little was Durant's General Manager for Buick) to produce it. Durant's objective for Little was to turn it into a Ford competitor. He believed that he could put Chevrolet's experiments to good use, along with Louis's well-known name.

The Chevrolet Motor Company was established in 1911 with Louis Chevrolet serving as a director. Durant integrated Chevrolet into his Little operations in 1913, and by 1915 he discontinued Little production, focusing fully on Chevrolet.

The Chevrolet Motor Company and its profits would ultimately be the lever that Durant would flip to regain control of General Motors. But he would do so without Louis. Unlike Henry Ford and Ransom E. Olds, who battled with investors over their conviction to create inexpensive, lightweight cars for the masses,

Louis Chevrolet during his early racing career (left) and in 1920 (right).

Chevrolet suffered the opposite frustration. Durant pushed him to design and develop lower-priced automobiles, but Louis had no interest in compromising his standards. So he simply sold his stock and resigned.

He returned to his racing roots and was soon back on the track. He created the Frontenac Motor Corporation (named after the bicycle he built back in France) with his brothers, Arthur and Gaston, and became a regular at the Indianapolis 500. He was not allowed to use his own name due to his previous obligations to Durant, but by 1920 he was once again in the winner's circle, this time with his own creation and his brother, Gaston, behind the wheel.

To help pay the bills, Frontenac also produced a line of Model T Ford speed parts. During the late 1920s, Fronty-Fords were barnstorming fairgrounds and local tracks all across the country and regularly winning. Marine and aero engine development was also part of the Chevrolet Bros. Mfg. Co. portfolio, as were a few bankruptcies along the way.

Like so many others, Chevrolet saw the Great Depression wipe out what was left of his winnings. Meanwhile, Chevrolet had become a household name and there were millions of cars and trucks on the roads across America and around the world bearing his melodic, Swiss surname. By 1934, however, Louis was reduced to working as a line mechanic in a Chevrolet factory, and he was forced to retire in 1938 due to illness.

Louis Chevrolet died in Detroit at age 62 on June 6, 1941, due to complications from surgery, supposedly, to amputate a leg. Only a small stone marks his unassuming grave at the Holy Cross and Saint Joseph Cemetery in Indianapolis.

In an effort to recognize his long-overlooked and forgotten career of achievement, the Indianapolis Motor Speedway Hall of Fame Museum erected a memorial in his honor in 1975. It bears the inscription "Never Give Up."

But Cinderella must have really been waiting for the Series D, which appeared in late 1917 as a 90-degree three-main bearing overhead valve V-8. Hopefully, she didn't blink and miss her ride to the ball, though, because fewer than 3,000 were produced through the next year or so. It was the answer to the question no one ever asked, because by now Chevrolet was well established as a mass-market brand with sales volume on the order of 150,000, as opposed to a luxury contender.

The 1920s were an unsettled time in Chevrolet history. The hostilities of World War I may have ceased, but not those in the competitive marketplace. The economy was suffering, as were new car sales.

After a stock slide from $400 per share to $12, Durant was done for a second time at General Motors. Perhaps he spent too much time focusing on yet another far-flung idea, the development of the Samson tractor. Pierre DuPont took over, and would soon bring in Alfred P. Sloan. Chevrolet sales had dropped to under 100,000 units per year, while Ford exceeded 1,000,000 annually.

Nineteen twenty-three was a year that would be forever remembered—and best forgotten—at Chevrolet. Although that's when Sloan arrived at GM, it also saw the debut of the air-cooled "Copper Cooled" Series C. With copper fins bonded to cast iron cylinders, the differential of thermal expansion across the two materials ensured that the fins would dislodge from the cylinders over time. As if that weren't enough,

The Chevrolet Brothers, Louis, Gaston and Arthur, entered two cars in the 1916 Indy 500, one driven by Arthur and the other, shown here, driven by Louis.

the overhead valvetrain defied any air cooling advantage because the airflow went from the bottom of the crankcase up to the top of the head, which meant it was preheated by the time it got there!

Back in the boardroom, William S. Knudsen had been brought on board to accelerate manufacturing efficiency. He was the right man for the job, having previously served as Henry Ford's production manager, and would lead Chevrolet into its second decade of success. Before long, production figures were in the 300,000 range.

By now Sloan had already begun to theorize on General Motors' mission in the market. In addition to establishing regimented financial controls, he concluded that GM should offer a car for every purse and purpose. Chevrolet's role would be to give "more for the dollar than Ford."

An early example of that effort began in the 1920s when an expanded Chevrolet color palette, beyond just black, was offered. But even more recognized was the arrival of the delicately designed Capitol Series AA in 1927, "the Most Beautiful Chevrolet Ever." Almost 700,000 were produced.

Even crafty and cantankerous Henry Ford got caught off guard by Chevrolet's next move. While he was busy retooling for the 1928 Model A, Chevrolet was already planning its response: a six-cylinder engine for the price of a four. The 1929 Chevrolet included what became known as "the Cast Iron Wonder." Annual production now exceeded one million, and Chevrolet was now truly gaining ground.

The well-deserved market response to the lovely Capitol Series and six-cylinder International Series that followed convinced Chevrolet that styling would be its next product "differentiator." So while Ford was racing to respond to the six with a V-8 in 1932, Chevrolet was incorporating chrome hood vents, trumpet horns and bright design cues derived from more upscale models within the GM portfolio. Unfortunately, due to the Depression, the general sentiment at the time didn't lend itself to such visual celebration.

Chevrolet would soldier on, though, and play tit-for-tat with Ford forevermore, including up until today. Like salt and pepper, or ketchup and mustard, the two would be forever linked as a long-standing business barometer for the automotive industry.

Knee-action suspension was introduced in 1934, and the one-piece, Fisher Body "Turret Top" arrived in 1935, the result of improved metal drawing and stamping techniques. Aerodynamic elements began to be included in 1936 in the form of V-windshields and smoother, softer styling. Hydraulic brakes were specified a year later, along with an upgraded six-cylinder engine. By now, Chevrolet sales eclipsed Ford's in the popular car category. Its 1937 "Diamond Crown" family design was svelte and streamlined, and incorporated safety glass all around.

The approach of World War II would have a somber effect on Chevrolet. A new "Royal Clipper" look was initiated in 1940, with its now traditional "alligator-opening" hood. It created a more upscale and refined appearance. A longer and lower impression was incorporated in 1941, and by 1942, Chevrolet was cautiously conservative with a more integrated approach (such as fender caps back into the doors). Before long, manufacturing would be redirected to support the war effort.

Production resumed for 1946 with warmed-over 1942 models to simply satisfy insatiable demand. When true postwar offerings finally arrived for 1949, they would set a new styling standard in the popular priced category. By now, Chevrolet evolved into one of the bookends that would ultimately anchor and bracket General Motors' leading position in the marketplace. Cadillac was on the other end, with the remainder of the brands in between.

The big news just after the war did not concern cars; instead it arrived in an advanced array of Chevrolet trucks, which were put into production in mid–1947. Again, cleaner and crisper styling was the order of the day and the "Advance Design Series" did not disappoint. They were so successful that they would be retained through mid–1955. From now on, light trucks would enjoy an even more prominent place in Chevrolet model hierarchy.

The 1949 Chevrolet automobile that followed proved to be an efficient and appealing package. Chevrolet could do no wrong. In the words of *Mechanix Illustrated's* Tom McCahill, "it's not dazzling…. America's number one family car is functional, reasonably tough and as utilitarian as a spittoon. With proper care, it will last about the lifetime of a horse." Fourteen variations were offered, including 2-door sedans, 4-doors, wagons and convertibles.

A 2-door hardtop joined the mix in 1950, along with the Powerglide automatic transmission and hydraulic valve lifters. The standard 216 cid six engine was upped to 235 cubic inches when mated to the Powerglide.

The 1950s would go on to be a defining decade for the bowtie brand. The first shot over the bow was the two-passenger Corvette, which joined the fleet in 1953. At first, it was nothing more than a flicker in Chevrolet's automotive arsenal. Powered by a Blue Flame six, the fiberglass sports car was first built in Flint, but production soon moved to St. Louis after the first 300.

The Corvette is also incredibly significant because it's the first real example of Chevrolet's diversifying into an adjacent automotive market space. Generally speaking, by now economies finally forced most mass manufacturers to build one basic car (in various body styles and maybe wheelbases, with perhaps an engine choice or two). It set the stage for not only platform diversification, but staggering model proliferation that would evolve into an industry norm.

A second series of sedans, convertibles and wagons also appeared in 1953 as the successors to the first postwar passenger cars in 1949. As in the Corvette, the Blue Flame six resided beneath the hood, featuring aluminum pistons.

Nineteen fifty-five was a pivotal year for Chevrolet. Not only was the full-sized sedan series redesigned, but the now legendary small-block V-8 was introduced, Chevy's first V-8 since the unfortunate 1917–1919 experience. The 265 cid engine benefited from then cutting-edge thin-wall casting technology, which made it light yet strong. It was 41 pounds lighter than the Chevrolet six, even though it was 30 cubic inches larger and delivered almost 40 horsepower more. The rocker arms were stamped, and pivoted on ball sockets.

The 1955–57 series of full-sized Chevrolets is often referred to as "The Hot One" in the hobby. The Corvette, too, enjoyed an upgrade in 1956. With all due thanks to Eric Clapton, and in the words of former Chevrolet General Manager, Jim Perkins, "nobody ever wrote a song about a '57 Ford." It's no wonder that everyone wanted to "See the U.S.A. in a Chevrolet."

The rest of the 1950s and early 1960s were a dizzying delight of versatile

1954 Corvette.

Chevrolet design direction and engineering innovation. The 1958 Chevrolet was yet another triumphant tour de force and an all-new extreme. A 283 cid Ram-Jet fuel-injected V-8 option was carried over from 1957, while a 348 cid big-block entered the fray. The El Camino arrived in 1959, then disappeared (for a while) after 1960.

Chevrolet transitioned into the decade ahead with a longer and wider example of its full-sized family sedan with an attitude that was all about fins, but also with a new air-cooled compact car called Corvair. In an effort to counter the then-burgeoning wave of European imports, the rear-engined flat six was Chevrolet's answer to the four-cylinder Volkswagen Beetle and Renault Dauphine. Unlike its competitors, the Corvair was specifically designed for the U.S. operating environment and its extremes. So it was well suited to the vast American highways and byways. Certainly, it was controversial when compared to its play-it-safe domestic rivals, the Ford Falcon and Plymouth Valiant. History has shown, however, that the Corvair's ultimate undoing was clearly the case of too much technology, too soon—despite what Ralph Nader had to say.

Chevrolet's quick response to consumer uncertainty was the Chevy II in 1962. Likewise, the full-sized sedans were updated. By now, the market was starting to fracture into still smaller and smaller segments to satisfy each and every interest, as competition and demand escalated.

Inspired by the XP concept car(s), the Corvette Sting Ray rose to the surface in 1963. The mid-sized Chevy Chevelle followed in 1964, along with an El Camino variant.

During the mid–1960s, Chevrolet matured even more. Crisp edges made way for more elegant European-inspired executions. The Corvair was totally revamped in 1965, while the full-sized sedans enjoyed a more flowing expression of design detail. In response to the Ford Mustang, the Camaro arrived in 1967.

Chevrolet couldn't have been better prepared for what happened next. Amid an ever-changing automotive industry landscape in Detroit, horsepower wars erupted and there sat the bowtie brigade with readily available high-output V-8 alternatives and an abundance of body styles in which to stuff them. The Chevrolet Super Sport, or "SS" series, would take center stage and settle right within the ranks of the muscle car uprising. It was a glorious time all up and down Woodward Avenue, but it wouldn't last long.

By now, the Chevy small-block V-8 engine architecture had proliferated from 265 cubic-inches to 283, to 327, to 302, and would eventually go on to 350, 307, 400 and 305 derivatives. And in the land of wide open spaces where bigger is always better, the original 348 cid big-block would be enlarged into a fine 409 and 427. A second big-block series arrived with the 396, which would later expand into a 427, a 454 and more.

In 1968, Chevrolet ushered in its next-generation Corvette. In 1969, it unfortunately said "so long" to the controversial Corvair. At the end of the day, offerings with such unique powertrains as the air-cooled, horizontally opposed six-cylinder could never qualify as a profitable business case amid ever-increasing corporate governance. The more mundane Monte Carlo personal luxury coupe was launched in 1970.

By now, America was under even more pressure than just fiscal constraint. The postwar baby boom led to a population explosion. In addition to 2.3 children, two cars in every driveway began to severely tax the U.S. infrastructure and environment, not to mention causing a gas crisis or two.

Emerging regulatory requirements forced automakers to immediately shift gears and redirect their engineering effort from increased horsepower to reduced emissions. Chevrolet, having carved out a specialty as an industry performance leader, had to rapidly reinvent itself. And if that weren't enough, ever-increasing safety requirements added yet another complication to the already emasculated American automobile.

Chevrolet launched an interesting early offensive with the Vega in 1971. Well received on its introduction, it failed to live up to its rising star recognition since quality and reliability problems required numerous recalls and redesigns. At least it was a worthwhile effort to create an innovative entry into a new segment. Other initiatives at the time were certainly not as compelling—such as the 1976 Chevette, or the downsizing of the American family sedan. In Chevy's case, that meant that its full-sized 122-inch wheelbase diminished to 116 inches in 1977. The Malibu intermediates were a foot shorter overall in 1978, too.

Then came the Citation, Chevrolet's first front-wheel drive offering. It also enjoyed a successful launch—so much so that *Motor Trend* named it "Car of the Year" in 1980. It was a huge undertaking, requiring all-new manufacturing methods and design/development techniques. Unfortunately, chasing so much change in such short order caused the "X-Body" to also suffer from numerous quality concerns. Merriam-Webster's definition, "a formal statement of achievement," may have been misplaced on the Chevrolet Citation. Shrunken sedans and contracted coupes of dodgy build quality proved to be a compromise that many Americans just weren't willing to make, and the great exodus to imports really accelerated.

The Cavalier J-body subcompact appeared in 1981 as a 1982 model, while the

2011 Corvette ZR1.

X-body led to the bigger badge-engineered front-wheel-drive A-body—the Celebrity, for 1982—that Chevy shared with Buick (the Century), Oldsmobile (the Cutlass Ciera) and Pontiac (the 6000).

Keeping on with the compact collaboration, the diminutive S-10 light truck series landed in 1982. If that weren't enough to demonstrate where the industry was headed, Chevrolet partnered with Isuzu in 1985 on the Spectrum and with Toyota to create the Freemont, California–built Nova. At least an all-new Corvette found its way to the showroom floor for the 1984 model year.

Coincidentally, this is just about where we draw the line on our 25-year-old antique automobile interest and affection. During the 25-plus years that followed, Chevrolet would enter the most tumultuous time in its history. Unparalleled competitive pressure, extensive overcapacity, an implosion of available credit, labor unrest and much, much more would all contribute to its, and General Motors', near demise.

As you know, the bowtie brand survives to this day. A new lease on life has given Chevrolet renewed spirit and vigor. If you're proud to be an American, you have to be proud of all that Billy Durant's dream achieved, because the one thing that can never be taken away from Chevrolet is its reputation as an American

Chevrolet collage.

industrial and cultural icon. It was acquired the old-fashioned way, during the past 100 years—it was earned, and well earned, indeed.

So happy birthday, Chevrolet. You've graced us with a century's worth of "more for the dollar," just as Alfred Sloan said you would.

The heart beats on…

The 10 Most Significant Automobiles That Influenced the American Automotive Industry

September/October 2014

Curved Dash Olds

This was the first affordable series-produced car with interchangeable parts, and the Curved Dash provided the opportunity of automobile ownership for the masses. The single-cylinder tiller-steered Oldsmobile was known for its utmost simplicity. It

Curved Dash Oldsmobile.

paved the way for the Model T and proved to be a successful competitor to its nearest market rival at the time, that being the horse.

Ford Model T and Model A

As the first affordable mass-produced car, the Ford Model T literally put America on wheels and its impact on social and industrial history is second to none. Henry's "Tin Lizzie" proved so ubiquitous that it was marketed as "The Universal Car." But the Model T is also essentially inseparable from the Model A Ford, because together they are well recognized as the backbone of the antique automobile movement.

Ford Model T (West Peterson photo).

1912 Cadillac

Recognized as the first production car fitted with an electric starter and integrated electrical system, the 1912 Cadillac provided the solution to what had previously been a precarious starting ritual. Hand-cranking was not only strenuous and potentially dangerous, but it also contributed to the then-limited market appeal and potential of the internal-combustion-engined automobile.

1912 Cadillac.

1922 Essex

In harmony with the self-starter, the arrival of the affordable, enclosed car for the masses catapulted the market acceptance of the automobile from a seasonal

1922 Essex.

alternative to a bona fide year-round proposition. The 1922 Essex is credited with providing this innovation to an anxiously awaiting audience.

1927 LaSalle

Generally cited as the first production car to be truly and consciously "styled," the 1927 LaSalle was the product of General Motors' then-new Art and Colour Section. It was influenced by the Hispano-Suiza and served as a more dynamic, yet still elegant, companion car to Cadillac. It was also the first aggressive attempt to market exterior design as a competitive advantage for mainstream consumption.

1927 LaSalle.

Cord L-29

This was the first series-produced American car with front-wheel-drive that was available in some quantity (5,000). Then the technology effectively migrated back to Europe and overseas where it matured as the drivetrain of choice, with its inherent manufacturing, packaging and efficiency advantages. It has since returned here and become a staple of the American automotive ownership experience.

Cord L-29.

1929 Chevrolet

With its standard six-cylinder engine in response to the four-cylinder 1928 Model A Ford, this was one of the most egregious and calculated early marketing shots-over-the-bow between mainstream competitors. Of course, Henry responded

1929 Chevrolet.

with the world's first mass-produced V-8 engine in 1932, and so began the tit-for-tat Ford-Chevy rivalry that continues to this day.

1949 Cadillac

The arrival of the overhead-valve V-8 in 1949 was yet another milestone that cemented the "great coming" of the Cadillac marque, and set the stage for the General Motors juggernaut that ultimately redefined the luxury car class—so much so that by leveraging its engineering might, marketing strength and purchasing power, GM essentially pushed companies like Packard to insolvency.

1949 Cadillac.

1955 Chevrolet

The small-block Chevrolet V-8 that first appeared in 1955 advanced engine technology to the extent that it's been called "the self-perpetuating marvel of automotive history." With its compact and lightweight design and the use of thin-wall casting techniques, it unlocked a previously unknown combination of performance, reliability and manufacturability. As the darling of the aftermarket, it helped fuel an entire industry of hard-core performance parts and specialty equipment to cast the die that's still followed to this day.

VW Beetle

While recognized for numerous attributes, the Beetle's most significant impact on the American industry led to the creation of the mass-market compact car category. Certainly, small cars had been offered to American consumers numerous times before, but it was the domestic industry's response to the Volkswagen that finally brought success and sustained viability to the compact segment.

The 10 Most Significant Automobiles

1955 Chevrolet.

VW Beetle.

Note: The 1895 Duryea, America's first automobile to be commercially produced, is not included on the list because its significance has already been well recognized by AACA, with the incorporation of its image as the organization's logo.

What the Heck Is a Hotchkiss?

MARCH/APRIL 2015

Of the thousands of automobiles beneath the AACA umbrella, the vast majority deliver power to their wheels by means of a system called Hotchkiss Drive. No doubt you're familiar with it, even if you don't know it by name.

It's the most common configuration for the front-engine, rear-wheel-drive chassis and features an open driveshaft with a pair of basic cross-type universal joints at each end. In addition, the driveshaft includes an internal slip-spline arrangement to allow its length to fluctuate in concert with rear axle deflection. That's because the live-beam rear end is mounted to a pair of inline semi-elliptic leaf springs that also serve to counteract the torque windup of the axle with load applied on acceleration. Torque arms can also be included if coil springs are utilized in place of leaf springs.

Prior to this design, driveshafts were enclosed in structural steel torque tubes and only included one universal joint at the tail of the transmission. The torque tube was rigidly attached to the rear axle/differential assembly and rear end torque thrust was therefore transmitted back up the tube to the transmission and engine mounts.

A simple and strong solution, the arrival of the open driveshaft improved serviceability, absorbed shock loads better, improved ride quality and resulted in more carefully calibrated leaf spring rates. But there's much more to the Hotchkiss story than just its effective, and ultimately universal, driveline arrangement.

The Hotchkiss clan dates back to the mid–1600s and hailed from Connecticut, of all places. Records indicate that Samuel Hotchkiss settled in New Haven in 1641. Almost 200 years later, Benjamin Berkeley Hotchkiss was born in 1826. His father, Asahel Hotchkiss, established a hardware concern in the northwest corner of Connecticut (in Sharon) during 1829.

It wasn't long before Benjamin found himself apprenticed to the hardware enterprise. He also did a stint at the Sharps rifle factory, along with the Colt company, so it's no surprise that he took an early interest in firearms and armaments. His experimentation in cannon ammunition in Connecticut found its way to Mexico, in support of the liberals, which led to small contracts from Japan and America in 1860. As a result, a dedicated manufacturing enterprise was soon established on the eve of the Civil War. Benjamin's timing was impeccable. He made a fortune by

What the Heck Is a Hotchkiss?

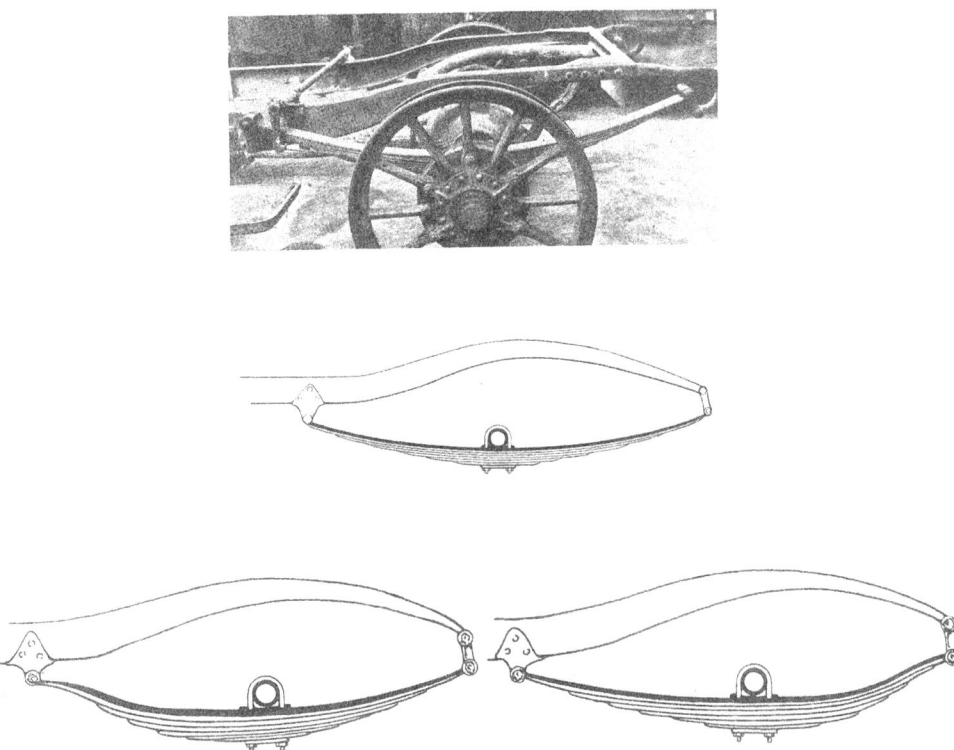

Hotchkiss drive.

supplying more cannon shells to the Union army than all the other manufacturers combined.

America had little interest in further armament development after its bloody Civil War, so Benjamin Hotchkiss took his expertise to Europe, just in time for the Franco-Prussian War. He established Hotchkiss et Cie in 1867 outside Paris in Saint-Denis. A revolving-barrel cannon was quickly developed and became known as the Hotchkiss Gun. A magazine rifle followed, with patent rights sold right back to Winchester in Connecticut.

Hotchkiss had struck gold again and was now recognized as one of the world's leading armament experts. He found time to marry Maria Harrison Bissell, an American heiress and philanthropist whose family descended from Illinois statehouse stock.

But in 1884, Hotchkiss suffered a stroke while in Paris. Maybe he overextended himself a bit, having become a recognized bigamist by marrying a woman from New York in a French ceremony. He died a year later. With an obvious focus on his own self-interest, it seems that he forgot to prepare a will. Following extensive legal haggling, his first legal wife, Maria, assumed a good bulk of his fortune. She took her inheritance and established the private Hotchkiss School in Lakeville, Connecticut, which remains on an incredibly lush 827-acre tract to this day. She also founded the Hotchkiss Library in nearby Sharon in 1893.

Hotchkiss et Cie soldiered on in France. With an established infrastructure for precision machining, they branched out and began manufacturing crankshafts for Panhard et Levassor and De Dion-Bouton. Before long they were building complete engines.

What was described as "an embarrassment of profits" drove the firm to diversify from armaments and explore the idea of manufacturing a complete car. Such a thought was not without precedent. Folks like F.N. in Belgium and Stevens-Duryea in America did likewise, as Saab (Bofors) ultimately did later on in Sweden.

Having procured an early Mercedes for inspiration, Hotchkiss et Cie set out as an automobile producer in 1903. They assumed a cross-cannon brand emblem as a proud badge of recognition for their armament origins. Hotchkiss ambitiously employed ball-bearing technology wherever it could, even in its first T-head four-cylinder offering. By building cars in the Paris area, the first cradle of the world's automotive industry, it's no surprise that they were soon drawn to racing. That's where the idea of the Hotchkiss Drive system originated, in preparation for the 1905 Gordon Bennett Cup, which ultimately proved to be a bitter disappointment for Hotchkiss. Ironically, the system would go on to make its mark in the more mundane application of volume automotive production the world over, for decades and decades that followed.

As so many boutique French producers discovered, the idea of building a handful of quality cars to attract the few wealthy enthusiasts that existed was a recipe for disaster. Quantity, not just quality, was necessary to make a successful go of it. Thus, Hotchkiss soon languished, innovative drivetrain technology aside.

The arrival of World War I pushed the Hotchkiss focus back to armaments. The management of the Hotchkiss automobile activity ultimately ended up in the hands of Harry Ainsworth, an Englishman with early ties to the Saint-Denis firm, who was also the nephew of the company's British sales agent. Ainsworth was desperate to inject vitality into the old cross-cannon company and soon established Hotchkiss et Cie of Coventry (England) as something of a "Hail Mary" expansion tactic. Then he had to figure out what to do with it.

The answer came in the form of an engine manufacturing agreement with Morris cars, along with B.S.A. Long story short, the quality-oriented Hotchkiss concern was ill-prepared to deal with the quantity demands of this leading mass-market manufacturer. A disaster in the making, Hotchkiss-Coventry ultimately became an engine division of Morris Motors, as settlement for financial liabilities incurred due to its failure to deliver.

Back in France, Hotchkiss was preparing a postwar plan with the introduction of an attractive yet conservative one-model range, though still in the upmarket category. And that it did, but the strategy was stillborn. Carryover powertrains were updated with minor lubrication and electric improvements, while coachwork was embellished to attract the landed gentry. By now, Hotchkiss had long abandoned its ball-bearing crankshaft configuration due to cost. The end result was an overweight and underpowered alternative.

Saint-Denis management responded by trying to drop down into the mid-market with a model that was more affordable, the 2.4-liter AM four-cylinder. The engine was also provided to Sizaire-Naudin and Tracta.

A 3-liter overhead-valve AM80 six-cylinder would enter the equation in 1928. By 1935, the engine was expanded to 3½ liters, but as was already so well proven by other specialist marques, Hotchkiss unfortunately didn't enjoy the infrastructure to exploit the opportunity. Even though *The Autocar* magazine concluded that it was a car "that invited one to drive it to the limit," without manufacturing efficiency and economies of scale, the weapon maker's automotive endeavor certainly wasn't exploding on the sales front. In fact, it was on its way to imploding financially.

Fighting for survival, Hotchkiss then tried to go down-market further still with a 2.0-liter, while simultaneously heading the other way with a Monte Carlo Rally–inspired AM80S six-cylinder (where it won in 1932, 1933 and 1934). While all this was going on, the armament side of the enterprise was nationalized under French government control in 1936. Then, Amilcar was absorbed by the Hotchkiss automotive operation in 1937.

By now, Hotchkiss was well recognized for its handsome horseshoe-shaped grille. It replaced the much earlier round radiator and hood, which actually predated Delaunay-Belleville, Spyker and Franklin designs. A joint venture, front-wheel-drive project was also pursued with J.A. (Jean Albert) Gregoire as a result of the Amilcar alliance, but went nowhere. Then another war came and went as well.

1938 Hotchkiss at an auto salon.

World War II was not kind to Hotchkiss. Without the financial wherewithal of the armament operation to prop it up, the automotive firm resorted to dusting off prewar designs yet again. Hydraulic brakes and independent front suspension would not arrive until 1949. Peugeot sniffed around for a possible acquisition and made a small investment, while two more Monte Carlo wins followed in 1949 and 1950.

An "austerity facelift" followed in 1951, according to automotive historian Michael Sedgwick (*Classic Cars in Profile*, Number 47). He went on to define Hotchkiss styling as the combination of "French austerity with near–British conservatism" and concluded that Hotchkiss ultimately set itself apart through the "combination of high performance, superior handling, and durability without recourse to complexity or eccentricity." Another last-ditch effort was the aerodynamic Hotchkiss-Gregoire flat four-cylinder, with just 250 produced.

1949 Hotchkiss.

In 1954, Hotchkiss merged with Delahaye to create Société Hotchkiss-Delahaye. Car production ended in 1955, and the firm never did achieve the stature of Delage or Delahaye alone, particularly within the collector car community. To help stem the tide, an agreement was reached to produce jeeps under license as a result of an H. Ainsworth encounter with Willys-Overland in Canada. Medium-duty trucks were also being manufactured. Production ultimately ceased after 1970, while the firm served as the French sales arm for Leyland truck.

Hotchkiss remains best remembered by what was historically a superior powertrain configuration that's since been superseded by more efficient front-wheel-drive technology. Unless, that is, you're familiar with the fireworks that followed after an

American armament engineer emigrated to France, enjoyed the thrill of victory on battlefields around the world, along with the agony of defeat on the home front due to a degree of personal impropriety—which ultimately fueled a philanthropic family and betrayed widow up in northwest Connecticut to shoot the works with an endowment in perpetuity for elite education!

Ending up as a resident of the Plaza Hotel, Maria Harrison Bissell Hotchkiss died in 1901, in New York. It's well known that "hell hath no fury like a woman scorned," especially one with an armament-fortune inheritance, demonstrating that there's more than one way to transmit power with purpose … via Hotchkiss drive.

1951 Hotchkiss.

Life's a Learning Experience

SEPTEMBER/OCTOBER 2015

I'm pleased to report that my new-found interest in linking automotive history to today's developing technologies and recent model offerings has not only been fascinating, but paying great personal dividends as well. Areas of automotive heritage on which I never would have even cast an eye are now coming into critical focus, and if Shakespeare was correct when he said "knowledge is the wing wherewith we fly to heaven," then I'm certainly soaring high. Here are a few examples why…

The History of Hyundai…

I have to confess I've never paid much attention to Korean cars—like a lot of you, perhaps. But after spending some quality time behind the wheel of a 2015 Hyundai Santa Fe, I now realize how foolish that was, particularly since they've been in this market for almost 30 years and early examples now enjoy antique status, if you can find one.

Although the company was founded as an engineering and construction concern in 1947, Hyundai's automotive roots date back to 1967, when the Hyundai Motor Company was established. Korea's first automaker, they set their sights on the entry level market to fill the void in a country that was completely dependent upon imports.

In 1968, Hyundai entered into a technology-sharing arrangement with Ford, which allowed them to start production of the European Cortina, and later the Taunus, in Korea. Hyundai describes their initial alliance with Ford Motor Company as the place where they "apprenticed."

After the enterprise was up and running, Hyundai immediately had a vision to develop its own offering and hired George Turnbull, a former British Leyland executive, along with a small team of other English-industry veterans. Although that may have helped expedite the creation of their first homegrown car, tapping into then-existing British tribal knowledge may have not been the best strategic maneuver. What followed was the Hyundai Pony in 1975, with underlying architecture somewhat based on the Austin-Morris Marina. Neither one would go down in history for

Hyundai Excel.

superlative quality, but Hyundai's sense of urgency to succeed would soon become the basis for its future behavior.

Export of the Pony to Canada began in 1983, and the car proved to be a somewhat good seller because it was inexpensive. Its poor in-use quality was even tolerated on occasion because it was at least better than the then-available Eastern Bloc price leaders like Yugo.

The Hyundai Excel followed, and the powertrain was revised from the Pony's rear-wheel-drive arrangement to front-wheel drive. After establishing a beachhead in Canada, Hyundai Motor America was established in 1985 and then the Excel entered the U.S. market in 1986. At a mere $4,995, the good news—and bad news—was that 168,882 were sold during that first year.

The car was plagued with a multitude of mechanical concerns, along with poor fit and finish, from the get-go. Hyundai ultimately had to resort to an extended warranty strategy to help woo back buyers and regain trust.

But inroads were established, and a dedicated ethic of continuous improvement soon followed. After bouncing back from its early quality debacle, Hyundai has aggressively accelerated forward ever since. Its first technical center was opened in California, and two parts distribution centers followed in 1988. Hyundai Motor Finance was created in 1989 and ground was broken in Montgomery, Alabama, in 2002 for its first Hyundai Motor manufacturing plant on U.S. soil. Then a 4,300-acre test facility was opened in California, along with a Michigan-based technical center in 2005.

Meanwhile, to address the sales slide as a result of the poor in-use performance of those early Excels, Hyundai began covering scheduled maintenance requirements at no cost to the owner in 1991. In 1994, the Hyundai Protection Plan was created, going beyond the standard warranty. Then came the Hyundai Advantage, with 10-year/100,000-mile powertrain protection, 5-year/60,000-mile bumper-to-bumper coverage and 5-year/unlimited mileage roadside assistance in 1998. It now also includes 7-year unlimited-mileage perforation protection.

In the end, you couldn't even call the Advantage offensive a calculated risk. Since product quality was improving so rapidly, Hyundai transformed public perception from what was a lemon and turned it into lemonade. The Hyundai Advantage evolved into a marketing coup at minimal expense, because the products ultimately proved to be superior in service. For example, the company rose from 19th to 11th in the leading sales and customer satisfaction survey in 1994, which was the highest rate of improvement ever. Everything from J.D. Power quality awards to North American Car of the Year accolades would then follow.

Hyundai's sales are now on the order of 725,000-plus units per year in the U.S, which is well ahead of Volkswagen and Subaru. Since 1986, almost 10 million have made their way to these shores. Hyundai now also owns a 34 percent share of Korea's other car company, Kia.

It's no wonder. The truly premium leather-clad 2015 Santa Fe Limited Ultimate I've been driving runs down the road in all of its active on-demand/all-wheel-drive and gasoline direct-injection glory with a sophisticated level of comfort, convenience and performance that's on par with the best in the business. All of this is achieved at two-thirds the price of its entrenched industry adversaries.

So consider me a late bloomer for just figuring out what many of you already knew, judging by Hyundai's inspired sales success. But having watched from afar for so long, I can now at least offer a fresh perspective. I'm quite confident that the Koreans have the ability, and aspiration, to inflict serious harm to the Japanese auto industry, just as the Japanese did to us. History does repeat itself, even automotive history.

They're well on their way already. With only Hyundai (and to a lesser extent Kia) to their credit, Japan's saving grace is the fact that the Koreans don't have the scale and scope of Toyota, Nissan and Honda, et al. ... at least not yet.

...and Then Along Came Lexus!

Another marque that just achieved antique automobile status is Lexus. Founded as the luxury division of Toyota, the brand began in 1989 and its intended target was specifically the United States. Honda had set the stage for an upmarket offensive from Japan with the formation of its Acura Division in 1986, by exporting a revised edition of what was the Honda Legend sedan along with Civic-related Integra hatchback. Toyota would do better.

After extensive market analysis and consumer research within the luxury segment in America, Toyota began preparing itself to unleash an industry flagship. In harmony with the extensive engineering development that was going on at the time, a

Lexus LS400.

totally new brand and sales network were created simultaneously. Attention to every detail from the beginning was such that even the development of the very name itself, Lexus, was an invention, intended to evoke an image of luxury and technology.

The first Lexus was the LS400 sedan, which arrived in the U.S. for the 1990 model year. The *Orlando Sentinel* on September 6, 1990, summed it up this way: "Toyota makes the best Mercedes-Benz you can buy. It's called the Lexus LS400."

In the same way that Korea's Hyundai sent the Japanese industry into a scramble, Lexus posed a new threat to luxury automakers, particularly Mercedes-Benz. But whereas Hyundai began by plugging a gap in the home market, the mission for Lexus was to establish a new and higher stature for Toyota on the world stage, outside of Japan. In fact, Lexus didn't appear on the island of Japan until 2005.

History records that Lexus began its ascent as a luxury leader by taking the best that Mercedes, BMW and Jaguar had to offer, and using that level of specification not merely as just a benchmark, but the starting point. From there, they relentlessly pursued perfection, as the advertising tag line later claimed.

The rest of the story is well known. Lexus managed to elbow its way into the luxury-car establishment, becoming a competitive force of the highest order. By comparison, the co-conspirators of that Japanese assault on the upscale segment at the time, Acura and Infiniti, never fully found their way. Longer term, those who would suffer the most from all the upheaval would be Cadillac and Lincoln, and when the dust settled there would be a new hierarchy among the luxury leaders.

In the end, the pendulum would swing the other way. Mercedes-Benz clawed its way back and regained its prominence by demonstrating sustained superiority. The gloves came off. Last year, Lexus sold a total of 311,389 new vehicles in America, compared to Mercedes' 330,391.

That certainly doesn't diminish what Lexus achieved in the American marketplace after a mere 25 model years. Unlike the hapless Hyundai Excel example, don't be surprised if you soon see a 1990 Lexus LS on an AACA showfield.

Market Miss, and the Opportunistic Fit That Followed

Once upon a time, there was a car company called Saab. It originated in a far-off place called Trollhättan, Sweden, after World War II, in the interest of motivating the local populace toward four-wheeled mobility. In 1956, Saab established itself in America on Park Avenue in New York. Shortly thereafter in 1961, the U.S. organization pushed its way on up to 100 Waterfront Street, New Haven, Connecticut. People in the Northeast began to take notice, as a result of its go-anywhere Swedish foul-weather heritage.

After tying off along the docks of the Elm City, it would take Saab more than 15 years to finally drop anchor and make a more prominent name for itself on U.S. soil. It rode a turbocharged wave of prosperity beginning in 1978 with the arrival of the 99 Turbo, and the 900 convertible would follow in 1986 to rewrite the rules for up-scale European alternatives with drop-tops. Saab was on an ascent, and industry powers paid attention.

With automotive acquisitions being all the rage at the time, General Motors came knocking and purchased a 50-percent stake in the Swedish automaker during 1989. Shortly thereafter, in what was an absolutely frivolous and foolhardy faux pas, the General opted to knock Saab off of its New England foundation and moved the American operation to Atlanta to create a new U.S. corporate culture in what was, historically, its single biggest market.

Saab would go on to effectively maintain its relative sales pace, but lurking behind the numbers was a dirty little secret. Traditional buyers who were behind the offbeat brand through thick and thin were being displaced. In their wake, GM employees began to arrive and got behind the wheel of the then-available 9-3 and 9-5 models. After years of Chevrolets, Pontiacs and Buicks ad nauseam, they exercised their annual employee lease benefits in favor of the new kid on the block, even though it was a little quirky, and marched to its own drummer.

Before long, Saab's largest selling dealer in America went from being in its traditional northeast hotbed to the greater executive suburbs north of Detroit. Loyalty was replaced by curiosity, and the desire to simply drive something different for a year. Among other challenges, the market would be burdened by an abundance of low-mileage, off-lease vehicles in a territory with a relatively low Saab absorption rate: the Midwest. Residual values tanked, and to add insult to injury, headquarters then moved to the Motor City, after GM assumed full ownership.

Meanwhile, Subaru stuck to its no-frills all-wheel-drive ethic and, together with its ambitious New England distributor, it soon began filling the void that Saab left behind. Before long, the college professor and save-the-whales set was driving flat-four-powered cars that hailed from a company called Fuji Heavy Industries.

Today, Saab is no more. Management and marketing misfires took it down a road less traveled that turned into a dead end. At the close of 2011, bankruptcy was declared. Scooby—or, Subie—owners, on the other hand, remain enamored with their distinctive cars, which led to the company's most recent advertising campaign: "Love … it's what makes a Subaru a Subaru." U.S. sales more than doubled between 2009 and 2013, and the brand has become one of the industry's fastest-growing franchises ever. Subaru is now the darling of New England.

The Saab-Subaru saga will probably go down in automotive history as a textbook case for not only a marketing miss of epic proportions, but for the opportunistic fit that was then seized and capitalized upon in its wake.

Is This the Solution for My Long-standing Motorcycle vs. Car Conundrum?

When I first got involved in the hobby, I was purely a car guy. My focus (no pun intended, read on) was specifically on four wheels, and it ran the gamut from turn-of-the-century antiques to modern-era exotics—and it certainly still does. Somewhere along the line I became infatuated with motorcycles as well.

Since it seemed as if I was participating in a lot of events by myself anyway, I slowly migrated to two wheels. With all of the visceral feel and dynamic lean angles, I found that there was certainly great fun riding motorcycles. There was also a lot to learn because many of the manufacturers, being rebels with a cause, went their own way in devising technical solutions and applying production techniques that translated into unique brand identities and personas that were out there, just ready and waiting to be discovered and enjoyed.

Meanwhile, I found that the spirit and soul that came with motorcycling brought a special degree of camaraderie along with it, too. Yes, you can meet the nicest people on a Honda, and oh, by the way, you can also store six or so motorcycles in the garage space that would normally accommodate just one car. To say I was hooked would be an understatement.

After some 30 years my personal M.O. (modus operandi) ultimately evolved into "when the task revolves around touring, take an antique car, but when the mission is rooted in the intent of burning up the pavement in search of satisfaction and fun, ride a motorcycle." So, to quench my high-speed thirst along twisty two-lane roads, two-wheelers have routinely been my weapon of choice. Lately though, I'm not so sure.

Plant yourself into the purposeful Recaro seat of something like a 2015 Ford

Ford Focus SVT.

Focus ST with EcoBoost and you'll soon learn that the historic performance gap between affordable four-wheelers and exotic hyper-bikes ain't what it used to be. In the case of the Ford, the migration of cutting edge technologies (like turbocharging) down into the mainstream marketplace has transformed what was previously a grocery-getter into an absolute barn burner that's a bargain, to boot. I should know, because I'm on my second SVT Focus, the predecessor to the new ST. Plus, I also happen to have a garage full of motorcycles with which to compare. Let me tell you, the difference between the then-and-now is not only amazing, but astounding.

So, as times goes on, I'm probably going to have to reassess my priorities when it comes time to scratch my frenetic itch, in favor of four wheels in lieu of two.

And Finally, a Lasting Legacy Endures...

Unfortunately, it's not as common as you might imagine. An automotive icon continues and sustains itself despite the drama of an ever-changing industry stage set—the result of long-term economic agitation and social transformation. While there might be market-driven adjustments, model repositioning and costume changes along the way in response to the critics, the DNA never deviates and the bloodline remains pure and uninterrupted.

So it is with Jeep, America's war-spawned workhorse. The show goes on. From the seven-slot grille to its generically-styled rectangular taillights that look like they came off of a utility trailer, to such design cues as exposed hood latches, a folding windshield and solid axles in between, it's obvious that the identity of this industry

Top and above: Jeep, past and present.

immortal has never wavered. Corporate ownership most certainly has, and on more than one occasion(!), while the Jeep brand has controversially proliferated in an effort to conquer a broader array of market segments. Though through it all, the CJ-inspired Wrangler has remained "authentic to the core," maintaining its trail-rated provenance since 1941.

While so many have succumbed to the ultimate and final curtain call, others have tried to return with an encore performance. Even such legendary superstars such as the Thunderbird, Camaro and Continental were diluted, neutered and ultimately put out to pasture after being washed up, only to be rewritten back into the script. And though absence makes the heart grow fonder, the cast is never the same when it attempts a comeback. Once the lineage is broken, awareness and investment erode and the sales gap inevitably leads to lost equity. We'll see how the above referenced epilogues play out. The unfortunate storyline was already outlined for the short-lived Lincoln LS–derived T-Bird, even before its patron pulled out.

Jeep, on the other hand, enjoys the distinction of having weathered the storm. Despite the way Kelly Clarkson sings it, German philosopher Friedrich Nietzsche was right: "That which does not kill us, makes us stronger." Staying the course and remaining true to gut instinct requires courage and commitment, which is a rare commodity in today's research and data-driven world of product planning.

I guess it's just "a Jeep thing," which also includes the sincere appreciation and simple affirmation of a wise purchase decision with each and every wave from fellow four-wheeler aficionados as you cross paths along the highways, byways, and sometimes even when you're sideways.

So depending upon what you choose to drive, these can still be the good old days. You just need to search for those few extraordinary rays of automotive limelight that still burn bright, and go back to the future to find them.

Yeah, but … It's Only a Model T

MAY/JUNE 2017

>No man making a good salary will be unable to own one.—Henry Ford

Walking down an aisle of entries at a local antique car meet, I heard it yet again from a couple of show-goers who were just ahead of me. "Yeah, but … it's only a Model T. Let's move on to the more important stuff."

Excuse me? Obviously, such sentiment demonstrates not only a lack of appreciation and respect, but more critically sheer ignorance when it comes to the Model T Ford and its extraordinary contribution to automotive history.

I'm confident that the vast majority of *Antique Automobile* readers agree, because the Model T (and in addition, the Model A) remains the bedrock on which America's car club foundation was built. Henry Ford's Universal Car has been a staple that's brought a vast majority of enthusiasts into our fold, created enough critical mass to routinely drive shows, meets and tours, swelled swap meet spaces with pieces and parts, filled pages in publications and newsletters, turned neophyte wrench-twisters into accomplished mechanics, stimulated the T-shirt trade, fueled an aftermarket supply chain, generated incomparable camaraderie (the world over) and racked up millions of miles and smiles. For decades. The hobby just wouldn't be the same—or perhaps, even exist—without Ford's flivver.

It all began in 1908 at the corner of Piquette Avenue and Beaubien Street in Detroit, Michigan. That's when the first Model T made its inaugural descent down the elevator at Ford's fledgling three-story Victorian-style Piquette plant. The new arrival was announced in the *Saturday Evening Post* on October 3, as a 1909 model. And so began an unparalleled ascent that put America on wheels.

Fifteen million would ultimately be made by the end of 1927, the vast majority hailing from nearby Highland Park. That Ford factory quickly superseded the Piquette Plant (visit FordPiquetteAvenuePlant.org) in 1910, and was purpose-built around the Model T manufacturing method. Piquette was inspired by New England mill experience, because there was no established standard for an automotive factory when it was conceived in 1904.

Henry Ford amassed his experience from three incorporated (though two

Ford Model T (West Peterson photo).

previously unsuccessful) attempts to establish himself as an auto maker. He surrounded himself with a small cadre of the best and the brightest that he could trust and leveraged the good graces of the 15-horsepower Models N, R and S. They successfully corrected the ill-fated course that was taken with the B, F and K, and led Henry instead toward his crowning achievement. In the early days, over half of the cars on the road would be Model T's. As a result, Ford went on to become the world's first billionaire, though it's possible that John D. Rockefeller can claim that achievement.

Away from prying eyes, the Model T went from mere inspiration to a practical reality in a small "secret room" (said to have been about 12' × 15') in the back corner of Piquette's third floor. It was held under lock and key, and Henry comfortably oversaw design and development from all the reassurance that his mother's old rocking chair could provide. Unlike its immediate predecessors, the Model T would carry four or five early automobilists on a right-sized 100-inch wheelbase, instead of just two or three aboard a small 84-inch span. That's merely the first inkling of the universal appeal that would champion its acceptance as the motorcar for the multitude.

The Tin Lizzie was anything but. It relied upon copious quantities of vanadium steel, which was both light and tough. This high- (tensile) strength alternative was proven in European race car competition, which was then at the cutting edge of automotive innovation. With the deplorable conditions of American roads at the time (if you could even call them roads), it was clear that "light was right" when it came time to navigate the mud-pocked cow paths of the day. That's also why Ford dictated plenty of ground clearance for the gangly T touring from the get-go, along with the landaulet, coupe, town car and roadster that soon followed.

Ford combined the Model T's tall ride height with an incredibly compliant three-point suspension system. The triangular front and rear arrangements included transverse-mounted leaf springs, which allowed the T to articulate up and over the worst of obstructions and simultaneously conquer colossal craters and deep ruts. It was powered by a 20 hp four-cylinder engine that ushered in the breakthrough production efficiency of a block that was cast as a single unit, in mass quantity, with a detachable cylinder head, as opposed to being built with individual cylinders or in pairs, which was common practice at the time. The powertrain was also fully enclosed, which isolated it from the elements and further contained vital lubricant.

The Model T included a purpose-built magneto that was flywheel-mounted, in the interest of simplicity. Current flowed through four individual coils and was distributed by a timer on the front of the engine to each spark plug. It was deemed more reliable and cost-effective than what was then traditionally sourced from an outside supplier. The Model T magneto became the stuff of legend. John Steinbeck surmised in *Cannery Row* that "generations of Americans knew more about the Ford coil than the clitoris, about the planetary system of gears than the solar system of stars."

But the flywheel magneto proved much more significant than just an electrical subsystem, or cultural barometer. Ford targeted magneto manufacturing as the incubator for his experiments with scientific management of the production process.

By dividing and subdividing work tasks into smaller and smaller fragments, and sequentially placing machine tools to allow for progressive production, the moving assembly line was adopted as a Model T method, thereby creating an automotive manufacturing milestone. The technique was previously employed in manufacturing munitions, sewing machine production, and other products.

Henry Ford didn't invent mass production, not even for the automobile. But after the time to assemble a Model T magneto went from 20+ minutes to 13, the principle was deployed throughout the Highland Park complex. From its original announced price of $850 for a touring car down to what would ultimately be $260 for a runabout in 1926, "Model T costs got driven so low that it cost less per pound than a wheelbarrow," according to A.J. Baime in *Go Like Hell*.

When it came to Steinbeck's other observation, Ford chose the planetary transmission because he believed that it would be easier for the great unwashed inexperienced operators—which were the vast majority, back then—to master. He learned that from the very beginning with his first Model A in 1903, and extended the idea up through the N, R and S. "This advantage lies in the longer life of such a transmission—stripped gears impossible—and the smooth velvety action as opposed to the vibratory jerky action of other types, which racks transmission, engine, gears and axles," according to 1909 Ford promotional material.

Production techniques didn't allow for the sliding-gear transmission to be made very precisely, in quantity, or with much cost-effectiveness. With only 20 horsepower on tap, frictional interface for drive proved effective enough, so the hard engagement between gear sets was unnecessary in this application.

The Model T was also responsible for harmonizing the driving position in America to left-hand steering. As traffic density began to increase with the arrival of the Ford flivver, it became more important to gauge the clearance between you and the car coming toward you on the inside, as opposed to worrying about where the rut was along the road on the outside. As Model T sales began to accelerate, left-hand steering became the de facto norm throughout the American automotive industry.

Sales then went into overdrive. More than 50 percent of new cars sold during the Model T's heyday were Fords. According to Upton Sinclair in *The Flivver King* published in 1937, "the rise of Model T mass production was the equivalent of a second Industrial Revolution." Meanwhile, production efficiency continued to rise and Henry Ford was adamant that savings would be plowed back into the business and thus passed on to consumers through lower prices—even if it meant getting sued by stockholders (like the Dodge Brothers), because he held back dividends to spark his plan for the $5-a-Day work wage. While that's another story in itself, the result helped fuel the creation of an American middle class. In fact, the Model T's impact on our society and culture is immeasurable.

"A new era dawned in which the gulf between the idle rich and the common man would cease to yawn so widely. Ultimately the former would virtually disappear, and the latter would take for granted a way of life previously reserved for a privileged class. The Model T played two roles in this changing pattern of life: It provided the common man with his first and biggest symbol of freedom and power, and it accelerated a new development of the industrial system that diffused wealth in a manner that made the new order possible," according to Frank Donovan in *Wheels for a Nation,* published in 1965. Yes, Henry Ford "democratized" the affordable automobile with the arrival of the Model T. Nowadays, we'd call it a game-changer or market disrupter ... think Microsoft, Amazon, et al.

Obviously, the Model T provided more than just basic transportation. It rewrote the rules by putting its best wheel forward. It became the farmer's friend as a workhorse, particularly when a PTO (power take-off) was employed to drive things like pumps and saws. Crops were ferried to market in it, and the T also took the family to town on Sunday outings. Instead of waiting for the local doctor to come by and make his rounds, the Model T allowed for more immediate medical attention by taking the patient right to the source of treatment.

The vast multitude of Fords helped pave the way into new reaches of unknown America, such as south Florida and the westward expansion. Many a dustbowl migrant went in search of a better life behind the wheel of a Model T. John Steinbeck wrote about that, too, in *The Grapes of Wrath.* The province of roadside America would soon follow, as did suburbia. The Tin Lizzie and Tin Can Tourist would prove inseparable.

Meanwhile, the celebrated U.S. Postal Service creed could have just as easily been written around the Model T. "Neither snow nor rain nor heat nor gloom of night stays these couriers from the swift completion of their appointed rounds." Of course, the Model T unshackled what was then a parochial existence. It was a lightning rod for a newfound appreciation of the outdoors and the personal freedom to head for the hills, in the interest of simple relaxation and enjoyment. It also allowed young courting couples to while away the hours in escape of parental scrutiny. In doing so, it certainly helped make the world a kinder and friendlier place.

While it might not be readily apparent, the Model T also set the standard for what is now a common consciousness of continuous improvement at the same time industry pioneer Ransom E. Olds unfortunately advertised his 1912 Reo as follows: "It embodies the best I know. It marks the limit, I think, in motor car engineering. It is My Farewell Car." Unfortunately, Olds thought wrong. There was plenty of upside ahead, and he went on to suffer the consequences. The casual observer might believe otherwise, but Ford updated the flivver incessantly, sometimes in minute detail, throughout its entire life. Why? To provide a better product at lower cost, of course.

Due to the consistent basic design throughout its 19-model-year lifespan, the Model T also proved simple to service, particularly because replacement parts simply fit. No filing or grinding required, which was pretty much the norm back then. Having existed for so long as such a basic car, the T then became the blank canvas for inventors and tinkerers who tried to improve upon the Ford's foibles and performance. Thus, a meaningful aftermarket industry was established around it, and the

Model T advertisement showing a 1926 roadster.

Model T jump-started the careers of many a motorsports competitor. It's well known what the Chevrolet brothers accomplished with their Frontenac hop-up business, but few are aware that America's first Formula 1 champion, Phil Hill, cut his teeth on America's favorite fixer-upper. He learned to power-slide his 40-dollar Model T at age 12 around the horse track on the William Randolph Hearst estate.

The routine control of component parts is another Ford legend. "Tiny trickles of parts flowed into small streams of components that flowed into rivers of larger and larger components, which in turn flowed into the main estuary of final assembly," according to Stephen Meyer, in *The Five Dollar Day: Labor Management and Social Control in the Ford Motor Company,* published in 1981. This is why Henry Ford fought so hard to vertically integrate his supply chain domain.

One of every six businesses in America would go on to be linked to the production, distribution, service and use of the automobile, and one-seventh of wage-earners' employment would be dependent upon it as well. Considering that the car also became the largest consumer of plate glass (70 percent) and rubber (60 percent), not to mention more than 20 percent of steel production, it's no surprise that Ford set such a parts-sourcing precedent. Just think about the economic impact attributable to the Model T all across America!

Some of the more modern manufacturing processes that have been credited to the Japanese automotive industry were, in fact, derived from the Model T experience. The Toyota production system relies on "just-in-time delivery," which is a carefully choreographed flow of components from factories and suppliers directly to the production line. It reduces accumulation of inventory throughout the supply chain. The fact is, that too was a Ford innovation that was deployed during Model T production.

According to Henry Ford from *Today and Tomorrow,* published in 1926, "The extension of our business since 1921 has been very great, yet in a way all this great expansion has been paid for out of money that, under our old methods, would have lain in piles of iron, steel, coal, or in finished automobiles stored in warehouses. We do not own or use a single warehouse. Our finished inventory is all in transit. So is most of our raw material inventory. The average shipping time between the factory and the branches is 6.16 days, which means that there is an average of a little more than six days supply of parts in transit. This is called float." It turns out that one man's "float" is another's just-in-time delivery.

Unlike any other car, the Model T was the subject of numerous books of jokes. As opposed to being antagonistic and just plain critical, in fact the majority were a testament of admiration, because so many were heartfelt testimonials, if not, endorsements, of its idiosyncrasies. E.B. White looked back and fondly reminisced in his "Farewell to Model T" published in *The New Yorker* in 1936: "There was never a moment when the [planetary transmission] bands were not faintly egging the machine on. In this respect it was like a horse ... if the emergency brake hadn't been pulled all the way back, the car advanced on you the instant the first explosion occurred and you would hold it back by leaning your weight against it. I can still feel my old Ford nuzzling me at the curb, as though looking for an apple in my pocket." Despite the chuckles, it was all free advertising.

And finally, on the eve of the arrival of the Model T, Ford's St. Louis branch established what historian David L. Lewis asserts in *Ford Country*, published in 1987, is the first single-marque car club. In mid–1908, that city's 300 "Fordists" were invited

Model T touring for $295.

to a nearby resort, "where a club was organized, membership and tourist committees appointed, and an identifying radiator emblem selected."

Henry (and Edsel, of course) went on to make a "lady out of Lizzie" with the arrival of the Model A, as Walter O'Keefe's lighthearted song lyrics (in "Henry's Made a Lady Out of Lizzie"; New York: De Sylva, Brown and Henderson) touted in 1928. The ubiquitous Model T was put out to pasture, and Ford Motor Company accelerated ahead with bigger and better things to come, toward future fortune as a global, industrial powerhouse, and into the annals of automotive history.

Yeah, but…

A Pullman for the People

May–June 2018

A journal entry from an early railroad traveler by the name of Samuel Breck describes what it was like to travel en masse in 1835: "This morning [July 22] at nine o'clock I took passage on a railroad from Boston for Providence. Five or six cars were attached to the locomotive, and uglier boxes I do not wish to travel in. They were made to stow away some thirty human beings, who sit cheek by jowel as best they can. Two poor fellows who were not much in the habit of making their toilet, squeezed me into a corner, while the hot sun drew from their garments a villainous compound of smells made up of salt fish, tar and molasses." Breck concluded that "The rich and the poor, the educated and the ignorant, the polite and the vulgar, all herd together in this modern improvement in traveling…."

As train travel gained popularity, public demand dictated improvement from what Mr. Breck experienced on his excursion out of Boston, because in addition to the incessant irritation of uneven track, there was suffocating smoke, stuffy dirt and dust, oppressive heat, bitter chill and soot thrown in for good measure. And new challenges arose with the arrival of extended and overnight service.

Early sleeper cars were little more than the typical day coach with bunks and mattresses scattered about, with a shared wash basin at one end. Candles provided light, and wood- or coal-burning stove boxes generated warmth. Obviously, it was a makeshift solution at best, and it was advisable to bring your own linens, because there were none.

Then along came George Mortimer Pullman. Born in Brockton, New York, in 1831, he was a cabinet maker who often rode the rails in search of a broader market opportunity than his sleepy little upstate New York Great Lakes community could provide. This quest for clients and contracts exposed Pullman to the vagaries of overnight travel, and all the hardships that went along with it.

His life journey took him to Chicago, and in 1858, Pullman got the chance to remodel a pair of coaches for the Chicago & Alton Railroad and turn them into sleepers. Innovative convertible upper berths were included, which could be closed and stowed out of the way during the daytime. The public embraced these cars immediately, and thus a Pullman dynasty was born.

As time went on, the Pullman coaches not only became more luxurious and elaborate, but exorbitantly expensive as well, to quench the thirst for ever-increasing creature comfort. According to railroad historian Joseph Husband in his book *The Story of the Pullman Car* (1917), "George M. Pullman not only evolved a type of railroad car luxurious and beautiful in design and embracing in its construction patents of great originality and ingenuity, but, in addition, evolved the rudimentary conception of a system by which passengers might be carried to any destination in cars of uniform construction, equipped for day or night travel…."

But such "private varnish" opulence was only within reach of a rarified few presidents and tycoons. In words from Smithsonian.com, "one name was synonymous with comfortable train travel: Pullman." Fast forward some 100 years and the lessons learned upon the iron rails would be barreling their way out along the interstate to yet another flagship of the fleet, which would instead provide an experience that was accessible to all, in keeping with our creed of American democracy and equality.

After the arrival of the internal combustion engine, the mechanization of America accelerated exponentially. The country quickly went to free-roaming wheels with the newfound freedom to traverse this great land … wherever, and whenever. Gone was the restriction of going only where the railroad track was laid.

Thus, the bus became the prime mover of choice to transport groups of people throughout cities and urban environments along with longer-distance routes. Traditionally utilitarian by design, buses would become more refined as road quality improved.

The arrival of postwar prosperity prompted a war-weary middle class to search for enjoyment and entertainment in oh so many ways. The freedom of the open road called as folks looked to get their kicks along Route 66. Simultaneously, they were now also mobile enough to seek out new opportunities for a better life across the country. A burgeoning roadside America was the result of unprecedented pent-up yearning for socioeconomic expansion, which fueled the interstate highway system.

As a transportation service provider, Greyhound Lines was in the right place at the right time. Founded in 1914 as an intercity bus company first serving the rural communities of Hibbing and Alice, Minnesota, Greyhound went on to challenge the railroad by taking a broader nationwide approach across a farther-reaching network of local destination points over a continually improving road system that was publicly funded with widespread acceptance and generous political support.

That's not to say that bus lines weren't challenged by the convenience of personal transportation. More and more consumers were realizing the American dream of "a chicken in every pot, and a car in every garage," so bus companies had to aggressively market themselves to compete.

A great deal of time, effort and money was put into promotion, to inform consumers that bus travel was safe, reliable, flexible, comfortable, clean and courteous. According to Margaret Walsh of the Economic History Association,

> The bus industry adopted a fresh approach to consumer relations in the late 1950s and the 1960s. The Greyhound Corporation led the way. Its new advertising agency, Grey Advertising, developed a novel and long-lasting campaign using a real dog, "Lady Greyhound," rather than the traditional silhouette in bus publicity. The corporation was able to portray "Lady Greyhound" as a caring and sharing personality as she gave press and radio "interviews," opened bus stations, civic events and charity functions and replied to the members of her fan club. The implications were that Greyhound and the bus industry were equally concerned about "people." More dramatic was the contemporary 1960s campaign to attract the young, foreign visitors, those who did not drive and the poorer groups in society. "Go Greyhound and Leave the Driving to Us" and the offer of up to 99 days bus travel for $99 were attractive proposals. By now the bus industry was differentiating among its clients.

But Greyhound was preparing to distance itself even further from the competition—be it automobile, air, rail or other bus lines—by not only raising the bar, but by raising the roof. *Literally!*

The domed observation car had long been a staple within the railroad industry. Essentially an iteration of the parlor car with a panoramic view, "Skytops," as they were sometimes called, allowed operators to upcharge passengers for the privilege of riding in them, because they were routinely mixed in among standard passenger cars. These special streamliners were considered "the finishing touch to the perfect train" because of the exclusive enjoyment they offered. Sightseeing would never be the same.

At the time, existing bus architecture was comparatively straightforward. The driver sat up front at the controls, the engine was out back and passengers climbed up onto a high floor, which allowed luggage to be carried below. GM's Truck & Coach Division was the industry's dominant supplier and served as Greyhound's exclusive provider. Just after the War, GM was commissioned to develop a new form of "Highway Traveler," as the project was dubbed, which would accommodate more riders and thus generate greater revenue, but legal implications over anti-trust concerns would force General Motors to turn the effort over to Greyhound.

So the bus line contracted Raymond Loewy to complete what would become the GX-1 (the first Greyhound Experimental) prototype. As you might be aware, Loewy had a hand in various Studebaker designs, the famous Coca-Cola bottle, Lucky Strike cigarette packaging, ongoing railroad engine enhancements, and more. Essentially a single-box double-decker design, the GX-1 looked like a rolling loaf of Wonder Bread and carried 50 passengers … 37 up above, and 13 on the main level. The norm at the time had been 35-ish.

Providing adequate power for the new "Compartment Coach," as Greyhound referred to it, proved problematic. According to Paul Niedermeyer's informative Scenicruiser history from Curbside Classic (curbsideclassic.com), twin six-cylinder engines from Aircooled Motors (formed by Franklin Automobile Co. employees who purchased the company's engine assets in 1937) were specified. They'd function in tandem on long grades, and revert to single engine operation over flat terrain. It was an idea that proved to be too far ahead of its time, due to primitive 1947–era control capability, and the GX-1 was too tall for existing service bays, which would obviously run counter to the business plan.

Greyhound wouldn't be denied. In a commitment to continuous improvement, they went back to the drawing board with Loewy. The now-familiar aerodynamic split-level design with its dramatic and dynamic observation deck was the result. The futuristic tri-axle (two in the rear), lower-profile prototype appeared in 1948, and was designated GX-2. Like the first Pullman, it was built in Chicago.

Now free of previous U.S. legal wrangling, GM rejoined the project and brought forth a proposed solution to the driveline shortcoming, a pair of Detroit Diesel 4–71 four-cylinder engines synchronized through fluid couplings that relied on a common gear train. Configured as a complete power pack, the entire drivetrain could be easily removed as a unit for quick service and minimal downtime. In fact, the cargo bays under the passenger compartment were designed to hold replacement engines when needed in remote locations.

Produced in series from 1954 to 1956 as the Scenicruiser, 1,001 were ultimately built. Greyhound was justifiably proud of its compelling semi-monocoque (unibody) 40-foot creation that made "every highway a strip of velvet" for 33 passengers who sat up high, and 10 more on the first level. The Raymond Loewy industrial design influence extended into the interior as well, including stairwell improvements, a fully integrated bathroom, and materials with bright yellow and white patterns (instead of the more mundane earth-tone fabrics of the day) that would minimize visible staining and spotting.

The streamlined aluminum-clad deck-and-a-half Scenicruiser was billed as "the most beautiful and luxurious motor coach ever built." With its raised panoramic observation window roof, sumptuous air suspension, complete washroom facility, reclining "body-contoured easy chairs" and air-conditioning, Greyhound offered an exclusive experience that couldn't be beat. In addition, unlike the railroad industry, customers didn't have to pay extra to enjoy it. Thus, the distinctive and ever-memorable American icon was born.

Original television footage from the fabulous fifties confirmed that the ride was as "smooth as a feather, and as comfortable as floating on air." It was also reported that the Scenicruiser delivered a "year-round, all-weather dependable way to travel in comfort, plus." Clearly, poor old Mr. Breck, as referenced earlier, could never have dreamed about sightseeing from Boston to Providence in such splendor.

The exquisite 1954 Scenicruiser featured here was restored by Pfahl's Mack & Antique Truck Restoration in Bethlehem, Connecticut. This bus, number 5465, first traveled on the New York-to-Miami run. Eventually it was pressed into service along every stretch of east-to-west route that Greyhound operated. It ultimately ended up in Oklahoma, where it was operated by an independent line. But its journey didn't end there.

It finally made its way to Pennsylvania. After a few false starts, restoration

Top and above: 1954 Scenicruiser. GM built 1,001 for Greyhound in series from 1954 to 1956.

attempts stalled. In the process, unfortunately, it was dismantled and stripped to such an extent that it became an almost unrecognizable shell of a Scenicruiser.

As is often the case within the hobby, an extremely dedicated enthusiast with the ways and means came to the rescue. The current owner and caretaker, John Webb, Jr., of Fishkill, New York, enjoyed many a fond memory of being aboard a Scenicruiser as a child, and after a successful business career decided to not only plow his passion into the neglected Greyhound, but get behind the wheel as well. That's when Matt Pfahl and company were commissioned to reincarnate the dilapidated Scenicruiser.

Seven years and 25,000 hours later, 5465 was brought back to its former king-of-the-road magnificence. Along the way there was a 3-year wait for 46 pieces of custom-made glass. Extensive 40-foot sections of wiring loom were required to tie the electrical subsystems together from stem to stern, along with 15 gallons of paint to embellish the outside and 10 gallons to coat the inside ... not to mention 45,000 rivets to piece the entire puzzle back together! Extensive aluminum straightening, stretching, fluffing and buffing was involved, too. Obviously not for the faint of heart, the scale and scope of the restoration, along with its incalculable intricacies, was immense.

Like so many Scenicruisers, 5465 was re-powered with a single 8V71 V-8 diesel engine, along with a 4-speed manual transmission. The conversion was done by Marmon-Herrington in 1961 and 1962 to all Scenicruisers still in operation

Initially powered by a pair of Detroit Diesel 4–71 four-cylinder engines synchronized through fluid couplings that relied on a common gear train, Scenicruisers had their engines replaced in 1961 and 1962 by Marmon-Herrington, who equipped the buses with a single 8V71 V-8 diesel engine, along with a 4-speed manual transmission.

(roughly 980). The twin 4-cylinder diesels that were originally specified proved just about as ineffectual as the GX-2 prototype's pair of air-cooled sixes. As a result, an extremely serious falling out occurred between Greyhound and GM. If that were not enough, the original air-conditioning was, in fact, unfortunately anemic in the face of the raised roof's greenhouse effect. Thus, numerous overhead skylights were routinely painted white, and the openable panoramic windows (which were glare resistant) were fixed shut.

The restored Scenicruiser made its debut at the 2017 AACA Eastern Fall Meet in Hershey, Pennsylvania, where it received a First Junior award. It appeared in Greyhound's period yellow-stripe livery and was met with a never-ending throng of showfield onlookers, who stood in line to capture a peek inside. It then secured an AACA national award (the Bus Award, for "most outstanding bus") at the 2018 Annual Meeting in Philadelphia, that followed.

Back to the Scenicruiser story itself: Beyond 5465, other such Greyhounds would go on to become the tour bus of choice for celebrities like Hoyt Axton, Arlo Guthrie, James Brown and Kool and the Gang after the last one was removed from service in 1975. The Rev. Billy Graham relied on one as well, according to *Greyhound Scenicruiser* by Tom McNally and Fred Rayman.

The bus's cult following further extended into Hollywood film, when one made a cameo appearance in Alfred Hitchcock's *North by Northwest*, after dropping Cary Grant off in the middle of nowhere. The Greyhound hallmark was also featured in *The Rat Race*, which starred Tony Curtis and Debbie Reynolds, while Groucho

A view from the aisle toward the front.

Left and right: Greyhound flashing neon sign.

Marx and Steve Allen appeared in period TV commercials to promote the savings and affordability of "going Greyhound."

To this day, in addition to buses themselves, enthusiasts remain in hot pursuit of Scenicruiser collectibles. Everything from scale models and battery-operated tin toys to period manuals, schedules, postcards and luggage tags are fair game. For the trivially astute, the bus's panoramic proportions most likely inspired the raised skylights on the 1964–72 Oldsmobile Vista Cruiser station wagon and the 1964–69 Buick Sport Wagon.

According to BluehoundsAndRedhounds.info, a one-stop source for Greyhound history, the Scenicruiser remains the most "remarkable and recognizable highway coach of all time." Together with General Motors and Raymond Loewy, Greyhound used innovation in the same way that George Pullman did to set itself apart and make a meaningful difference in the history of mass transit. Obviously, their contribution went beyond the well-heeled to instead provide a Pullman for the people.

"Making every mile," in the words of Greyhound, "a magnificent mile." For every one, and all…

Been Thinkin' About Lincoln

July/August 2018

American automotive history is littered with brand names and model designations. Some have withstood the test of time and prospered. Others are best left forgotten. The care and feeding of brand identities is a marketing science in itself, that the *Ward's AutoWorld* trade magazine describes as "a consistent focus on the value, integrity, positioning and image of the brand. The goal is to manage these four variables to maximize both sales and profitability."

When it comes to brand management, you would think that Lincoln would be as consistent and as stable as the Rock of Gibraltar. Unfortunately, though, Ford's luxury purveyor of upscale automobiles has performed like a roller coaster through a combination of sales triumph and marketing surrender ... while simultaneously struggling through the ups and downs of mother company compassion followed by periods of parental neglect.

In a sense, the Lincoln story began on February 16, 1843, the date on which Henry Martyn Leland was born. A Vermont native, Leland displayed an early aptitude for mechanics and, at the age of 14, began cutting wooden wheel spokes in Worcester, Massachusetts. The works where he was employed also manufactured looms, and it wasn't long before young Henry became an apprentice machinist. That lead to an assignment at the Springfield Armory where Leland began turning out gun stocks.

It would be Leland's first foray into the art of engineering intricacies and the science of manufacturing precision. He took to it like a duck to water. By 1865, Leland found himself at Colt's Mfg. Co. in Hartford, Connecticut. It was there that he was first exposed to the ideas of assembly lines and interchangeable parts.

Along the way he married Ellen Rhoda Hull and fathered three children: Martha Gertrude, Wilfred Chester, and Miriam Edith. With such new-found responsibility and obligation, Leland looked to better himself, and by 1872 (the year Miriam Edith was born), assumed a more far-reaching role with Brown & Sharpe in Rhode Island. It was there that he started to contemplate the advancement of manufacturing methods and management theory.

It wouldn't take long before Brown & Sharpe sent Leland out into the field as a manufacturing representative and troubleshooter. He was soon visiting clients and prospects throughout a territory that extended from Pittsburgh to St. Louis, and now had the skill and experience to achieve his life goal—to establish his own enterprise. In 1890, he settled in Detroit. The city's open-mindedness, thriving nature, financial wherewithal and pleasant waterside existence were all attractions that drew Leland to what was rapidly becoming a Midwest manufacturing mecca.

The firm Leland, Faulconer & Norton was established that same year. Robert Faulconer, a Michigan lumber baron from Alpena, was the primary financial backer. Charles Norton was a former colleague from Leland's Brown & Sharpe days who ventured west. The pioneer machine shop specialized in toolmaking, and one of the earliest employees to learn an exacting trade within its four walls was Horace Dodge. It's well known that Horace and his brother John would go on to form a machine company of their own, with lessons learned from Leland.

Norton would go back East in 1894. Now known as Leland & Faulconer, by the turn of the century the company would be recognized as one of Detroit's leading precision shops. Henry Leland's son, Wilfred, was now engaged there as well. At this point the firm set itself apart with the addition of a state-of-the-art foundry, which was based on exacting New England casting and machining principles, standards that just didn't exist in Detroit, or hardly anywhere else, at the time.

Leland also specialized in automatic gear-making machinery that was bought by everyone from Colonel Albert Pope in Hartford, Connecticut, to the Geo. N. Pierce Company in Buffalo, New York. Then, Ransom E. Olds came calling. He was experiencing transmission troubles with his Curved-Dash Model R and turned to Leland & Faulconer for improved gear sets. Careful re-engineering produced gear sets that were not only quieter, but interchangeable as well.

In 1902, the directors of the now defunct Henry Ford Company (Henry's second attempt) approached Leland to appraise the remaining assets in preparation for liquidation. In a twist of fate, the owners decided to reorganize and make another attempt—if Henry Leland would take over and run the establishment. It was the result of the confidence he inspired. Simultaneously, Leland & Faulconer sensed opportunity and proactively developed an improved single-cylinder engine for the Curved-Dash Olds, which Ransom E. rejected. Olds was already selling everything he could produce, so the remains of The Henry Ford Company were combined with the enhanced Olds engine, and the Cadillac Automobile Company was incorporated.

Leland's influence on the fledgling Cadillac concern is well recorded. It was there that he solidified his status as a "Master of Precision," as his memoir by Mrs. Wilfred C. Leland (his son's second wife) and Minnie Dubbs Millbrook is entitled. Cadillac's British distributor took it upon himself to dispel the prevailing opinion in England that American automobiles were of inferior quality. In an age when plenty of filing and grinding of individual parts was employed during most assembly processes, the Royal Automobile Club established a standardized test for manufacturing accuracy. Three identical Cadillacs were entered, disassembled and their parts were then randomly mixed. They were easily reassembled of their components, then driven around

1902 Cadillac prototype.

the Brooklands track for 500 miles, and the "Standard of the World" was established. Cadillac, due to its interchangeability of parts, was awarded the RAC's Dewar Trophy in 1908 for unprecedented manufacturing precision.

More corporate milestones would follow. Cadillac was absorbed into William C. "Billy" Durant's General Motors empire later that year. The price tag was $4.5 million. Battery ignition, the self-starter (which earned Cadillac yet another Dewar Trophy in 1913), V-8 engines and other innovations would follow. Henry and Wilfred Leland were sittin' pretty, and remained active in Cadillac affairs.

The father and son team persevered through Durant's management mischief until 1917. A lack of General Motors interest in support of the World War I effort led the Lelands to part ways with the company. Durant was quoted as saying, "This is not our war and I will not permit any General Motors unit to do work for the government."

Henry and Wilfred went to Washington and ultimately secured a contract to build V-12 Liberty aircraft engines. To do so, the Lincoln Motor Company was created in September 1917. As a young man working in the armory during the Civil War, Henry admired Abraham Lincoln and reached the age of 21 in time to vote for him in the 1864 presidential election. As a lifelong admirer of Lincoln's, Leland named his company to finally convey his heartfelt admiration.

At war's end, the Lelands found themselves with an empty factory. At a time when most men would already be enjoying a well-earned retirement, Henry dove in head first and reentered the automobile business at age 76. The 60-degree fork-and-blade V-8–powered Lincoln Model L debuted in 1920. To give you an idea of what

Leland intended to achieve with Lincoln, his objective was as follows: "…dimensions of certain Lincoln parts are defined by measurements as fine as three-tenths of a thousandth, or about one-tenth the diameter of a human hair. By actual count there are more than 5,000 operations in which the deviation from a mean standard is not permitted to exceed one-thousandth, and more than 300 in which one-half of one-thousandth deviation from a mean standard is the extreme limit of tolerance."

All good intentions, indeed. Unfortunately, to achieve such exacting standards, the Model L launch was plagued by delays in achieving such tolerances in quantity, which resulted in cash flow concerns. The

Top and above: Henry Leland, in a portrait photograph and with a 1906 Cadillac Model H coupe.

company thus went into an immediate financial crisis, particularly since deliveries didn't materialize until September, thereby missing the height of the selling season. Lincoln, and Henry Leland in particular, would pay an unfortunate price for such an insistence on perfection.

Adding to the inability of Lincoln to gain initial market acceptance was its staid styling. With such extreme focus on technical merit, the Model L's aesthetics were an afterthought—so much so that Leland left the Lincoln's styling in the hands of his son-in-law, Angus Woodbridge, whose only qualification was his training as a ladies' hat maker. If that weren't enough, there was a burden of outstanding Liberty engine tax liens against the Lelands.

Henry and Wilfred soon found themselves in the role of fund-raisers, a position at which they were unaccustomed and inexperienced. Salvation could be found in the form of refinancing, but the Lelands were not keen on the idea of relinquishing management control to investors, so the Lincoln Motor Company went into receivership on November 8, 1921.

A lifeline arrived in February 1922. Putting $8 million on the table, Henry Ford assumed ownership of Lincoln. It was a gesture that was believed to be both strategic and magnanimous in nature. By all indications, Henry and Wilfred were to remain with Lincoln and retain management responsibility, but the operating doctrine that the Lelands established was quickly overridden by Ford methodology.

In March, purchasing operations were incorporated into the Ford corporate function. By May, the sales department was moved to Highland Park … and in June, Wilfred Leland was dismissed. Henry Leland then resigned in protest. Ford was now free to imagine the future state of Lincoln, and he assigned much of the responsibility to his son Edsel. It took a while for Ford management to adapt its mind-set from marketers and manufacturers of "The Universal Car" to purveyors of a prestige product.

Much of the early influence to reposition the product portfolio was the result of Edsel's influence. His artistic sensitivity and flair was put to good use, and new body designs were introduced in 1923. Simultaneously, efforts were made to upgrade the dealer body in keeping with the brand's premium pretensions. It was the beginning of the Model L evolution. From 5,626 Lincolns sold in 1922, 8,858 hit the street in 1926. Henry Ford went on to make a lady out of Lizzie with the arrival of the Model A Ford. Many of its design details were derived from Edsel's Lincoln styling direction, so much so that the handsome entry-level auto was sometimes referred to as a "little Lincoln."

The L was succeeded by the Lincoln Model K in 1931. Wheelbase was extended from 136 inches to 145, while the V-8 engine was enhanced with improved carburetion, intake, exhaust, starting and generating systems, and more. A year later, the range was expanded to include a V-12. It was longer, lower and more road worthy than its predecessor, and period press reports concluded that the Model K "is as impressive in performance as it is in appearance…."

1924 Lincoln.

Most critically, the mass market Ford enterprise was vindicated at last from the assumption that it would ultimately besmirch the Leland standard for Lincoln. Instead, Ford clearly enriched the luxury brand's stature. Unfortunately, however, times being what they were in the Depression years, premium Lincoln sales for the remainder of the decade never exceeded the 5,311 that were delivered in 1931, a good deal fewer than in the Model L's heyday.

Red ink ensued. Something had to be done. The answer arrived in 1936, while the Model K was still in production, with the Lincoln-Zephyr. It was intended to be in the mid-market, and with a more attainable price was slotted between the Ford DeLuxe and Lincoln K. It was derived from a Briggs body design exercise created by John Tjaarda, which was "productionized" by yacht designer and Brewster & Company alumnus E.T. "Bob" Gregorie. Originally summoned to Ford to design the European Model Y, he had gone on to become the head of the design department in 1935.

Named for Zephyrus, the Greek god of the west wind, the Zephyr was intended to compete with the likes of the Packard 120 and the LaSalle, albeit with a much more dynamic design. The New York Museum of Modern Art considered it "the first successful streamlined car in America." It included a 75-degree V-12 engine.

In 1938, the wheelbase was extended, the car was enlarged and a fresh new defining face for Lincoln appeared. Zephyr production continued through the shortened 1942 production run, with just over 100,000 produced. It finally brought Lincoln the

1939 Lincoln Zephyr Continental prototype.

success and critical acclaim it so very much deserved. The stage was now set for Ford's luxury arm to up the ante and deliver what would become an automotive milestone.

Among his other assignments, Gregorie would routinely come up with one-off specials for Edsel's personal pleasure. In preparation for the junior Ford's 1938–1939 winter sojourn to Florida, a Lincoln Zephyr was "imagined" as a European-flavored convertible coupe. It was therefore dubbed "Continental," and became the talk of the Palm Beach social circle. As a result of such unsolicited encouragement, Edsel ordered it into production for the 1940 model year.

It became an instant classic and remains so to this day. According to historian Maurice Hendry, "The original Continental filled a gap in the passenger car market by offering a vehicle whose beauty lay primarily in its honesty and simplicity of line … and the Lincoln quickly became a symbol of luxurious elegance." Unfortunately, the years that followed were not all that kind to it.

The early Continental's expressive and aerodynamic design elements soon gave way to a more massive, blocky and ungainly appearance. The car might have appeared bigger, but was it any better? Fans of the original exquisite design think not, but the full line of 1940–1948 Lincoln Continentals were immediately recognized as Classics by the Classic Car Club of America (CCCA), and for many years stood as the only postwar car to have the honor.

In preparation for postwar recovery, Lincoln was busily preparing for its next installment in a story that had thus far read like a soap opera, full of unqualified design and engineering success combined with what was often disappointing market erosion. Fresh, fully enclosed (pontoon) bodywork was employed for the new flagship. The name of the new model very much defined its spirit and demeanor of what was intended to be a citizen of the world, that being the 1949 Cosmopolitan.

Front-opening rear doors were included in the bathtub design brief, as were "Frenched" (recessed) headlights and taillights. Front coil springs and a V-8 engine with an available automatic transmission rounded out the specification. A more rakish Cosmopolitan Capri model was also offered, along with a less expensive Lido. Unfortunately for Lincoln, a good bit of the design language was shared with the lower-priced Mercury. Oops.

A second generation came along for 1952. The redesign was even more conservative and in addition to sharing styling cues with Mercury, it was further based on generic corporate Ford architecture. And it showed. Oops, again. The new model set itself apart, however, dynamically. It was powered by an overhead valve Y-block V-8 engine and *Motor Trend* concluded that "Without a doubt, the most outstanding characteristic of the Lincoln is its handling ability … at top speed and high cruising speeds the Lincoln feels very safe." Thus, the moniker "Hot Rod Lincoln" was born. These latest Lincolns also distinguished themselves in Mobilgas Economy Runs and in places like Pan American Road Races.

It was the arrival of the Continental Mark II in 1956 that reversed Lincoln's design fortunes. As an incredibly exclusive personal luxury car it truly set Lincoln apart, so much so that it was sold through its own Continental Division, further separating it from Ford Motor Company. It debuted at the Paris Auto Show and retailed for a staggering $9,695—the most expensive offering in America.

Some 3,000 were produced through 1957, and it was clearly of world-class caliber, on par with the best and most prestigious alternatives that Europe could offer. The press concluded that "The spirit of modern traditionalism has returned" with the Continental Mark II. But it didn't last long, because it wasn't a money maker. Then, Lincoln would soon lose its way again.

The controversial third-generation Continental and Premiere models were introduced in 1957. Inspired by the Lincoln Futura dream car, they were overweight, overstyled and overembellished, and at the time, the biggest cars ever built by Ford. They were deemed the "slant-eyed monsters" within Ford Design, and the Continental was specified with a Mercury-inspired reverse-slant "Breezeway" roofline. Here's what *Road & Track* had to say about them: "In traffic one soon becomes used to the sheer bulk. We didn't try any exuberant cornering, for obvious reasons.…" What were they thinking? Once again, it was back to the drawing board.

Lincoln rapidly rebounded with the all-new Continental in 1961. After a staggering $60 million loss between 1958 and 1960, it was finally realized that if Lincoln were to succeed, it was going to have to distance itself from Ford and Mercury.

1956–57 Continental Mark II.

Referring back to Maurice Hendry's analysis once more, "Styling of the 1961 Continental was striking in its simplicity. Modern classic was a good description, as was the catalog claim that it was 'low, clean-lined with beauty inherent in its design, avoiding excess ornamentation.' In June 1961, it was awarded the Bronze Medallion of the Industrial Design Institute." Now iconic, front-opening rear doors were once again employed.

This latest and greatest Continental was produced, with significant changes, through 1969 and established another important Lincoln precedent to help drive profitability: a long lifespan with consistent styling and design continuity. All were common considerations in Europe's premier car category, by the way. The end result? Over 330,000 were manufactured.

The 1969 Mark III personal luxury coupe picked up from where the Continental left off as far as market impact is concerned, and created another Lincoln design dynasty. In one form and then another, the two-door extension of the brand portfolio would roll on through 1998.

After that, Lincoln reverted to a manufacturing-driven strategy of platform-sharing—essentially, selling rebadged Ford/Mercury models that were trimmed into Lincolns. Thus, the brand floundered. They even dabbled with a misguided Ford F-150–derived pickup. Not once, but twice!

Most recently, as stated by the company's newest executive management team, Lincoln's market performance has traditionally been "a collection of sprints … followed by, for various reasons, a bit of an energy lapse." But Ford CEO (not a car guy)

Jim Hackett has instilled a new-found "focus for fiscal and operational fitness," with which Lincoln will clearly comply. It's purely business. Emotion is out, as is any loss leader reverence in the interest of heritage, because in Dearborn these days, it's all about dollars and sense.

When it comes to Lincoln's standing in today's competitive marketplace, Hackett and company have confidently concluded that, "We have a long-term strategy now." A wave of new product introductions and mid-cycle refreshments will extend into 2019 and beyond "with more investment than ever." Like a lot of other car companies, Lincoln looks to derive greater revenue from existing sales volumes as opposed to chasing pure sales numbers through discounts, subsidies and other short-term brand-tarnishing tactics by considering "the overall quality of the sale" instead.

One example of such new-found focus is the arrival of the latest Aviator sport utility, which Lincoln recently unveiled at the New York Auto Show. Essentially the size of a Ford Explorer, the Aviator rides on an all-new platform that will no doubt see service beneath the next Explorer, as well. It is reassuring that it debuted with Lincoln.

Just as the recent Lincoln Continental was seemingly inspired by Bentley design language, the new Aviator tends to take a bit of its styling inspiration from Land/Range Rover, which isn't all bad. According to *Automotive News*, the Lincoln Aviator was "the star of the New York Auto Show."

Having just spent some quality time with a 2018 Continental, I can confirm that Lincoln has upped the ante in the premium car category, too. Unlike so many others, including their crosstown competitor, they've avoided becoming yet another Mercedes-Benz/BMW wannabe. Instead, they've delivered their interpretation of what a modern American luxury car should be—right down to its dignified grip-worthy door handles that convey an image of being chiseled out of a chunk of billet. Giving credit where credit is due, the Continental certainly stands out by countering conventional me-too luxury car wisdom. There's even talk about returning to (hold on, wait for it) … front-opening rear doors!

Then there's the most recent Lincoln Navigator. It's literally the flagship of the fleet, particularly with its "Yacht Club" interior accoutrements that include Coastal Blue Venetian leather captain's chairs, micro-perforated comfort-carrier seat cushions with nautically inspired piping and stitching and whitewashed teak detailing. From stem to stern, the new Navigator is the reincarnation of four-wheeled American luxury. Finally!

If you wonder whatever happened to the unparalleled elegance and exquisite opulence of coachbuilt Pierce-Arrows (America's Finest Car) and custom made Packards (Ask the Man Who Owns One)—not to mention the Lincoln KA and KB—look no further than the new Navigator. It's a glorious rebirth of U.S.–made grand luxury and pampered tranquility that's come to fruition before our very eyes, coincidentally even down to its classic seven-passenger seating configuration, active front grille shutters and power-actuated running boards. Internally, the company is committed to an ethic of what they now refer to as "quiet luxury," which is dignified indeed.

Lincoln is struggling to keep up with Navigator demand (the 2018 North American Truck of the Year), though admittedly at some $100,000 per copy, it plays in a thin, rarefied market segment. They only stay on dealer lots for an average of 10 days, so you can be sure that there's not much price negotiation going on. Cadillac has quickly countered with sales incentives on the order of $10,000 per copy of their own, to help buyers embrace its competitive Escalade offering.

Meanwhile, the Navigator's magnificent profit margin contributes rather heavily to Ford Motor Company coffers, which is what the role of the Lincoln brand should be all about, not trying to slug it out with the masses in near-luxury segments as it has been for far too long.

We'll now be watching and rooting as the brand shifts gears and accelerates ahead, ascending back to a grand classic future through the likes of Aviator, Continental and Navigator, and fanatically coddling customers along the way.

Go big or go home—the proof within the premium segment is in the product and the ownership experience, because if it fails to perform in these challenging times, with impatient new Ford management that's long on fiscal responsibility and short on traditional emotion and patience, the final fate of the marque might just be in the question, "So other than that, Mrs. Lincoln, how did you like the play?"

People and Personalities

My 10 Favorite Car Quotes

January/February 2015

There's nothing quite like the proverbial quotation, a succinct, sometimes witty insight that's become a routine part of our art of expression—particularly, for us, when its inspiration is automotive!

Often bolstered by attribution to a well-known and respected source, the quote can crystallize a slice of life into a powerful, yet compact, revelation. Quotes serve to support arguments and move meaningful, motivational messages—so much so that many of them have become a part of our everyday vernacular.

The 10 that follow are merely the ones that reside top of mind … in *my* automotive mind. No doubt, this list could therefore spark a fair degree of discourse since your idea of pithy car quotes may differ vastly. In all fairness, to prepare for the cards, letters and e-mails that might logically follow, let me set the stage with yet another quote: "Opinions are like birthdays, everybody has one."

So without further ado, a David Letterman drum roll, please, for my 10 favorite car quotes:

> "A chicken in every pot, and a car in every garage."
> —Herbert Hoover

Although often attributed to Hoover as a direct quote, this was actually an excerpt from one of his 1929 presidential campaign flyers (an example of which appeared in the October 30, 1928, edition of the *New York World*). It was intended to convey a position of anticipated Republican prosperity, should Hoover get elected, and the party worked hard at moving more like-minded messages at the time such as "Republican efficiency has filled the workingman's dinner pail—and his gas tank, besides." Interestingly enough, both were knocked off from King Henry IV, of 17th-century France. He proclaimed, "I want there to be no peasant in my realm so poor that he will not have a chicken in his pot every Sunday." It must have sounded, if not tasted, just as good in 1928, because the campaign succeeded and drove Hoover to the White House in style. Unfortunately, Wall Street crashed shortly thereafter and he failed to get re-elected in 1932 for the term beginning in 1933.

Herbert Hoover.

"We are the first nation in the history of the world to go to the poor house in an automobile."
—Will Rogers

Best remembered as an American humorist and social commentator, this famous Oklahoman often expressed the views of the common man. He was grounded in traditional morality, family values and the innocence of ordinary life, and remained close to his cowboy-inspired upbringing. Will Rogers (1879–1935) was justifiably proud of the success that the typical American could achieve through hard work, determination and pure grit. In this crisp conclusion, he was simply extolling the virtue of hope during the Depression era by trying to convince his audience that things weren't as bad as they might have seemed.

"Friends don't let friends drive drunk."
—The Ad Council and the U.S. Dept. of Transportation

Intended to create awareness of the seriousness and dangers of operating an automobile while intoxicated, this message was part of a public service announcement launched in 1983 by the above-mentioned authorities. Since the movement began, more than 68 percent of Americans have tried to prevent someone from driving after drinking. Appealing to the conscientiousness of friends, family and loved ones—since it's useless to appeal to the impaired judgment of the one who's already inebriated—this saying remains a powerful deterrent to this day.

"What's good for General Motors is good for the country."
—Charles E. Wilson

In 1953, President Eisenhower nominated General Motors CEO Charles Erwin "Engine Charlie" Wilson (as opposed to Charles Edward "Electric Charlie" Wilson, CEO of General Electric during the same period) to serve as Secretary of Defense. During his confirmation hearings, the public-spirited Wilson was asked if he would be prepared to make difficult decisions, even if they caused negative impact to GM. He responded affirmatively, because he could never imagine such a situation arising. In his words; "I cannot conceive of one, because for years I thought what was good for the country was good for General Motors and vice versa." Unfortunately, this not only became the critically acclaimed misquote that's presented above, but it further fueled then-existing opinions of General Motors' corporate arrogance. Even though a full transcript of the hearing was released a few days later, the quote—again, actually a misquote—just plain stuck. Despite the injustice, Wilson was confirmed by a Senate vote of 77 to 6.

Will Rogers.

"A car for every purse and purpose."
—Alfred P. Sloan

Alfred Sloan is well known as the architect who instilled a sense of business process into the chaos that was created by Billy Durant during the formative years of General Motors. The company having grown too complex and unwieldy to run from Durant's corner office, Sloan introduced a sweeping series of modern management principles in an attempt to tame the beast. GM ultimately went from a behemoth that couldn't get out of its own way to a cutting-edge corporation that grew into an automotive powerhouse. "A car for every purse and purpose" was Sloan's way of defining GM's multi-brand and price-range segmentation strategy. It certainly was in bold contrast to Ford's stark, universal Model T car proposition, a vision which ultimately became outdated as America evolved and matured through the Roaring Twenties. This simple, clever quip, as presented in 1924 to GM shareholders in the annual report, was the foundation of the Sloan strategy that would go on to propel General Motors to a position of industry dominance.

Alfred P. Sloan.

"Any customer can have a car painted any color that he wants, so long as it's black."
—Henry Ford

This line originated in *My Life and Work*, the biography written by Henry Ford in collaboration with Samuel Crowther (first published by Garden City Publishing, 1922). In the chapter entitled "The Secret of Manufacturing and Serving," Ford was outlining his quest to go beyond just bringing the car within reach of any man. His vision was to serve the needs of everyman; thus the demand for minimal variation and fast drying paint was something he had set his sights on early in the Model T evolution, despite internal protests from his sales department. Students of Ford history are well aware that the above quote really only applied to those Model T's built between 1915 (approximately) and 1925. When production began in October 1908 at the Piquette Avenue plant in Detroit (see FordPiquetteAvenuePlant.org), the color palette ranged from red to green to gray as a function of body style. A blue hue was added in 1911. On the other end of the run, Windsor Maroon and Channel Green joined black as color choices for 1926. In 1927, brown and blue were added, along with other shades of maroon and green, not to mention Fawn Grey.

Big car with big engine.

"There's no substitute for cubic inches."—Anonymous

My pal Russ Calamari is the sort of renaissance man who's quite comfortable, and exceedingly capable, talking about almost anything I might care to hear about. Be it cars, boats, engines, outboard motors, motorcycles, guns or airplanes—not to mention local, military or world history—Russ can hold his own with the best of 'em. He says he got smart by listening. So when I told him that I was putting this piece together he immediately shot back with the above, an old adage that's now very much a part of the automotive racing and performance-car lexicon. The same sentiment is sometimes referred to as "There's no replacement for displacement." Either way, it's certainly a self-explanatory automotive expression. Thanks, Russ.

*"Two roads diverged in a wood, and I—
I took the one less traveled by,
And that has made all the difference."
—Robert Frost*

Although not specifically a car quote, this one's pretty personal. The thought of following the road less traveled is something that's been with me throughout my entire automotive existence. It began more than 40 years ago when I was trying to learn anything and everything I could about Triumph sports cars, Volkswagen Beetles, Alfa Romeo sedans and Saabs. Meanwhile, everyone else was enthralled with

Corvettes, big-blocks and pure automotive Americana. Not that there's anything wrong with that, but it's always seemed that my DNA's been wound around engineering elegance as opposed to brute force and bridge-truss–like car construction. It's also an ethic that's routinely taken me off the interstate, in favor of twisty two-lane back roads.

*"Lead, follow,
or get out of the way."*
—Lee Iacocca

Dick Bauer is chief of the Killingworth, Connecticut, Volunteer Fire Company, so he obviously knows a thing or two about mobilizing men and inspiring team spirit. Like Lee, his personal code of conduct is often exemplified by this compelling quote, which is why I wasn't surprised when he reminded me of it. It was part of a 1992 corporate advertising campaign, when Chrysler was desperately trying to communicate that

Robert Frost.

Lee Iacocca.

it had reinvented itself for the better. The complete copy reads; "In the car business, you lead, follow or get out of the way … and Chrysler intends to be a leader." Right out of the chute, however, it seemed that Chrysler chose to follow when it came to the creation of this passage. "Lead, follow or get out of the way" was first attributed to Thomas Paine (1737–1809), an English-born American political activist from the Revolutionary era. Prior to Chrysler's pirating, General George S. Patton took his own liberties with Paine's prose when he said, "We herd sheep, we drive cattle, we lead people. Lead me, follow me or get out of my way."

> *"History is bunk."*
> —Henry Ford

This is another one that's not specifically about automobiles, but since it's been so indelibly linked to Henry Ford, it might as well be. In context, what he actually said was "History is more or less bunk. It's tradition. We don't want tradition. We want to live in the present, and the only history that is worth a tinker's dam is the history we made today." Henry Ford made this observation in an interview with the *Chicago Tribune* on May 25, 1916, to convey a message of how to best live life in the present, as

Henry Ford.

opposed to the past. He thought the way that history was being taught in school, with a focus on medieval kings, Egyptian pyramids and the Roman Empire, neglected the contribution made by ordinary men with common tools. That's why he established the Edison Institute in 1929, which went on to become the Henry Ford Museum & Greenfield Village (now known as The Henry Ford: visit TheHenryFord.org), to preserve and share America's industrial heritage. Obviously, a concerted automotive influence remains there to this day, along with enticing, interpretive examples of the car culture that we all so much enjoy, just like what appears throughout the pages of each and every issue of *Antique Automobile*. No, history is not bunk—particularly when it pertains to antique automobiles!

Enzo Ferrari in Emotion and Feeling

JANUARY/FEBRUARY 2016

Like a lot of you, I've long followed the fortunes of Ferrari from afar. Race reports, show highlights, road test reviews and an occasional sighting here and there have kept me up to speed on the Maranello-based manufacturer of exotic luxury sports cars. My interest and awareness has routinely been rooted in the company and its cars. Particularly after Ferrari's acquisition by Fiat, I never paid much attention to the people behind the products.

Then, I stumbled across Enzo Ferrari's autobiography. Originally published in Italian by Casa Editrice Licinio Cappelli in 1962, its first English edition appeared two years later from The Macmillan Company in New York. Not only does it provide an insightful look into the life and times of Il Commendatore, but from Ferrari's writings I was able to gain an understanding of the spirit, soul and sensitivity of the man behind the prancing horse.

The Enzo Ferrari Story is therefore just as much of a personality profile as it is a career history. It was written after the death of his son, Dino, because in Enzo's words, the "sadness forced reflection." So to give you an idea of what made this guy tick, I thought I'd share an interesting assortment of excerpts that help translate the emotions and feelings that ultimately forged the legend of "Il Grande Vecchio" (the Great Old Man).

- Although his official birth date is February 20, 1898, Ferrari was actually born on the 18th. It took two days for his parents to reach the Modena Hall of Records because of snow.
- His boyhood ambitions were to become an opera singer, sports writer or racing driver, in that order.
- He went to his first car race in 1908 at age 10, and he was intrigued by early safety technology. While everyone else was watching the competitors speed by, he noticed that the ground alongside the most dangerous corner of the circuit was flooded with a foot of water, for a length of 40 yards. He recognized that this not

only helped keep spectators a safe distance away from the spectacle, but provided a deceleration mechanism in the event that a car went off course.

- Enzo took his first job in Turin testing bare truck chassis that were bound for Carrozzeria Italo-Argentina in Milan, where they turned them into torpedo-bodied cars. Ferrari was enthralled by this cultural and business center in northwestern Italy, known as "the cradle of Italian liberty."
- Shortly thereafter, he moved to Milan and joined Costruzioni Meccaniche Nazionali (C.M.N.) as a test driver.
- He got behind the wheel of his first race car, a C.M.N., in 1919 and finished fourth at Parma-Berceto. Later that year, while competing in the Targa Florio, he was stopped mid-race by the Carabinieri and forced to wait until Italian President Vittorio Emanuele Orlando finished a speech before he could proceed.
- In 1920 he joined Alfa Romeo in Milan and began building a performance powerhouse by pilfering the best and the brightest from Turin-based Fiat, including Vittorio Jano. Ferrari felt that the ambiance and rhythm of Turin culture and its people were not only a peculiarity, but a gift that he wanted to harness and transfer into industry. He felt that such spirit did not exist in Milan.
- The prancing horse logo came from Italian ace Francesco Baracca's fighter plane, which was shot down. In 1923, Ferrari met his mother, Countess Paolina Baracca, who urged him to put the emblem on his race cars for good luck.
- Ferrari spoke no English. Besides Italian, he could communicate in French.
- Scuderia Ferrari, the racing team that took over Alfa Romeo racing exploits from the factory, began in 1929 and ran through 1939.

Driving Tipo-B P3 Alfa Romeos, the Scuderia Ferrari team of Achille Varzi, Louis Chiron and Carlo Trossi at the 1934 French Grand Prix. Team Scuderia Ferrari adopted the prancing horse logo from Italian ace flyer Francesco Baracca's fighter plane.

Enzo Ferrari behind the wheel of a 1931 Alfa Romeo.

- Enzo drove in his last race during 1931.
- His personal sentiment toward Alfa Romeo was one as "the adolescent tenderness of first love."
- The first time that Scuderia Ferrari beat the factory Alfa Romeo racing effort, the guilt was such that Enzo exclaimed, "I have killed my mother."
- Since success can indeed breed contempt, Ferrari began to encounter bitter feelings from within Alfa Romeo management. When Wilfredo Ricart was brought in as an additional technical resource, he met with Ferrari, who concluded his handshake was the equivalent of "grasping the cold, lifeless hand of a corpse."
- Ferrari parted ways with Alfa in 1939 and was forbidden to engage in racing or reconstituting Scuderia Ferrari for four years. He found opportunity in machine tools by pirating German grinding equipment designs, and began to produce ball bearings in 1944.
- Auto Avio Costruzioni was founded at the war's end. The Ferrari influence toward 12-cylinder engines came from Packard, even though Enzo felt uncomfortable with the premise of more power than a chassis could capably handle.
- Ferrari certainly demonstrated great respect and compassion for his son, Dino. "When I was worried about something, he would say 'don't let it

Enzo Ferrari in 1952.

get you down, Things always come out all right if you only give them time.' He was young, but he always had the right word ready at the right moment."

- "My son naturally worked in the factory, where he gave the best of himself. His last work was done in the long and snowy winter in which his ailment, a nephritis virus, kept him almost constantly confined to his bed. I and my old friend Jano spent long hours at his bedside. I remember how carefully and with what competence Dino read and discussed all the notes and reports that were brought to him daily from Maranello."

- "I had deluded myself—a father always deludes himself—that we should be able to restore him to health. When Dino died, I simply wrote; 'the race is lost.'"

- "Leaving me his great spiritual inheritance, my son above all taught me that we remain children up to any age, until, tried by some great sorrow, we suddenly learn the meaning of goodness, renunciation, charity and duty." Alfredo "Dino" Ferrari was born in 1932, and died in 1956. Because V-6 engines were one of his passions, the series of road and racing Ferraris that were so specified were named in his honor.

- Ferrari then began to be concerned over the fate of his firm once he was gone. He was very much aware of what became of Bugatti, whom he recognized as "the French artist of eclectic genius, whose unique philosophy died with him."

- Concerning the topic of technology, Ferrari believed that "there is little remaining to be invented in automobile engineering, although there is still much room for improvement." He further recognized, however, that his interest to put something new into each car every morning was "an inclination that terrifies my staff," since it would bring production to a standstill.

- When it came to racing cars, he realized that such a machine does "not come into being as the creation of a superior mind, but is always the compendium of the common, unflagging and enthralling work of a team of men fired by a common enthusiasm."

- His opinion of drivers was that a "bond of understanding, of solidarity, necessarily exists between all racing drivers." He didn't believe that there could be deep friendship "between men whose job obliges them every weekend to pit their skill and courage one against the other and risk their lives in doing so." Rather, he thought they coexisted in an environment of "comradeship."

- On the subject of team talent, Ferrari went on to conclude that "there is a species of psychosis for racing cars that will eventually evolve into habits and create a breed of its own"—a combination of blood, brains and rebellious character that's required to build race cars.

- Ferrari withdrew from active participation himself in motorsports in 1932, when his son Dino was born. But he always had doubts in regard to his capability as a driver, because he knew that "I always drove with consideration for the car, whereas to be successful, one must on occasion, be prepared to ill-treat it."

- Ferrari felt that it was his "bounden duty" to find out why racing accidents

occurred, because he assumed a "heavy responsibility" when he turned over one of his cars to a driver.
- Team orders did not exist during Enzo's era because he recognized that a driver's greatest ambition was/is to catch and overtake his teammate, thereby demonstrating his worth as number one.
- He was also aware, however, that internal rivalry could destroy all the work that the team had done together throughout the season.
- As a patriotic Italian, Ferrari was proud of the fact his race and sports cars provided more than just good publicity for the company; in addition, they brought recognition for the country's engineering prowess.
- When Pirelli pulled out of racing, Ferrari concluded, "when men of one generation leave a company, one often finds that in place of old friends, one is instead faced by a wall of ice, the frosty barrier behind which the big joint-stock companies entrench themselves."
- To defend himself against corporate espionage, Ferrari simply chose to tell the truth. With his reputation of being shrewd and complicated, competitors commonly viewed his remarks with suspicion and quite often went in search of hidden meaning, when there was none.
- He believed that "the ability to compromise can be confessed without any feeling of shame, for when a man is prepared to sacrifice some of his pride to achieve his purpose—a purpose aimed at technical superiority that will ensure supremacy in sport—he can be considered morally justified."
- Even more tellingly, Ferrari said that he was "thin skinned" and that personal insult and attacks "hurt my feelings, immensely."
- In Ferrari's words, not mine: "Cars are female—we always refer to them as she—and like all females they're likely to let you down when you least expect it. In the motor racing world there are enough complications as it is without bringing women into it to create more."
- But meanwhile, he simultaneously confessed, "I think that it's we men who are inferior, if not in intelligence, at least in vitality and hardiness. Women are more astute, more cautious, more practical-minded, and—what is very important—more painstaking in their attention to details." Yes, he was a complicated fellow.
- Ferrari defined his friendship with Pininfarina, the Italian car body builder, as one of complementary interests: "Pininfarina was routinely seeking beautiful women to dress, while I was in search of high-class couturier to dress her."
- Although a lot was written about the historic Ford-Ferrari feud, the latter was very well aware that the former voiced the following opinion: "I wonder whether it is really worthwhile spending so much money on advertising, when Mr. Ferrari gets space free of charge every Monday morning in newspapers all over the world."
- Mercedes was certainly a long-time adversary. Concerning Team Manager Alfred Neubauer, Ferrrai said, "in pace with the growing strength of Mercedes and Germany, Neubauer grew steadily fatter and fatter and became increasingly more

authoritarian and dictatorial. He and Mercedes and Germany seemed to grow as they were one, pound by pound, success after success, mark by mark."

- Ferrari was convinced that racing stimulated technological progress, encouraged the development and application of new materials, revealed hidden dangers to improve safety and provided a good degree of entertainment.
- "I race because I am an enthusiast, whereas others do so as a business. I have, in fact, no interests in life outside racing cars." In his spare time he liked to read.
- As Ferrari looked out toward tomorrow, he concluded, "Today's work conditions the future. It stands as evidence that men pass, but their work remains. And each example of this work, created for the present, is a step on the stairway of the future."
- A final and rather telling closing sentiment: "I feel alone after a life crowded by so many events and almost guilty of having survived. And I feel, too, a certain detachment, for in this arid earth that is myself, the plant of hope can only thrive if watered by a son's love."

Enzo Ferrari died in 1988. His death was made public two days later, to compensate for the delayed registration of his birth, 90 years before.

From Office Machines to Automobiles, Part I

May/June 2016

The trajectory of talent that fueled our favorite industry in its infancy has been well documented. Mechanics, bicycle builders, carriage makers, engineers, impresarios, and—in the words of Beverly Rae Kimes—sometimes even scoundrels all played a part not only in the invention of the automobile, but also in ratcheting it up into a commodity for mass consumption. But there's another group of pioneers that deserve overdue consideration for their contribution—those that came along via the avenue of office machines.

Of course, it makes perfect sense that such pathfinders would play an important part in the development of the American automobile industry. Office machines were mechanical in nature and built with precision. They were produced in quantity and distributed locally through agents and outlets all across the country and around the world. As in many other industries, the overseers of the office machine industry were part of an exclusive club that was all their own. It was a big fraternal business.

Some of these executives are familiar names who have been well recognized within the ribbon of automotive history, but not as individual keystrokes in this vein. So in the interest of bookkeeping accuracy, let's hit the return and tabulate those who were included in the exclusive register that went from office machines into automobiles.

Hugh Chalmers, 1873–1932

There's probably no better place to start our reconciliation than with Hugh Chalmers, who's best remembered by his namesake automobile. Chalmers was a product of National Cash Register (NCR), of Dayton, Ohio, where he was born in 1873. He began there as an office boy at age 14 and rose to the position of general manager in 1900. He was recognized for his expertise in marketing.

NCR was formed in 1884, and by the time Chalmers came along, the company was enjoying a near monopoly. Considered a high-tech concern in its day, its manufacturing muscle flexed over 51 acres of floor space and the firm would ultimately be challenged by Sherman Antitrust claims by the time the second decade of the 1900s arrived. Before that, Hugh had the foresight to move on in 1907, in a time and place where cash was king. As a result of his 20-year tenure, he certainly left as a victor with abundant spoils.

In search of his next conquest, Chalmers came across the struggling Thomas-Detroit enterprise, which had evolved as an offshoot of the Buffalo, New York, E.R. Thomas Motor Company. Roy D. Chapin and Howard E. Coffin were actually running the Michigan manufacturing activity at the time, though Thomas retained sales and marketing control from afar. As industry pioneers, Chapin and Coffin were destined for greater things and found in Chalmers the perfect partner. He was a proven salesman with an interest in investing, but had no intention to meddle in their operational affairs. Chalmers-Detroit was born in 1908, leaving Thomas to focus on his business back in Buffalo after being bought out.

A vintage cash register (West Peterson photo).

Coffin and Chapin proved restless, however, and soon focused their effort on Hudson in 1909, in the interest of developing a lower-priced offering with broader market appeal. Hugh Chalmers was the second largest investor in Hudson (of the 9,000 shares issued, department store magnate Joseph L. Hudson held 1,584 while Chalmers had 1,334). But having already succeeded in industry on a grand scale, Chalmers preferred to concentrate on marketing and sales campaigns for his more expensive Chalmers-Detroit products rather than struggle with a start-up.

Various stock swaps and financial maneuvering ensued, along with some design and patent exchange, and by the time the dust settled, Chapin and Coffin formally parted ways with Chalmers. With cars that have been described as "decently assembled and well-priced," what was now known as Chalmers Motor Company soldiered on. But it would never enjoy the success that Hudson achieved. By 1917, an agreement was reached with Maxwell (the sole survivor of the United States Motor Co.), whose sales were soaring. Chalmers' excess production capacity would be employed by Maxwell, while the latter's dealer body would be utilized to help support lagging Chalmers sales.

Hugh Chalmers.

Maxwell would go on to absorb Chalmers in 1922, and Hugh retired to his palatial 10,000 square-foot Albert Kahn–designed mansion in Detroit's Indian Village enclave. He passed away in 1932.

Harry Ford, 1880–1918

No, not Henry ... Harry. In case you were unaware, Detroit had another early automotive entrepreneur by the name of Ford, though there was no relation between the two. Harry Ford was born in 1880, and originally hailed from Missouri. After a stint with Western Union Telegraph Co., in 1905 he, too, found his way to Ohio and NCR. While Harry was at NCR, he made a positive and memorable impression on Chalmers; when Hugh was later in need of an advertising manager, he sent for Ford.

Harry went to Detroit in 1909. Enamored by the fledgling auto industry, Ford quickly began studying engineering, production and procurement in preparation for

Harry Ford took control of low-priced car manufacturer Saxon.

his next move. Hugh Chalmers would go on to name him assistant general manager in 1913.

Simultaneously, Chalmers had been contemplating the need for an entry-level alternative (having watched Hudson's success from the sidelines) to share the showroom with his more upmarket alternative. Thus, the Saxon Motor Car Co. was created on November 1, 1913, and Harry Ford was named president. Perhaps the Ford name was leveraged to lend it an immediate air of credibility, though in fact, by this point Harry had already established himself as a quite capable and respected automotive authority.

Two years later, Harry bought out Hugh and took control of what was now the Saxon Motor Car Corp. The Saxon enjoyed immediate success as a well-made, cost-effective competitor that had a good look about it as an alternative to the category-killer Ford Model T. But the novelty soon wore off in the quest to mass produce this low-priced car. Saxon was quickly challenged by material supply problems, and then, more critically, by a shortage of capital and, finally, profit.

Harry Ford then grappled with financial control of the firm, went on to serve in the military and became seriously ill by 1917. He died at the end of 1918, and Saxon would cease to exist by 1922.

Ned Jordan, 1882–1958

Yet another alumnus from the halls of National Cash Register emerged from somewhere East of Laramie. Wisconsin native Edward S. "Ned" Jordan was schooled in Madison, and simultaneously served as university correspondent for the *Wisconsin State Journal*. Before long, a series of eloquent editorials began to appear beneath his byline. It was the beginning of a career that would change the way in which words would be romantically entwined to market automobiles through advertising expression.

After graduation, Jordan joined a Chicago-based publication by the name of *Inter Ocean* and then began submitting stories to *Collier's Weekly*. He then moved to Cleveland with the *Cleveland Press,* and after that he was editing the house publication for NCR at double his previous salary. At age 23, Jordan was inspired by NCR's president, John Patterson, who believed that a most effective business principle would always be simple honesty. Jordan then concluded that in keeping with that ethic, there were only four fundamentals of human motivation: love, money, adventure and religion.

In 1907, after a year, Jordan parted ways with NCR and made his way to Kenosha, Wisconsin, home of his wife's family. He joined the Thomas B. Jeffery Co. (producers of the Rambler, which would go on to become the Jeffery) as advertising manager. There, he demonstrated inexhaustible energy, and before long, hungered for still further fulfillment. He would go on to become secretary and general sales manager for Jeffery.

By 1915, Jordan was of the opinion that the industry was maturing toward saturation with manufacturers. Becoming restless as the industry evolved, Ned decided to act before it was too late. He left Jeffery on his own accord on January 13, 1916, to form the Jordan Motor Car Co. His proven sales skills brought immediate investment in an enterprise that would be distinguished by "smart looking cars." And the rest, as they say, is history—automotive advertising history, that is.

Although it was an assembled car, the Jordan was distinguished by the way it was marketed. Jordan knew that quantity would most likely elude him, so he focused on quality and healthy sales margins to help sustain his company. He was careful to appoint fewer dealers with bigger territories, to reduce the chance of their battling one another and discounting his automobile.

In harmony with that innovative approach, once the company was up and running and on solid footing, Jordan began to reposition his cars with alluring and evocative names. Playboy, Sport Marine, Tomboy and Blue Boy were examples of how Jordan tried to separate himself from the rest. To help communicate their virtues, he then began to leverage those impassioned motivators he so very much believed in, particularly love and adventure.

In lieu of simply spouting specifications, he instead capitalized on human emotion in his advertising copy. Exquisite artwork and imagery were combined with flowing and flowering copy. Jordan tugged at heartstrings, with the hope that buyers would then respond by opening their wallets. His "Somewhere West of Laramie" ad from 1923, which featured "a bronco-busting, steer-roping girl" to promote the Playboy, became the stuff of advertising legend.

In my opinion, a later little-seen ad with the headline "In the Middle of the Night" from 1927, which featured a closed sedan on a snowy road with no occupants visible, is even more socially significant, if not powerfully provocative. The copy begins, "After the dance—when tiresome chaperons [sic] have gone to bed—and youth will have its fling—let's wander away." From there, it goes on, "Down the moonlit ribbon of a magic road…" and the suggestive ad was ultimately banned by the New York Society for the Suppression of Vice.

Jordan continued to stretch the advertising envelope, but his company's fate was sealed when it entered into bankruptcy in 1931. Ned Jordan was right, way back in 1915. The market was oversaturated, and the Great Depression would go on to suffocate many of the smaller independents that were already out of breath, including the Jordan Motor Car Company.

In summary, a wonderful period-assessment of attributes that led to Ned Jordan's landmark contribution to, if not the invention of, automotive "image" advertising appeared in *Automotive Giants of America*, by B.C. Forbes and O.D. Foster (published 1926, by B.C. Forbes Publishing Co.). His genius was defined: "Racing side by side with Jordan's keen merchandising sense is his vivid love of the open, his vigorous interest in play, his keen knowledge of the call the primitive has for the human, his quick analytical sense of values, and back of it all is the impelling urge generated by his love of adventure…."

Albert R. Erskine, 1871–1933

Underwood is another office equipment manufacturer that helped typecast a chapter in the formative years of American automobile history when Albert Russel Erskine was written in as leading man to the Studebaker story. He was born in Huntsville, Alabama, on January 24, 1871, and at the age of 15 he began work as an office boy at the Huntsville office of the Mobile & Ohio Railroad. Erskine went on to become head bookkeeper with the railroad and then served as chief clerk with the St. Louis–based American Cotton Company. Expanded roles as general auditor and operations manager soon followed. When American Cotton went bankrupt in 1904, Albert R. moved on to the Yale & Towne Mfg. Co., a hardware and lock concern, as treasurer.

He then joined the Underwood Typewriter Company in 1910 as vice president and assumed a seat on its board of directors. Erskine quickly jumped to the South Bend, Indiana, automaker in 1911 as treasurer. By 1915, he was named president of Studebaker.

Although he bore more than just a passing resemblance to W.C. Fields, in fact he was all business. Erskine demonstrated a polarizing personality while at the helm of Studebaker. He was recognized for his managerial genius and laser-like focus on the fiscal side of the business, though simultaneously he could be ruthless, vindictive, overbearing and ill-mannered.

Erskine is credited with injecting vitality and style into the staid South Bend, Indiana, wagon maker's operations. He was heavily influenced by the more dynamic French automotive industry and introduced the stylish Erskine during 1926, in an attempt to take Studebaker into a more mainstream marketplace, which included aspirations in European sales. Dubbed "The Little Aristocrat," it was produced from the 1927 model year through 1930.

In 1928, under Erskine's direction, Studebaker gained control of Pierce-Arrow.

From the "if at first you don't succeed, try, try again" files, a second Studebaker attempt to enter the lower-priced but broader field arrived with the Rockne during 1932 and 1933. Profit never materialized with Pierce and the Rockne was hardly what would be considered a touchdown play. In fact, it never even got near the end zone. With the Depression now in full effect, a few more financial blunders followed, including Erskine's approval to pay healthy dividends, despite being in the middle of a severe cash flow crisis.

Studebaker went into receivership in March of 1933, and Pierce-Arrow went back to Buffalo in the hands of a management syndicate. Battling insurmountable corporate financial woes, staggering personal debt and ever-increasing heart and diabetes complications, Erskine took his own life later that year, at the age of 63. According to the July 2, 1933, edition of the *South Bend Tribune*, "his pride and spirit had been crushed by the tide of adversity that had overtaken him in the past three years."

... *to be continued*

Studebaker President Albert Erskine (right) and humorist Will Rogers in front of a 1927 Studebaker (courtesy Studebaker National Museum.

From Office Machines to Automobiles, Part II

JULY/AUGUST 2016

Alvan Macauley

Alvan Macauley's early business background can be traced back to Burroughs, and before. James Alvan Macauley was born in 1872 in Wheeling, West Virginia, where his father served as the first state treasurer. He was schooled in Washington, D.C., went on to earn an engineering degree from Lehigh University, and followed that with a degree in law from Columbian University (now George Washington University) in 1892. As we learned in Part 1, National Cash Register in Dayton, Ohio, was fast becoming a breeding ground for automotive pioneers, and Alvan joined NCR as a patent attorney.

Alvin Macauley.

In 1901, he moved on to assume management responsibility for the American Arithmometer Company in Missouri. The company was founded in 1886 by William S. Burroughs, who passed away in 1898. By 1905, business was booming and Macauley looked to expand the firm's operations. The move was blocked by the St. Louis city fathers, the result of nagging political pull from Macauley's predecessor, who had a falling out with the company when he left.

To give you a feeling for the moxie from which Macauley was made, he instead set his sights on

Detroit. Having secured a suitable location for what was then a growing American Arithmometer, one quiet night after the close of business, he had the entire contents of the factory loaded onto boxcars and whisked away to Michigan with all the employees onboard a special train called the "Clover Leaf Express." The following morning, city officials awoke to a surprise, to say the least! The company was then rechristened Burroughs Adding Machine Company, in honor of its founder.

In the meantime, Henry B. Joy was ambitiously turning Packard into one of the industry's foremost luxury car makers. A wealthy and influential Detroiter, Joy became fixated on providing the kind of product that those who traveled in his social circle might enjoy. He liked what he saw in the combination of Macauley's character, confidence and charisma, traits that would go on to earn him a reputation as "The Gentleman from Detroit." Joy enticed Macauley to join Packard in 1910 as general manager.

Three years later, Macauley was named vice-president, and by 1916 he assumed the role of president. The June 3, 1916, edition of *Automobile Topics* indicated that Joy "suggested the election" of Macauley "in recognition of the splendid work he has done…." At the time, Joy was instead engrossed in issues of military preparedness and the Lincoln Highway, and needed a capable individual to whom he could turn.

Macauley thus stepped up when Packard's serious upmarket ascent had just begun to accelerate. The first six-cylinder arrived in 1912, and the Twin Six (12-cylinder) appeared in May 1915. He would then go on to move the marque into overdrive. *Automobile Topics* reported that Macauley was a "student of big affairs" and specifically credited him with "the development of the Twin Six and the rapid expansion of the company since its introduction."

The enduring eight-cylinder engine was added to the stable in 1924 and it was under Macauley's watch that the memorable "Ask the Man Who Owns One" advertising slogan (which began around 1903) really gained momentum. It helped position Packard at the helm with the arrival of the Classic era.

It was also Macauley who guided the company's repositioning into the mid-market with Junior offerings, thereby protecting Packard's prosperity (as much as it could be protected) in response to the devastating Depression. He further supported Packard's production of the Liberty engine during World War I and got behind Packard's version of the Rolls-Royce Merlin engine, which would go on to see action in the P-51 Mustang during World War II. At that time, he was head of the Automotive Council for War Production.

Macauley served as Packard's president through 1939. After stepping down, he remained on the board of directors until 1948. He also served as president of the American Automobile Manufacturers Association and the National Automobile Chamber of Commerce. Alvan Macauley died in 1952.

Jesse G. Vincent

Hot on the heels of Macauley's arrival at Packard, another member of the Burroughs Adding Machine brotherhood soon followed. Jesse Gurney Vincent joined the house of the Red Hexagon on July 29, 1912, after a stint as acting chief engineer for the Hudson Motor Car Company in 1910. He enjoyed early success—if not what's been called immortality—with not only the creation, but the production of the Liberty V-12 aero engine. Legend has it that it was designed in five days.

Born in 1880, he was a native of Charleston, Arkansas, and received an engineering education through International Correspondence Schools. He began as a machinist tool designer at Burroughs and soon rose to the rank of superintendent of inventions. When he joined Packard, he assumed the role of chief engineer and became vice president of engineering in 1915.

Although he was an early member of the Society of Automobile Engineers, his interest in engines went beyond automobiles and into aircraft and marine applications. So when the SAE became known as the Society of Automotive Engineers as we now know it today, with its early logo depicting a focus on land, sea and air, Vincent became a staunch supporter of the organization. He was named first vice president for SAE in 1917 and went on to become its president in 1920.

Vincent was instrumental in all of Packard's engineering affairs. His fingerprints

Jesse Vincent.

were on everything. In addition, under his umbrella, Packard went on to develop four-wheel brakes in mass quantity, worm-drive rear axles and air conditioning. Ultimately, his name appeared on 206 patents for Packard and more than 400 in total including his batch from Burroughs, but it's been said that many were actually the work of others, and appeared in his name as a result of his position as engineering leader. Jesse Vincent retired from Packard during 1946 and served as president of the Automobile Club of Michigan in 1948–49. He died in 1962.

Edward A. Deeds

In the annals of office machine to automotive history, lesser-known Edward Andrew Deeds still deserves his fair share of recognition. Together with Charles Kettering, he co-founded Dayton Engineering Laboratories Company (Delco) in 1908. In fact, it was Deeds who initiated the idea and helped orchestrate the initial investment capital necessary.

He served as the chief of construction and development for National Cash Register and was responsible for the electrification of NCR facilities, beginning in 1899. He hired Charles Kettering in 1904 to further develop his Deeds-patented prototype electric motor, which would go on to power cash registers. When Kettering was in the process of developing a more exacting engine ignition system and then the revolutionary electric starter—which was a derivation of cash register motor principles—Deeds provided workshop space in his barn. There, Boss Kett could complete evening and weekend experiments.

Deeds resigned from NCR in 1915 to run Delco full time; in fact, it was Deeds' Packard that was used as a test bed, particularly for ignition system developments. After Delco was later sold to Billy Durant's United Motors Company for $9 million in cash and stock, Deeds stayed on as a member of the board of directors.

During World War I, Deeds entered the army as a colonel and assumed the role of chief of aircraft production. He oversaw the

Col. Edward A. Deeds.

development of Liberty engine manufacturing for U.S. war planes, which of course flew out of automotive industry plants, and also directed army aircraft research. Deeds returned to National Cash Register in 1931 as president, where he remained through 1940. During World War II, NCR played a pivotal role in cracking the German Enigma code that was used for U-boat (submarine) communications. He continued as honorary NCR chairman through 1957, when he retired. Born in 1874, he died in 1960 in a place then known as Kettering, Ohio.

Charles F. Kettering

When it comes to gravestones, it's been recognized that the most important part is the dash between the birth date and year of death. It's shorthand for a lifetime of accomplishment. Concerning Charles Kettering, his lifeline spanned the years between 1876 and 1958 and yielded 186 patents along its 82-year path.

The fourth of five children born to Jacob and Martha Kettering, Charles Franklin Kettering was burdened with poor eyesight as a child. His vision problems interrupted his studies at Ohio State University and forced him to make his way beyond just a classic curriculum; instead, he discovered and developed his own aptitude for learning and intellectual exploration.

Kettering persevered, however, returning to Ohio State after a stint as foreman with a fledgling telephone exchange, and graduated at age 27 in 1904. The career that followed was certainly never constrained by convention, and thus delivered immeasurable dividends. Kettering was driven by the quest to achieve solutions, instead of simply trying to identify improvements.

As superintendent of National Cash Register, Edward A. Deeds was on the lookout for new talent. He recruited the newly-minted electrical engineer and brought him 150 miles west from Loudonville to Dayton. His first assignment was to complete what Deeds had been trying to do himself: electrify the cash register drawer.

After achieving that, Kettering remained with NCR for another five years, though he never aligned himself with engineers or other inventors while there. He instead spent his time with the sales team because he believed that they were the ones who really understood what the market wanted, and what people *really* wanted in the first decade of the 20th century were automobiles.

Recognizing the immense potential of the automotive industry in its infancy, Kettering began experimenting in "solutions" to existing auto problems. With Deeds' encouragement, along with workshop space that he provided in his barn, they set up shop to pursue commercial possibilities.

What began with an improved ignition system in 1909 led to the creation of the Dayton Engineering Laboratories Company (Delco), after Henry Leland ordered 8,000 (ignition) sets for Cadillac. Kettering left NCR and introduction of the self-starter soon followed, in 1912.

Charles Kettering with self-starter.

By 1919, Delco had established so much equity within the industry that General Motors bought the business, outright, from Billy Durant's United Motors Company, which had been formed in 1916. Kettering remained as the head of GM's new research division for the next 25 years. Many more technological milestones, if not marvels, followed: quick-drying paint, which allowed for a significantly increased production pace; Chevrolet's copper-(air) cooled engine experiment (well, you win some, and you lose some); the discovery of Tetraethyl lead as an antiknock agent (more on that to follow) for improved performance; the creation of Freon as a refrigerant; and the lightweight, high-speed diesel locomotive engine. They were all examples of innovations that catapulted Kettering to a *Time* magazine cover, which recognized him as America's best-known engineer.

If that weren't enough, his dedication to medical research resulted in what is now known as the Memorial Sloan Kettering Cancer Center. Kettering retired in 1947 and became sought after as a public speaker, particularly concerning topics of industrial progress and scientific research. As an end result of his incredible career, Kettering amassed a fortune to the tune of $200 million in post–World War II dollars. He routinely preferred to drive a low-line Chevrolet to avoid being "conspicuous." Without a doubt, engineer extraordinaire Charles Kettering proved to be National Cash Register's greatest graduate.

William A. Chryst

After six months with National Cash Register, Kettering was promoted to head of the inventions department and named William "Bill" Chryst (1877–1958) as his chief assistant. In the same way that C. Harold Wills' brilliance took Henry Ford's ideas and turned them into reality, Chryst did likewise with Kettering, first at NCR, and then later at Delco.

Chryst began his career as a messenger at the cash register concern, and then became a machinist. Beyond his acumen for invention and innovation, it was Chryst who came up with the "Delco" acronym, as an influence from the name "Nabisco" (coincidentally, it was Wills who created the Ford logo script). Deeds originally wanted to call the company Dayton Laboratories and Engineering. Among others, Chryst was also moonlighting as part of the "Barn Gang" behind Deeds' house and formally joined Delco at the end of 1911.

During World War I, General Pershing had Chryst dispatched to France as an on-site ignition expert. In 1928 he was in Russia overseeing testing and servicing for Liberty aircraft engines that the Soviets had purchased. He went on to become chief engineer and retired from Delco in 1947.

Thomas Midgley, Jr.

Yet another NCR alumnus was chemist Thomas Midgley, Jr. (1889–1944). A former draftsman and designer at the company's Dayton, Ohio, headquarters, he moved over to Delco

Thomas Midgley, Jr.

in 1916. With more than 100 patents to his name, Midgley was instrumental in the 1921 discovery of Tetraethyl lead as an antiknock agent for gasoline, under the direction of Kettering, who was by then head of research for GM. Midgley went on to serve as vice president of the General Motors Chemical Company. Decades later, Midgley's two foremost inventions, leaded gasoline and chlorofluorocarbons, would be globally banned after wreaking havoc on both public health and the world environment.

Levitt Luzern Custer

Even as a child, L. Luzern Custer was recognized for his inquisitive nature. Born in 1888, he inherited his intense curiosity from his father, Levitt Ellsworth Custer, who was an Ohio dentist and balloonist. Ellsworth not only experimented with aerial torpedoes, but is believed to have been one of the earliest proponents in the use of the X-ray in dentistry.

Luzern took to the sky as well, particularly after graduating from Massachusetts Institute of Technology (MIT) in 1913. By the time he was 24, he invented the bubble statuscope, a device that determined whether a balloon or dirigible was ascending or descending. He would go on to produce it for the U.S. Navy.

For a short time, he was employed by National Cash Register. As often occurs in a game-changing engineering enterprise with an abundance of strong-willed individualists, Custer soon left after a patent dispute with Charles Kettering.

The Custer Specialty Company was then formed in 1916. Beyond just being an incubator for invention,

Levitt Luzern Custer.

the first indoor miniature golf course was included within its walls along with an "oceanarium," which housed more than 100 tropical fish tanks. Yes, Luzern Custer marched to a different drummer—his own.

With the cruelty of World War I, he recognized that there was an unfortunate abundance of invalids among the ranks of returning doughboys. It prompted him to create the Custer Invalid Chair, a three-wheeled battery-powered vehicle that provided mobility for veterans and others around the world. It went on to be upgraded with a Briggs & Stratton engine and achieved speeds of 10 mph.

The two-wheeled Custer Scooter followed and was eventually licensed to Cushman. It would attain speeds of 60 mph, but suffered early teething problems through its transmission of power. The result was the development of the centrifugal clutch. The Scooter led to the Custer Car, a small four-wheeled electric vehicle, along with the Comet, which was intended for those who needed to scoot around large factories or warehouses.

Luzern Custer continued to invent, with more than 20 patents to his credit. Amusement park rides, pontoon boats, radio sets and certainly more balloon innovations kept him busy until 1962, when he died in Dayton.

Richard H. Grant

Automotive Hall of Fame inductee R.H. ("Dick") Grant was dubbed "America's No. 1 Salesman" by automotive and business writers in the 1920s and '30s. His ascension to that lofty status started with his birth in Ipswich, Massachusetts, in 1878. A Harvard education armed him for what would prove to be an unparalleled career. Upon graduation in 1901, he landed a job in a Boston multi-goods store in the book department. It wasn't long before he discovered what would become his life-long obsession ... *selling!*

On a tip from a friend, Grant then applied for a job at National Cash Register and assumed the role as a clerk in the sales office. He went to Dayton in 1904. Before long, his superiors realized that he'd deliver more by being out in the field than from behind a desk. Nine years later he was named general sales manager.

Charles Kettering and Colonel Deeds were paying attention and enticed him to join Delco in 1915. Further tenure with Delco Light and Delco-Frigidaire followed, and then General Motors stepped in. Grant was ultimately tapped to lead the Chevrolet sales charge in 1924. By 1927, Chevrolet was outselling Ford for the first time. It would continue to do so, on and off, and in 1929, he became a GM vice president. Walter P. Chrysler responded with the statement, "If it were not for Dick Grant, I wouldn't have to work so hard."

Dick Grant remained as the head of Chevrolet sales through 1944, though he stayed on GM's board of directors through 1953. Even with his executive status in Detroit, he continued to live in Ohio and commuted. Recognized for his ability to motivate the sales force, he was also well-remembered by his clever quips which became known as "Grantisms": "A salesman, like the storage battery in your car, is constantly discharging energy. Unless he is recharged at frequent intervals, he soon runs dry." Or "Carry an order blank in your nightshirt pocket, in case you walk in your sleep."

Under Grant's guidance, modern sales methods resulted in GM's market share expanding from 12 to 43 percent, with Chevrolet becoming the largest volume seller. In preparation for his future, Grant personally purchased controlling interest in a company called Reynolds & Reynolds, in 1939. The firm specialized in automotive dealer accounting systems and further migrated into the operations/enterprise and information management company that it is today. Coincidentally, it's headquartered in what is now Kettering, Ohio.

Richard H. Grant.

R.H. Grant, Jr., went on to lead Reynolds & Reynolds after Dick Grant pursued yet another passion, his 780-acre Normandy Farms Dairy in the Dayton area. He passed away in 1957.

Innovators, entrepreneurs and industrialists all, who went from office machines to automobiles. It all adds up…

Technicalities

The Roll of the Radio

March/April 2013

In addition to antique cars, vintage motorcycles and old outboards, another affliction that occupies my existence here in Connecticut, and competes for a fair share of my all-too-elusive budget, is tube-type radios, particularly those that were made between the late 1950s and early 1960s. That's when the FM (frequency modulation) band became commonplace. After that, the transistor soon sucked the life out of the vacuum tube, even faster than fuel injection killed the carburetor.

It seems that I've been listening to old radios for as long as I've been chasing (even older) cars. Come Friday night, they're on throughout the house—throughout the weekend. In addition to the incomparable warm sound quality, they also radiate a steady glow from the front dial face, while creating wonderful wall art from the light emitted through the ventilated rear cover. Certainly, there's no better way to listen to things like Garrison Keillor's "Prairie Home Companion" and Click and Clack's "Car Talk" on NPR. And if your heater fails, they'll even help keep you warm. So it's funny that it's only taken me 40 years to recognize the remarkable role that the radio simultaneously shared with the evolution of the automobile!

Both the radio and the automobile were products of our last century's unprecedented industrial juggernaut. Inventions that transformed the quality of life quickly proved to be prized possessions because they delivered revolutionary value. The personal mobility offered by the automobile accelerated social change and brought cultures closer together. Likewise, the arrival of the radio and its almost magical wireless voice transmission was the equivalent of unleashing the genie from a lamp that had previously only emitted an odd assortment of dots and dashes for communication.

By 1920, the automotive age had truly taken hold. Already a proven product, the automobile was being embraced by an ever-increasing audience. The radio, meanwhile, was just beginning to evolve from such experimental applications as ship-to-shore to the commercial reality of a living room aspiration. It would take another 10 to 20 years for the gramophone and piano in the parlor to really be superseded by the radio, because it required the development of a broadcasting industry to fuel it—the radio's own "Good Roads Movement," if you will.

Like the invention of the automobile, the earliest less-is-more link between the

Arvin car radio ad.

horse*less* carriage and the wire*less* set was the result of tinkerers and self-taught engineers. To them, the thought of mobilizing the airwaves was as natural as harnessing an engine to a buggy because they recognized that together with the automobile, the radio could provide utmost public service. So the radio got its start on four wheels as more of a transmission device, as opposed to simply a receiver. Broadcasters realized that they could provide reports right from the source. The combination of radio and car also quickly distinguished itself during emergency scene assessment and as an enforcement tool for authorities.

But that's not to say that the thought of simply enjoying the radio's virtue as an entertainment and information vehicle was not a factor to help get it out of the house. As early as 1922, a Chevrolet Superior sedan could be outfitted with a Westinghouse radio set. It may have been an ungainly installation with its bank of supplementary batteries and speaker horn perched precariously on the floor of the back seat, not to mention its roof-mounted antenna net, but its primary claim to fame was its portability. It supposedly could do double duty at home or on the move.

By the late 1920s, the radio was on the cusp of becoming a staple of American life. In combination with the car, it would go on to help eradicate the isolation of rural life and bring communities closer together. And both could take you away to far-off places ... either real or imaginary. It was obvious that there was an immediate affinity between the automobile and the airwaves.

The first commercially available set specifically for automotive applications is believed to have been the Transitone, from 1927. It was a product of the Automobile Radio Corporation, which went on to acquire the patent for dashboard installation in an automobile. Recognizing the potential gain of just such an automotive opportunity, the Philadelphia Storage Battery Company (Philco) tuned right in and acquired Automobile Radio by 1930.

Meanwhile, around the same time, the Galvin Manufacturing Corporation of Chicago was producing a device called the battery eliminator. It allowed battery-powered direct-current radio sets to be used with the alternating current that

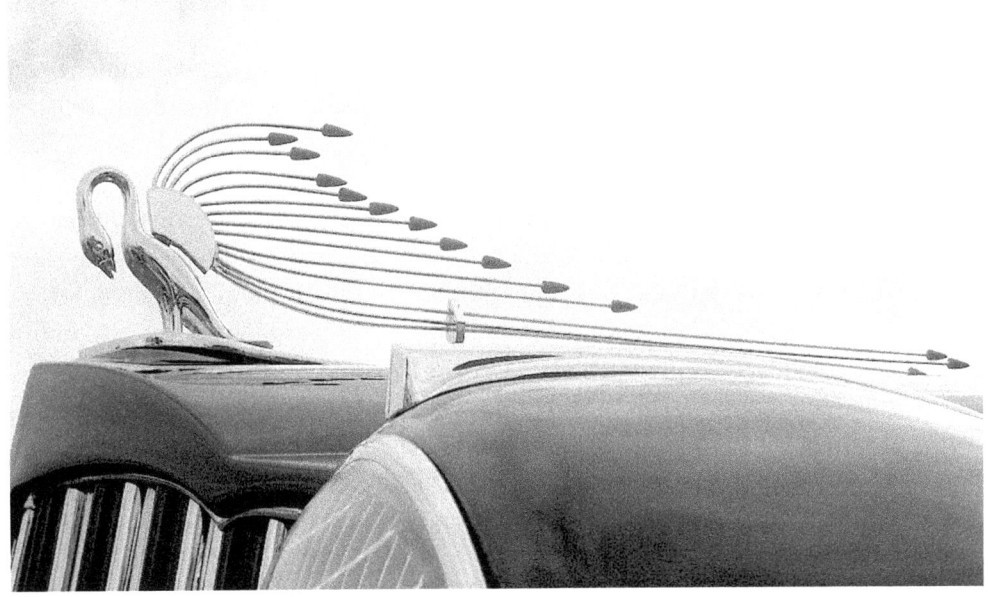

Packard cormorant hood ornament with radio antenna wings.

was finding its way into many households. Unfortunately, the Depression was just about ready to short-circuit the under-funded Galvin concern.

In an effort to stave off its own crash and inspired by the fact that "radio shops were installing sets in cars," the company quickly developed an affordable offering that could be universally installed in almost any automobile. To bring it to market, they coined the catchy name Motorola to convey the combination of motion and radio. There was already a familiarity in the marketplace with such established products as the Victrola (from the Victor Talking Machine Company) and the Radio Corporation of America's (RCA) Radiola.

A tidal wave of enthusiasm began to swell around the self-contained radio at the time, which accelerated its popularity for automotive use—so much so that it amplified small startups like Motorola and skyrocketed them to success. It drove Cadillac to list the availability of a radio application in 1931 with "price on application." And Powel Crosley, Jr., offered his Roamio set for any make of automobile. To no one's surprise, all the attention meant that pretty soon, Big Brother would be listening in too.

Radio history runs rampant with indiscriminate stories of government concern over the control of airwaves on a grand scale. But it was unimaginable when George A. Parker, the Massachusetts registrar of motor vehicles, proposed local legislation to address drivers distracted with car radios in 1930. It didn't stand much of a chance due to the clamoring public's insatiable appetite for more and more radios. The volume on the decree was soon squelched by Clarence E. Colby, a lobbyist for the Radio Manufacturers Association, who quickly proclaimed that "the radio knob is as easy to use as a choke handle." Parker went on to pursue drunk drivers instead, and the legislation thereof, proving once again that history does repeat itself.

It was another piece of world history that would soon have utmost influence on the developing four-wheeled radio drama. The approach, and ultimate outcome, of World War II would put the automotive radio industry into high gear.

Obviously the operating environment for a typical automotive radio application was more extreme than the confines of a typical living room. Dust, dirt, vibration, moisture and temperature variations wreaked havoc with early radio sets and speaker cones, which were quite fragile to begin with. Technical advances in radio development that were conceived for military specification in preparation for war also found their way into automotive applications.

Smaller and more efficient tube designs were made to be more robust. Improvements in tuning sensitivity and the invention of signal-seeking technology likewise proved advantageous in the automobile, as did local versus long-distance selectivity. The automotive application also benefited from the latest improvements to suppress noise interference.

Beyond just electrical functionality, the war effort also contributed to more modern dial-face design, the arrival of aircraft inspired foot controls, and, more

Crosley touted its $28.98 price and suitability for a wide range of cars.

importantly, pushbutton tuning. But it was plastics, of course, that proved to be another pivotal milestone in the state-of-the-car-radio-art, just as they did for the rest of the automobile.

Antenna technology advanced from the radio body itself and roof-wired mesh systems to running board-mounted solutions, to what became the common stick or

Philco advertised its radio as "Custom Styled for your car."

wand aerial. Even radiator ornament alternatives were tried. The unfortunate glass-mounted antenna experience was still a ways away.

Postwar prosperity only added to the appreciation of automotive audio. With America's manufacturing might already primed to run at a fever pitch, economies of scale drove the price of auto radios down to a level for even more mass-market acceptance. Affordability was the answer to ensure that radio installations in cars would become the norm, not the exception. Due to the then-abundance of disposable income—and if not, due to what quickly became an exponential acceptance of the oh-so-enticing installment plan—they did.

The automobile and the radio became inseparable in other ways too. The captive audience within a car became a prime target for advertisers, much to the dismay of what had been a flourishing newspaper industry. Advertising spending began to shift from pure print to more dynamic, and thus influential, audio. It was just the beginning of a mega-media trend to follow, particularly when it came to pitching automotive products. Memorable ad campaigns, such as Autolite's sponsorship of the *Suspense* mystery series and the B.F. Goodrich backing of *The Shadow* exploits, became as much a part of radio folklore as the shows themselves ... *Kimo Sabe*.

Then came the practical transistor in the late 1950s and early 1960s, and the rolling radio industry would soon accelerate into overdrive. As cars became more complex, instrument panel real estate came at a premium, so compact and lightweight radios elbowed their way in between instrument clusters and the glovebox. Ever-improving power, performance, efficiency and control were not just confined to the engine bay and chassis. The transistorized radio had as much appeal as horsepower, and wattage would come to be leveraged as a competitive advantage, as well.

The combination of revved-up cars and cranked-up radios was very much an American invention. While other parts of the world were levying supplementary user taxes on cars with radios and legislating noise limits, another wave of personal freedom washed up on these shores, sparked by a car/surfer counter-culture and fueled by the radio. The little old lady from Pasadena could jump into a little deuce coupe and have fun, fun, fun 'til her daddy took the T-bird away. So the radio also served as a creative outlet on the hot rod scene, romanticizing the automobile lifestyle even more, which helped sell more cars—with radios.

Out on the open road, in-car audio would earn its keep to help reduce monotony and boredom, and help travelers keep up with current events. Closer to home, its ability to provide timely traffic and weather reports would allow operators to drive around ever-increasing congestion, road closures and other unexpected impediments.

The radio would go on to become a fully integrated entertainment system to include a multitude of strategically placed and tuned speakers. Over the years, everything from turntables to 8-track players to cassettes, CBs and CDs would be incorporated. And that's just what was offered in what we recognize as 25-year-old "antique" automobiles. Then there would be telephones, docking stations, video, surround sound, navigation, voice activation, satellite radio, and more. Now the sky's the limit for the future of auto entertainment ... pun intended.

Originally, it was the go-anywhere advantage of the automobile that took the radio along for the ride. But with the arrival of advanced electronics, the radio moved into the driver's seat and earned its place as a constant companion in what used to be an automobile, and what's now become a complete cloud-connected audiomobile.

Requiem for the Running Board

SEPTEMBER/OCTOBER 2013

When you enter my garage from the kitchen of my house, the first thing you bump into is my 1922 Wills Sainte Claire A-68 roadster. The product of Childe Harold Wills from Marysville, Michigan, this fine car of distinction is best remembered by its Hispano-Suiza–inspired overhead cam V-8 engine. It set itself apart from the pack even further by numerous other innovations, such as its generous use of molybdenum, the first standard application of a back-up light, and one of the earliest factory-specified rumble seats. But for me, one of its greatest assets happens to be its running board.

Set within the Wills' 121-inch wheelbase, the 10-inch wide running board abuts the gentle valence that spans the frame rail. Together they embrace the front fender, which arrives at a thoughtful 45-degree angle—coincidentally, just about identical to the inclination of the comfy cedar Adirondack recliner out on my deck.

So it should come as no surprise that I often find myself out in the garage lounging around on my Wills Sainte Claire running board, leaning back against the satisfying slope of its beefy left-front fender. Even better, as the cowl and hood tuck inward to enclose the narrow-angle engine, the valence turns horizontal, leaving a comfortable perch for my left elbow. And if you know anything about Wills Sainte Claires, you can just imagine that the unique, cowl-mounted courtesy light might even make a great reading lamp!

My garage is more of a palace of personality and passion, my garage is more of a "palace of personality and passion" than just a basic storage shelter, so there simply isn't a better seat in the house—I mean, garage—particularly when the lights are low and the stereo's going. Pass the chardonnay, please…

There's certainly no other icon that typifies antique car construction like the beloved running board. Its history is well known, but it's rarely been written about. Like an old Rodney Dangerfield joke, the running board "just don't get no respect."

Going back to the beginning, the lack of proper roads and the fact that carriages were horse-drawn meant that step plates were necessary to board tall wagons and coaches with high ground clearance. Once the horse was liberated from the carriage, the step plate evolved as speed increased and vehicles got closer to the ground. The

Running board and supplementary step plate on brass-era car.

running board offered easier access and better protection from the elements, particularly when combined with an enveloping fender, enclosed frame valence and splash aprons. According to the *Dictionary of Automotive Engineering* (1989) published by the Society of Automotive Engineers (SAE), it's defined as a "lengthwise horizontal step at sill level to facilitate access to a vehicle."

The running board was soon an integral automotive design element and would go on to become the stuff of legend. It would also serve as the primary platform to carry tool boxes, acetylene tanks, luggage and Boyco (gas/oil/water) service sets.

But beyond that, vivid *Grapes of Wrath* images remain of dust-bowl migrants carrying everything including the kitchen sink on the running board. Tin Can Tourists routinely used them as a foundation for mounting bunks and tents. Who can't picture machine-gun-wielding gangsters on the running board of the getaway car, while running from the long arm of the law? Think of all the old family photographs that were taken with the kids on a running board ... that are now a true reflection of America's social history as well. At one time or another, who hasn't ridden on a running board just for fun? (Not that we're recommending that.)

To this day, the running board remains a popular perch for an afternoon picnic, or the most expedient place to take a load off (particularly if you forgot to bring a lawn chair). Go to any antique car show and see for yourself. I just did—the Klingberg Vintage Festival in New Britain, Connecticut, where I saw my friend George Dragone enjoying the expansive running board of his 1921 Locomobile (which is what got me to thinking about writing this column in the first place).

The side-mounted spare tire also found a home within the confines of the running board/front fender wheel estate. It made perfect sense. Cars were getting

Top and above: Running boards have carried tool boxes and furnished convenient temporary resting spots (above: West Peterson photo).

longer and more refined, and traveling farther away from home. Greater emphasis was being placed on giving the real estate in the rear to a flush-mounted trunk and luggage rack.

The side-mount was certainly a costly alternative, requiring more complicated fender tooling, associated mounting hardware and, in many instances, the inclusion of a cloth cover or metal enclosure. That's why side-mounts were, and still are, most appropriate on the grand marques, where cost was less of a concern. And yes, they do work on Model As, too, thanks to Edsel Ford's instinctive design sense.

So the good old-fashioned running board would go on to serve as a design cue for the classic automotive era, as well (late 1920s and early 1930s specifically). When specified with a side-mount, though, it would be to the detriment of someone like me who might prefer to otherwise use the running board/front fender combination as a casual recliner (how crude).

Riding on a running board in a 1923 cartoon.

These days, side-mounts are somewhat akin to Shelby Mustangs and continental kits—there are many more out there than were ever built in the first place. Unfortunately, some of them have been ill-applied. Small series Buicks, Cadillacs, Chryslers and Packards with dual side-mounts, for example, come across (to me, at least) as the equivalent of a bimbo sporting a pushup bra.

In the end, time wouldn't be kind to the running board, either. It was the combination of art and science that would be its undoing. During the late 1920s, an

The running board evolved from individual horseless carriage step plates to include a full length frame valence and side-mounted spare tires (photograph © Michael Furman).

emphasis on automotive design began to evolve. The industry realized that aesthetic differentiation could, in fact, serve as a competitive advantage. Since "they all look alike to me" was an all-too-common sentiment, as reported by Consulting Body Engineer William H. Emond from the floor of the National Automobile Show in New York in 1929 (*Autobody Magazine*, May 1929 edition, as published in George Hildebrand's *Golden Age of the Luxury Car*). He went on to say, "After you've seen about four exhibits you have seen the whole show." Similarly, there was a good deal of dissension among the ranks at that year's Society of Automotive Engineers (SAE) semi-annual meeting about what was considered as the "deadly similarity" of body design.

It's well known that General Motors established its Art and Colour Section (the industry's first formal styling department) in 1927. Lawrence P. Fisher, Cadillac's then general manager, convinced Alfred P. Sloan (GM's president at the time) of the importance of appearance. He then got him to agree to commission Harley Earl in 1926 to design the upcoming companion car that would go on to become the LaSalle.

After the LaSalle's sensational debut in March 1927, Earl was brought on board to run the new design group. Sloan realized that "unifying the various parts of the car from a standpoint of appearance" would help General Motors stand out.

Engineers began to consider the car as a whole, as opposed to the sum of its parts. In a presentation before the Metropolitan Section of SAE on November 15, 1928, Amos Northup (formerly of Murray Body and serving as art director and chief designer for Willys-Overland) used an analogy from the field of architecture to share his vision for the future of automotive design. "Just as the foundation and the house must be in perfect proportion, so must the chassis … the foundation of the body … be in perfect relation with this body. There should be no apparent dividing line between these two parts of the whole."

With roads continually improving, he further professed, "By lowering the body and by eliminating the side aprons (which are not only unnecessary, but which prevent harmonious design) the entire picture will be changed. But it will be changed to most perfect advantage. At this stage we can really create the exact relation of

Franklin dropped door skins to the running board, putting the company "in the forefront of fashion" in 1931 by creating a more modern, integrated running board (photograph © Michael Furman).

the foundation to the house, producing a whole in as perfect relationship as can the architect."

Hugo Pfau, in his well respected work *The Custom Body Era* (published in 1970 by Castle Books), credits the Dietrich-designed Franklin Pirate as "the first American car with doors running down to the running boards, a style which eventually led to the complete elimination of the running boards." It was a trend that actually began in France, at the Paris Salon. The positive response from automotive critics at the time is clearly evident in this January 18, 1930, excerpt from *The Montreal Gazette*: "Such new features as the concealed running boards … [will] definitely place these new Franklin types in a conspicuous position in the fine car field." The Syracuse, New York–based car maker's sales materials boasted that concealed running boards put them "in the forefront of fashion."

Taking door skins down to the running board would become the state of the body engineer's art, even though it could result in a somewhat bulbous appearance in certain applications, particularly as time went on. With ride heights remaining somewhat high, however, running boards still offered a practical advantage even though no one wanted to look at them. Ignoring if not hiding them was the designer's path of least resistance, not to mention the most cost-effective short-term solution.

With the arrival of the streamlined, aerodynamic age of the mid–1930s, the running board lost what little respect it had left and then really got stepped all over. What had proven to be a valuable, in-use asset quickly turned into a showroom liability. Cars with running boards were soon considered out-of-date. The newfound sense of fashion and style had very much invaded the automotive industry, and the running board was an early casualty.

The quest for aerodynamic efficiency dictated that cars get lower to the ground and hug the pavement. The curved, organic shapes of the next cycle of postwar body tooling spelled the end of the running board. Integrated designs moved more toward

1933 PIERCE SILVER ARROW

Going ... going ... gone. When a few Pierce-Arrow "Silver Arrow" show cars were built in 1933, it foretold that cars would become lower to the ground and more aerodynamic as speeds increased. The body and chassis would become "one harmonious whole" ... and the running board would disappear.

streamlining (defined by industrial designer Norman Bel Geddes as "when an object passing through a fluid such as air creates the least disturbance in the fluid") and away from old-style coachbuilding techniques.

Fenders began to be better integrated within the body envelope in the interest of improved airflow management. Although tooling constraints at the time severely limited the ability to achieve an ultimate teardrop shape on a grand scale, fender designs evolved into more and more of an aerodynamic enclosure, while still ensuring that the front wheels could turn. In the rear, removable skirts could be applied.

With vehicle speeds routinely on the rise as the industry matured and roads improved, Amos Northup further predicted that "wing-like fenders that would seem to lift the car up in the air as it moves along" would make way for "fenders so designed to help keep the car on the ground where it belongs ... more in harmony with aerodynamic lines." That proved to be the ultimate demise of the running board, "the result of an effort to weld into one harmonious whole the body and chassis...."

Ironically, it was the logical next step. Engineers who previously only considered simple construction and assembly details were soon supplanted by stylists who were instead focused on the more sophisticated science of surface development. And the rest, as they say, is history.

Truck designs, due to their practical nature and higher ride heights, were able to soldier on with running boards. Among the last vestiges would be the step-side pickup and the original Volkswagen Beetle, of course.

Today, running boards have made a resurgence, due to the myriad of light trucks and sport utilities that have saturated the marketplace. But history has a way of repeating itself, and automotive progress has taken a turn toward the past. Ride heights are heading the wrong way, going back up. Fuel economy and vehicle dynamics be damned, the buying public's infatuation with four-wheel-drive means that it's getting harder to get in and out of tall trucks and big honkin' SUVs.

Though the term "running board" is now a misnomer, today's running boards are nothing more than glorified step plates. Most of them are tubular, and some will even retract beneath the rocker/frame rail when not in use. But what good is that, when I'm out in the garage with the lights dimmed low and the stereo going, looking to enjoy a glass of chardonnay?

A New Beginning

July/August 2015

Automotive history is full of examples of technologies that were propelled to the forefront after migrating from boutique builders to mainstream volume producers. It's no wonder, innovators often operate more nimbly with a high degree of daring, and enjoy limited-production runs with carefully managed market allocations. This allows them to better manage their products in the field by providing an opportunity for more hands-on control when issues inevitably come up in daily use.

Likewise, technologies often trickle down from upscale specialty manufacturers who have the ability to charge and derive revenue from cutting-edge solutions to those who ultimately strive for mass production. Since smaller companies have limited marketing resources, it simultaneously allows them to generate a brand or portfolio distinction that they might otherwise not afford, to further drive their identity and awareness in what's become an even more competitive marketplace. Such is the case with exhaust-driven charge boosting, or turbocharging as it's more commonly known.

The turbocharged engine accelerated to the commercial forefront during World War I in aircraft applications. The quest to provide seamless output at altitude was satisfied through forced induction, which compensated for the natural reduction in air density. The exhaust-driven turbocharger was utilized to compress the inlet charge of air, thereby packing a greater mass of air into the intake system. More air meant that more fuel could be supplied, which generated more power.

Although the domestic industry toyed with the turbocharger over the years, it took Sweden's Saab to really turn it into a viable success in the automotive marketplace. Saab enjoyed the unique advantage of having roots in the airplane industry, and simultaneously benefited from an alliance with a well-regarded heavy-diesel truck manufacturer (Scania-Vabis), where turbocharging excelled and was certainly put to good use.

Always the innovator, Saab essentially civilized the turbocharger for automotive applications by leveraging its relationship with the experienced Scania and relying on a supplier partnership with the then-pioneering Garrett Airesearch organization (now owned by Honeywell International). Due to packaging constraints around its

Sanford Alexander Moss, the person most responsible for development of turbosupercharging in America, was born in San Francisco on August 23, 1872. At the age of 16 he got the idea that if fuel was burned in compressed air, its energy output could be increased. This idea followed him through his engineering training at the University of California to Cornell, where he wrote his 1903 Ph.D. thesis on the gas turbine. For the turbocharged Liberty engine (above), Moss used a cluster of small-diameter tubes that functioned as a heat exchanger to pressurize the carburetor, which was positioned downstream of the turbo.

backward-mounted inline four-cylinder front-wheel-drive specification, turbocharging was the only logical near-term alternative to satisfy Saab's quest for improved performance. It was strategically being utilized as a springboard to move the brand upmarket after the positive response to its Saab 99 EMS model.

The Saab 99 Turbo made its debut in U.S. market in 1978 and was quickly superseded by the 900 Turbo in 1979 with improved under-hood elbow room. Although rather rudimentary when looked upon today, the turbocharger as applied to the Saab was relatively large, hung off a corner of the engine, suffered from lubrication challenges, spun up relatively slowly—which resulted in what was deemed "turbo lag"—and could sometimes whistle a sound resembling a siren. It did work, and well enough to set the stage for what would become a literal rebirth of the brand.

Today, turbocharging is much more of a norm, and not an exception. Technology has advanced to the extent that turbochargers are much more integrated within an engine's basic design. They're smaller with less rotational inertia and together with modern electronic engine management, charge-boosted engines now offer efficiencies that Saab—and folks that followed—could only envision.

Saab 99 Turbo combi coupe (courtesy Saab).

I recently experienced what is perhaps the most ambitious turbocharger application in modern times, the 2015 Ford F-150 pickup. You can't get more run-of-the-mill than an F-150, and this latest iteration offers the option of a 2.7-liter twin turbo.

The basic engine is a V-6. I've never been a fan of these wee-vees because they're never as refined as an inline-six, and they're always in the shadow of the more meaningful V-8 (from which they've often been derived). There have certainly been some sweet V-6s such as Alfa Romeo's 2.5 and 3.0 and Lancia's ground-breaking example from 1950, which was the industry's first; but for the most part, the V-6 has been more functional than fun—case in point, GM's old 3800 standby.

The new Ford convinced me otherwise. Simply put, the performance of this new powertrain is absolutely outstanding! With a small turbocharger for each bank of three cylinders, combined with sophisticated electronic control, there's no such thing as a torque curve. The output of this engine is instantaneous, and if you had to chart it, the torque diagram would no doubt look like an immediate plateau, instead of an old-time curve, that builds as the revs do. With recent advances in manufacturing technique—down the level of superior materials and lubricant properties—you'd be hard-pressed to realize that this new F-150 was a mere 166 cubic inches as it puts out 325 horsepower and 375 lb.-ft. of torque.

Ford is positioning the new engine architecture under the "EcoBoost" badge, and it sets up what will go down in automotive history as yet another great marketing war between Ford and General Motors. Before this, the two Michigan manufacturers drew pickup truck battle lines around the V-8. Chevrolet and GMC stuck to their small-block pushrod roots while Ford ventured into the realm of aluminum overhead cam technology. Though there were projections that Ford would ultimately suffer low-end torque consequences as a result—which is certainly not good in a pickup—the sales results speak otherwise.

This time, however, the boys with the blue oval have yet another ace up their sleeve. The 2015 F-150 body is constructed out of aluminum, which is reputed to provide a 700-pound weight savings. It's quite a bold strategy, particularly when packaged with the twin turbo EcoBoost engine, so it's no wonder that GM has immediately responded with aggressive advertising that boasts about the advantage of high-strength steel construction, particularly for a pickup. In addition, the light-duty pickup has a maximum payload rating of 2,250 pounds and maximum tow rating of 8,500 pounds.

It's going to be fun to watch how this latest Ford vs. Chevy skirmish gets settled by the marketplace. In the meantime, though, I believe that the V-6 engine has finally found its true calling as a result of twin turbochargers—in the mass market, no less. With the efficiency of an inline twin overhead cam four-cylinder, the effectiveness of a pushrod V-8 and the magnificence of the V-12, when combined with sophisticated electronic control, I predict that the demonstrated maturity of today's twin turbo V-6 will result in its recognition as tomorrow's next classic engine configuration. It's that good.

Have you driven a Ford lately?

The End of an Era...

From what might very well evolve into a breakthrough motoring milestone, we now move on to another bit of unique engine engineering that has accomplished its own intended mission, but has now run its course. If you're familiar with the likes of Armstrong Siddeley and Bristol you might be aware of it: the five-cylinder engine. Though in their case, these were radial engine designs intended for British airplane applications, that didn't stop Dubuque, Iowa's, Adams-Farwell from stuffing a rotary version of their own design into the back of roadsters and touring cars between 1906 and 1912.

Mercedes-Benz finally liberated the five-cylinder engine from the sky and brought it down to earth in the first meaningful way. In 1974, their 300 Diesel was launched with a quintuplet of cylinders, though arranged in-line, and by 1978, turbocharging was applied for improved performance. The long-standing, Stuttgart-based stalwart stressed that it was a "characteristically unconventional" design, and judging by the industry adoption rate that followed, they were right.

As a compromise between the four- and six-cylinders, the five was deemed to offer better performance than the former and provide improved operating economy over the latter. In addition, there were weight and packaging advantages in its favor and it also allowed engine makers to gain modular efficiencies in casting and machining techniques on the production line through common bore spacing. In

Five-cylinder Diesel engine from Mercedes.

certain respects, a five-cylinder can also generate less vibration than a four, though in other instances it can create more. They're also known to be rather reliable since they've often been relatively low stressed.

Volkswagen-Audi joined the fledgling five-cylinder fraternity in 1977 with the Audi 100, and then with the 5000 models that followed, along with various other applications over the years. Acura took the pledge but didn't matriculate very far with their Vigor in 1992. Other, European-inspired diesel alternatives such as Land Rover's Defender and Discovery, along with a VM Motori-powered version of the Jeep Grand Cherokee, helped round out the exclusive Class of 5.

More recently, General Motors' Atlas family of modular in-line engines included dual-overhead cam Vortec 3500 and 3700 five-cylinders that found their way into the Chevy Colorado, GMC Canyon, Hummer H3 and Isuzu i-350/370. Fiat/Lancia has also been known to deploy the same configuration in Europe and Brazil, and Ford has as well, in light vans. Not to be left out of the Asian equation, South Korea's SsangYong Motor Company has relied on old Mercedes tooling for a limited version of their own example of the in-line quintuplet through an alliance with Daimler-Benz.

The last gasp for the ever-functional five-cylinder appears to be the current Volvo S60, V60 and XC60 platform with all-wheel drive. The Gothenburg, Sweden–based and now Chinese-owned manufacturer has relied on a modular five since 1992, starting with the 850 model. All the pre-existing logic in support of its specification continues to roll on (pun intended; the word Volvo translates to "I Roll"), with performance, economy, packaging, weight, reliability, etc., in comparison to the four or six.

Technology aside, however, the marketing challenge has always been to entice four-cylinder economy-minded aficionados to move up, or convince those with more refined six-cylinder intentions to move down. Unfortunately, the folks at Volvo have traditionally been light on marketing muscle. So the five-cylinder has proven to be somewhat of a jack of all trades and a master of none. And that's too bad, because Volvo's current 2.5-liter, complete with a turbocharger, generates a capable 250 hp and 266 ft.-lb. torque along with respectable fuel economy of 23 mpg combined and 29 mpg highway on regular octane.

But if you can't beat 'em, you might as well join 'em. The evergreen Swedish automaker now plans to write its next chapter of automotive history around four-cylinder turbocharged technology—only this time with direct injection—along with a six-cylinder alternative. They're also experimenting with a future-think three-cylinder, as did Adams-Farwell (in rotary form, however), way back before 1906. Surprise!

...and Finally, Less Is More

Meanwhile, another interesting trend that's developing in today's automotive industry is the migration from super-sized sport utility vehicles and pickups to those with more logical and modest proportions. Drive through any mature subdivision or developed shopping mall and you'll find streets stuffed with obscene SUVs and parking lots bulging with trucks that barely fit between the lines of a space. No wonder so many vehicles now come with retractable side-view mirrors! So it goes here in America, the land where bigger is always perceived as better.

Lately, however, there's been a move afoot to offer more rational alternatives for those who remain sensitive to the footprint they leave behind, not to mention the interest to quench the thirst at the gas pump. The marketing departments at many of the industry's leading automotive companies have now seized on what's called the "cute-ute" category: more diminutive yet stylish sport utility vehicles that not only offer reduced operating expense, but are more spirited, youthful and fun to drive as well. It's the fastest growing sector in today's automotive industry.

One of the early players in the segment happened to be Mitsubishi, which has offered their Outlander Sport since 2011. Named one of the "10 Most Affordable SUV's" by Kelley Blue Book, the Outlander Sport has been recognized for its "compact size that makes it a breeze to slip into any space in the lot, along the street or in the garage between the snow blower and lawn mower," according to the *Chicago Tribune*.

Surprisingly, though, if you rewind through automotive history and go back to the very roots of the sport utility segment, you'll find that the 2015 Mitsubishi

Outlander Sport has something in common with the 1940s–60s Willys Jeep station wagon! At least dimensionally:

	2015 Mitsubishi Outlander Sport	*1950 Willys Jeep station wagon*
Wheelbase	105.1"	104.5"
Overall Length	169.1"	174.0"

Certainly beyond its depth and breadth, there's very little similarity between the Outlander Sport and the Willys Jeep wagon. The Mitsubishi obviously performs better, is safer, more fun to drive, offers so much more in the way of comfort and convenience, and lots, lots more—which is what you'd expect from twins that were separated by 65 years of evolutionary development. But it's interesting to realize that today's new segmentation architecture is nothing more than yesterday's mainstream market specification.

The same goes with current compact–mid size trucks (with regular cabs), which run down the road on what was essentially early postwar pickup parameters. Take a look:

	Toyota Tacoma	*1955 Ford F100*
Wheelbase	109.4"	110.0"
Overall Length	190.4"	189.1"

Like the Mitsubishi/Jeep wagon comparison, the '55 Ford functionally pales in comparison to today's Toyota Tacoma, which leads the compact–mid size category by a wide margin. It turns out that Ford discontinued their similarly sized Ranger, while General Motors just inflated the proportions of its new Chevrolet Colorado and GMC Canyon siblings to almost full-size status, leaving what's left of available truncated trucks to the more old-school Toyota and Nissan incumbents.

It really is too bad that so many American consumers have been coerced by modern marketing magic. When you see 1950s or '60s pickups today, they just seem so small compared to everything else that's now out there on the road. But the Toyota Tacoma demonstrates that it sure is nice to be able reach over the side of the bed and haul out all the trash on a Saturday morning at the town transfer station without the need for a step ladder! Just like an old Chevy step-side.

So let us never forget that all of the above discussion conclusively demonstrates the importance of lessons learned from antique automobile history. To remain as a viable competitor and succeed in today's automotive industry, you might sometimes have to go back to the future to accelerate ahead.

Three-Peat

July/August 2016

As car makers continue to search for enhanced manufacturing efficiency and owners look for improved economy of operation, automotive history has once again come to the rescue by repeating itself. Witness the increasing availability of three-cylinder engines.

The inline three-cylinder goes back to the dawn of the automotive industry. Early on, engine cylinders were produced individually and assembled modularly. A set of three was a compromise that a few adventurous pioneers employed to satisfy space, weight and complexity constraints. Having met with minimal success, the triple crown of combustion chambers is now a forgotten footnote from the era of anything-goes experimentation (see sidebar).

As manufacturing methods and material science improved, engines began to be cast with a common crankcase. Simultaneously, better carburetion, ignition and production accuracy led to higher outputs and increased engine speeds that exposed the three-cylinder's most critical shortfall: imbalance around its middle piston, which led to rough running. According to *Fundamentals of Automotive Engine Balance* by W. Thomson (published by Mechanical Engineering Publications, Ltd., 1978), "The couples (the combined primary and secondary forces of the three-cylinder combustion process) do not provide such a happy picture … the distribution of forces along the crankshaft produces couples of varying magnitude as the crankshaft rotates … which tends to displace the engine upwards … pitching and yawing couples arise."

Before long, the monoblock four-cylinder would become the predominant powertrain of choice, not only because the two-cylinder alternative was already overtaxed, but because of the arrival of the en bloc Model T Ford, which quickly met with universal acclaim. Of course sixes, eights, twelves and even sixteens would go on to further power the industry as it matured; thus the three-cylinder was unceremoniously superseded.

Some 40 years later, the three-cylinder began to enjoy a slight resurgence, particularly as Europe started to rebuild after World War II. With a good portion of its heavy industry reduced to rubble, simple and cost-effective solutions (such as bicycles, scooters and mopeds) were called upon to put the war-torn weary back

With plastic body, the DKW 3=6 Monza set some speed records in 1956.

on wheels. Beyond that, not simply the three-cylinder but the even easier-to-manufacture three-cylinder two-stroke began to be deployed in some small select cars.

Memorable examples include the DKW 3=6 from 1953, which displaced 896cc and generated 34 hp. The model designation was marketing speak to help communicate that its three two-stroke power pulses per crankshaft revolution were the equivalent of six four-stroke expansion cycles. As a two-stroke, the three-cylinder proved smoother because combustion forces were better spread. In addition, with only seven moving parts, the minimalist message was further promoted in such advertising campaigns as "The Remarkable DKW from Dusseldorf."

Based on DKW designs, Sweden's Saab followed suit with a three-cylinder two-stroke when the 93 model arrived in late 1955 as a 1956 model. East Germany's Wartburg and the Polish FSO (Fabryka Samochodów Osobowych, or Passenger Automobile Factory) also relied on three-cylinder two-strokes during their embattled existences, for exactly the same reason: because they were easy and inexpensive to produce and operate.

By the 1960s, impending clean air legislation and/or social-corporate upheaval—depending upon the country of origin considered—would finally push the three-cylinder back into automotive oblivion, where it would remain until a global gas crisis or two later.

Early American Three-Cylinder Cars

1905–1906	Adams-Farwell (Rotary) (Dubuque, Iowa)
1905	Ariel (Boston, Mass.)
1908–1910	Atlas (Springfield, Mass)

1902–1903	Baldner (Xenia, Ohio)
1903–1904	Caloric (Chicago, Ill.)
1905	Cameron (Pawtucket, R.I.)
1904–1907	Compound (Middletown, Conn.)
1900–1908	Duryea (Reading, Pa.)
1906–1909	Elmore (Clyde, Ohio)
1908	Euclid (Cleveland, Ohio)
1907–1909	Eureka (Beavertown, Pa.)
1905	Gaeth (Cleveland, Ohio)
1902	Gasmobile (Marion, N.J.)
1903–1904	Howard (Yonkers, N.Y.)
1903	Jaxon (Jackson, Mich.)
1909–1912	Jonz (Beatrice, Neb.)
1910–1913	Kearns (Beavertown, Pa.)
1913	Lambert (Anderson, Ind.)
1901–1903	Long Distance (Jersey City, N.J.)
1909–1910	Paige-Detroit (Detroit, Mich.)
1903–1905	Phelps (Stoneham, Mass.)
1905	St. Louis (St. Louis, Mo.)
1904	Thomas (Buffalo, N.Y.)
1903	Toledo (Toledo, Ohio)
1903–1905	Waterloo (Waterloo, Iowa)
1904	Woodruff (Akron, Ohio)
1905–1906	Zent (Bellefontaine, Ohio)

Source: Standard Catalog of American Cars, 1805–1942, *by Beverly Rae Kimes and Henry Austin Clark, Jr.*

The world was a changing place, and fresh eyes took a new look at the economical three-cylinder, particularly upstart manufacturers who had minimal investment capital and were looking to elbow their way into the industry. Japanese automaker Daihatsu introduced its 843cc Charade in 1977. Suzuki followed with its own subcompact in 1983, which appeared in the U.S. under such designations as Geo Metro, Chevy Sprint and Suzuki Swift. The 997cc three-cylinder Subaru Justy appeared a year later. Not to be left out, Ford introduced its Mazda-designed but Kia-built Festiva in 1987, and then the Aspire in 1993.

Mitsubishi in particular has maintained a strong commitment to the three-cylinder and continues to do so. Its Colt evolved into what is now called the Mirage, but it's certainly no figment of the imagination. Having spent some quality time behind the wheel of one, I can confirm that it's simply a fine small car for its intended purpose, despite its inherent lumpy idle. *Motorweek TV* describes it as an interesting fit, for perhaps this audience in particular. "The Mitsubishi Mirage is a bit of a throwback to a simpler time when small cars were bought purely on price as basic transportation," which I can confirm, along with having also enjoyed its 40+ mpg fuel economy capability.

Among other places, the 400cc-per-cylinder 1.2-liter took me from eastern Connecticut across New York's Tappan Zee Bridge and down along the Palisades Parkway into New Jersey. Then we went way out west across Route 80 toward the Delaware Water Gap. Keeping up with traffic all the way, the mini Mitsu simultaneously returned that "best fuel economy for a non-hybrid" performance about which the company boasts. Okay, so it may not be the fanciest thing on four wheels, but with a starting price of $12,995, you really can't go wrong. As Garrison Keillor's tasty Powdermilk Biscuits ads proclaim on NPR's old-time radio re-creation show *A Prairie Home Companion*, the Mitsubishi Mirage has "the strength to get up and do what needs to be done."

In fact, it gets it done better while in sustained forward motion along the open road. I can easily imagine that in continuous bumper-to-bumper traffic, its erratic idle might turn into an irritation. So the Mirage's final assessment is really a function of the specific demands that the end user will ultimately place upon it. I will say, though, it worked for me.

But turning back to Mr. Thomson's *Fundamentals of Automotive Engine Balance* tutorial, his prediction from 1978 would ultimately be proven wrong: "Three-cylinder engines are normally chosen because of their simplicity and it is doubtful if the complexity of an auxiliary balancer shaft would ever be acceptable…." The fact is that the engine's legacy bugaboo—vibration—has become a more recent focus for further improvement. During the 2000 model year, a jewel of a 1,000cc (1.0-liter) three-cylinder was specified for the landmark Insight hybrid, which included a balance shaft. Leave it to Honda's engine wizards to likewise "get up and do what needs to be done."

Today, the effort to quell the three-cylinder's bad behavior goes beyond just the balance shaft. Harmonic crankshaft dampers, active engine mounts, turbocharging and direct injection are enhancing the refinement and performance of the three-banger. And as Honda so clearly demonstrated, the three-cylinder engine architecture is particularly appealing in hybrid applications.

The improvements are readily apparent. Ford's current Fiesta, for example, generates 128 hp compared to Daihatsu's old-school 53 hp, from an engine of the same size. Mini is now employing the three-cylinder for those customers who are demanding utmost operating economy, and it's an integral part of Daimler's Smart car specification.

In addition, as you might expect from their social and environmental consciousness, Europeans have now taken to the three-cylinder in an even more meaningful way. Since small is nothing to be ashamed of on the streets of places like Paris, Berlin and London, Peugeot, Citroen, Renault, Opel, Volkswagen, Seat, Skoda and Opel all offer trios of piston and connecting-rod packages, as do Toyota, Nissan and Hyundai over in Asia.

Meanwhile, the three-cylinder also found a welcome home within the world's

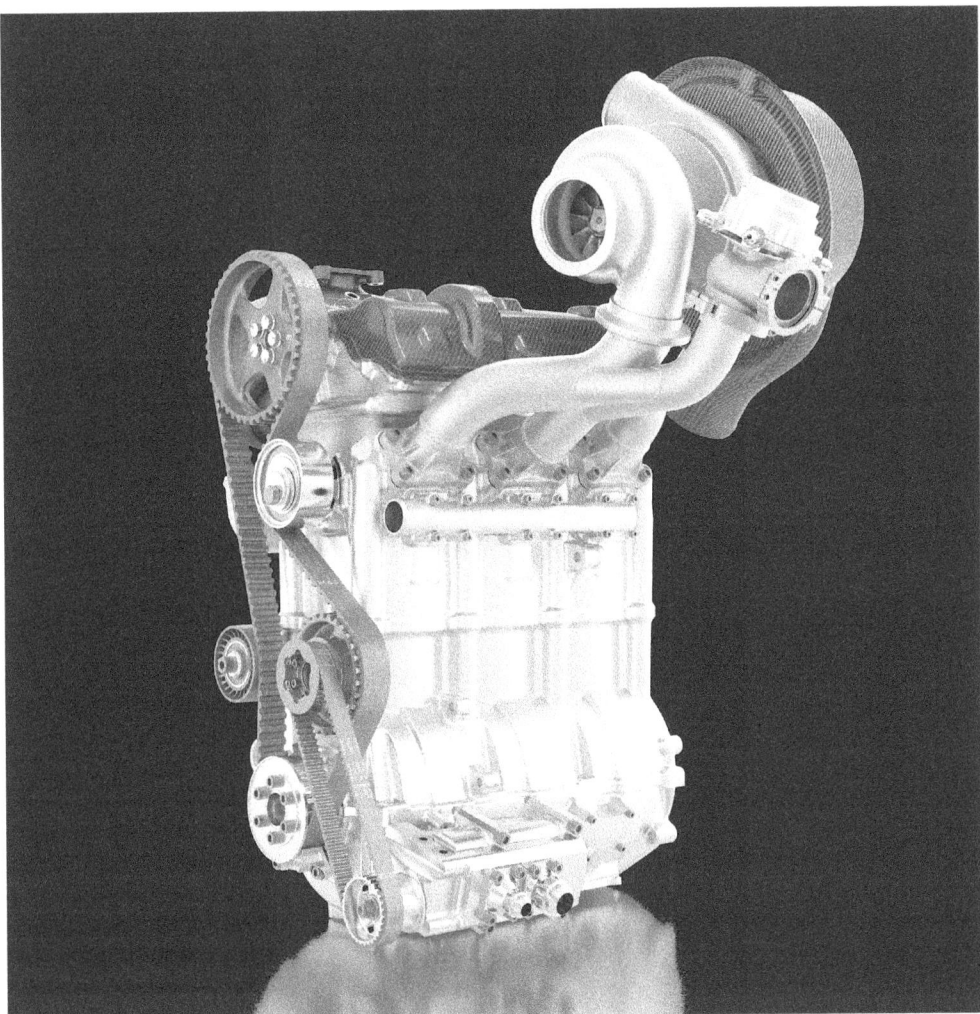

Nissan's 1.5-liter three-cylinder turbo DIG-T R weighs only 88 pounds and measures just 20" × 16" × 8", but it produces 400 horsepower. At Le Mans in June 2014, it helped Nissan make history in running a complete lap around the circuit purely on electric power (186 mph on the Mulsanne Straight). For each hour that the DIG-T R 3-cylinder engine was used, the car would generate enough electricity to run the car for one lap solely on electric power. Sadly, the car's gearbox failed after just 23 minutes, only five laps into the endurance race.

motorcycle manufacturing establishment. Italy's lusty Laverda is best remembered by its triple, as is Kawasaki's ferocious 250, 350, 500 and 750 range of two-strokes. The BSA Rocket 3 and Triumph Trident featured just such a triumvirate, and now a good number of the current Hinckley-built Triumphs do as well. BMW and MV Agusta have both been known to offer three-cylinders, as did recently reincarnated Benelli. Finally, Suzuki GTs featured them and Yamaha repeated its previous XS specification as part of its new award-winning FZ-09 sport standard.

As technology continues to accelerate and the quest for clean air and improved economy remains forever in the forefront, the three-cylinder engine has come back to the future and looks like it's here to stay. Another advantage is that the three's small cross-section results in more concentrated and controlled cockpit intrusion in the event of a severe frontal collision, thereby further isolating occupants from harm. Continuing advances in manufacturing technique and engine management hold even more promise for the pipsqueak powerplant.

Hopefully, we'll start to see a growing acceptance of the three-cylinder as a compelling proposition here in the U.S., mirroring the logical adoption rate that it's enjoying all across Europe and throughout Asia. Though I'm sorry to say, American amnesia seems to be setting in again with the current state of low gas price affairs. Buyers are now turning their attention toward big sport utilities and big pickup trucks once more, and in a big way. So plans for three-pot engine applications are unfortunately being scuttled as we speak, in fear of market backlash—such as a range-extending option for the newly updated Chevy Volt. Certainly, nobody's aggressively advertising that they offer a three-cylinder engine.

That's too bad because good things have, still do and will continue to come in threes.

Talking About Torque

MARCH/APRIL 2017

From "She's Real Fine, My 409" by The Beach Boys to Jim Wangers' memoir (of Pontiac GTO fame), *Glory Days: When Horsepower and Passion Ruled Detroit*, displacement and power have historically received their fair share of attention as engine performance parameters, particularly when it comes to advertising and promotion. In the words of Rodney Dangerfield, however, torque just "don't get no respect!" And that's too bad, because for every man and every woman out there every day, it's certainly the most crucial consideration.

According to Professor Edward F. Obert and his landmark *Internal Combustion Engines* treatise (International Textbook Company, 1944), "torque is a measure of the ability to do work, while power is a measure of the rate at which the work is done. Putting this in another way, the torque determines whether an engine can drive a vehicle through sand or other obstacles, whereas power determines how quickly the car progresses over the obstacles." So in a simple sense, horsepower picks up where torque leaves off. Torque drives acceleration, while horsepower ultimately determines sustained top speed.

As a unit of measure, torque predates horsepower and displacement. It was first quantified by Archimedes, who analyzed its influence in his study of levers. Mathematically, torque is defined as the rate of change of angular momentum of an object, which is why it's also referred to as moment, since it's the tendency of a force to rotate an object around an axis.

Regrettably, torque's status as a second-class specification is well rooted in the annals of engineering history. C. Lyle Cummins, Jr. (the son of diesel engine pioneer Clessie Lyle Cummins) observed, "Horsepower was, unfortunately, a magic word in the nineteenth century as well as the twentieth, but the torque or turning effort of an engine is a primary performance factor; horsepower is a derived function of torque and engine speed" *(Internal Fire: The Internal Combustion Engine, 1673–1900,* Carnot Press, 1976).

You don't need to specifically measure torque to understand its consequence, because you can feel it in the seat of your pants. Even in a Model T Ford, you learn to manipulate the throttle and spark advance to operate on the peak of the engine's performance curve. It's a delicate visceral balance that was similarly referred to as being "on the pipe" in a two-stroke engine.

But that was back in the day when engines actually had torque curves. Unlike horsepower (HP = RPM × Torque ÷ 5252), torque is not speed (RPM) dependent, so the torque peak is normally at a lower engine speed than the power peak, which would usually occur either at or near the maximum engine speed. Thus, torque is a more usable commodity. Variables such as camshaft profiles and intake/exhaust manifold lengths and cross-sections have often been manipulated to help position or broaden a torque peak, as a function of application demands.

With the arrival of electronic control and new technology, however, engines no longer have what could be considered a traditional torque curve. A torque plateau is more like it, with output in abundance from the get-go, and then all across the engine's full operating range. Here are three recent examples that I had the good fortune to evaluate, which demonstrate the point:

Jeep Grand Cherokee EcoDiesel

The Jeep Grand Cherokee is recognized as the standard bearer in the invention of the luxury sport utility vehicle (SUV) segment, so much so that it clearly inspired Mercedes-Benz to create the M-Class, which went from competitor to corporate cousin after Daimler-Benz acquired Chrysler. Though that's another story, it does serve to illustrate the global reach and influence of the Jeep brand. So it's no surprise that "the toughest four-letter word on four wheels" has dabbled with a bit of diesel development over the years, on the world stage, in the interest of providing utmost hauling and towing capability—most recently as an outgrowth of current FCA (Fiat Chrysler Automobiles) Group ownership.

Coincidentally, if not conveniently, within the FCA portfolio, there's a wholly-owned diesel engine subsidiary known as VM. Founded in 1947, VM Motori S.p.A. hails from Cento, Ferrara, Italy—the same ingeniously fertile region which spawned Ferrari, Lamborghini, Maserati and Ducati—and was created by Claudio Vancini and Ugo Martelli.

With a design philosophy that's been grounded in a modular manufacturing ethic, VM has produced diesels in 1, 2, 3, 4 and 6-cylinder configurations. From industrial and marine applications, they ventured into the automotive domain in 1979 through a relationship with Alfa Romeo. In 1995, Detroit Diesel acquired VM, and an alliance with Chrysler began. DaimlerChrysler assumed ownership of Detroit Diesel and VM in 2000, but by 2003, Penske stepped in and assumed a 51 percent stake. In 2007, GM took control of Daimler's equity. Then, in 2011, Fiat bought out Penske's interests and VM is now a 50/50 joint venture between GM and Fiat. In addition to Jeep, VM also currently supplies Maserati and Lancia with diesels and has had previous contracts with Chrysler, Dodge, Land Rover,

Jeep Grand Cherokee EcoDiesel (FCA Chrysler).

Toyota, Ford and Opel. They've also licensed their technology to Hyundai and Daewoo.

Earlier on, Jeep did the diesel dance with England's Perkins engine concern (Perkins Engines Company, Ltd.). The CJ was coupled with the Perkins 4.192 (4-cylinder, 192 cid) from 1961 to 1969. The same engine was used in a Massey-Fergusson tractor. It was a match that clearly wasn't made in heaven. *FourWheeler* magazine projects that slightly fewer than 2,000 were produced. A 2.1-liter Renault turbodiesel was later offered in the Cherokee from 1985 to 1987. From the "if at first you don't succeed, try, try again" department, a 2.8-liter inline four-cylinder VM diesel appeared on the Jeep Liberty equipment list for 2005 and 2006.

But back to the future: VM launched a new line of V-6 diesels in 2011. An improved example of that 60-degree 3.0-liter engine is now optionally available in upmarket Grand Cherokee variants, such as the Limited and Summit editions, etc. It develops a tenacious 420 lb–ft torque @ 2,000rpm and delivers a best-in-class 30 mpg highway. Horsepower in comparison? A more than adequate 240 @ 3,600rpm.

With such gutsy lowdown grunt, Jeep's four-cam EcoDiesel provides a category-leading towing capacity of 7,400 pounds and delivers an operating range of up to 730 miles, while simultaneously meeting stringent Euro emission standards. The diesel's compression ignition clatter is evident, but it's not overly intrusive. The VM alternative is a $4,500 option.

Ward's Auto named the VM 3.0-liter one of the industry's "10 Best" engines for

2014. They concluded that, "ideally mated to an 8-speed automatic transmission, the 3.0-liter turbodiesel goes about its business with little effort or humdrum...."

But perhaps Jeep has best summed up the VM engine's virtues—the gift that just keeps on giving with a mere press of the accelerator pedal—in its most recent marketing campaign. "Forget what you thought about diesel. The available Jeep EcoDiesel engine offers efficient performance that increases range and improves power—all while leaving little trace of being there."

Like a lot of underappreciated antique cars of today, however, the Jeep EcoDiesel and its wonderful treasure trove of torque may leave little trace tomorrow because its sales penetration has proved minimal. Before the recent VW diesel debacle, the VM V-6 represented a mere 8 percent of total Grand Cherokee sales. No doubt, the bad press that's since engulfed the oil burner engine has had a negative impact on Jeep's results, too, just as it has for every other diesel provider.

Sometimes they're rare for a reason. In this particular case, it's perhaps an unfortunate example of collateral damage, especially for the sport utility enthusiast who wants to go anywhere with giddy-up and gusto.

Dodge Challenger Hellcat

Certainly, a torque monster that won't soon be forgotten is the Dodge Challenger Hellcat! From the legendary high-winged Charger Daytona to more recent V-10 Vipers, Dodge has traditionally erred on the side of overkill, if not the outrageous, to set itself apart in an overcrowded marketplace. So when GM and Ford arrived with big-blocks, for example, Chrysler responded with a big-block Hemi.

Now here comes the Hellcat, with an incredible 650 lb–ft of ground-pounding tire-squealing torque and 707 hp from its 6.2-liter V-8. It's a modern take on such previously referenced classic torque manipulation techniques "as camshaft profiles and intake/exhaust manifold lengths and cross-sections ... to help position or broaden a torque peak." Only, to the extreme!

Yeah, the Hellcat's got a Hemi, but this latest iteration includes a twin-screw supercharger that drives nearly 12 pounds of boost pressure through the inlet tract, via a grille-mounted air-catcher inlet port. Separate water-to-air intercoolers with high-speed variable-flow water pumps are mounted on both sides of the supercharger to feed each bank of cylinders with cool dense air. An electronically controlled bypass valve keeps all the induction magic in accord ... a long way from old-school manifold length alterations.

Meanwhile, spent gas exits the aluminum cylinder heads through double-walled exhaust manifolds and a 2.75-inch straight-through dual exhaust system that includes twin electronically controlled exhaust valves. In addition to improved performance, it regales with a combustion concerto. Remember something called the

Dodge Challenger Hellcat (Stellantis Media).

exhaust cut-out? Well, this is a modern interpretation, which actively reroutes flow through solenoid flap valves instead of dumping to atmosphere.

Again, the days of simple exhaust manifold alteration to unlock hidden torque advantage are long gone. And it's all under the control of a sophisticated electronic engine management system that's sealed and locked from the factory, to avoid aftermarket access and tuner tampering. The Dodge Hellcat derives its name from Grumman's World War II F6F carrier–based fighter plane, which was powered by a 2,000 hp Pratt & Whitney R-2800 Double Wasp radial engine. The same engine was used in the Corsair and the P-47 Thunderbolt. The Hellcat was credited with taking down more than 5,000 enemy aircraft.

Even though I've spent some quality time on the Autobahn in more exotic offerings than the Dodge Challenger, I can confirm that the Hellcat is the fastest car I've ever driven from a kick-in-the-pants point of view. It'll smoke the tires throughout the rev range and, with suggested retail pricing starting at $64,195, it's guaranteed to cross the finish line in a flash as a future collectible, since it's been seriously selling out. And an enthusiast buying public is clamoring for still more.

In a segment that's known for inevitable one-upmanship, it's currently the most powerful production muscle car of all time.

Ford Focus RS

Of course, a mere glimpse of a car like the Dodge Hellcat quickly defines its performance intentions and allows you to accurately level-set your king-of-the-hill

Ford Focus RS (Ford Motor Company).

expectations, but there are other recent examples of underhood torque manifestation that have also pegged the dynamometer needle. They require a bit more understanding to fully appreciate, because their missions are less familiar to the American buying public.

Ford Motor Company has had a long history in World Rallying, the form of motorsport that relies on heavily modified production-based cars or purpose-built specials that are street legal. Street legal in places like Europe and Asia, that is, because significant portions of the rallies take place on public roads, and run from point to point (referred to as stages) at wide open throttle, instead of on an enclosed circuit, like NASCAR racing.

Ford has been participating in the World Rally arena since the days of the Falcon and even before, with such winning campaigns as Monte Carlo in 1936 by a privateer entry. From the Escort RS to the Sierra RS Cosworth, and on to the Group B RS200, the Blue Oval brigade has been power-sliding its way to the forefront of rally history for decades.

It's very much been in pursuit of the classic "win on Sunday, sell on Monday" sales formula, because the cars do look somewhat stock. Ford won the World Rally Championship (WRC) for manufacturers in 1979, 2006 and 2007. It took WRC Drivers' Championships in 1979 and 1981, with Björn Waldegård and Ari Vatanen behind the wheel, respectively. From 1999 to 2011, the company's rally offensive was fueled by the Ford Focus RS—think Subaru WRX STi or Mitsubishi Lancer Evo competitor. Rule changes have resulted in the Fiesta becoming the weapon of choice from the Ford arsenal, though the latest Focus street offering that I drove pays homage to a grand WRC heritage.

Along with the Jeep Grand Cherokee EcoDiesel and the Dodge Challenger Hellcat, the Focus RS demands its own amount of specification respect because it delivers 350 lb–ft of torque @ 3,200 rpm, and coincidentally 350hp, from a 2.3 liter engine! Think about that. It's an engine that's 37 percent of the size of the Hellcat's, but cranks out 54 percent of the Challenger's torque.

Ford has opted to elegantly re-engineer the four-cylinder (from the Mustang) EcoBoost engine's intake architecture with a low-inertia twin-scroll turbocharger and a peak boost pressure of an astounding 23 psi! Intercooling low-restriction manifolds and a large diameter exhaust with a pair of four-inch outlets are further employed to produce its performance plateau. Again, the days of the classic torque curve are over.

In addition, Ford has upped the torque management ante by including a proprietary performance all-wheel drive system that includes Dynamic Torque Vectoring. In a nutshell, it pushes torque from the front to the rear wheels, and then to the outside rim, to improve turn-in by pushing the rear end around. According to Ford, it's a performance advantage that's achieved by "combining outstanding traction and grip with unmatched agility and cornering speed." I can confirm that it works.

Until recently, the Focus RS had long been forbidden fruit on U.S. soil due to homologation and profitability concerns, but American enthusiasts can now get behind the wheel of this rally-inspired hot hatchback and be just like Björn or Ari, among others. It's the latest in a long lineage of 29 predecessors that have proudly worn the ever-special Ford of Europe RS (Rallye Sport) emblem. Yet again, it's an example of accelerating ahead by redeploying old engineering insight through the use of more modern technology, to become tomorrow's next collectible … today.

Talk about a twist of torque!

Power Density
Lessons Learned from Automotive History

SEPTEMBER/OCTOBER 2017

I recently spent some quality time behind the wheel of a 2017 BMW 530i test car. No surprise, it's a rich and refined four-wheeled magic carpet that does justice to the brand's "Ultimate Driving Machine" mantra. It whisked me back to the fall of 1997, when I was working for Mercedes-Benz of North America at their Montvale, New Jersey, headquarters.

In preparing for the launch of the 1998 E-Class, we grappled with the challenge of introducing a new V-6 engine in the E320. It replaced a well-respected inline six-cylinder icon that was recognized for its silky smoothness. We were quite aware that BMW would seize the opportunity to come after us competitively, because, in the words of W. Thomson in his 1978 book *Fundamentals of Automotive Engine Balance*, "The six cylinder inline engine has always been regarded as belonging in the luxury class...."

At the time, the industry was on the hunt for modular manufacturing efficiency as the then-current engineering summit to be scaled. Building a V-6 engine off of V-8 architecture was a logical tactic in the effort to optimize production by leveraging common tooling. Cylinder bore spacing could be shared, ancillary equipment and associated drives could be harmonized, packing considerations could be rationalized, weight was reduced and the broader frontal area of a V-6 provided better deformation management in the event of a frontal collision.

The 1998 E320 was at a crossroads of the brand's compactness because it featured the first Mercedes-Benz–built V-6 engine. In the interest of niche segment sanctity, BMW stuck with tradition instead and retained its tried and true inline six. Recently, they've even gone so far as to offer one in their K-Series motorcycle range because of the turbine-like refinement and emotional driving/riding experience that it provides.

Imagine my surprise when I popped the hood on the latest Munich-made sport sedan and found a 2.0-liter turbocharged four-cylinder "Efficient Dynamics" engine! It also features twin cams and four valves per cylinder, to the tune of 248 horsepower and 258 lb–ft. torque—and a lot of empty engine compartment space around it that would otherwise be occupied by a straight-six or V-8. Why in the world is it under the hood of a new BMW 5-series? Is it a marvel, or a munchkin?

Very simply, it's because the pursuit of power density, and all the efficiency that comes along with it, has driven the automobile since its inception. Speaking with the conviction "to do more with less," Robert Bryce observed that such innovation is always "improving the conditions of humankind" in his 2014 book, *Smaller Faster Lighter Denser Cheaper*. "The age of steam was yielding to the age of the automobile. While Benz kick-started the era, an American, Henry Ford, brought motive power to the masses. In doing so, Ford offered consumers a durable internal-combustion engine that was Smaller Lighter Denser than the steam engines that birthed the industrial revolution."

As the gasoline engine accelerated, the steam car pioneers valiantly fought back, with a vengeance, through innovation. For example, Stanley literature at the time promoted the fact that when it came to power, internal combustion engines were only efficient at certain speeds. They argued that the steamer was the answer to the density dilemma, because it had the ability "to store power, which is generated in advance and is instantaneously available for use in any desired quantity when the driver wants it."

The point was proven in 1906, when Fred Marriott set a two-mile-a-minute (127.66 mph) land speed record in a 1,600-pound Stanley "Rocket" streamliner at Ormond Beach, Florida. Two years prior, Henry Ford had achieved 91.37 mph along the ice outside of Detroit, but it required 1,156 cubic inches (18.9 liters) of four-cylinder internal-combustion engine displacement to do so!

Despite the fact that steam cars also had the ability to "distinguish themselves by the silence and dignity of their behavior," their inconvenience and impracticality were just too much to overcome, and the accepted belief is that it led to the demise of the steamer. But the truth of the matter is that the art of internal-combustion engineering had also begun to rapidly mature in a quest to derive more from less, which sealed the unfortunate fate of the steam engine as a viable automotive power source.

The internal combustion engine was not only improving, but improving faster than its alternatives through advances in material technology and manufacturing precision, which allowed engineers to venture into the realm of combustion control. Lighter (soon to be aluminum) pistons, improvements in fuel metering and careful ignition control were merely precursors of what would follow.

Twin overhead camshafts with four valves per cylinder arrived when the industry was still in its infancy. A Peugeot so specified won the 1912 French Grand Prix and repeated the performance in Indianapolis a year later. As is now the norm, such new technology would soon appear in elite upscale entries for the rarefied few who could afford it, before trickling down and finding its way into more mainstream applications.

From the mighty Duesenberg to the exquisite DV-32 Stutz, the twin-cam engine would evolve into more attainable offerings like Fiat and Alfa Romeo, before making

The first known use of supercharging on automobiles appeared with the 1908 Chadwick Six. While it appears here in a race car during the 1908 Vanderbilt Cup race, it is believed that the blower was also available on production runabouts for an extra $375.

its way toward workhorses like the Saab 900 and General Motors' Quad 4-powered Oldsmobiles, and more. Today, the twin-cam mill is now run of the mill, found in almost everything, down to the middle-of-the-road Honda Civic. As such, it's often barely even referenced as a differentiator within competitive spec summaries.

Supercharging is another example of technology that was harnessed early on to wring out more from what was then the norm. The supercharger achieved acclaim in aircraft applications as a way to combat decreasing air density at altitude. Pressurizing the inlet air tract made up for the natural reduction in air mass, particularly as pilots strove to fly higher. A mechanically driven impeller, powered by the engine itself, provided the impetus. By simultaneously providing more fuel, performance was maintained and allowed barnstormers and aces to continue to climb. The supercharger enjoyed its aviation heyday between the two world wars.

It then spilled over under the hoods of Duesenberg race cars in 1924, followed by production Duesenbergs, Auburns, Cords and Grahams, and later Studebakers, but before that it was Pottstown, Pennsylvania's, Chadwick that generally gets credit for the world's first automotive supercharger application, despite scant details that can clearly confirm it. Lee Sherman Chadwick's racer dates back to the 1908 time frame, and made its mark in hillclimbs, followed by the Vanderbilt Cup. Mercedes then brought automotive supercharging into its first recognized series production run during the early 1920s, even though Chadwick listed it "for an extra $375 on the production runabout," according to a definitive Beverly Rae Kimes account that appeared in *Automobile Quarterly*'s Vol. IX, No. 2 issue (1970).

In 1955, another milestone was achieved as the power density quest progressed. Chevrolet's small-block V-8 would revolutionize Detroit's engine engineering ethos. According to Pat Chappell's landmark *The Hot One: Chevrolet 1955–1957*, it was considered an "economy engine ... cheap to build, and efficient in operation."

Innovative thin-wall casting allowed the 265-cubic-inch V-8 to shed 41 pounds compared to the inline-six that it replaced. Meanwhile, it cranked out 26 more horsepower. In lieu of traditional rocker arm shafts, the small-block employed independent rocker arms that were stud-mounted and retained by fulcrum balls and nuts. Cylinder heads were interchangeable, pushrods were hollow and the compact yet powerful configuration made the small-block Chevy V-8 the Motown poster child for engine packaging efficiency, and thus improved power density.

In 1957, it would achieve what was then the elusive one-horsepower-per-cubic-inch threshold with 283 hp when its displacement was increased to 283 cubic inches, with fuel-injection applied (Chrysler also achieved the milestone with their 354 cid V-8 in 1956). Many of its innovations and design details remain with us to this day. Obviously no munchkin, it would instead go on to achieve affectionate, if not iconic,

The 1955 Chevrolet 265 cid V-8 was nicknamed "Mighty Mouse" not only for its efficiency in producing power, but also because it was inexpensive to produce. Weighing 41 pounds less than the six-cylinder engine that preceded it, the lightweight V-8 cranked out 26 more horsepower. In 1957, fitted with fuel injection and with an increase in displacement, it produced one horsepower per cubic inch.

appreciation as America's "Mighty Mouse," because it was both powerful and small/lightweight.

Following in the footsteps of the supercharger, the turbocharger likewise increases inlet air density through forced induction. In this case, though, it is the expansion of spent exhaust gas that drives the compressor instead of mechanical means. Therefore, the parasitic loss from engine drive, as in a supercharger, is avoided. Yet again, *smaller faster lighter*, and while not necessarily *denser*, maybe *cheaper*? It, too, is an outgrowth of world war aircraft inspiration.

Employed in heavy trucks by the late 1930s, the turbocharging technique came to American cars with Chevrolet's Corvair Monza and the Oldsmobile Jetfire from 1962 to 1963. The F85 Jetfire went as far as to include water injection to quell the concern of temperature rise within the inlet tract under pressure, an iteration of the intercooler concept. Read on.

Demonstrating that there's no such thing as a free lunch, a regrettable byproduct of supercharging and turbocharging is temperature rise during pressurization of the inlet charge, which compromises intake density. The intercooler arrived as a device to deal with that type of density conundrum. To help make more from less, a passive heat exchanger known as an intercooler is commonly plumbed somewhere within the inlet tract, thereby cooling the path of forced induction to increase air density. It also reduces the danger of detonation. By the late 1900s, air compressors already included intercooling.

Also along the way, there were parallel efforts to address the incessant power density debate. Light and compact, the two-stroke engine was employed during the earliest days of engine development and went on to reappear in the 1940s, '50s and '60s because of its ability to deliver a power pulse with each rotation of the crankshaft (as opposed to every other revolution, like a four-stroke). By the 1970s, the Wankel rotary engine was being heralded as a likely successor to the reciprocating four-stroke engine as a result of its power density proficiency, along with other advantages. Essentially, it delivered three power pulses per revolution from its epitrochoid combustion chamber geometry and three-lobe rotor that circulated within it. In the end, both met with limited commercial success, particularly due to ever-increasing emissions constraints.

Ultimately, it was the advancement of electronic engine management combined with the tried-and-true four-stroke engine that turned the page and brought us to the unparalleled state of the art that we enjoy today, particularly when specified with such enhancements as supercharging and turbocharging. Even the language of engine output expression has been forever altered.

We used to talk in terms of horsepower per cubic inch. There was a time (as with the previously referenced Chevrolet small-block) that generating one horsepower for every cubic inch of engine displacement was a big deal. Well, our above-mentioned BMW example blows that accomplishment into the weeds, because the new 530i delivers slightly more than two horsepower per cubic inch.

And what about engineering history's illustrious torque curve? The sophistication of modern electronic control, and particularly its authority over induction and exhaust flow, has left us instead with what can now be considered a torque plateau. Instantaneous response off idle, followed by a surge of thrust all through the rev range.

Power-to-weight ratio is yet another parameter that many of us used to consider sacred. Today it's more a part of the historical record than it is the specification page, because reduced weight and increased power are merely the price of admission in the modern automotive industry, like meeting safety and emission standards.

So the attention to optimize engine power density has clearly been a mainstay in the automobile's rite of passage. Similar to the lithium battery, the ability to deliver more output from less mass brings peripheral advantages with it. With the li-ion battery, a new world order has been established in power tool opportunity and cell phone performance. When applied to the automobile, compact powertrains with greater power density will reduce weight, redirect packaging emphasis from under the hood to the passenger and luggage compartments instead and will further improve operating efficiency.

I'm going to go confirm that now because there's a new Volvo S90 waiting outside that delivers a marvelous 316 horsepower from its cast-aluminum 2.0-liter four-cylinder engine. That's more than 2.5 horsepower per cubic inch from a Swedish family sedan! It's been made possible by what is now traditional twin-cam four-valve-per-cylinder technology combined with supercharging, turbocharging and intercooling, within a single engine package. Don't those technologies sound familiar?

These well-established solutions have simply been redeployed by going back to the future and diving into the toolbox of automotive history. Only now the combination is being amped up through modern electronic integration and management.

The vacuum tube was displaced by the transistor. The flash bulb and rolls of 35 mm film were superseded by the diminutive digital camera. So it's no surprise, in the words of Robert Bryce's book title, that our automotive heritage remains an ever-progressing adventure of Smaller Faster Lighter Denser Cheaper innovation. The spirit and intent of continuous automotive improvement was born in America when brothers Frank and Charles began work on their second Duryea in 1894. And the journey hasn't ceased since.

Lessons learned ... indeed.

Third Time's the Charm!

January/February 2018

Automotive history has clearly proven that the electric car has never been quite ready for prime time. Despite all the interest and enthusiasm, it's an idea that's always outpaced available technology. Though I'm pleased to report that recent engineering advances will finally allow the electric to move from a curiosity to a commodity—within reason, that is.

The origin of the electric automobile dates back to the very beginning of the industry. Early experiments certainly demonstrated the potential. *The Western Electrician* reported in 1892, "The sight of a well-loaded carriage moving along the streets at a spanking pace with no horses in front and apparently nothing onboard to give it motion, was a sight…."

The distinct advantage of electric propulsion was, of course, that it was clean, quiet, smooth, refined and easy to master, with no gear changing and effortless starting. It was not only efficient, but impressively effective, as well. It's well known that the first closed-course auto race in America, the 1896 event at Narragansett, Rhode Island's Trotting Park, a one-mile oval, was won by an electric car that was built by the Riker Electric Motor Company. The Riker Electric Vehicle Company was subsequently formed in 1899. The first car to set the land speed record at more than 100 kph (62 mph) was Camille Jenatzy's torpedo-bodied "La Jamais Contente" electric, that same year.

According to James Rood Doolittle in his book, *The Romance of the Automobile* (1916), "there is no practical means of mechanical locomotion that is more highly developed or more evenly balanced in all its parts than the electric automobile itself. As a piece of mechanism it is so nearly perfect that he would be a rash prophet who would undertake to point out the direction of future improvements." So, compared to its then-current steam-powered and gasoline-fueled contemporaries, the electric car came charging out of the starting gate at the dawn of the automobile age.

But it was the limitation of operating range, of course, that would constrain the ultimate success of the electric. While it proved useful within city confines, it was also employed in commercial applications that included taxi service. Doolittle would observe, "The growth of the business has never taken on boom proportions.

The Riker Electric Vehicle Company built more than a dozen types of electric cars and trucks. This Riker, ca. 1900, was a gift to the National Museum of American History (Smithsonian Institution) by its original owner, Mrs. Herbert Wadsworth. It is not currently on display.

The increase in the demand for electrics has been sufficiently moderate...." The technology just wasn't there, and even ideas like battery exchange stations did little to enhance achievement. Electrical engineers just didn't have the innovative wherewithal or manufacturing means to keep up with the exponentially improving gas engine and its subsystems. Not to mention that as a fuel source, gasoline was simultaneously becoming easily affordable and more widely distributed at the time.

Early electric automakers were known to be quite conservative compared to the more adventurous gasoline car builders. Range limitations essentially excluded electrics from reliability runs and cross-country tours, which proved to be a principal marketing method of the day. In addition, electric car makers couldn't buy enough advertising to compete with the headlines that essentially endorsed the in-use integrity and "win on Sunday, sell on Monday" success that gas and steam alternatives enjoyed.

Electric automobile acceptance was further stymied by unfortunate social stereotype. According to David Gartman in *Auto Opium: A Social History of American Automobile Design* (1994), "Even more influenced by carriage design than the first gasoline-engined autos were the electric vehicles. Early vehicles with electric motors had the advantages of being silent, and easy to operate, making them popular with the upper class, especially the women. Electric autos quickly became part of the bourgeois social scene and were consequently fitted with the elegant handcrafted coachwork to which this class was accustomed in horse-drawn vehicles ... the cultural connotation of femininity that the electrics acquired was also a handicap in an industry with a pronounced masculine bias."

It should also be remembered that the electrical infrastructure along Main Street, U.S.A., was in its infancy then. Home electrification was coming into vogue during the second decade of the 20th century, which was a necessity for owner/operator recharging. By then, however, the gasoline automobile had proved its superiority and accelerated to the industry forefront.

If that weren't enough of a challenge, the arrival of good roads ignited a wanderlust among early automobilists, with new horizons to explore both far and wide, which would prove to be the death knell for the battery-driven variant. The uncertain electric would be kicked to the curb as a result of its limited operating range.

By the 1920s, the intrepid old guard like Detroit Electric (Anderson Electric Car Co.) was desperately fighting for survival, and in a last-ditch effort to attract attention and improve acceptance, they went so far as to update antiquated carriage-inspired coachwork with faux radiators, along with mainstream Dodge sheet metal. After the Depression, Detroit Electric production was curtailed to a pitiful "by subscription only" basis. Having manufactured some 13,000 vehicles since 1907, Detroit Electric

1937 Detroit Electric in the Armacost Museum in Kansas City, Missouri. In the end, they were still using ca. 1930 Dodge bodies (West Peterson photo).

would deliver its last car in 1939. The golden age of the electric automobile was over.

The second coming of the electric alternative arrived during the 1960s and '70s amid ever-increasing environmental and fossil fuel concerns. Perhaps the earliest and most recognized example was the Henney Kilowatt, which went on sale in 1959. To say that its brief existence was the result of circuitous origin would be an understatement.

It was developed by the National Union Electric Company, and was inspired by the firm's president, C. Russell Feldmann (who had an early interest in Winton Engine and Transitone Auto Radio). National Union was a conglomerate with ties to Eureka Williams (vacuum cleaners), Emerson Quiet Kool (air conditioners) and the Henney Motor Company (coachworks and professional cars), among others. Joining forces with the Exide Battery Corporation (National Union built their batteries), Henney assembled the Kilowatt at its subsidiary Oneida School Bus factory in Canastota, N.Y.

The Renault Dauphine was chosen as the donor car because it was compact, lightweight and inexpensive. The combination of its commodious rear engine compartment and spacious front trunk provided an expansive platform for battery trays and electrical infrastructure. The four-door Dauphines were supplied by the French automaker sans powertrain. Renault was ready and willing to accommodate National Union because it happened to be saddled with an abundance of inventory at the time, as their American interests began to wane.

The Kilowatt was introduced with a 36-volt system (18 2-volt batteries) that could propel the car to 40 mph, replaced by a 72-volt (12 6-volt batteries) alternative a year later that supposedly attained 60 mph. Operating range improved from roughly 40 miles per charge to a claimed 60.

The Henney Kilowatt attempted to leverage all of the established electric attributes, so it was promoted as "Completely Uncomplicated! Completely Undemanding! Completely Electric!" It was billed as the answer for everyone and was even pitched as an in-plant appliance, which could be used under the roof in a factory and from building to building in a campus environment, since it was so silent and emitted no exhaust fumes. In reality, it pretty much proved to be "Completely Impractical!"

All the marketing hype couldn't improve the perception of its limited range and pathetic performance, and when it comes to what could be considered risky new technology from an unknown car company, perception very much drives reality, because there are no other attributes on which to rely. Apparently, Henney couldn't profitably produce the Kilowatt at its suggested $3,600 price point, either. It's been said that just 100 Renault Dauphines were electrically equipped, with only 47 ultimately being sold. Most went to utility companies.

Timing is everything in the automobile industry, and the Henney Kilowatt proved that the timing for the American market to embrace an electric car was still not right. Yet again, it was a case of too little technology, too soon, and the venture failed after a mere two years of existence.

Fifteen years later, Florida's Sebring-Vanguard fared a little better. Like the Henney Kilowatt, it arrived in response to a fuel crisis. Yes, it was based on Club Car golf cart concepts and features, but was inspired by the battery-powered Lunar Rover. The firm was founded by New York Chrysler–Plymouth dealer Robert Beaumont, who was intrigued with the idea of an affordable electric vehicle for every man and woman. He was of the opinion that if the idea was good enough for the moon, then why not try planet Earth?

The Citicar featured a Cycolac plastic (a polymer known to be both tough and stable) body that was "styled as the most efficient package for a seated human form," according to Sebring-Vanguard Director of Operations Bob Sanders. It tipped the scales at just 1,300 pounds, of which 520 was battery weight. Early examples were driven by a 2.5 hp motor from a 36-volt supply, though that was soon updated to 3.5 hp and 48 volts. Eventually, a 6 hp offering appeared.

Original sales literature indicated that it was "Easy to Drive, Downright Cheap to Operate and [required] Virtually No Maintenance." Sound familiar? The company was also quite clear to point out that it was indeed "licensable," because at first glance, potential buyers probably wouldn't/didn't think so.

Car and Driver (1977) described the diminutive "volt wagon" as such: "As long as you accept the limited speed and range, the wonkey cartoon styling and the idea of plugging in the extension cord every night, the Citicar is an ecologically minded method of zipping around town. It's kind of like walking sitting down." With what was said to be a 35 mph top speed (on level ground) and 40-mile operating range, *Consumer Reports* deemed it "foolhardy to drive." Unfortunately, the shortcomings of the "cheese wedge on a golf cart chassis" (*The New York Times*, 2011) Citicar were all too familiar.

Around 2,200 Citicars were built between 1974 and 1977. Another 2,000 followed from 1979 to 1982, after Commuter Vehicles, Inc., acquired the assets from what was then a bankrupt Sebring-Vanguard and renamed it Comuta Car. They also produced a Comuta Van in an attempt to expand the market. Those improved examples are easily recognized by the battery box being relocated behind the bumper. But to no avail. Commuter Vehicles soon ran out of energy and unplugged its enterprise, as well.

Beyond that, there were a few other organizations and inventive entrepreneurs who dabbled with the idea of electric propulsion, to round out this unsuccessful second wave. That includes a project between American Motors and battery-maker Sonotone that developed a run of electrified Jeeps for the U.S. Postal Service, along with a couple of GM concept cars called Electrovair and Electrovette.

Italy's Zagato design house created the fiberglass Zele microcar, which was marketed in the U.S. as the Elcar (not to be confused with the Elkhart Carriage

"As long as you accept the limited speed and range, the wonkey cartoon styling and the idea of plugging in the extension cord every night, the Citicar is an ecologically minded method of zipping around town."—*Car and Driver*

Company's Elcar, which was produced from 1915 to 1931). The Elcar (electric car) was built between 1974 and 1976, and about 500 were manufactured. Otherwise, there wasn't much else to write home about during this particular phase of auto electrification.

Then along came the third iteration of electric automobile development. It began with General Motors' rolling EV1 experiment in 1996. The idea originated with the teardrop-shaped Impact show car, which debuted at the Los Angeles Auto Show in 1990 and was derived from World Solar Challenge experience. It's been said that GM leveraged the Impact in an attempt to politically influence the California Air Resources Board. CARB stipulated that two percent of new cars produce "zero emissions" by 1997. GM countered that it put its best foot forward with the EV1, but voiced concern that its market viability and technical capability were unproven—which is why GM only made 1,117 EV1s available via a carefully scrutinized lease promotion. They further suggested that, as a result, the California regulation needed to be delayed, if not rescinded.

It's well known that General Motors would go on to struggle throughout the early years of the new millennium that followed. After GM pulled the plug on the EV1 in 2003, an incredible amount of controversy ensued, including conspiracy theories and a belief that the General self-sabotaged the project. A documentary film even appeared in its wake, titled *Who Killed the Electric Car?* and recounting a supposed GM strategy to demonstrate that there was no demand for an EV.

Ultimately, the bulk of the EV1 fleet was scrapped, despite impassioned pleas of former lessee devotees. In 2006, then–GM chairman and CEO Rick Wagoner concluded that the worst decision ever during his tenure at the helm was "axing the EV1 electric car program and not putting the right resources into hybrids."

No wonder. While GM zigged by trying to outmaneuver California bureaucrats, Honda and Toyota zagged and were quietly preparing for an ambitious, electrified future—an electric hybrid future, that is.

Honda arrived at the forefront here in 1999 with its Insight as a 2000-model-year vehicle. Like the EV1, it was an aerodynamic exercise that would accommodate only two passengers. In addition to a 3-cylinder engine, it featured an electric motor between the engine and transmission to provide a power assist on demand, called Integrated Motor Assist (IMA). It was the equivalent of an electric turbocharger with regenerative braking that supplied instantaneous torque at the stab of the accelerator pedal.

The Insight was optimized for utmost fuel economy, and constructed with aluminum and plastic panels. To shed weight, door pockets weren't even specified and air conditioning was an extremely hard-to-find option. In the interest of full disclosure, I must admit that I own one, and its license plate proudly proclaims "61 MPG." With an EPA estimate of 61 mpg city/70 mpg highway, it was the most fuel-efficient gasoline-powered automobile in America at the time.

So it's hard for me to accept that it was a failure. Being so heavily skewed toward the fuel economy end of the equation, though—down to a carrying capacity of just a driver and single passenger, and barely a bag of groceries—it never met Honda's sales expectations. Only about 3,500 or so were produced annually in the same Suzuka, Japan, plant that assembled the Acura NSX and Honda S2000, in a first-generation model run that would last through 2006.

Meanwhile, Toyota took a more conservative approach, and would follow some seven months later (here in the U.S.) and ultimately win the marketing war. It built the Prius (which means "first" in Latin) to be more real-world family friendly with four doors. It had been on sale in Japan since 1997. A redundant powertrain was included, that would switch from gasoline to electric propulsion, and vice versa, or engage both in parallel. The Prius would go on to be recognized as the generic de facto category equivalent for hybrids as Kleenex is to tissues. After living with a new Prius Prime for a week, I can understand why.

But a hybrid is not fully electric, so the subject might appear to be a bit off topic for this discussion. In my opinion, the idea of parallel powertrains is certainly not the most elegant engineering solution, since one—the electric one—can't go the distance. Though in fact, the hybrid appears to be the missing link that's ultimately going to allow the electric automobile to finally assimilate.

Of course, hybrid technology is nothing new. It dates back to such innovative experiments as the Bridgeport, Connecticut–built gasoline-electric Armstrong from 1896, not to mention the 1901 Lohner-Porsche Semper Vivus. One could perhaps argue that the 1909 Woods and the Owen Magnetic produced from 1915 to 1922 qualified, having relied on a combination of gasoline and electric drivetrain technologies. Unfortunately, commercial viability was never a strong suit for any of them.

Returning to Toyota and Honda, though: Their marked success, even as a halfway house, has played a pivotal role in familiarizing the buying public and the automotive infrastructure with the trials, tribulations and virtues (of course!) of electric propulsion. In addition to convincing buyers that they're feasible, engaging them from behind the wheel with compelling charge indicators and regenerative braking monitors and enthralling them through unparalleled fuel economy, automotive technicians have learned how to respect and service high-voltage powertrains. First Responders know how to approach a hybrid electric in the event of a serious collision, tow operators can now contain and transport them, insurance companies understand the true extent of their in-use liability and even municipal governments have gotten on board the electric bandwagon with incentives and tax breaks to advance the ultimate objective of improving economy and reducing emissions. Going green has never felt so good.

We're now in a world that's completely different from the market that met the first two attempts to electrify the automobile. Time has marched on, both practically and philosophically, in this internet age of digital dependence, clearly facilitating the acceptance and success of this third wave of electric automobiles—because we've now been conditioned to do so.

Cars like the Nissan Leaf, Mitsubishi MiEV (for the record, I own one of those, too), Hyundai Ioniq, BMW i3 and more have begun to contribute to electric automobile adoption, but none of them are the ultimate answer, due to the inherent anxiety over their limited range. But technology continues to advance at an unabated pace. Ever-improving operating range, vehicle performance and recharging capability are all hurdles that are within the grasp of the automotive engineering community.

Battery packs are getting better and better, with ever-increasing power density, and manufacturing costs are coming down. Lithium-ion is just the beginning. Electric motors are becoming more efficient. Control system capabilities are being augmented even further through innovative software management solutions. Hybrids have contributed to much of this technological advancement by being rolling test beds in daily service.

In the grand scheme, if the new Chevy Bolt is any indication, 200-plus miles between charges is no longer unthinkable, and can indeed be affordable. More such GM derivatives are in the works. The upstart (if not industry disrupter) Tesla, of course, has certainly achieved such performance, but at a price. While they are trying to move downmarket, they've simultaneously excited electric aspiration and inspired awareness in their effort to "accelerate the world's transition to sustainable energy."

When you consider either execution, congratulations are certainly in order for both!

I believe that we are finally on the eve of a meaningful electric-car era. The third time's the charm as a result of 21st-century technological progress and an auspicious stepping stone known as the hybrid, but I predict that more widespread adoption will only be achieved when a multinational industry leader like Mercedes-Benz raises the Tesla bar, and then pushes such technology down through the entire mainstream marketplace on a global basis.

Innovation requires a lot of investment, which comes from cash reserves, venture capital or other assets. Tesla has proven to be an incredible competitor, but they've yet to turn a profit, nor do they have the distribution model to sustain an electric assault on a grand scale. I'd be hard pressed to assume that General Motors has enjoyed any return on investment with the $38,000 Chevy Bolt. Sales incentives are already being applied, and unfortunately, Chevrolet doesn't play on the world stage. The continuation of federal government motivation via mandated tax breaks for buyers of electric autos also remains a critical wildcard.

In the foreseeable future, electric automobiles will end up supplementing gasoline-powered alternatives. In fact, they've already begun to find their way within brand portfolios. Manufacturers will offer a mix of cars, trucks, sport utilities, hybrids, electrics, etc. The gasoline engine won't go away because it has too much of a head start, and it's just too good, which is also the result of electronics. With gasoline remaining at around $2-plus per gallon and pickup truck/sport utility sales continuing to surge, consumers will continue to choose as they see fit.

Meanwhile, the hybrid has already morphed into its own subset, because "plug-in" hybrids (they can be recharged through an external power source) have now been added to the mix, as well, with vehicles such as the Chevy Volt. According to Hyundai, "electric power helps you go farther on a gallon" with a hybrid, while a plug-in provides "Electric when you want it. Gas when you need it." This was proven to me in no uncertain terms, when I was recently serenaded by a sweet rendition of just such a Sonata sedan, from the Korean car maker.

So GM Chairman Rick Wagoner's EV1 observation from 2006 was most prophetic. Variety will remain the spice of life within the automotive marketplace because the electric has clearly elbowed its way into the arena as an alternative. It's finally here to stay. After a l-o-n-g look ... back to the future.

Persistence Pays Off
The V-6 Saga

MAY/JUNE 2018

Truth be told, it's taken me more than 30 years to warm up to the idea of a V-6. In my mind, such engine architecture was simply a compromise from the get-go, offering manufacturers a clear economic advantage but with little practical upside for the poor consumer. Though in fact, the V-6 is a poster-child for the thin reality that separates marketing genius from engineering insanity—that being *success!*

It was yet another invention that was ahead of its time, which can now be accurately interpreted and brought into focus by looking back to the future. By honing in on its origin and evolution, we can gain a greater understanding, if not appreciation, of the V-6 engine's fortitude and foibles.

Leave it to Lancia to cast the first stone, if not the initial casting die, for just such a tooling pattern. Always the innovator, the Italian automaker's original intention was certainly sincere when it began development of the 1950 Aurelia. In an attempt to attract new clientele by distancing the company from prewar principles in a postwar economy, Gianni Lancia (founder Vincenzo's son) was now in charge. He was quite ready to go beyond the firm's well-established, narrow-angle V-4 engine formula to deliver further refinement and performance.

Francesco de Virgilio, working under Chief Engineer Vittorio Jano, specified a six-cylinder with two banks of three cylinders, which were set at an included angle of 60 degrees. Hemispherical combustion chambers were incorporated, as was a two-barrel downdraft carburetor and a single camshaft.

Recognized as the first series-produced V-6 (Marmon made a few around 1905, as did Deutz during the decade that followed), the Aurelia was known for its smooth running nature, due to the even firing intervals across its six individual offset crankpins. A slight horizontal rocking couple was deterred by resilient rubber engine mounts.

It was also narrow enough to fit quite comfortably beneath the compact hood of the lovely Lancia, which also included an interesting rear transaxle arrangement with inboard brakes. What began as a 1.8-liter evolved into 2.0, 2.3 and 2.5 liter

Lancia was a V-6 pioneer; shown here is an Aurelia B24 spider (Shutterstock.com).

displacements. Obviously, the engine was shorter than an equivalent inline six-cylinder. Even back in 1950, the V-6 engine's packaging efficiency, reduced mass and minimal moment of inertia were its most significant engineering assets.

Great Britain's *Motor* magazine confirmed in its May 3, 1950, issue that Lancia was well known for "unorthodox design, but of genuine practical merit." For example, after easily winning its class in the 1950 Mille Miglia, a 2.0 liter Aurelia came in second overall in 1951 behind a 4.1 liter Ferrari America. Numerous other podium celebrations would follow throughout the life of the Aurelia.

With such an auspicious start, you would think that the V-6 would be bound for immediate automotive glory. Unfortunately, the idea was unwittingly detoured early on. General Motors exploited the engine in the interest of manufacturing efficiency, with some unfortunate consequences.

At the outset, GM was drawn to the V-6 as a matter of minimal investment and utmost engineering expediency in response to the early 1960s import onslaught. For the 1961 model year, General Motors launched a triumvirate of compact cars: the Buick Special, Pontiac Tempest and Oldsmobile F-85. Each brand and model would offer its own signature specifications, which would include a V-6 engine for Buick in 1962.

It was derived from what was then a recently-released new generation aluminum 215 cid (3.5 liter) V-8. By essentially removing two cylinders, the Buick eight-cylinder block turned into a 90-degree V-6, which was thus hampered with an uneven firing pattern with only three crankpins, set at 120 degrees apart. Opposing pistons

and connecting rods each shared a crankpin. The cast-iron "Fireball" V-6 displaced 198 cubic inches (3.2 liters), and developed 135 horsepower and 205 lb.-ft. of torque. It was the first mass-produced American V-6 car engine. GMC previously developed a heavier duty 60-degree V-6 for truck applications, starting in 1959.

In use, the entry-level six-cylinder Buick Special demonstrated good performance and respectable fuel economy. *Popular Mechanics* claimed that it was "an exceptionally able and thrifty performer," in their October 1961 issue, and *Motor Trend* followed up by naming it "Car of the Year" in February 1962.

They also concluded that Buick's "V-6 has many claims to fame, not the least of which is that it was

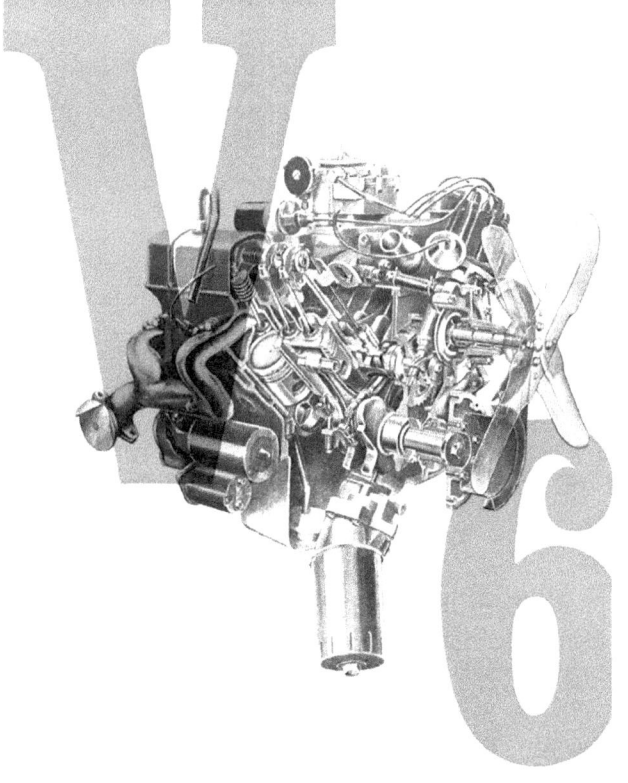

Top, left and right and above: Buick developed its V-6 in the early 1960s (Buick Heritage Alliance images).

probably developed faster than any engine in the industry's history. Thus did the V-6 borrow all the months and months of research, designing, engineering and testing which had created the companion aluminum V-8, to so save a whole year in its own development." *Uh-oh* ... If Paul Masson would "sell no wine before its time," as the TV ads announced, why would General Motors uncork an immature engine?

Despite *Motor Trend's* honorable accolade, the fact is that it's tough to short-circuit any engine's necessary gestation cycle. After all the initial excitement subsided, the Buick V-6's arrival proved premature. In the words of one industry executive, it was "rougher than a cob."

So while GM was able to compete with the imports, and Buick set itself apart from Pontiac and Oldsmobile, the cast-iron V-6 failed to truly distinguish itself within the competitive marketplace. While it might have been a functional workhorse, in its early life, it was never an engine that inspired enthusiasm or the aspiration to actually own one. Unlike the sweet six that Lancia enthusiasts still lust over to this day, the GM V-6 was simply the standard engine in a Buick Special that was not-so special as a result of it, even though sales performance would ultimately prove otherwise. Exacting engine-mount calibration was the secret to its interim success.

In 1967, Kaiser-Jeep would begin using the rumbly Buick V-6. Perhaps the thought was that Jeep buyers would be a bit more tolerant of a rough-running engine, so GM sold them the rights to its V-6. Jeep designated it the "Dauntless," and it certainly helped the struggling automaker defer investment expense. By now, a beefier 225 cid version with a heavier flywheel helped quell the shake, rattle and roll, while Buick would quietly retreat and revert to an inline-six (Chevrolet's 250 cid engine) during that same year.

It would take an early 1970s fuel crisis, or two, to get GM to take a second look and rethink the V-6. They bought back the tooling from what was now a subsidiary of American Motors and returned the engine to production for 1975, then bit the bullet in 1977 and redesigned the crankshaft with split pins that were offset from one another by 30 degrees, thereby resulting in more even cylinder firing. The need was further driven by the imminent demand to downsize, which resulted in General Motors' seismic platform-shift to front-wheel drive, where yet again, with what was now at 231 cid, the V-6 engine's inherent packaging advantage would be put to good use.

Meanwhile, despite GM's sidestep, the Italians were not standing still. Ferrari picked up where Lancia left off and engaged Vittorio Jano in its engineering effort. Enzo Ferrari's son, Alfredo, was enamored with the idea of a V-6 engine for Formula 2 racing during the late 1950s and began consulting with Jano. Alfredo, who was nicknamed Alfredino, thus "Dino," took ill at the time and Jano ended up as more than just an engineering consultant. In fact, he became Dino's bedside confidant.

Between the two of them, a plan was formulated to create a purpose-built 1.5-liter racing engine, which was splayed at 60 degrees. Such a narrow angle in a racing application, however, resulted in a compromised intake tract because a simple

Ferrari's Dino (Shutterstock.com).

carburetor would obviously never do. So the engine was opened up to 65 degrees to further optimize inlet flow. Unfortunately, Dino didn't live long enough to see the end result.

To satisfy GT-class homologation requirements, 500 roadgoing examples of the V-6 were required, but Ferrari was certainly in no position to produce such quantity. So they turned to their compatriots in Turin, and the Fiat Dino was born in 1966. The same 2.0-liter V-6 then made its way into the Ferrari 206 in 1968, with 178 horsepower.

To deal with the fuel metering challenge of overlapping induction strokes, three two-barrel Weber carburetors were included. Twin overhead camshafts were also fitted, and the "Dino," as the new Ferrari sportscar was also affectionately dubbed in honor of Alfredo, gave an early inkling of the V-6's true performance potential, specifically when it was not only balanced, but allowed to breathe properly. The more potent 2.4 liter, 195 horsepower 246 would follow a year later and the Ferrari V-6 would go on to dominate the World Rally scene via the Lancia Stratos, in which it was also installed.

Of course, anything Ferrari could do, and Lancia before it, Citroën felt it could do, too. So when Citroën assumed Maserati ownership in 1968, they immediately went in-house and assigned long-standing engine engineer Giulio Alfieri to design a cutting-edge powerplant for the upcoming SM executive express. In accordance with then-existing French tax restrictions, the end result was a 2.7-liter V-6 that first appeared in 1970.

Under significant time constraints, like Buick, Alfieri utilized V-8 engine tooling (from the Maserati Indy) as a foundation, so the Modena-made V-6 was yet another example of 90-degree architecture. One of the SM's critical constraints was for an engine that would be as short as possible, since it was intended to be mounted longitudinally in support of a front-wheel drive powertrain. Like Ferrari, a pair of twin-overhead camshafts were included, along with hemispherical combustion chambers and three Weber two-barrel carburetors, in the interest of generating a gentrified 170 grand-touring horsepower.

Yes, it too was plagued by vibration concerns due to uneven cylinder firing. Citroën expert/specialist Dave Burnham, of Delanson, New York, is of the opinion that the SM's interesting engine-mount orientation helped even out the odd-firing engine. Its real Achilles heel was its timing chains, particularly its primary crankshaft chain. Updated chains and automatic tensioner technology on the primary addressed that shortfall.

The Maserati V-6 would expand to a 3.0 liter displacement, which was then also fitted to the mid-engined Merak from 1972 to 1983, with as much as 217 horsepower on tap. Yet again, it was becoming apparent that the V-6 engine had plenty of upside opportunity if it was carefully considered, as Alfa Romeo would attest with its sensuous 2.5 and 3.0 liter alternatives that followed.

Peugeot would get into the act as well, in cooperation with others. The Peugeot Renault Volvo (PRV) V-6 saw the light of day in 1974. It would appear in a variety of examples from all of the above, not to mention the rear-engined DeLorean.

By now, GM and Buick would return to the fold and redeem themselves, most significantly with what eventually became known as the 3800. It would be thoroughly revamped from what was previously the 231 (231 cid = 3,785 cc). General Motors had reassumed ownership of its V-6 tooling, as previously mentioned, and reinstalled the production line in the same Flint, Michigan, factory and in exactly the same place where it was originally, in time to reintroduce the engine in the 1975 models.

Along the way, a turbocharged V-6 was added to the Buick engine list in 1978. By 1984, the slender six began to carve out a new identity for itself with the arrival of the Grand National which included sequential fuel injection and computer-controlled ignition, in addition to turbocharging. It developed 200 horsepower. Buick V-6 pace cars and race cars would appear along the way in Indianapolis as well.

It took until 1988, though, for the Buick V-6 to cement its status as a mass-market milestone. GM began to get serious with improved machining tolerances, reputedly to be on par with Japanese manufacturing precision, and introduced multi-point fuel injection and a balance shaft. A balance shaft is an eccentric weighted counter-rotating shaft that offsets vibration impulses. It was developed by the eclectic English aeronautical and automotive engineer Frederick Lanchester in 1904. The naturally aspirated 3800 now developed 165 horsepower.

But it was the ultimate iteration that debuted in 1995 that catapulted the Buick

In the 1987 GNX, Buick's 3.8 liter V-6 generated 245 horsepower.

V-6 to world-class status. The block was heavily redesigned to reduce weight and overall dimensions. Furthermore, there was a concerted effort to improve volumetric efficiency by incorporating new cylinder heads, which featured larger valves and an increased compression ratio. Once more, the V-6 would benefit from better breathing, improved engine management and more precise fuel metering, which resulted in an output of 205 horsepower and improved fuel economy. By now, the wide 90-degree V-angle was an asset because it allowed for improved inlet tuning with the enhanced technology of the time.

Ultimately, GM produced more than one million V-6 engines a year, while total production would go on to exceed 25 million, according to the industry trade journal *Automotive News*. *Ward's Autoworld* would routinely name the 3800 as one of the industry's "Ten Best Engines of the Year." Limited production, performance variants such as the ASC/McLaren Buick GNX and the 4.3-liter GMC Syclone/Typhoon combination would go on to command a cult-like following.

While GM was finally getting its V-6 act together, Maserati was still toiling away with its wee-V intentions. In an attempt to set itself apart, the Italian automaker came up with the idea of hanging twin turbochargers (one off of each bank) on their V-6 engine. At the time, turbocharging technology was such that inertia within the turbine impeller resulted in "lag" upon acceleration. To ensure that the turbo system

Maserati Biturbo engine.

would spool up as fast as possible, Maserati concluded that two smaller units would prove more advantageous.

The result was the Maserati Biturbo, which was produced from 1981 through 1994. The world's first twin-turbo V-6, it also included three valves per cylinder, another first. Although it was originally carbureted, the Biturbo was soon updated with fuel injection in 1987. Little did anyone know that Maserati would be responsible for letting the genie out of the lamp and unlocking what had been an untapped potential of the V-6 engine.

By now, you might also be wondering where Ford and Chrysler fit into the V-6 story. The boys behind the Blue Oval opted to rely on their international operations to provide such an engine offering—specifically, the German-made 60-degree V-6 that debuted in 1965.

Unlike General Motors, which shrank an existing V-8 into a V-6, Ford did the opposite. Originally intended for the stillborn front-wheel drive Cardinal project, a V-4 appeared in the Ford Taunus in 1962. It was then enlarged into a V-6 and went on to see service in numerous iterations, from 1.8 to 4.0 liter sizes. Best remembered here as the Cologne 2.8, it found its way underneath the hood of everything from the Ford Pinto and Mercury Capri to the Ranger pickup, Bronco II sport utility and Aerostar minivan.

Ford also produced V-6 versions in Great Britain, which were known as Essex engines, from the Dagenham, Essex, plant that gave them their name. These, too, were configured in a 60-degree format, beginning in 1966, and spanned 2.5 to 3.4

liter displacements. They appeared in such U.K. cars as the Ford Consul and Zodiac, along with the Transit van.

Chrysler, meanwhile, would not witness its first Detroit-designed V-6 until 1987. With such a heavy reliance on the Slant-6, a page was taken out of the Buick book when a six-cylinder version was derived from the 318 V-8. It was fitted in the Dodge Dakota pickup and displaced 239 cu.in. Like the later version of the Buick V-6, the 90-degree engine included split crankpins for better balance.

Then there were the Japanese. Nissan gets credit for the first mass-produced Asian V-6 in the Maxima during the 1985 model year. Honda followed suit later that year with its Legend model, which arrived in the U.S. as a 1986 Acura. Yamaha supplied a 3.0-liter dual-overhead cam 60-degree V-6 for the Ford Taurus SHO (Super High Output), beginning in 1989. It generated 220 horsepower.

Today, the V-6 has matured into a powertrain of choice. Technologies such as electronic engine management, direct injection, variable valve timing, four overhead camshafts, four valves per cylinder, twin turbochargers, a balance shaft (when necessary) and more have turned the V-6 into the industry's preferred platform for tomorrow. Such legacy advantages as compact dimensions for improved packaging, reduced weight and thus inertia (less weight in the nose of the car for better handling dynamics); the efficient balance between output (power density) and economy; manufacturing optimization, with shared ancillary and accessory drives (together with the V-8); and a broad physical cross-section that reduces body penetration

The 220 hp, 3.0 liter Yamaha V-6 of the 1989 Ford Taurus SHO.

possibilities in the event of a front-end collision (compared to an inline-six) add up to an engine opportunity like no other.

Recently, I've had the good fortune to experience the state-of-the-art V-6. It began behind the heated steering wheel of a 2018 Dodge Challenger GT. Packaged together with standard all-wheel drive, the new GT redefines what was previously an ill-mannered muscle car by exchanging burnout aptitude for four-season finesse.

The 24-valve 3.6-liter V-6 has been matched with an 8-speed automatic transmission and offers up 305 horsepower. More importantly, the GT delivers a proper balance between outright performance and everyday prowess, by combining capability with confidence. It's not the usual sort of association that we've come to expect from such alternatives as its Hellcat hell-raising brethren, but so it goes, by pairing V-6 engine technology with all-wheel driveline ability.

It's still a portly 4,000-pound-plus 2+2 coupe, and it's certainly not a Jeep. But give Fiat Chrysler credit for trying to at least accommodate the demands of real life, as opposed to continually challenging conventional wisdom. A Dodge Challenger with snow-covered winter weather congeniality? Who would have thunk it? Credit the civility of the V-6.

Then there's the Kia Stinger GT. Another all-wheel drive V-6, this one further includes twin turbochargers to the tune of 365 horsepower. While not even established as an automotive entity when the V-6 story began, the Korean car maker has now put on the gloves and stepped into the grand touring ring with its new 5-door hatchback that "floats like a butterfly, and stings like a bee," as Muhammad Ali once evangelized.

In an attempt to create an "icon of street style," according to Kia, the Stinger signals a more ambitious, if not aggressive, approach for Korea's number-two automobile company. Think of it as a more attainable Audi S-line. By selecting the V-6 twin turbo for its foundation, I can confirm that this thing is fun to drive … with a capital F!

In the same way that I prefer transverse V-twin and single-cylinder motorcycles to all others, my now favorite modern automotive engine configuration is clearly the twin turbocharged V-6. The epiphany was sparked by the Ford F150 EcoBoost V-6 (but that's another story for another time), and fueled by ever-improving electronic control, sophisticated engine management systems, advanced manufacturing precision and new-found marketing strategy.

The V-6's engine integrity is also routinely demonstrated on many a Sunday afternoon, so it can then be sold on Monday morning. Since 2012, it's been the engine of choice in INDYCAR racing. Chevrolet and Honda are the current providers. A 1.6-liter turbocharged V-6 also superseded the 2.4-liter 8 in Formula 1 beginning in 2014.

In the end, perhaps Jan P. Norbye and Jim Dunne foresaw the future of the V-6 saga best in their book, *Buick: The Postwar Years*, when they concluded that the engine's ultimate promise was as "an ugly duckling that turned into a swan."

It now has taken wing after almost 70 years of enduring persistence.

Here's to the Hobby

The Antique Automobile Hobby
The 10 Best Things That Ever Happened

July/August 2009

This may be a matter of personal perspective, so accept it as just one member's opinion of the top 10 things that have happened to the antique automobile hobby:

The Ford Model T and Model A

If one were to search for the underpinnings of the entire antique automobile hobby, there's no doubt that the Model T and Model A Ford would be the two most compelling cornerstones beneath its foundation. Their contribution remains unparalleled.

Both the Model T and Model A have been the entrée for many an enthusiast because they were, and still are, quite plentiful, relatively affordable, extremely functional, incredibly durable and easily serviced. Replacement parts are only a phone call away, and just about everybody knows somebody who knows a bunch about them.

Local club and region memberships have been built around them, and they remain an absolute staple of the antique automobile scene. Just think about what any weekend antique car show or tour (other than a single-marque event, of course) would be without these familiar Fords.

Hemmings Motor News

Often referred to as "the Bible" of the antique car hobby, *Hemmings Motor News* was founded in 1954 by Ernest Hemmings in Quincy, Illinois. It began as a four-page newsletter for those like-minded enthusiasts who were in search of antique cars and parts. Fifty-five years later, it still retains what became its familiar phone-book-style and newsprint-like presentation. Nowadays your fingertips no longer get black

A 1971 issue of *Hemmings Motor News*.

from the ink off the paper, and its plain brown wrapper has made way for four-color covers.

Certainly the electronic age has had an impact. In an effort to maintain its full phone-book format, editorial content (also in glossy color) has been added to replace those classified ads that have since defected to the Internet. Hemmings launched a host of other specialty collector publications such as *Special Interest Autos* (now *Hemmings Classic Car*), *Muscle Machines* and *Sports & Exotic Car*, after being acquired by American City Business Journals in 2002. They've also aggressively pursued their own world wide web presence.

But who doesn't anxiously await the arrival of "the Bible," still, each and every month?

Hershey

Officially known as the AACA Eastern Fall Meet and hosted by the AACA's Hershey Region, "Hershey" is considered the granddaddy of antique automobile events in America, if not the world. Like a pilgrimage to mecca, attending Hershey is a rite of passage for any antique automobile enthusiast.

The Hershey meet has been taking place since 1953 and is held the first full week of October. It now includes some 9,000 flea market spaces, 1,500 car corral spots and almost 1,500 show-car entries.

Every year, old acquaintances are renewed and new friendships forged. What's gone missing, though, is mud. Hershey mud is the stuff of legend, and while its demise has been universally welcomed, some of us still miss it (well, just a little, maybe). After all, with a bit of adversity comes adventure! Think about all those war stories back at the hotel that are no more (fortunately).

No doubt, some enterprising flea market vendor will probably start bottling and selling mud, though. After all, you can buy just about anything and everything pertaining to the antique car experience at Hershey! That's what Hershey is really all about, and many of us just wouldn't miss it.

Personally, I just celebrated my 30th consecutive year, and I'm sure proud of it.

Reproduction Tires

When I'm out on the road or noodling around the neighborhood, I'm often asked, "Where do you get tires for that thing?" It turns out that thanks to the dedicated effort of those like Tom Lester, Harold & Corky Coker, John Bohmer and Ann Klein, tires are perhaps one of the easiest items to acquire for our antique automobiles.

Believe it or not, back in the day, collectors were often forced to cut down or replace wheels on antiques and classic-era vehicles because they just couldn't find proper replacement tires. It wasn't uncommon for some to resort to truck-sized alternatives.

Wide whites, redlines, bias ply and nostalgia radials—they're not only all available, but have remained true with period tread patterns and sidewalls for that authentic appeal. They're reproduced from original molds, though they're now much improved as a result of modern manufacturing methods and rubber compounds.

You'll be amazed how fresh reproduction tires will transform your antique automobile, even if you've been riding on what appeared to be a set of seemingly good (but perhaps petrified) tires. Certainly, the safety factor alone is worth the investment.

Antique Auto Insurance

Like reproduction tires, where would we be without the availability of antique automobile insurance? Off the road, no doubt, because most of us would never be able to afford the premiums!

Antique automobile insurance is priced around the premise (and actual claim experience) that antique cars are gently and minimally used in relatively controlled environments, are highly prized by responsible and mature owners and are well maintained and properly stored. Risk is essentially managed and minimized by careful and considerate owners, and they are essentially rewarded for it, thanks to companies like Condon & Skelly, Grundy, Hagerty, Heacock and J.C. Taylor.

Modern Fuels and Lubricants

Once upon a time, there was an incredible amount of controversy surrounding the removal of lead in gasoline because of the anticipated impact it was going to have on our antique automobiles. Now it's the reduction of Zinc Dialkyl Dithiosphosphate (ZDDP) in motor oils and gear lubricants that's causing concern. ZDDP is an additive that protects sliding surfaces and high pressure friction points. It has also been found, though, to damage today's catalytic converters.

There's no doubt that the argument around ZDDP is going to rage on for some time, just as it did for lead. Everyone's entitled to an opinion here, but I believe in the simple truth: modern fuels and lubricants are infinitely better than anything that was available back in the day.

Low-speed engines with minimal compression ratios (say, 5:1 vs 11:1), that are used incredibly conservatively (perhaps, at 4,000 rpm maximum engine speed vs. an 11,000 rpm redline), are hardly taxing the full capability of modern formulations. Then there is the reality that antique automobiles don't need to dissipate as much heat, since they're just not as efficient. Many continue to function just fine with thermo syphoning cooling systems.

Maybe it's something to be concerned about if you're going vintage racing, but then you should be relying on performance lubricants, anyway. For the rest of us, modern fuels and lubricants are a miracle. Stick to the recommended straight viscosity instead of going multi-grade, change your lubricants on a regular basis and use your vehicle often (or rely on fuel stabilizer) and I'm confident that you'll be just fine.

The Battery "Tender"

What could be more frustrating than anxiously awaiting the arrival of a wonderful weekend or the spring season itself, going out in the garage and turning the key (if your antique has a self-starter), and hearing … "click." That was quite often how it used to be, but it most certainly doesn't have to be anymore. The smart battery tender is a simple and affordable trickle charger that every antique automobile owner should have. Not only are they fully automatic with quick disconnect convenience, but tenders extend battery life by maintaining full charge at all times. They ultimately achieve a storage/float charge mode, and signal such a state via a green diode. Battery tenders even adjust their charge rate to compensate for changes in ambient temperature.

The days of acid spitting out from beneath the battery caps due to overcharging are one antique automobile annoyance that need not be preserved. Fool around with old cars long enough, and the use of a tender will evolve into an instinct.

HPOF

For those of you who may be unaware, the HPOF show category refers to "Historic Preservation of Original Features." Formally recognizing those vehicles that retain a good portion their originality (at least 65

1915 Overland representing Historic Preservation of Original Features (HPOF) (West Peterson photo).

percent) was truly a masterstroke, and has since led to a passionate subculture of "barn finds." Of course they're only original once, and HPOF initiated a whole new consideration of automotive history and its well-being by focusing on as-manufactured condition. Books have now even been written on the subject.

By creating a defined venue for the historic preservation of original features, HPOF deferred what can only be considered as the needless and unfortunate restoration of original automotive artifacts, vehicles with the wonderful and irreplaceable patina of age.

HPOF continues to flourish, and eligibility is reserved for antiques that are 35 years old or older. For a lot of us, they're now the highlight of many antique automobile events. In the interest of historic preservation, I only wish the category had arrived sooner.

A Cell Phone

Speaking from years of experience, I can attest to the fact that an antique automobile is a wonderful ice-breaker when you're stuck near or in front of some stranger's house. Been there, done that, with everything from a 1930 Franklin to a 1967 Alfa Romeo. But nowadays, unfortunately, knocking on somebody's door in search of a phone or a gallon of gas may not be the most cordial or comforting experience. "*Gee* ... could I possibly use your bathroom, too?"

Your best insurance is to always have a cell phone with you when you're out and about in your antique automobile ... assuming that you're not simultaneously stranded by a lack of cell service, that is.

They come in handy, too, at shows and flea markets when you're trying to rendezvous with a friend, or if you stumble across a long-lost find that you know he just won't be able to live without.

AACA

Established in 1935, the Antique Automobile Club of America (AACA) is America's oldest and largest automotive historical society. It's a nonprofit corporation with members in all 50 states and more than 50 countries, and there are more than 400 AACA regions and chapters. A national headquarters, library & research center and museum are all assets employed to foster the preservation of automotive history, not to mention its impressively revamped magazine and its other publications.

Personally, I believe the AACA has done more for our antique car hobby than any other organization or influence ... *ever* ... which is why I became a contributor to this fine magazine (*Antique Automobile*).

The AACA mandate to welcome any and all passenger vehicles makes it all-encompassing and, simultaneously, all-inclusive. That ensures that it stands alone to "further the interest in and preservation of antique automobiles," and moreover the Antique Automobile Club of America remains dedicated to "promoting the sportsmanship and good fellowship" of its members.

Who could ask for anything more?

Our Greatest Asset

January/February 2012

For many of us across America and around the world, another old-car season has come and gone. While all the shows, swap meets and tours may be history, that doesn't mean we have to hibernate, like the old iron that's tucked away out there in the garage. AACA membership is the spark that ignites our hobby, particularly during the off months.

The very magazine you hold in your hands (*Antique Automobile*) is our lifeline. But notice that a considerable part of its focus is really not about old cars. It's about old-car enthusiasts—people who have participated in events, people who have restored old cars and want to share their experience in their own words, people who are looking to hopefully buy or sell another antique car or component through the always-enticing classified ads.

The AACA Annual Meeting is another example of the power of our people. For a few days every February, we're drawn to Philadelphia—coincidentally, the City of Brotherly Love—to simply share among ourselves. All of the workshops, meetings, awards and trade vendors celebrate the spirit of our community, not necessarily the automobile itself.

Online forums keep the chatter going as the snow flies, and teeth are chattering, too. Our collective consideration for cold hard steel makes way for an unparalleled exchange of information. Although the dialogue may be about how to rebuild a transmission or where to find a head gasket, what's really going on is people helping and supporting people. The AACA Forum (forums.aaca.org) is a wealth of information. It ensures that the passion persists, and it's worth a visit to further help escape the harsh reality of winter.

The AACA Museum is quite a destination in Hershey, Pennsylvania, as is the AACA Library & Research Center. In addition to the hard-working employees, they're fueled by still more people—*volunteers*.

AACA's 400-plus regions and chapters certainly fan the flames and keep the home fire burning during the downtime. The opportunity to personally interact with like-minded individuals all year long is a huge part of our existence. The AACA ethic of inclusion also recognizes any and all antique automobiles, trucks and motorcycles, and their owners, all 60,000 magazine readers.

AACA membership gives back as much or as little as you care to commit to it. You will always derive the greatest return by getting more involved, especially during this time of year.

So as we turn the calendar to 2012 and anxiously await the return of shows, meets and tours, remember, when it comes to the antique automobile experience, our greatest asset is *each other*.

Old Habits Die Hard

July/August 2013

It's April 28 and I've finally had the good fortune to walk my first flea market for 2013. After a wild and wacky winter here in the northeast, the age-old Mark Twain adage was proven true: "If you don't like the weather in New England, just wait a few minutes." It routinely changed, but for the worse.

The opportunity to break the ice this year came with the 39th running of the Belltown Antique Engine Show in East Hampton, Connecticut. The last time I took to the turf in search of treasures from that all-too-elusive category of collectible compulsion that I call "early miscellaneous" was at the AACA Eastern Fall Meet last October, at my 33rd (speaking of old habits) Hershey. So in the interest of accuracy, I guess that should have really read, "took to the tarmac."

That said, I stepped onto the field with that fond feeling of déjà vu. As a guy who's demonstrated a keen ability to buy high and sell low, I find the first flea market of the year can be a perilous pursuit. After all, there's a lot of pent-up enthusiasm there—an itch that needs to be scratched, if you will.

Picture-perfect weather made for a superb Sunday morning. With old single-cylinder industrial engines firing away at random in the background, it seemed as if the show was being sustained by a heartbeat all its own. Then, after bumping into a few good friends, I realized that after years of scouring the nooks and crannies of sale tables, milk crates and mystery boxes, the fortune that lay before me was in more than just the rusty relics of a distant automotive past. For a lot of us, a swap meet is just as much a social gathering as it is parts hunt. Acquaintances and friendships that have been forged along the aisles are reunited through a common bond … the antique automobile experience. I've been blessed to have found a number of lifelong friends on the flea market field, not to mention a comparatively inconsequential carburetor or two.

That's just not the sort of camaraderie you can create when you're huddled behind a flat screen scrolling through page after page of eBay listings. The sedentary sensation of a couple of keystrokes is just no substitute for mixing it up among like-minded gearheads, which is why I guess I'm destined to be a flea market rat forever. And perhaps it's also because getting up early and out the door fast for such a special occasion is usually accompanied by a hot ham, egg and cheese breakfast sandwich from the local deli.

Another rite of passage for me is the old-fashioned classified antique auto ad, which still appears in print. In every magazine or publication I get, including this one, I always go right to the rear pages to see all the unobtanium that really is still out there. Of course, I go back to the days when you could buy cars off the pages of *Road & Track* and *The New York Times*.

Certainly today's online alternative is incredibly effective, and yes, I do use that resource as well, but for me, the simple pleasure and anticipation of what awaits just behind the next page in the classifieds is like unearthing the prize in a Cracker Jack box.

So I can still be easily entertained by a copy of *Hemmings Motor News*. My wife is well aware that the day I stop looking at antique cars for sale is the day that I will undoubtedly be meeting my maker.

Being a creature of habit, used car lots are another institution to which I subscribe. I've craned my neck so many times while perusing the back row when driving by that the intention could probably justify as some trendy exercise regimen. At least it helps keep me loose and limber.

In my case, being always on the prowl for another now-antique Saab or Volvo, it doesn't get any better than spending a Sunday afternoon kicking tires out among the rows of rejuvenated rides at some local lot. Each one presents a demeanor and persona of its own, with some offering more appeal than others by pulling at your heartstrings. But how many more orphans can I adopt? If they could only talk, I'd love to know where they'd been, and where they're going.

My first car came off just such a used car lot in Hempstead, New York, at a nearby Renault dealer. That 70-dollar Dauphine may not have been much to most, but it launched my own 40-plus-year obsession with offbeat automobiles.

As time went on, there were certainly many other more meaningful would've-could've-should've moments among the multitude of used car memories. Like the 1960s Ferrari 250 coupe that was at an independent lot on automobile row in Denver. At the time, during the late 1970s, it was the meager (but not to me) $8,000 asking price that kept us apart, since it was just another tired, old, used car. Or the aluminum-bodied 1937 Adler streamliner that my good buddy Buck Mook and I discovered out in the wilds of lower Michigan. That's just the tip of the iceberg, and I could go on and on. Suffice to say … I have a soft spot for used car lots.

When I moved to Michigan for the first time, back in 1976, my old pal Randy Mason (former curator at the Henry Ford Museum) introduced me to the idea of the "finished" garage. I'm not talkin' just sheetrock and fluorescent lighting, here. I mean the garage as an inner sanctum and extension of one's lifestyle space, complete with art, heat, floor coverings, stereo, refrigeration, furnishings, dimmer switches, liquid refreshments and perhaps even hot and cold running water.

Today, they're often referred to as "man caves," but to me, Randy's Roost was

My ultimate garage, which served as the prototype for the *Ultimate Garages* book.

simply the equivalent of stumbling on the Emerald City of Oz. I was green with envy, and spent as much time there as I possibly could.

Fast forward, as time has its own habit of doing, and it turns out that museum-quality garages and I have been inseparable ever since. As someone who's lived through five corporate moves in nine years, that's quite an accomplishment. Not only was there a lot of heavy iron to lug around, but all the painting, refinishing and re-hanging of wall art could have qualified as a second career.

In fact, my "ultimate garage" served as the prototype for my friend Phil Berg's very first book of the same title back in 2006. His photo session at my house helped sell the publisher on the concept that there was truly a fascination in such palaces of personality and passion. And the rest, as they say, is history. So among other inclinations, I'll always be a garage guy.

Doing my own oil changes is yet another affliction that's been with me for years. Even though an entire industry of convenient, quickie-lube joints has sprung up in the interim, I still prefer being on my back aboard a nice piece of fresh cardboard.

Despite the fact that I sometimes say, "I'm getting too old for this" (particularly during January or February), I can at least be sure that the job gets done right. I can also specifically select the quality of oil and filter I want. No matter what the manufacturer's recommendations are, I have always gone with my own simple-to-remember 5,000-mile intervals.

You also have the opportunity to get up close and personal with your antique car on a regular basis when you change your own oil. I can't tell you how many times I've discovered other faults or concerns, from frayed fan belts and leaky clutch hydraulics to blown bulbs, by being under the hood doing such simple routine maintenance as an oil change.

Shifting gears (pun intended), manual transmissions have long been, and will no doubt always be, my gearbox of choice. Essentially everything I own, except for the Citroen CX (which should just naturally do everything *for* you) and my old GMC dump truck, includes a clutch.

Truth be told, I enjoy driving. *A lot!* The ability to appreciate a closer engagement with the automobile has routinely led me to seek out sticks because direct drive communicates feedback more effectively than a slushbox does. And since all the old iron in my garage is devoid of any advanced electronics and controls anyway, it remains up to me to work the gearbox around the engine's available torque curve for optimum output—which is not only fun, but quite gratifying as well, when done right.

Certainly automatic transmissions have gotten better and better since the days of the original Hydramatic and Dynaflow, and in fact, are now superior to manuals in most applications when it comes to performance and fuel economy. But as a guy who's always done all his own maintenance, I've also done my fair share of clutch replacements over the years, though I'm certainly not about to rebuild an automatic transmission in my driveway.

Due to the fact that nowadays, most kids don't know (or even care to know) how to drive manuals, I also don't have to worry about anybody at home absconding with my antiques! And I'm also doing my part to help ensure that the lost art of double-clutching doesn't disappear.

In the March/April 2008 issue (Volume 72, Number 2), I wrote about my penchant for garage gazing. Not much has changed since, and what I said then still goes: "For me, the best thing about a lazy tour around town at this time of year is the opportunity to finally see what's been hiding behind all those garage doors for the past months. With the surrounding foliage still at a minimum, you can always discover another garage, barn or even an old car or antique tractor out there on the back 40."

Don't get me wrong, it's not as if I'm some sort of peeping tom … but if I could get away with riding around carrying a pair of binoculars, I probably would. Certainly, I've made a few friends and acquaintances by pulling into a driveway unannounced to inquire about a diamond in the rough, or two.

I'm also pleased to report that in the five years since that column was written, I can still say, "Though I have not been invited, no one has ever reached for their shotgun … not yet, anyway." Fortunately, I can keep my eyes peeled because my neck is already "loose and limber" from scoping out all those used car lots.

Lessons learned early on often stick with you, and also become part of your m.o. (*modus operandi*). In my case, one example is the importance of investing in quality trailers and transport.

A long time ago I used to work the pits at Watkins Glen during club races. On one such weekend up there in the Finger Lakes, I bummed a ride back to Long Island with a somewhat disheveled racer. It soon became apparent that his attention to mechanical detail was on par with his commitment to personal hygiene.

At about 2 a.m. during a torrential downpour, I awoke in the passenger seat when he slammed on the brakes. He came to the realization that his trailer and F-Production racer were no longer in tow behind the van! Doubling back up Route 17, we came upon the rig about 10 miles later ... wrapped around a bridge abutment.

It turned out that the nut vibrated loose and fell off the trailer ball. At the next bump that followed, the trailer tongue simply lifted off the receiver hitch taking the ball and threaded stud with it. Safety chains? We don't need no stinkin' safety chains! Incredibly, the ball was still clenched by the trailer tongue, amid the wreckage, when we found it.

The experience has stayed with me ever since, and I've become somewhat of a stickler when it comes to trailering. Quality components, extra backup straps for added insurance, proper tire inflation, supplementary mirrors, a spare tire and heavy-duty tools with which to install it, routine maintenance and conservative speed are all a part of my towing ritual.

So you can imagine my surprise when the last car that went out of here, bound for California, got picked up on little more than a three-vehicle flatbed. Instead of relying on a recognized, antique automobile transport specialist, the buyer opted for an online auction gypsy. I've seen cars removed from a local accident scene restrained better than this potential cross-country catastrophe. As time goes on, you come to realize that you usually do get what you pay for. As a result you get a good night's sleep, as well.

Finally, I really don't know where I'd be without all the club memberships and magazines I've enjoyed for so many years. I've learned so much and met so many wonderful people that the connection to the club scene is as natural as the air I breathe, and is buried deep within my DNA.

Many of my fondest memories and dearest friends are the result of car clubs. Guys with whom I was autocrossing back in high school at the old Mitchell Field Air Force Base on Long Island, such as Triumph devotee Bill Sohl and fellow industry veteran/barn-find friend Tom Cotter, remain an integral part of my ongoing existence—and that was 40 years ago!

My long-standing AACA membership, along with having been a part of the other, broad-based antique organizations such as HCCA and CCCA, joining a myriad of single-marque clubs, enjoying local chapter activities, participating in a growing number of online forums, showing cars and motorcycles, walking swap meets, touring, serving on various boards and in club offices, and writing articles, all have helped define who I am, and always will. Such good old habits do indeed die hard because they're a return on investment that gets given back, and sustained, by the gift of years.

An Alternative for the Armchair Enthusiast

September/October 2015

Although I've attended many automobile auctions, I must admit I've never been that big of a fan. No doubt they're incredibly exciting, highly entertaining and growing by leaps and bounds, but I put more contemplation into my antique car-buying decisions than the auction format generally allows.

Nowadays, antique automobile auctions have matured to the fine art of merchandising of what is essentially fine art. The auction scene excels as a sales machine to move old iron with expedience, and it's generally the consignor's decision to hold out for a price by listing with a reserve, or instead deciding to just take the money and run.

The buyer's position is a bit more tenuous, since there are limitations, indeed, on how much mechanical inspection can actually be performed, let alone any ability to really road test, pre-sale. Many auction companies have been doing a good job of scrutinizing the merchandise before they accept the consignment, but the intentional fast pace of the offerings that proceed over the block, with patrons who are well lubricated with alcohol (no coincidence), obviously sets up a buyer-beware scenario. Meanwhile, there's even more intensity while trying to keep up with absentee phone and internet bidders, along with the fever pitch of, more often than not, an auctioneer with a proper English accent.

It truly is quite a spectacle, fueled by both seller and buyer commissions, along with things like gate/catalog fees, trade vendors, souvenir and premium sales, food services and more. After all, those big extravagant tents that are set up at the best-of-the-best venues, where these high-end extravaganzas often take place, are expensive! Antique automobile auctions also serve to satisfy that basic human idiosyncrasy of instant gratification, where machinery is immediately transformed into money and magnificent collections can be built, or disposed of, in short order. If you've never been to one, I urge you to go.

I prefer another type of antique automobile auction, that being the ones that cater to literature and automobilia. More of a get-down gritty affair, an automobilia auction is often old school, more like a traditional farm or estate sale. There's something for everyone at an automobilia auction, from lots of sales literature and boxes of brochures to milk crates full of license plates and signs galore, all at more attainable price points, so many more of us can participate.

Instead of a cash bar, sometimes there's a hot dog truck out in the parking lot. If there is a catalog, it's normally a black-and-white photocopied consignment list, no glossy color.

A typical automobilia auction can have in excess of 500 lots. Plan on a long day. The nice thing about automobilia is that it also allows enthusiasts to play in the hobby at a much lower overall cost of entry. No supplementary state registration fees, insurance premiums or maintenance requirements follow—nor flat tires and batteries, either—and there are certainly storage advantages with automobilia over autos. You can also touch and feel everything to your heart's content at the preview before you bid/buy.

Like an automobile auction, automobilia sales often offer phone and internet bidding opportunities. The arrival of the smartphone has certainly helped attendees craft their bids. You'll see many of them scouring around on eBay in an attempt to assess market value before the hammer drops.

If you're like me, you can enjoy the automobilia you've purchased at auction day-in and day-out, right from the comfort of your own armchair. My house, for example, is full of it. There's no need to go out to the garage to partake of your pleasure.

Here in Connecticut, our craving is satisfied by Automobilia Auctions (AutomobiliaAuctions.com), particularly when the weather goes sour over the course of the long winter. Local antique automobile auctions such as Dragone Classic Motorcars (DragoneClassic.com) are starting to include their own fair share of automobilia inventory. Likewise, all the big boys—RM Sotheby's, Barrett-Jackson, Mecum, etc.—are also including automobilia. If pure ephemera is more of your passion, there are general events such as PaperMania (PaperManiaPlus.com) and other printed-matter fairs that can sometimes include automobilia, to help get you through the off season.

So even if you're an armchair enthusiast, you can still get your fill of the antique automobile experience through an automobilia auction.

SOLD!

At the Crossroads

In Between the Car Show and the Concours

March/April 2016

There's always one, if not more, every weekend. Local car shows, meets, tours and swap meets are the lifeblood of the antique automobile hobby. As time marches on, such tradition is being superseded by a new world order of automotive events and activities. Some local car shows are starting to struggle because, as indicated above, there are simply too many of them, and they often haven't kept up with the times.

First and foremost, some of the typical Sunday car shows may be in jeopardy. One problem is that by the crack of noon, many a show field begins to dwindle. No one's getting any younger, and many elderly show-goers are running out of gas. Certainly, a little seating and some shade would go a long way, not to mention a complimentary bottle of water with admission, to help sustain the festivities.

Then there's the fact that such shows try to be all things to all people, and thus end up being a master of none. Without some kind of special attraction, even if it's as simple as a small feature or category, your average run-of-the-mill antique car event ends up being exactly that: an average run-of-the-mill antique car event. After all, how many Model T Fords, '57 Chevys and '65 Mustangs can you admire? Not that there's anything wrong with the more popular collectibles, since they're truly the anchors of our interest. But...

Beyond a myriad of well-established AACA region and chapter activities, a good example where opportunity has been seized is at shows like the Old Car Festival in Dearborn, Michigan—this country's leading early automobile extravaganza, which caters to pre–1933 examples, exclusively. Then there's Ypsilanti's Orphan Car Show that recognizes only now-defunct car and truck brands, and is put on by the Ypsilanti Automotive Heritage Museum in Ypsilanti, Michigan.

Here in Connecticut, the Klingberg Vintage Motor Car Festival in New Britain includes a special focus on Connecticut cars, while East Hampton's Belltown Antique Car Club will feature antique automobiles that were produced in the New England area in honor of its 50th anniversary show this August. The Larz Anderson Museum in Brookline, Massachusetts, has enjoyed spectacular success with its ongoing and distinct series of lawn events on spring/summer/fall weekends that include everything from microcars to a Swedish-exclusive day. A little bit of focus can go a long way since none of us can attend them all, and we're often forced to pick and choose. You might not want to hear it, but it has become inevitable that car shows are often in competition with one another as they vie for our attention.

No doubt, there will always be a place for single-marque club events because there's an overriding enthusiasm that drives such concentrated participation. Generally speaking, attendees will go the extra mile and come from further afield with the confidence that they'll be able to get up close and personal with those unique antiques that they love best, because they're guaranteed to see what they came looking for at such single-marque meets. However, in many cases, these are shrinking a bit, too, with ever-aging club member demographics.

Likewise, events with such following and fortitude as the AACA Eastern Fall Meet in Hershey may be on very solid ground, and the multitude of dedicated members making the pilgrimage to Pennsylvania will never wane. Although Hershey continually seems to get bigger and better, more and more 1950s, '60s and '70s cars are finding their way onto the field, which is to be expected. It's no surprise with the passage of time, an aging audience is of concern here as in the rest of the hobby. But proactive innovations such as the Historic Preservation of Original Features class (HPOF), Driver Participation Class (DPC), vintage race car activity, motorcycle features, and more have certainly added fresh vitality to this milestone celebration. Yes, it pays to create unparalleled distinction, particularly when it comes to the early, offbeat and more interesting automotive icons. Thank you, Hershey Region!

On the other side of the equation, the high-end concours have certainly grown by leaps and bounds during the recent past. There are now something like 40 of them here in the U.S. alone. In case you were unaware, the concours d'elegance is derived from the French "competition of elegance," which dates back to the 17th century, when horse-drawn carriages were paraded and reviewed by and before the upper crust.

These days, it's quite common for a concours to have a specific theme, an honorary grand marshal, and a direct connection to a major charity. Pebble Beach, for example, began in 1950 and has donated more than $16 million to charitable causes. Amelia Island has been in existence for 25 years and has already brought forth more than $2.5 million to charities and is recognized for its always compelling annual features, thematics and celebrity marshals. And let's not forget The Elegance at Hershey, now in its sixth year with charitable donations amounting to $740,000. The list goes on and on, and the concours is the place to be if you want to see the best of the best, and the most preeminent automobiles.

Most of the major concours have a featured tour, vintage racing event or, in the case of The Elegance, a hill climb. There's an incredible array of peripheral activities that have spun out from under the concours umbrella, making a destination such as

At the Crossroads

Never know who you're going to bump into at a concours event.

Pebble Beach more of a spectacle of attraction and distraction. With a literal week's worth of fun and frolic to peg your passion meter, from Concorso Italiano to Concours d'LeMons, Monterey is an incomparable happening within the old car community. So be prepared to strap in and hang on! It can be overwhelming.

Perhaps most surprising, however, has not just been the arrival but the explosion of the auction scene, as yet another alternative of enthusiastic attention. Putting aside my personal preference in the manner in which I choose to buy and sell, and having previously dismissed the auction as a place to merely move iron, I had the good fortune to attend this year's October extravaganza at the Hershey Lodge as a guest of RM/Sotheby's. Prior to that, I dropped in on the always enjoyable up-close-and-personal Dragone Auction in Westport, Connecticut, in May, along with the gargantuan Mecum sale in Kissimmee, Florida, in January.

As indicated by the title of this column, I've recalibrated and come to the conclusion that the antique automobile auction is now, in fact, at the crossroads between the car show and the concours, because where else can you see everything from a Dodge to a Duesenberg parked bumper to bumper? If not, how about a Delahaye and DKW nestled side by side? And perhaps even an assortment of vintage motorcycles from around the world to round out the offering?

Truth be told, for those of us who suffer from extremely diverse tastes in automotive expression, an auction's inventory can be the best source to satisfy such affliction and enjoy everything from the brass era to ultimate exotics. You can usually roam around burgeoning pre-sale tents to your heart's content, and if you want to actually follow the proceedings and experience the real-time drama as the live auction unfolds, admission can usually be had for less than the cost of a high-end concours ticket, because the expense to host the event is offset by car sale commissions.

Many of those aging show-goers referenced above (in fact, they're the earliest collectors) are now shifting life-journey gears, and it's their collections of the rare and exceptional—which have often been out of sight for too long—that are now fueling the auction proceedings. In addition, most auctions include plenty of vendors and exhibits, offering everything from literature and automobilia to car-care products that help enhance the attraction even more.

Beyond just aiding and abetting the sales process, comprehensive catalogs are often part and parcel of an auction. In addition to describing each lot and setting a price estimate, they can include an interpretive history of each item consigned and are often beautifully produced—depending upon which house publishes them, and for which specific event they're intended. Judging by the lusciously exquisite hardbound *Driven by Disruption* catalog (with a die-cut cover, no less) from RM Sotheby's crème de la crème December 10, 2015, sale in New York City that I have the good fortune to be holding in my hand as I write this, auction catalogs promise to be the next hotly-contested collectible that anyone would be proud to have on the shelf. I strongly suggest that you do whatever it takes to get your hands on one if you attend an auction, because it will really add to the learning experience, if not the memory. There's always a website listing that you can follow as well. Those are just some of the embellishments that you just won't find at a car show or concours.

Meanwhile, there's no peer pressure to compel you to don an obligatory blue blazer and straw hat at an auction, yet celebrity sightings will still abound among the miles of aisles of antiques. No surprise, there's also good food and drink to be had, which will draw you in even further, instead of having to tolerate the tried and true car club hot dog truck.

Just as Pebble Beach has turned into a week-long spectacle of automotive indulgence, the auction arena has as well. Just consider what takes place in Arizona every January. In fact, there the model has now been reversed, with a new high-end concours supplementing all the auction action, making the Scottsdale/Phoenix area yet another car collector's dream destination. That is, if your calendar can cooperate. At least the weather most likely will. Though, either way, Arizona is now the world's single largest gathering of old cars, aficionados and fanatics.

So the auction has accelerated from what had simply been an antique automobile sales vehicle into what is now a full-blown car-crazy lifestyle experience. If you can't make it out west, there's live wall-to-wall television coverage to guide you through select steals and deals, and help you avoid missing the least little bit of excitement.

These days, it's not just about what crosses the block, and a bidder's paddle is no longer a prerequisite, so don't be intimidated. You don't have to be a buyer to participate, so adjust your thinking. If you want to be able to say you've really been around the block, come to the crossroad and check out a modern antique automobile auction. You won't be disappointed, and you'll find yourself comfortably in between the car show and the concours—along with a magnificent mix of Dodges to Duesenbergs, Delahayes and DKWs, et al.

ON THE ROAD AGAIN

Survival of the Fittest

JULY/AUGUST 2008

The regional jet on which I was flying home after an AACA meet was into its final approach. As the runway appeared ahead, the pilot suddenly pulled the nose up, increased air speed, aborted the landing and hauled you-know-what out of there. It seems that there was a smaller, prop-job ahead that we were rapidly running down. To avoid having any possibility of two planes occupying the same spot on the runway at the same time, evasive action was in order.

Such a speed differential between airplanes sharing the same airspace is really no different than the deviation we routinely encounter out on the open road with antique automobiles as we attempt to intermingle with modern traffic. Though our situation is, in fact, more hazardous.

Today's cars and trucks are faster and more refined than ever. Drivers are also increasingly harried and frazzled, and if that's not enough they're often distracted by cell phones, PDAs, GPS programming and who knows what else. So while you and I are out there in the equivalent of a propeller-driven airplane (something like a Piper Cub comes to mind), everyone else is buzzing by in Learjets … and quite often, with half a brain paying attention and one hand on the controls.

Whereas the Piper pilot has three dimensions of freedom for avoidance, you and I in our old cars are limited to only two degrees of motion, and restrained by the very road itself. As the tarmac turns, so must we.

Here are a few thoughts on how to deal with the ever-increasing differential we face behind the wheel of an antique auto:

Level the Playing Field

Before you even begin to consider driving an old car in today's traffic, take a step back and make sure you really understand what you're up against. Basically, you're going to be competing for the same space with all the latest and greatest iron while driving a 25- to 100-plus-year-old car.

I happen to live in a small, New England village environment with low traffic

You won't be keeping up with modern cars.

density, so I can get away with chugging down to the post office in a brass-era car or heading over to the hardware store in a Model T. Those of you in more crowded conditions may not have the same luxury.

So first and foremost, think about where you're going, plan a route around those locales with the heaviest density (if possible) and do your best to stay out of harm's way. The road less traveled may not be the fastest way between point A and point B, but it will certainly be safer, and quite often, more scenic and enjoyable as well.

A good rule of thumb is to simply avoid roads that were laid down and built after your car was. This way, you'll always avoid the eight-lane interstate with your 20-horsepower antique.

Choose Your Weapon

Okay, you live just outside of the city center, where the average speed is normally 60 or 70 mph, if not more. Romping around in a 35 mph car will probably not contribute to your long-term well being.

It's no wonder that as time marches on, interest in the fabulous 1950s–era antiques has now advanced to the 1960s and '70s as well. And it's no coincidence that the street rod scene has exploded, too. Certainly there are many reasons, including baby-boomer owner demographics, but there's no doubt that later cars will do a better job out there on the open road.

So if you intend to use an old car to simply go wherever you want, whenever you want, an early antique auto probably shouldn't be your weapon of choice.

Recognize the Reality

There you are, sitting at a stoplight, and it goes green. You open the throttle, advance the spark, and begin to pull away. The guy behind you in the modern car (with instantaneous torque) is immediately up your tailpipe. Then you back off and attempt to find second gear.

It's not a pretty picture, but we've all been there. There's not much you're going to be able to do about it, other than perhaps try to stay to the right and keep your wits about you. Being constantly focused on your surroundings, having the awareness of situations developing around you and driving with forethought are imperative. Don't become a victim of circumstance on the road.

The Best Defense Is a Good Offense

In addition to fooling around with old cars, I also routinely ride motorcycles. Regularly taking to the two-laners on two wheels is perfect training for like-minded enthusiasts who prefer four wide-whites instead. Why? Because when you operate a motorcycle, you very much do so with the idea that everyone's out to get you …

100 percent of the time. Those of us who drive old cars should behave with the same mindset.

It's so easy to just hop into an old car and run down the road with the same thought process as you would with your everyday iron. After all, it's a very similar scenario: you open the door, step in, sit down and hit the gas.

Motorcycle riders instead do things like check the weather and give the tires a once-over before they even get on board. Then, once in motion, a highly choreographed process begins that really doesn't stop until the motorcycle stops. Scanning the pavement ahead and reading the quality of its surface, looking left, looking right, checking the mirrors, being always aware of who's ahead, behind, and beside and then doing it all over again and again. Of course, you also never believe or trust traffic lights, stop signs or center lines when you ride a motorcycle, and always assume that oncoming motorists are simply going to go right through or over them—which they often do.

If you think motorcycle riding is only about heading off into the sunset to smell the roses, it's not. Antique auto operators need to assume the same responsibility. Your senses need to be amped-up. You never want to drive an old car on autopilot, like a lot of us usually do on the way to work.

Understanding the Enemy

Many assume that the difference in speed between old cars and modern iron is our chief concern out there in the real world. The speed differential is a serious problem, but it's the rate of speed gained or lost that's our ultimate enemy. I've described what can happen when the light turns green, but even more dangerous is the deviation between us and them when it comes to braking!

You're driving down the road with the flow of traffic when the guy in front of you slams on his four-wheel, antilock, power assisted, ventilated disc brakes (with ceramic pads) to dive into the Dunkin' Donuts for a double latte. You respond by applying your lowly, four-wheel (hopefully) mechanical drums, which are probably out of adjustment and have glazed/petrified brake shoes. You haven't got a chance.

Most critically, stopping an old car is more serious than starting it. Your V8-engined antique may be able to keep up with modern traffic, but its braking capability is strictly yesteryear. And those skinny, 6.50–16 bias-plys are only going to make matters worse.

Modern car drivers have no clue about our dire circumstances. *Never* lose sight of that. For example, they don't give a second thought about going out around us and then pulling back immediately in front again, then hitting the binders. They just don't realize what we're up against. Do everything you can to always keep your distance, all the time and all around you.

Strength in Numbers

One of the best ways to enjoy old cars is in a group. It's also safer because you'll certainly be more visible and recognized. People will make way and give you a wide berth. There are plenty of good tours, for example, listed in this issue—and every issue—of *Antique Automobile*. Tour organizers do the best they can and spend a lot of time seeking out roads that are compatible with our old cars.

Still, be courteous. There's nothing more aggravating than a line of modern cars a mile long being held up by an oblivious operator of an antique. Move over and let them by on occasion. Yes, we have just as much right to use the road as they do. But the fact of the matter is, we're going to be on the losing end of any altercation.

Be Prepared

If the primary objective is to remain safe on the road, then you must take safety seriously. Keeping your antique auto in good working order is imperative, yet it's so easy to become complacent because you only take it out once in a blue moon, and only for a short hop.

Tours and group drives offer a measure of safety.

Sure, the tread on those tires looks fine, but are the carcasses 20 years old? Wonder how much of the hydraulics in the master cylinder and the rest of the system is actually brake fluid, and how much is now rusty water? Can anybody really see that little old tail light/brake light with the bad ground circuit—particularly when they're barreling down on you at 70 mph?

Simply put, a significant mechanical failure or incident at 50 mph is bad in any car. But it's even worse in an old car because it doesn't have the safety systems or structural integrity that a modern car has to back it up. Sorry, that's a fact.

In summary, yes, it's a jungle out there. But it can be tamed and enjoyed if you have the right attitude, ethic, awareness and equipment. Be ready, pay attention, think ahead and have a strategy, and you'll drive safely this summer in your antique automobile.

The Automotive Influence on America's Garden of Eden

May/June 2013

For the past few years I've been visiting Florida on occasion, between October and January. My business travels have confined me to Orlando and points south (by company decree). I usually try to avoid the mainstream and head for the hills in search of more interesting back-road destinations.

The first thing I always do in unfamiliar surroundings is aim for the nearest motorcycle shop. That's because motorcyclists know all the best places to go and the best two-lane twisty roads to get there. Unfortunately, though, I've come to learn that in South Florida there just aren't many. Everything is essentially flat and straight, and I'm not a fan of simply cruising A1A in stop-and-go traffic.

In lieu of a more energetic automotive experience, I've started to shift my focus in search of history, that being the influence of the automobile on the Sunshine State. And let me tell you, I've come to learn that it's rather fascinating.

At the turn of the 20th century, when the automobile was in its infancy, Florida was still a fairly wild and uncharted corner of our country. Rail service had made its way up and down the coasts, and east and west across the panhandle, to service sportsmen, speculators and those in search of an agrarian existence. Much of it had been laid by Henry Flagler, a partner of John D. Rockefeller's, starting in the 1880s. Having reached Key West by 1912, the wheels for future development were now adequately greased thanks to Flagler's personal fortune, which was derived from his association with Rockefeller in Standard Oil.

Flagler had the acumen to recognize the opportunity that Florida offered, particularly as a playground for the social elite. Isolated fishing and hunting camps attracted the heartiest (and wealthiest) of outdoorsmen, but they wouldn't be alone for long. Neither would those seeking fertile land on which to establish a homestead.

To further ensure a return on investment, Flagler's railroads quickly began to do what they so often did just after they laid track into the unknown. They built hotels to create destinations … and thus demand … to help sustain their reason for being.

As they did out west, the railroads also started to offload the excess tracts of land they had accumulated to lay down the routes in the first place.

To help do so, they needed to appeal to a wider audience and started to leverage Florida's idyllic climate to its advantage. According to Nick Wynne and Richard Moorhead's *Paradise for Sale*, then-recent developments in photography and printing allowed the Sunshine State to be marketed through a colorful palette of hue and tone, and the public relations machine went into motion. With a picture being worth a thousand words, there was a concerted effort to depict Florida as a virtual Garden of Eden, complete with beaches, bathing beauties and ever-sunny skies. Such illustrations of the "good life" often included an image of an automobile in the campaign.

After a slow start, Florida's first boom came with the arrival of the Roaring Twenties. Coincidentally, the automotive era was well established by this time and very much played a part in the growth of the state. As tourists flocked to the south, many opted for the road instead of the rail because of the well-appreciated freedom that it allowed. With a car, you could travel in privacy at your own pace, wherever there was a hard-packed path. And with more than half of the cars on the road at the time being Model T Fords, you could go even farther than that! But the automotive influence on the development of Florida went beyond its simple mechanical ability to traverse the topography.

A driving force came from as far away as Indianapolis. Carl Graham Fisher was the unique combination of pioneer and promoter par excellence. By the time he turned 30, Fisher acquired an interest in the acetylene headlight patent and his Prest-O-Lite company became the industry's primary supplier. He also played a part in the creation of the Indianapolis Motor Speedway and is credited with the idea of paving the track with bricks to improve the surface. Through his involvement with various automobile dealerships in the area, he masterminded an infamous automotive publicity stunt when he flew a Stoddard-Dayton over Indianapolis beneath a hot air balloon. As if that weren't enough to keep him busy, he also helped develop the Lincoln Highway.

Fisher had been vacationing in Florida since 1910. In 1913, Prest-O-Lite was sold to Union Carbide and provided him with the resources to fund his next big idea. Being familiar with Miami, he saw potential in the oceanfront area that lay just across Biscayne Bay. There was an effort underway at the time to provide access to it over a wooden bridge, but construction stalled due to lack of money. Fisher stepped in and provided cash to complete the bridge in exchange for land on the far side. Miami Beach, as we now know it, was born, but Fisher was just getting started.

Not ready to rest on his laurels, Fisher put his automotive millions to good use and began dredging the bottom of Biscayne Bay to create an even larger oceanside land mass, thereby artificially expanding his real estate holdings even more. In the words of Will Rogers, "Fisher was the first man to discover that there was sand under the water … (sand) that could hold up a real estate sign. He made the dredge the national emblem of Florida."

Luxury hotels would follow, along with an electric railway system to serve the fledgling resort community that catered to the wealthy. After he developed the north–south Dixie Highway system to allow direct access from the Midwest, snowbirds ultimately flocked to the pleasure paradise in droves. Fisher, the automotive tycoon from Indianapolis, acquired the nickname "Mr. Miami Beach" the old fashioned way—he earned it.

Glenn Curtiss was a well-recognized bicycle racer and motorcycle maker from Hammondsport, New York. His engine expertise led him into aviation, where Curtiss-Wright was ultimately formed through the merger of the Curtiss Aeroplane and Motor Company and the Wright Aeronautical Corporation. As a land speed record holder and aviation pioneer, his comfort with calculated risk would go on to serve him well.

Following in Fisher's footsteps, Curtiss, an avid hunter, got bitten by the Florida development bug after numerous adventures in the Everglades. Having cashed out of his Curtiss company in 1920, he went on to play an integral part in the creation of Hialeah (in 1921), Miami Springs (1923) and Opa-locka (1926).

Another early pioneer-promoter who was fascinated by Florida was Barron Collier, who amassed a small fortune from gasoline-fueled streetlights and an even bigger one from streetcar, trolley and subway advertising. He became Florida's single largest landowner by the 1920s, having amassed some 1.5 million acres in the southwest section of the state. Like Fisher, he recognized that improved access would certainly help develop his holdings, so he supported construction of the Tamiami Trail from Tampa to Miami.

Although the entire Naples–Marco Island expanse, and more, was named after him (Collier County), the family later became better recognized by automobile enthusiasts through the exploits of his sons. The Automobile Racing Club of America was founded in 1933 by C. Miles, Barron Jr., and Sam Collier. In 1944, it evolved into the Sports Car Club of America.

Ransom E. Olds, founder of Oldsmobile and then REO, took to the Sunshine State, too. In 1913, he purchased more than 37,000 acres in the Tampa–St. Petersburg area to create his "Oldsmar" community for the common man, as opposed to the wealthy. It was the same tack that he previously took during the development of the Curved-Dash Olds.

Olds promoted his oasis, thoughtfully planned with "beautifully planted medians and lovely oaks," as an ideal destination from which to promote "health, wealth and happiness." Originally, the area was platted under the name R.E. Olds-on-the-Bay, but it was soon called Oldsmar. In 1927, it became known as Tampa Shores, but reverted back to Oldsmar in 1937, as it remains today. Olds sold his last lot there in 1935.

Of course, it should come as no surprise that Henry Ford wintered in Florida, too, though his interest was in riches other than those derived from real estate speculation. Thomas Edison had been vacationing in the Fort Myers area since 1887, and

Ford followed his influential elder by acquiring an adjoining property in 1915; both remain on the National Historic Register to this day.

It was fertile soil and a climate that favored fast crop growth that led them to conduct botanical research there, in hopes of finding an alternative rubber source. Although a solution was not found, it certainly wasn't the illustrious automaker's final foray into Florida.

On the other side of the state, Ford set up shop to produce cars in Jacksonville. From 1925 to 1927, the Jacksonville Ford factory produced some 45,000 Model T's per year. In 1928, the plant shifted over to make the Model A. After 1932, the facility remained in operation through the 1970s as a distribution center.

But Ford was preceded in Jacksonville by a gentleman by the name of John Einig, who produced a gasoline-fueled steam carriage in 1896. A marine engineer by trade, Einig was fortunate enough to garner comprehensive coverage of his steamer in *Scientific American* magazine, which resulted in an order from an English subscriber. The export may have been Jacksonville's first overseas automotive exchange, but it wouldn't be the last.

Incidentally, M.C. Hutto built a few four-cylinder touring cars there in 1905, and a high-wheeler by the name of Southern was also produced in Jacksonville from 1906 to 1908. Coincidentally, Henry L. Innes formed the American Motors Export Company in the port city in 1920 for the sole purpose of producing a product for overseas markets. It was a small four-cylinder based on the Simms from Atlanta. As many as six prototypes were built. Unfortunately, the venture sputtered out when Innes died in 1921, after a brief illness. There would be more to follow from Jacksonville in later years, though; stay tuned.

Simultaneously, Florida became a haven for the wealthiest of families who were not in search of commercial opportunity. The privileged were merely looking for pleasure and the opportunity to enjoy the one-upmanship of outdoing each other with the most extravagant of estates. One of the earliest to arrive and invest in his own piece of the playground was William Deering, chairman of the Deering Harvester Company. After he settled in the Miami area, his sons Charles and James soon followed. He went on to become the first chairman of International Harvester after it merged with McCormick Harvester. Their mega-mansions upped the opulence ante to a new extreme.

All of this external expansion was achieved in partnership with internal combustion. The workers, construction materials and infrastructure improvements were all reliant on automobiles and trucks to carry out the necessary tasks of moving goods and providing services to achieve what became insatiable appetite for growth. Everything that was built and everyone that built it had some connection to the car, not to mention those who harvested fruit and raised cattle.

Lured by jobs, labor made the migration to Florida on four wheels as well. Many auto-camped along the way, using the car as a home-away-from-home with a tent slung off the side. Trailer courts, motels, fruit stands and roadside attractions from alligators to Indian enclaves began to appear to encourage the arrival of the automobile and accommodate its occupants even more.

Simultaneously, as witnessed by such accounts as *The Grapes of Wrath*, the automobile became the prime mover for those who were determined to do more than just explore. People took to the two-lanes in search of a better life. To "unite fraternally all autocampers," a national group called Tin Can Tourists was established in 1919. Though eager Americans were now touring to all four corners of the country, the organization was formed in Tampa. TCT's guiding principles included "clean camps, friendliness among campers, decent behavior and wholesome entertainment." Members could be easily identified by a tin can that they affixed to their radiator caps. Founded in Chicago in 1902, the American Automobile Association (AAA) is now headquartered in Heathrow, Florida, just outside of Orlando.

On the other end of the sleeping-under-the-stars spectrum, Glenn Curtiss (having settled in the Sunshine State as mentioned earlier) began production of a lavish travel trailer he called the Aerocar. Relying on established aircraft construction techniques with which he was obviously quite familiar, his Curtiss motor bungalow was both streamlined and lightweight. Production began in 1928, and the Curtiss Aerocar Co. was headquartered in Opa-locka through 1941. Lesser examples of such tradition have continued to this day with luxury van conversions by Coach House, Inc., of Nokomis and the assembly of upscale teardrop-shaped campers by SignaTour in Tampa.

Meanwhile, in the land of the perpetual party, the automobile also played a part in Florida's history of decadence and debauchery. The arrival of Prohibition would merely be a speed bump in the Sunshine State, as opposed to a roadblock. Rum-running became quite the sport, since South Florida was situated so close to places like Bermuda, Puerto Rico and Cuba.

It's said that Carl Fisher and his high-octane connections back in Indianapolis helped keep the rum-runners continually ahead of the authorities by out-muscling them with engines that would outrun the law. His recognized relationship with boat racer and marine designer Gar Wood probably helped, too.

Speaking of sport, motorsport would, of course, be yet another diversion for the Florida hoi polloi. To further promote his Ormond Beach Hotel, railroad magnate Henry Flagler built the Ormond Garage with the interest of supporting winter auto racing on the smooth hard-packed sandy surface of Ormond Beach. In fact, "Gasoline Alley" actually existed there before it did in Indianapolis.

The 1903 Challenge Cup race that was staged between the Winton Bullet and Olds Pirate put Ormond Beach on the motorsport map, and earned it the distinction of being the "Birthplace of Speed." In addition to American manufacturers and competitors, the beach became a proving ground for aspiring racers and hungry speed seekers from Europe. Among others, Glenn Curtiss, the Stanley twins, Henry Ford, Harvey Firestone, William K. Vanderbilt, Barney Oldfield and many more used Ormond Beach to demonstrate prowess, products and progress.

The Automotive Influence on America's Garden of Eden 321

This page and following two pages: A sampling of vintage Florida postcards.

S-81—Enjoying the Green Benches On the Sidewalks of St. Petersburg, Fla.

C-11—Worth Avenue Distinctive and Exclusive Palm Beach

Off to Sea with No Seasickness Over the New Overseas Highway on the Way to Key West, Florida

By 1911, Carl Fisher's other Indiana connection, the Indianapolis Motor Speedway, held its first 500 and was on its way to becoming the "Greatest Spectacle in Racing." Despite that, with Daytona just a short distance down the shore from Ormond Beach and offering a similarly solid sand advantage, beach racing would continue through the 1920s and 1930s. When speeds began approaching 300 mph, shifting tides and ever-changing winds forced record seekers to the more consistent

Bonneville Salt Flats in Utah. Obviously, though, that wouldn't be the last that would be heard from Daytona.

Despite his interest in Indy, Fisher, a full-fledged Floridian by now, would simultaneously work hard to ensure that there would still be a spectacle under the sun as well. From the earlier experience at Ormond Beach he continued the quest to create a winter racing capital of the world, so he began building a breathtaking board track called Fulford-Miami Speedway in 1925.

Designed by Indy 500 winner Ray Harroun, the expansive 1¼-mile North Miami track was an incredible sight to behold. For example, it included 50-degree banking that allowed sustained speeds to approach 140 mph! The inaugural, 300-mile Carl G. Fisher Cup Race was held there on February 22, 1926, and attracted 20,000 spectators. Barney Oldfield served as official flagman, and the race was won by Peter DePaolo in a Duesenberg. Unfortunately, the fabulous Fulford-Miami oval was reduced to splinters seven months later by the massive hurricane that hit South Florida on September 17, 1926.

Back in Daytona, in addition to one-way record runs, a 3.2-mile circuit was created. Part of A1A was used parallel to the shoreline, before heading toward the beach, appropriately enough, on Beach Street. From there, the racers ran along the sand and returned to A1A around what was called the North Turn. An early competitor there was Bill France, who was asked to manage and promote the course in 1938, due to alleged "inconsistencies" in timing and scoring by the previous management. Due to World War II, racing ceased after 1941 and didn't return until 1946.

Of course, France went on to found NASCAR (National Association for Stock Car Racing) in 1948. The last race on the beach in Daytona was in 1958. The first Daytona 500 was held on a new superspeedway with 31-degree banking in 1959, and the rest, as they say, is history. NASCAR remains headquartered in Daytona, and the 500 has evolved into the automotive equivalent of the Super Bowl.

Meanwhile, although it took 70 years, Carl Fisher's storm-damaged dream to serve the Miami motorsports market would be reinvigorated by still more of Mother Nature's violent wrath on the Sunshine State. Homestead-Miami Speedway opened in the wake of Hurricane Andrew in 1995 in an effort to revitalize the Homestead area after major destruction was caused by the storm.

Another form of racing that thrived beneath the Florida sun and elsewhere took place at air bases. An enthusiastic and motorsport-friendly air force general by the name of Curtis Lemay offered Strategic Air Command bases across the U.S. as venues for road racing. Coincidentally, the first such race happened to be at the MacDill Air Force Base in Tampa in 1953. The most memorable track, however, remains in Sebring, and events are still sanctioned there to this day.

Due to agreeable weather and flat terrain, speed bowls ultimately sprang up all across Florida to keep Friday night fans on the edge of their seats. From the ¼-mile speedway in Auburndale to the Youngstown ¼-mile dirt track in Panama City, more than 100 short-tracks have dotted the Sunshine State during the years. A good number are still in operation to this day.

There's no shortage of drag strips in Florida on which to run ¼-mile flat-out. Events sanctioned by the NHRA (National Hot Rod Association) take place at Gainesville, the Orlando Speed World and the Showtime Dragstrip (formerly the Sunshine Strip) in Clearwater. The IHRA (International Hot Rod Association) operates out of Bradenton, Orlando's Central Florida Complex, Countyline in Miami, Immokalee Regional Raceway and Moroso Motorsports Park (now known as Palm Beach International Raceway) in Jupiter. In addition to Daytona and Miami-Homestead, motorcycles also race outside of Tallahassee at the Jennings GP facility.

Street racing has been held on and off again—now, very much on—since 1985 in St. Petersburg. The waterfront sports car and open-wheel circuit includes 14 turns on a 1.8-mile course.

Going briefly back to air bases and agreeable weather, that was yet another important chapter in the automobile's influence on America's Garden of Eden. Many a serviceman was given the opportunity to get behind the wheel of a car or truck for the first time thanks to Uncle Sam, during military training at numerous outposts around the state. Having had a taste of the good life, they also served as goodwill ambassadors to promote the endless sunshine, open space and year-round warmth that Florida afforded. Many would return—by car, of course.

Some would be attracted by the various motor museums that opened around the state. One of the most memorable was opera singer James Melton's Autorama collection at Hypoluxo, in Palm Beach County. The museum opened in the 1950s and included nearly 100 antiques, along with toys, music boxes and carriages. When Melton died in 1961, so did his Autorama.

Back over in Collier County on the southwest side of the state, Miles Collier (son of C. Miles) opened his collection to the public in 1988. Today, the Naples facility serves as the home of the Revs Institute for Automotive Research. Their mission is "the scholarly study of automotive history," and they continue to host their Symposium on Connoisseurship and the Collectible Car, though the collection is now closed to the general public. It is, however, available for group tours.

In between, there's the Dezer Auto Museum & Event Space in North Miami, Don Garlits' Museum of Drag Racing in Ocala, the Elliott Museum in Stuart, the Fort Lauderdale Antique Car Museum, Muscle Car City in Punta Gorda, the Sarasota Classic Car Museum, the Tallahassee Antique Car Museum and the Tampa Bay Automobile Museum in Pinellas Park.

Unfortunately, what you won't see in most of these museums are examples of the all-too-few automobiles that were made in the Sunshine State. In addition to Jacksonville's previously mentioned Einig Steam Carriage, the Hutto, Southern's high-wheeler and American Motors Export, Joseph Forbes built Florida's first gasoline-powered runabout in 1896, in a place called Cromanton. It's now the site of the

Tyndall Air Force Base. But at least such recognized emergency vehicles like E-One fire engines and EVI (Emergency Vehicles, Inc.) rescue trucks are still manufactured in Ocala and Lake Park, respectively.

Florida is also home to prominent private collections such as Rick and Jim Schmidt's NPD collection in Ocala, and John Staluppi's Cars of Dreams in North Palm Beach. Having decided to shift gears, Staluppi recently put his extensive assemblage up for auction.

Speaking of auctions, houses such as Auctions America, Barrett-Jackson, Gooding & Co., Hollywood Wheels, RM (which handled the Staluppi sale), Mecum and the Zephyr-hills Autofest are now very much a part of the local automotive landscape. Some of them have ridden the tide of the growing concours d'elegance experience, which of course has proven to be a natural for Florida. Most significant is the success of the Amelia Island Concours, which is held outside of Jacksonville, and the more recent Boca Raton Concours.

By now you may have noticed that Jacksonville has played, and continues to play, a role in the evolution of the automobile in Florida. Trading has been going on there along the St. Johns River since 1565, which is why Jacksonville is referred to as "America's First Port." Although it's only the 36th largest port in the country and the third in Florida, it's the nation's second largest importer and exporter of automobiles, behind New York/New Jersey. Millions of cars and trucks have landed on these shores in Jacksonville, much to the dismay of Detroit.

The Sunshine State is also the home of Southeast Toyota Distributors (SET), the world's largest independent distributor of Toyota and Scion vehicles. They serve Florida, Georgia, Alabama, North Carolina and South Carolina and deliver 20 percent of Toyota's U.S. sales. SET is part of the Jim Moran JM Family Enterprises.

The Ford test track in the Everglades has also been a low-profile but enduring part of the Florida automotive landscape. It was purchased by Harley-Davidson several years ago, and is now owned by Chrysler-Fiat. This accounts for some of the interesting cars one may see running around on the streets of Naples. Up until recently, GM had a home under the sun as well. Its Latin American operations were headquartered in Miramar to oversee sales and support in Latin America, South Africa, the Caribbean and Middle East. As a result of GM's recent bankruptcy, the office was closed.

AutoNation, America's biggest group of automotive dealerships, is also headquartered in Florida. The Fort Lauderdale company represents essentially every automotive franchise through 227 stores across the country. At roughly 400,000 units retailed annually, no one sells more cars and trucks than AutoNation.

The South Florida Automobile Dealers Association has been hosting the Miami International Auto Show for more than 40 years in Miami Beach, each year with a huge display of antique automobiles gathered by the South Florida Region. No discussion about auto shows in the Sunshine State could be complete without recognizing the contribution of AACA's extensive array of 28 (!) regions and chapters. In addition to numerous local events, tours and cruise-ins, the AACA Winter Meet (hosted by the Orange Blossom Region) was recently held in Lakeland.

And finally, the automotive influence in Florida stretches even as far as space! All kinds of wheeled and automotive conveyances have contributed to the NASA cause, and when Apollo 15 took off from Cape Canaveral in Broward County, it took the Lunar Rover along for the ride—the most expensive car ever constructed.

So despite all the flat, straight roads, there are all kinds of compelling twists and turns in the state's incredible automotive story. They're just not along the asphalt. Cars and trucks helped Florida flourish, and Ponce de Leon was proven right. Florida truly is a flowery land, for antique automobile enthusiasts as well.

Shake, Rattle and Roll

May/June 2015

Enthusiasts of modern motorcars just don't know what they're missing. As primeval forms of machines, antique automobiles have a habit of communicating their condition in a very visceral way. By comparison, today's technology has diminished noise, vibration and harshness to the extent that a good deal of feedback has been isolated right out of the driving experience.

Antique automobiles engage their operators. For example, beginning in 1962, Chrysler engines were cranked by gear-reduction starter motors. These "Highland Park Hummingbirds," as they were sometimes called, spun up with a distinct discord that was truly unmistakable. Once you heard one, you'd never confuse it for anything else … but no more. To appease the demands of today's discriminating car buyers, such a racket would now be considered an unacceptable irritation.

Screeching caused by slipping V-belts used to be a clear signal that it was time for an adjustment, if not replacement. It was a natural form of mechanical connection that kept the operator up close and personally involved with his or her automobile. Now, with the arrival of serpentine belts, cars don't talk to their owners like that anymore. When those wide, multi-rib belts get to the end of their useful life they don't give the driver the courtesy of a warning.

The onset of valve clatter was a condition that would get you to consciously dig out the feeler gauge from your toolbox to take on the tappets, after pulling the oil dipstick first, just in case. And a little "morning sickness" from the power steering pump would also get you under-hood, to check those vital fluid levels as well.

Meanwhile, the diagnosis of exhaust backfiring, or spit-back through the carburetor intake, is now a lost art. It's no surprise, with such precise control of ignition timing and fuel metering these days. Get it right, and you'd have an easy starting and fine running antique. Get it wrong, and you run the risk of blowing the muffler off the back end, as I once did when I forgot to retard the ignition on my Model T. Too bad, because all the above experience was the best hands-on training ground that there ever was to understand the intricacies of engine management.

Even just the basic control of acceleration and deceleration was a science in itself. Manipulating a hand throttle, spark advance and gear change (remember those

Cover illustration for July 1929 *Motor* magazine.

things called manual transmissions?) as a mere rise in the road approached—let alone a hill—or reading up ahead and anticipating braking demands well in advance made you a key component of the operation of the automobile. What you got in return was the supreme satisfaction of a job well done as you successfully chugged your way up the incline. Yes, it was/is possible to run a Model T on the ragged edge of its torque curve because the car will still send clear signals that you can hear and feel through the seat of your pants.

Of course, sometimes what stood between you and starting the old thing in the first place was the mechanical advantage, or disadvantage, of a hand crank to help coax the four-wheeled nag into action. If you've never started a car with a hand crank, I urge you to do so. It really should be considered a rite of passage into the old car community, because the rudimentary handle also serves as a lifeline to connect your inquisitive spirit to the soul of the automobile.

Beyond just the engine dimension, there were other forms of automotive dialogue and disorder that have since been superseded by technology. For example, squeaking or (even worse) grinding brakes were always a conspicuous cacophony that sent antique auto owners to the service bay with immediacy. Integrated wear sensors now do to the same thing, some of which can also trigger a warning light on the instrument panel. As a result, from forever mindful, the code of conduct concerning brakes today is ignorant bliss.

The early exhaust cut-out not only helped sustain engine torque, but also served to warn those on the other side of the hill that a new form of trackless traction was fast approaching. Certainly, no one needs to be reminded that the automobile is on the verge of arriving these days. Performance-wise, superchargers and turbochargers now do some of the same thing (well, sort of), though with much more social restraint. But it's at the point where even recent "turbo whine," the whistle that's heard as the compressor spools up, is now a thing of the past. What fun is that?

The monotonous howl from the heavy studs molded into old, hard snow tires out back always reminded you to take it easy, while the rattling vibrato of a pair of tire chains at least inspired enough confidence to assure that you were going to make it home ... probably. These days, most automobile owners have been seduced into believing that their all-wheel-drive SUV with all-season tires of compromise construction (they're just okay in the summer, and just okay in winter) will defy the laws of physics. Too bad they've been isolated out of the operating equation to the extent that they simply don't even think to take it easy.

Surprisingly, clunky leaf springs which were calibrated with abacus accuracy proved more compliant and comfortable than one might imagine. Even though modern, computer-simulated and computer-developed suspension systems are certainly superior, many antique automobile designers compensated by over-engineering with what little material they had to work with in the first place. That's why Fafnir Bearing Company, for example, provided ball bearing-suspended spring shackles on cars like the Pierce-Arrow. Nowadays, automotive engineering is instead an art of optimization, right-sizing and critical extremes, with minimal overcapacity left in excess.

So speaking of which, how did we ever get along without automatic climate control? I'll tell you how—with a totally intuitive, three-knob or lever control system to simply regulate temperature, fan speed and air flow. Nowadays, we grapple with computer controls that seem to develop a calibration all their own, once sensing systems get dirty and later, drift out of design tolerance. Never mind, I'll just open or close the window instead, thank you very much.

But antique automobiles can further communicate in a most articulate way as well, where modern iron pales in comparison. The sweet, poetic syncopation of a whisper-quiet low-compression Pierce-Arrow or Packard idling its way across a concours field is still one of those old-car experiences to die for. And the gentle churn from an Hispano-Suiza–inspired bevel-drive overhead-cam Wills Sainte Claire V-8 or straight-eight Stutz has not only rarely been duplicated, it's virtually been forgotten.

If you ever get the chance, go storming down a dirt road and enjoy the sheer brilliance of a brass-era antique, shod with 34-inch tires on wood spoke wheels. With its exhaust cut-out wide open, of course. You'll immediately understand how an automobile can be instinctively attuned to its natural element.

Finally, cars can communicate in different dialects as well, and unfortunately, many of those have been lost. Consider the heavy clunk from a worn U-joint when shifting from drive to reverse, which has since been translated into a high-pitched clack from a worn constant velocity (CV) joint. You say tomato, I say *tomahto*.

In fact, the crude simplicity of an antique automobile and its inherent capability to communicate is truly something to celebrate. Like a metronome, where there's rhythm there's reason. Ford made 15 million Model T's, and Volkswagen built some 22 million Beetles. Why? Because they just plain worked!

Too bad they don't make 'em like they used to, because it's getting awfully lonely behind the wheel with no mechanical chorus…

From Here to Gone
Architecture's Influence on the Automobile

SEPTEMBER/OCTOBER 2016

Roger Sherman, editor of the Pierce-Arrow Society's quarterly publication *The Arrow*, recently devoted an entire issue to the ultimate demise of what's best remembered as "America's Finest Car." While P-A was certainly subjected to a maelstrom of obvious and cruel forces in its final post–Depression days, Sherman identified yet another under-appreciated influence that no doubt contributed to Pierce-Arrow's eventual undoing in 1938: Pierce's inability to leverage its existing manufacturing facilities to migrate from what had been a legacy wooden-framed-body build process in 1933 to a more modern steel-intensive upgrade for 1934.

According to Sherman,

> Pierce-Arrow, itself, assembled its automobile bodies to its own specifications, so it is easy to assume that they had a self-sufficient body plant. Looking at the factory diagrams of the mid-1930s, there appears to be no stamping plant with giant presses to produce the large steel panels needed in body construction. This suggests that many of those body panels were stamped out by subcontractors. While Pierce-Arrow had an experienced woodworking staff that was probably capable of making the precise, hardwood forms used to guide production of the dies to press out panels, the company had to farm out the die making to Detroit companies.

It really demonstrates how vital it was to have not only four proper walls, but an effective infrastructure within them. Beyond supporting the well-being of the existing enterprise, the very bones of such a building or manufacturing complex would be the foundation for the future sustainability of the company as technology evolved. Pierce was just not prepared to move into the realm of pressed-steel panels, which were essentially the industry norm, because their celebrated Buffalo, New York, base could simply not accommodate it. Of course, by the mid-1930s they couldn't afford to, either.

This got me to thinking. Although we normally devote most of our attention to the antique automobile experience and the people responsible for fueling it, I thought it was about time to take a little look at some special places that proved to be incubators for the automobile, after reading Series 16—Model 1 of *The Arrow*. Automotive brick and mortar may not be the most glamorous of subjects, but their historic significance cannot be overlooked when it comes to the manufacturing and market development of this incredible industry that we so enjoy, along with its associated products. And in so many instances, even though the wrecking ball may have erased the physical remains of many a structural relic from a bygone day, others have been spared, and perhaps some are even still awaiting rediscovery and eventual repurpose.

Either way, what's most important is that the memory of historically significant buildings and automotive institutions, along with their influence and contribution to the industry, remains preserved for the sake of historic interpretation and understanding. So here's a brief bit of contrast across four very different Detroit-area icons, from the files of the here and gone. The good news is that more of them remain here with us today, as opposed to those that have gone on into oblivion.

Thanks for providing the seed for such an idea, Roger.

Survived: Ford Piquette Avenue Plant

When Henry Ford began his third and ultimately successful automotive (ad) venture, it was housed in a rented facility on Mack Avenue in Detroit, which was made available through arrangements orchestrated by the company's principal investor, coal merchant Alexander Malcomson. The building, which was owned by Albert Strelow and situated across the street from Malcomson's coal yard, previously served as Strelow's wagon shop. Ford Motor Company moved in during April 1903. At the end of that year, a second story was added, and by the spring of 1904, some 40 workers were churning out 15 two-cylinder Model A's per day.

Already bursting at the seams, the fledgling firm moved quickly that same year in search of a more accommodating assembly solution. They ventured far off into the outskirts from what was then considered the city center (a mere three miles north of the Detroit River) and settled on a three-plus-acre parcel where two rail lines intersected, known as Milwaukee Junction. Bordered by Beaubien and Brush Streets, the property sat on Piquette Avenue and would be Ford Motor Company's home from October 1904 through 1910.

A purpose-built structure was erected, but at the time there was no established benchmark or blueprint for the construction of an automobile factory. So the tried-and-true New England–style mill building was pressed into service. A three-story brick factory was built. Its long and narrow proportions (388' × 56') allowed for an abundance of windows (355 in total), which followed New England tradition to provide good ventilation and plenty of natural light.

Despite the Piquette Avenue plant's old-world design details, Ford capitalized on some recent lessons learned in Detroit during its construction. Oldsmobile's factory near Belle Isle burned down in 1901, so the new Ford plant included a vault to secure documents and drawings, fire doors to not only segregate but isolate sections of the factory floor, and a very early example of a ceiling-mounted fire suppression system.

Ford Piquette Avenue Plant, then and now.

In addition to being the first piece of commercial real estate that the company owned, Piquette nurtured Ford from its origins as a simple start-up to its self-sustaining status as an industrial powerhouse, and from an adolescent assembler to avant-garde innovator, as well. All the early letter cars were built there: B, C, F, K, N, R and S. Most significantly, the plant was the birthplace of the legendary Model T. In addition, it's said that very primitive moving-assembly-line ideas were first experimented with at Piquette Avenue.

The first 12,000 Model T's were assembled at Piquette before Ford found itself in need of still more manufacturing capacity. It was a result of the universal acclaim that the Model T immediately achieved. Meanwhile, Ford also fought a good portion of the infamous Selden Patent suit from within the walls of Piquette.

Ford outgrew the Piquette plant and the company would soon move further out into what were then the Detroit hinterlands, up Woodward Avenue to what would become the Highland Park complex. The Piquette plant was sold to Studebaker in 1911, which owned it until 1933. Next 3M took it over and used it for only light storage until 1989. The fortunate result was that Piquette suffered minimal wear and tear during the bulk of its existence.

It then attracted the attention of a dedicated group of preservationists and local Ford historians who managed to take control and begin the task of stabilization. Those 355 New England–style windows, which had gone through 85-plus years of sweltering Detroit summers and wicked Motor City winters, needed a lot of attention! After securing the building, restoration followed, including a re-creation of its original facade.

Among other distinctions, the nonprofit 501(c)(3) Ford Piquette Avenue plant is now recognized as a National Historic Landmark and is on the National Register of Historic Places. It's open for informative tours, hosts regular events and is even available for group rental. Check out their website for further details.

It's well known that the tough and tumble Model T Ford had the ability to withstand all that Mother Nature and the natural environment could throw at her, which is one of the reasons why so many Tin Lizzies remain with us to this day. Likewise, the Piquette Avenue plant was able to endure the incredible ups and devastating downs that would ultimately redefine Detroit, with all of its spiritual and structural integrity left intact.

Perhaps the best way I can describe, if not, salute, the Ford Piquette Avenue plant is to say, If it were in a place like Stuttgart, Germany (the hallowed home of Mercedes-Benz), with its indisputable historic purity and unaltered original form, it would be celebrated as a national shrine. Do go and see for yourself.

No, you won't be disappointed. In fact, you'll be amazed. You can get involved by volunteering, becoming a member, adopting and helping restore a window and shopping at Piquette's marvelous online museum store.

More at **FordPiquetteAvenuePlant.org.**

Survived: Packard Proving Grounds

Within the American automotive aristocracy, the duel for supremacy between Packard and Cadillac is well known. In fact, Cadillac would ultimately be responsible for the passing of Packard, but along the way, the two raced to one-up each other in everything from engine cylinders to exquisite coachcraft.

When General Motors established its automotive proving grounds near Milford, Michigan, in 1924, as a result of Chevrolet's unproven copper-cooled engine fiasco, Packard stood up and took notice. According to author Michael W.R. Davis, "After learning of the GM Proving Grounds west of Detroit, Packard lost no time acquiring land [building] its own test track" (from *Detroit Area Test Tracks*, Arcadia Publishing, 2009).

The Packard Proving Grounds were established on 500 acres of rolling countryside in Utica, Michigan (north of Detroit), and opened in 1927. In keeping with the marque's prestige status, the facility's buildings, garages, gate houses and even landscaped gardens were designed by noted Detroit industrial architect Albert Kahn. One of the planted areas by the front entrance was even shaped like a Packard radiator shell.

Throughout the ebbs and tides of Packard's fortunes, the Proving Grounds routinely validated the firm's enduring answer of genuine quality for those who endorsed the brand through enthusiastic ownership. Ask the man who owns one, indeed.

In an attempt to upstage GM's Milford Proving Grounds, speed records were set in Utica with Miller Special race cars. Packard even went as far as staging airplane vs. automobile races along portions of the track to further demonstrate that its facility was faster, though in the end, such publicity stunts didn't prove much.

During World War II, Chrysler leased the facility and the track would suffer the injustice of being used as a venue for the testing of 30-ton army tanks, which severely damaged its pristine pavement. Packard, and eventually Studebaker-Packard (S-P), operated the Proving Grounds through 1956. As a result of a management agreement to help prop up the then-struggling S-P organization, Curtiss-Wright assumed day-to-day control and then took full possession in 1959. The Proving Grounds were sold in 1961 to Ford, which wanted the expansive property to build a manufacturing plant on its northwest corner.

Time marched on. To divest itself of excessive real estate holdings, Ford generously donated seven acres of Packard Proving Grounds property, including a small portion of the track itself and numerous surrounding structures, to the nonprofit Packard Motor Car Foundation in 1998. The group is "an educational organization, dedicated to the preservation of the products, history and properties of the Packard Motor Car Company." Ford's Land Corporation then sold the rest to housing developers.

The Packard Proving Grounds was added to the National Register of Historic Places in 2000. The site is part of the MotorCities National Heritage Area, which

Top and above: Packard Proving Grounds.

was established in southeast Michigan by the National Park Service. To help defray operating expenses, the venue hosts various shows, special events and activities throughout the year, including wedding rentals that may access the supply of vintage Packards for hire. The Foundation has also built a vital alliance with the local Shelby Township, and enjoys a strong sense of civic pride.

From club concours to Great Gatsby galas and farmers markets in between, it's obvious that the Packard Proving Grounds is in good hands. Sign on to become a "Friend" through an annual, renewable membership, and enjoy the ride.

More at **PackardMotorFDN.org.**

Survived: Miller Motors

Testing one's mettle and then manufacturing an automobile is obviously a critical accomplishment, but the cash register doesn't ring until a car or truck makes its way into the hands of an owner, which is why the local sales outlet is so significant. Wooing prospective buyers has been the challenge among competitive dealers on Main Street, all across America and around the world, and once those prospects become patrons, they need to be supported through service and parts operations.

Over the years, dealerships have come in all shapes, sizes and levels of sophistication. In the fast-paced world of automotive retail, when a "store" (as it's called in the trade) outlives its usefulness, it either gets upgraded, repurposed or worse, razed.

Miller Motors.

So it's a rare occasion, indeed, to come across an early car dealership that has withstood the test of time and been spared from the siren call of a shiny new façade, let alone ever-increasingly efficient reception lanes, service writer desks, wash bays and parts counters.

Ypsilanti, Michigan's Miller Motors is an exception. Carl L. Miller took over the facility at the corner of East Cross Street and North River, previously the home of the first Dodge dealership outside of Detroit, and moved his Hudson sales and service franchise there in 1933. Miller Motors proved to be a bellwether within Washtenaw County's automotive establishment. Ypsi was also the home of Preston Tucker, the Willow Run bomber plant, which Kaiser-Frazer bought after the War, and GM's Hydramatic Division. Corvairs were also produced there from 1959 to 1969, and then other Chevrolet and GM models followed.

In addition to taking on Rambler, Miller Motors would go on to be recognized as the last remaining Hudson dealer in operation. When production ceased in 1958, the Miller Motors showroom—in what is now historic Depot Town—transitioned to used cars, while its back shop simultaneously serviced Hudsons and supported owners.

Carl's son Jack took the reins and began to further position Miller Motors as the world's preeminent Hudson resource. He began buying inventory from other Hudson dealers who were stepping down (pun intended), and Miller Motors became an epicenter within the Hudson-Essex-Terraplane club community.

Jack Miller and Miller Motors served as two of the spark plugs behind the creation of the wildly popular Ypsilanti Orphan Car Show. Now in its 20th year, it's this country's leading show for automotive brands that are no longer with us, and is held each September in nearby Riverside Park.

Miller Motors morphed into the Ypsilanti Automotive Heritage Museum in 1995. A vacant postal service building further down East Cross Street was acquired, and a new structure was built in between to unify the two buildings and create what is now a non-profit collection of artifacts and archives.

General admission is only $5 per adult, with children under 12 being free, but joining with a museum membership brings free admission, a quarterly newsletter and 10 percent gift shop discounts.

More at **YpsiAutoHeritage.org**.

Razed: Hotel Pontchartrain

You might be wondering why a humble hotel is included among such an august group of Detroit-area automotive institutions like an early milestone manufacturing facility, a test track tour de force and illustrious sales outlet. It's because the original Hotel Pontchartrain was considered the "Mother of Motors," and the forefather of luxury hostelries for the elite in lower Michigan.

Hotel Pontchartrain.

According to HistoricDetroit.org, "the name dates to the city's founding in 1701," when explorer Antoine de la Mothe Cadillac approached French Minister of Marine Affairs Count Pontchartrain for permission to explore the Great Lakes. Some 200 years later, ground was broken to replace the landmark Russell House on the same site, which closed in 1905. The "Pontch," as it was often referred to, was not only the largest construction project ever undertaken in Michigan at the time, but also the most opulent. It opened in 1907 at the corner of Cadillac Square on Woodward Avenue.

But its place in automotive history was secured by its bar, not its bedrooms.

> Detroit was, for all intents and purposes, a small town when the industry began to grow. The nearest approach to a popular club was the Hotel Pontchartrain bar. Prospective motorcar builders came from all walks of life and professions. So did prospective stockholders, many of whom wanted to get rich quick. They learned a lot in the Pontchartrain bar. Automotive executives met there to discuss business and exchange ideas. If modern recording devices had been available then, they could tell of the formation of dozens of companies. Ideas were exchanged that were to form the basis of the modern automobile business. William J. Chittenden (Pontchartrain's manager), affectionately known as "Bill" to all of the would-be car manufacturers who frequented his club, could … really … be considered a pioneer in the industry [Eugene W. Lewis, *Motor Memories: A Saga of Whirling Gears*, Alved Publishers, 1947].

And here's how the *Detroit News* summed it up still further, in a feature from 1970: "the Pontch was the meeting place for the men who made motors hum—magnates and financiers, crackpots and geniuses, salesmen and go-getters. Horace and John Dodge, William Durant of General Motors, Louis Chevrolet and the Lelands of Cadillac were among those who rested their elbows on the bar. Henry Ford visited, too, though he didn't drink. He was there to network."

When the Statler Hotel opened in 1915 at Grand Circus Park, it offered the advantage of a private bathroom in every bedroom. Meanwhile, in an attempt to provide an alternative to the bars along Woodward Avenue used by what were now automotive aristocrats, the Detroit Athletic Club was completed in the heart of the city's theater and entertainment district during that same year, syphoning off the Pontchartrain's upper crust clientele.

The original Hotel Ponchartrain closed at midnight on January 31, 1920. It was demolished shortly thereafter. After a long hiatus, the name would reappear on a new Jefferson Avenue property in 1965, but that Ponchartrain Hotel was shuttered in 2009. Today, it operates under the umbrella of Crown Plaza Detroit Downtown Riverfront.

And the now-gone bar that put the world on wheels is a forgotten footnote in the annals of Detroit's antique automobile heritage.

More at **HistoricDetroit.org/building/hotel-pontchartrain.**

Cars on the Cusp

JANUARY/FEBRUARY 2018

After 385 miles, we pulled into the parking lot of the delightful Seal Cove Auto Museum in Seal Cove, Maine. As I got out of the car, another visitor called over to me, "Hey … it's almost an antique!" I wasn't sure if he was talking about me or my car.

In fact, as a 1992 model year (the car, not me), the Citroën XM we drove from Connecticut is now an antique, indeed. Right down to the state-issued license plate that clearly says so.

Unlike a lot of other antique auto excursions, the XM made its way to Maine like a magic carpet. Running along at a sustained 75 mph, we were riding in the lap of luxury. Automatic climate control kept us cool, the sumptuous leather seats kept us comfortable, the hydropneumatic suspension kept the potholes and road imperfections at bay, and the V-6/four-speed automatic powertrain combination kept the big French flyer running like a freight train. Some antique…

With the turning of the January calendar page, a complete new crop of cars and trucks arrive after 25 years of existence and enter the realm of antique automobile achievement. It's a well-earned rite of passage. Unfortunately, a lot of enthusiasts just don't think so, or refuse to realize it.

I, too, used to walk right by things on the show field like Dodge Aries, but if one considers the K-Car's contribution in bringing Chrysler back from the brink—along with models like it, and other offspring such as the Plymouth Reliant—it is more historically significant than you might ever imagine. True, they had their flaws and might not be everyone's cup of tea, but there are also those who scoff at the idea of driving a Model T Ford. Speaking of anachronisms and idiosyncrasies…

So there's a purpose and place for each and every antique: from brass-car tours and reliability runs to fabulous Founders Tours and glorious Glidden Tour revivals—if not cruise nights, grocery getting, or in my most recent case, ascending Camden, Maine's short-but-sweet Mount Battie Auto Road with the sunroof open and the FM radio keeping company.

Obviously, there are certain advantages of more modern antiques that can't be denied. First and foremost, many examples are quite affordable and easy to maintain, and therefore provide a great entree into the hobby. They're certainly more

***Top and above:* Citroën XM.**

roadworthy as a result of increased power and performance right from the factory—keeping up with traffic these days is a good thing—and they're also safer, due to enhanced subsystems from seat belts to windshield wipers and washers, in addition to better braking (both for stopping and for keeping the car stopped when parking on a hill), quicker steering and more precise handling.

Then there are the creature comforts: reduced noise, vibration and harshness goes a long way as the miles stack up, as does staying dry when the rain starts pouring. Being able to see out of a demisted windshield is nice, and so are effective climate and cooling systems when you get stuck in the middle of a summer traffic snarl. If your car does boil over, a replacement radiator hose or fan belt might be closer than Timbuktu—except, of course, in the case of a Citroën XM.

Recently recognized antiques are also great conversation starters. Such as when you're enjoying a wonderful stay at the sympathetically-restored 1950s–era Lincolnville Motel in Lincolnville, Maine. Ask me how I know.

We're now at an interesting crossroads when it comes to collectibles that are on the cusp of antiquity. The early 1990s is the time when manufacturers began migrating from R-12 air-conditioning refrigerant to the more environmentally friendly R-134a. According to Steve Schaeber, technical editor for the Mobile Air Conditioning Society (MACS), the 1991 Mercedes-Benz S-Class was the first car to be specified with 134a.

The transition was completed on December 31, 1995. The last holdout to convert from R-12 was the early 1996 model-year Jeep Wrangler. (Those that were produced after January 1 included 134a as a running change.) Our now newly arriving antiques might be configured either way, which can be a problem, since R-12 refrigerant has essentially been outlawed.

Other than buying old rusty cans of R-12 off Ebay, or from the flea market aisle (that have been languishing beneath someone's workbench), the only alternative has been an R-134a conversion, and that can be a bit of a crap-shoot.

In certain cases it can be as easy as changing the service fittings to the R-134a type and simply recharging with the new refrigerant and lubricant. In other instances, an old R-12 tube and fin condenser could prove ineffectual with more modern R-134a because today's systems are calibrated around parallel flow condensers, which provide for more efficient heat exchange across a greater surface area. MACS recommends consulting with the Alldata auto reference service or Mitchell manuals to see if any technical service bulletins exist with regard to converting specific vehicles.

Generally speaking, Steve Schaeber (MACS) believes that GM air conditioners will continue to function quite well with just a simple service fitting and refrigerant change, while Ford products can be a bit more particular. It depends on the individual car. You'll just have to give it a shot and see. The good news, however, is that the initial fear and worry of incompatibility between the two refrigerants has proven to be unfounded, so there's no problem, there, per MACS.

In addition to the great air-conditioning quandary, you might want to also familiarize yourself with the allowances of AACA's Driver Participation Class (DPC), particularly when it comes to the more modern antiques. Certain upgrades that contribute to improved safety and driving convenience are accepted and endorsed in this not-point-judged category, including "seat belts, seat coverings, turn signals, stop lights, sealed beam/halogen headlights, radial tires, alloy wheels of the same era and/

or same vehicle manufacturer, radio upgrades, electrical upgrades, brake upgrades (bolt on), steering upgrades (bolt on), air-conditioning, overdrive system and altered exhausts." No doubt, R-134a service fittings and refrigerant would be acceptable as well.

If you believe that traveling in a recent antique is taking the easy way out, think about romping around the wilds of the Maine coast in something as offbeat as a Citroën. As I often say, it's going to be an incredibly memorable experience, because only one of two things is going to happen. It'll either be a wonderful time and we'll/you'll return home unscathed, or, perhaps we'll/you'll make it back aboard a flatbed. Obviously, the counterman at the closest AutoZone isn't going to be of any help, unless we/you need something as simple as a hose clamp. So you might want to stock a few spares in the trunk, before you head for the hills in a newly minted antique.

Either way, old cars often provide fond memories, for sure. Have no fear, I'm not going to abandon earlier cars as a result of my Gallic sortie across mid-state Maine, and you shouldn't either, because older cars provide still more—if not better—memories and an even greater sense of accomplishment when you actually do complete the journey! The same goes for cranky old motorcycles too. Fortunately for us, there are alternatives, so there's no right or wrong answer when it comes to the provenance of your antique tour car choice. Just "run what'ya brung," as they say.

Even in its infinite wisdom, the Department of Motor Vehicles is aware that there's something special about 25-year-old automobiles and recognizes them with antique/classic license plates. The oldest antique car in my garage dates back to 1912, and now you know that the newest is from 1992. Along with the others in between, that's 80 years of progress and innovation, which translates into education, in my case, because I'm continually studying and exploring any and all antiques, and you might want to too.

Since this is the first issue of 2018, it's time to celebrate. So let's welcome the "Class of 1993." These are the newest entries to earn the enviable distinction of "antique automobile." If the idea of taking to the two-lanes in Aunt Mildred's untouched original 25-year-old Mercury Grand Marquis intrigues you, or putting, perhaps, a little gravel in your travel behind the wheel of the farm's well-worn workaday F-150 flareside that's earned its keep, I urge you to do so—even if it's on the cusp of collectibility, or almost an antique.

Like me…

Index

AACA (Antique Automobile Club of America) 7, 47, 78, 155, 166, 185, 291, 293–298, 296–297, 302, 305–306, 310, 326, 344
Abbott-Detroit 117
AC Cobra 56, 78
Acura 164, 287
Adams-Farwell 117, 249
Aermacchi 109
ALCO 40
Alfa Romeo 70, 86, 88, 90, 134, 202, 207–208, 246, 265
American League of Wheelmen 5
American Motors 33, 66, 274
Apperson, Edgar 5
Armstrong Siddeley 118–119
Armstrong-Whitworth 118
Arnolt-Bristol 121
Arvin Car Radio 230
ASC/McLaren 285
Aston Martin 89, 135
Auburn 28, 266
Austin-Healey 120, 134
Austin-Morris 162
Austro-Daimler 118–119
Automobile Body Builders 58
Automobile Radio Corporation 231
Automobilia Auctions 304
AutoNation 326

Belltown Antique Car Club 298, 305
Benelli 255
Bentley 70, 135
Benz, Carl 35–37
Bimota 107
BMW 63, 88, 132, 165, 255, 264–265, 268
Bollee 37, 112
Boyco 237
B.S.A. 158, 255
Buick 11, 20, 65, 67, 86, 88–89, 106, 131, 137, 166, 186, 280–285, 288
Burroughs Adding Machine Company 220–221

Cadillac 10, 44–45, 48, 53, 56, 65–66, 71, 88, 131, 150–151, 154, 165, 188–190, 197
Cadillac V8-6-4 19
Chadwick 266
Chalmers/Chalmers-Detroit 117, 212–215
Chapin, Roy D. 213–214
Chenard-Walcker 113
Chevrolet 18, 19, 48, 56, 68, 78, 90, 120, 131, 137–148, 153–155, 166, 228, 231, 250, 256, 277–278, 288
Chevrolet, Louis 139–140
Chevrolet Corvair 135–136, 145, 268
Chevrolet Corvette 144
Chevrolet TrailBlazer 25
Chevrolet V8 136, 144–145, 246, 250, 267
Chrysler 14, 21, 23, 54, 203, 287, 328, 336–337
Chrysler, Walter P. 13, 131
Chrysler K-Car 22, 342
Chrysler Thunderbolt 60
Chryst, William A. 225
Citicar, Sebring-Vanguard 274–275
Citroen 89–90, 100, 113, 133, 283–284, 301, 342–344
Classic Car Club (of America) 13, 52, 105, 193, 302
Clement-Bayard 112
Clement-Talbot 121
Click and Clack 229
Coffin, Howard E. 213–214
Coker 291–292
Collier Bros. 318
Columbia 3, 5, 7, 40, 114
Condon & Skelly 292

Corbin 40
Cord 29–30, 152–153, 266
Corporate Average Fuel Economy (CAFE) 18
Crane-Simplex 117–118
Crosley 14, 78, 232–233
Crow-Elkhart 118
Cummins 257
Curtiss, Glenn 318, 320
Custer, Levitt Luzern 226–227

Daihatsu 253–254
Daimler 5, 15, 35–37, 42, 120
Darracq 37
Datsun 86, 132
Dearborn-Detroit 118
de Causse, Frank 53
DeDion Bouton 112
Deeds, Edward A. 222–223, 227
Deering Harvester 319
Delage 37
Delahaye 37, 113, 160
Delaunay-Belleville 37, 112, 159
Delco (Dayton Engineering Laboratories Company) 222–225, 227
DeSoto 13
Detroit 6, 8, 10–11, 15, 17, 21, 46, 339–341
Detroit Electric 272
Deutsch-Bonnet 121
De Vaux 29–30
DKW 252, 307, 309
Dodge/Dodge Brothers 5, 13, 27, 68, 174, 260–261, 263, 288
Dual-Ghia 121
Duesenberg 265–266, 307, 309, 324
Dunlop 4
Durant, William Crapo ("Billy") 9, 11, 49, 115, 131, 137–139

Index

Durant-Dort Carriage Company 10
Duryea Brothers 5, 7, 38–40, 51, 155, 269

Earl, Harley 51–52
Elcar 274–275
Electric Vehicle Company 7
Elmore 131
E-M-F 116, 132
Environmental Protection Agency 18
Erskine, Albert A. 217
Essex 98, 151–152
Everitt, Barney 116

Falcon-Knight 56, 116
Ferrari 90, 134, 206–211, 282–283, 299
Fiat 15, 23–24, 134, 207, 265
Fisher, Carl Graham 317–318, 320, 323–324
Fisher, William A. 51–52
Flagler, Henry 316
Flanders, Walter 116
Ford, Harry 214–215
Ford, Henry 3, 8, 10–11, 41, 45, 47, 50, 99, 191, 201, 204–205, 265, 318–319
Ford F-150 246–247, 288, 345
Ford Highland Park 45, 48, 174
Ford Model A 55, 68–69, 78, 131, 142, 150, 153, 171, 178, 239, 289
Ford Model N 10
Ford Model R 10
Ford Model S 10
Ford Model T 10–11, 27, 45, 47–50, 52, 86, 88, 131, 137–139, 150, 171–178, 251, 257, 289, 311, 329, 331
Ford Motor Company 12, 14, 54, 61, 68, 131, 162, 188, 194, 250, 286–287, 326
Ford Piquette 48, 171, 201, 333–335
Ford River Rouge 13
Ford RS 261–263
Ford Skyliner 62–63
Ford SVT 81–84, 168
Ford Thunderbird 136, 170
Ford V8 56, 86
Franklin 25–28, 53, 87–88, 90, 94, 135, 159, 181, 241
Frayer-Miller 117
Frazer-Nash 121
Frontenac 176
Frost, Robert 202–203

F.R.P. (Porter) 126
FSO (Fabryka Samochodow Osobowych) 252

Galvin Manufacturing Corporation 231–232
Garford 132
Garrett Airesearch 244
Gaylord sports car 60
General Motors 7, 11, 12, 14–15, 20–21, 23, 25, 48–49, 51–52, 54, 131, 166, 186, 189, 248, 280–285
GM Art & Colour Section 51–52, 152, 240
GM EV1 275–276
GM Truck & Coach 181
GMAC (General Motors Acceptance Corporation) 23
GMC Truck 131, 250, 285
Good Roads Movement 5, 7, 229
Gordon-Keeble 121
Graham/Graham Brothers 27–30, 116, 266
Graham-Paige 28
Grant, Richard H. 227–228
Gray-Dort 119
Greyhound 180–186
Grundy 292

Hagerty 292
HAL 126
Harroun, Ray 324
Haynes-Apperson 6, 41, 113
H.C.S. 124–125
Heine-Velox 119
Hemmings 289–290, 299
Henney Kilowatt 273–274
Henry Ford Museum 299
Herschell-Spillman 117
Hispano-Suiza 87, 115, 152, 236, 331
Honda 21–22, 132, 164–165, 254, 276, 287–288
Hoover, Herbert 198–199
Horch 135
Hotchkiss 37, 60, 156–161
H.R.G. 127
Hudson 13, 32–33, 54, 58, 98, 131–132, 213, 338–339
Hupp/Hupmobile 28–29, 126
Hyundai 162–166

Iacocca, Lee 22, 203
Indian 4
Infiniti 165

International 90, 108
Isotta-Fraschini 113–114

Jaguar 90, 165
J.A.P. (Prestwich) 129
J.C. Taylor 292
Jeep 65, 68, 168–170, 248, 250, 258–260, 282, 344
Jeffery, Thomas B. 5, 132, 216
Jellinek, Emil 37
Jensen-Healey 120
Jewett, Harry M. 116
Jordan, Ned 215–217
Joy, Henry B. 220

K & N 74
Kaiser, Henry 13, 54, 66
Kaiser-Frazer 120, 339
Kawasaki 255
Kettering, Charles 222–227
Kia 288
Kimes, Beverly Rae 6, 212, 266
King, Charles 8, 41

Lamborghini 90, 134
Lancia 60, 90, 109–110, 134, 246, 279–280, 283
Land Rover 65
LaSalle 13, 29, 51–52, 152, 240
Lea-Francis 121
Leland, Henry 43, 116, 187–191
Lexus 164–166
Lincoln 60–61, 65–66, 71, 90, 100, 120, 165, 187–197
Little Motor Car Company 137–139
Locomobile 4, 40, 90, 237
Loewy, Raymond 181, 186
Lohner-Porsche 56, 277
Lorraine-Dietrich 112
Lozier 125

Macauley, Alvan 219–220
Malcomson, Alexander 42
Marmon 53, 90, 279
Maserati 90, 134, 283–286
Mason Motor Co. 137
Mathis 37
Maxim, Hiram Percy 4, 41, 114
Maxwell/Maxwell-Briscoe 120, 131, 139
Maybach, Wilhelm 35–37, 135
Mazda Miata 63–64
McLaughlin-Buick 119
Mercedes/Mercedes-Benz 37, 62, 64, 120, 132, 135, 165, 210, 247, 258, 264–265, 344
Mercury 68, 286, 345
Metzger, William 5, 116

Index

MG 134
Michelin 4
Midgley, Thomas 225
Mini 254
Mitsubishi 65, 249–250, 253–254, 262, 277
Morgan 90, 129
Morris 158
Mors 37
MV Agusta 255

NASCAR 324
Nash 32–33, 54, 131–132
Nash-Healey 120
National Cash Register 212, 216, 219, 222–223, 225–227
National Cycling Association 5
Nissan 21, 28, 133, 255, 277
Nokian 103
Northup, Amos 240, 242

Oakland 10–11, 131
Oldfield, Barney 5
Olds, Ransom E. 8–9, 41–42, 48, 318
Oldsmobile 10–11, 20, 68, 70, 123, 131, 149, 186, 188, 266, 268
Opel 5
Otto, Nikolaus August 34, 42
Overland (Willys) 13, 56, 66, 116, 131, 160, 240
Owen Motor Car 127

Packard 12, 16–17, 31–32, 53–54, 56, 68, 90, 130–131, 196, 208, 220–222, 231, 331, 336
Paige-Detroit 28, 116
Palmer-Singer 116
Pan-American 118
Panhard 37, 60, 112, 133
Peerless 5, 90, 130–131
Perkins 259
Peugeot 5, 37, 59–60, 89, 113, 133, 265, 284
Philco (Philadelphia Storage Battery Company) 96, 231, 234
Pierce 5, 115
Pierce-Arrow 28, 53, 80–83, 87–88, 90, 105, 130–131, 196, 217–218, 242, 330–332
Pirelli 4
Plymouth 13, 68, 70
Pontiac 55, 68, 131, 166, 257

Pontiac GTO 56
Pope, Colonel Albert A. 5, 7, 40, 49–50, 114, 188
Pope-Hartford 40, 49, 114–115
Pope Manufacturing 4, 7, 40, 114
Pope-Robinson 40, 49, 115
Pope-Toledo 40, 49, 115
Pope-Tribune 40, 49, 115
Pope-Waverley 40, 49, 115
Porsche 63, 135–136
Pratt-Elkhart 118
Pullman 179–180, 186
Pungs-Finch 119

Rambler 5, 54, 56, 132
Range Rover 65, 68
Rapid Motor Vehicle 131
Rayfield 93
RCA (Radio Corporation of America) 232
R.C.H. 127
Reliance Motor Truck 131
Renault 15, 37, 85–86, 145, 273, 284, 299
Reo 27–28, 54, 123–124, 175
Richard-Brasier 37, 113
Rickenbacker 118
Riker 270–271
RM Sotheby's 304, 308
Rochet-Schneider 37, 113
Rockne 218
Roger, Emile 37
Rogers, Will 199–200
Rolls-Royce 15, 40, 115, 135
Russo-Baltique 118

Saab 25, 33, 86, 90, 158, 166–167, 202, 244–246, 252, 266
Saxon 215
Scania-Vabis 118, 244
Scripps-Booth 120
Serpollet 37
Siddeley-Deasy 118
Sieberling 4
Sintz Gas Engine Company 8, 41
Sizaire-Berwick 112
Sizaire-Naudin 112, 159
Sloan, Alfred P. 9, 11, 13, 48–52, 60, 62, 115, 142, 148, 200–201
Smart 254
Smith, Samuel 42
Sorenson, Charles E. 48
Standard-Swallow 121

Stanley 265, 320
Stearns-Knight 116–117
Stevens-Duryea 40, 113–114, 158
Steyr-Puch 118
Stoddard-Dayton 115–116
Stromberg 73
Studebaker 14, 31–32, 54, 86, 217–218, 266
Studebaker-Packard 130
Stutz 54, 90, 124, 265
S.U. 79
Subaru 25, 164, 167, 262
Sunbeam-Talbot 121
Suzuki 253, 255

Talbot-Darracq 121
Talbot-Lago 121
Tesla 277–278
Thomas 5, 102, 213
Toyota 18, 21–22, 68, 132, 164–165, 250, 276, 326
Tracta 159
Trico 100
Triumph 86, 134, 202, 255
Tucker 54, 339
TVR 128

Underwood 217

Victor Talking Machine Company 232
Vincent, Jesse G. 221–222
VM Motori 248, 258–260
Volkswagen 15, 18, 85, 132–133, 145, 154–155, 164, 202, 248, 331
Volvo 63, 248, 269, 284

Wartburg 252
Watkins Glen 302
Weber 85
White 6
Whiz 95
Wilkinson, John 5, 136
Wills Sainte Claire 87–88, 225, 236, 331
Willys, John North 5, 13, 116
Willys-Knight 116–117
Wilson, Charles Erwin "Engine Charlie" 200
Winton 5, 6, 41, 130

Yamaha 255, 287

www.ingramcontent.com/pod-product-compliance
Ingram Content Group UK Ltd.
Pitfield, Milton Keynes, MK11 3LW, UK
UKHW050543150426
5217IPUK00026B/2054